P9-DDU-561

BEYOND SHANGRI-LA

—

AMERICAN ENCOUNTERS/GLOBAL INTERACTIONS
A series edited by Gilbert M. Joseph and Emily S. Rosenberg

This series aims to stimulate critical perspectives and fresh interpretive frameworks for scholarship on the history of the imposing global presence of the United States. Its primary concerns include the deployment and contestation of power, the construction and deconstruction of cultural and political borders, the fluid meanings of intercultural encounters, and the complex interplay between the global and the local. *American Encounters* seeks to strengthen dialogue and collaboration between historians of U.S. international relations and area studies specialists.

The series encourages scholarship based on multiarchival historical research. At the same time, it supports a recognition of the representational character of all stories about the past and promotes critical inquiry into issues of subjectivity and narrative. In the process, *American Encounters* strives to understand the context in which meanings related to nations, cultures, and political economy are continually produced, challenged, and reshaped.

Beyond Shangri-La

*America and Tibet's
Move into the
Twenty-First Century*

JOHN KENNETH KNAUS

With a Foreword by Robert A. F. Tenzin Thurman

DUKE UNIVERSITY PRESS   DURHAM AND LONDON   2012

**Cuyahoga Falls
Library**
Cuyahoga Falls, Ohio

© 2012 Duke University Press

All rights reserved

Printed in the United States of America on acid-free paper ∞

Designed by Heather Hensley

Typeset in Arno Pro by Westchester Book Group

Library of Congress Cataloging-in-Publication Data appear on the last printed page of this book.

All statements of fact, opinion, or analysis expressed are those of the author and do not reflect the official positions or views of the CIA or any other U.S. government agency. Nothing in the contents should be construed as asserting or implying U.S. government authentication of information or agency endorsement of the author's views. This material has been reviewed by the CIA to prevent the disclosure of classified information.

CONTENTS

ILLUSTRATIONS

Robert A. F. Tenzin Thurman

I am honored to herald Ken Knaus's masterful account of America's role in Tibet's agonizing and inspiring progress into a future that is still uncertain, either marvelous or horrendous! The world is undergoing dramatic transformations, and Knaus's well-researched and insightful narrative brings to life the human reality of key contributors to the outcome. I especially admire how he has skillfully drawn out, from the tangled web of events and ideas over the century, the central thread of America's hesitant and intermittent recognition of the human right of self-determination as being the seed of the solution to all the rush of tragedies.

Reading about the ups and downs of America's involvement in Tibetan affairs, ranging from W. W. Rockhill's 1909 conversations with His Holiness the Great Thirteenth Dalai Lama up to Barack Obama's 2010–11 meetings with His Holiness the Great Fourteenth, is like attending an epic recital, ending with the dramatic suspense of the unknowns we face everywhere today, confronting prospects of great danger and great potential. Knaus perceptively reveals the transformations that the Tibetan people have suffered through, and he is clearly appreciative of the struggles and achievements of their leader, the Dalai Lama, over six decades.

A distinguishing factor that enormously raises the value of the book is that Knaus, while having his eyes wide open about the foibles and virtues of the many actors in these events, actually likes the Tibetan people. He has known them well under life-and-death conditions by working with them as a CIA operative, trying to help them regain their freedom. Even though that help was discontinued long ago, he has subsequently given years of effort—hard thought, patient research, and courageous speaking truth to power—not to give up on the Tibetans, whose determination, human warmth, and bravery he came to admire. Governments may adopt and abandon people and nations as their leaders' perceived self-interest dictates, but the true human being, once finding friendship with others, never gives them up.

Knaus is restrained in his critique of some people he has less use for, depicting their shenanigans with a dry wit, while clearly indicating the consequences of their decisions and follies without belaboring or deploring. As for those he admires, such as the Dalai Lama himself, and the more worldly, irrepressible elder brother, Gyalo Thondup, he shows their effectiveness in action.

His mandate is to depict America's role all along in shaping Tibet's trajectory, in relation to China's grasping through conquest at the ring of being the "Great Power" it so anxiously wishes to become. So he does not so much address the role of Tibet in shaping America's and China's trajectories, the different perspective that I never tire in telling.

Readers will understand with total clarity how the Manchu empire, when firmly on top in China, also tried to invade China's mountain neighbor, Tibet; how Nationalist China, once free of the Manchu yoke, tried unsuccessfully also to be an empire and possess Tibet; and how Communist China succeeded in its own grab at imperial conquest, invading and occupying Tibet in 1950–51 and continuing a relentless attempt at the genocidal assimilation of the Tibetan people. The focus of the book is on the part played by American political and military actors in trying their best, with mixed results, to understand, handle, and, exceptionally, even prevent the crushing effects of the grinding wheels of the Chinese imperial chariot. We receive an insider's view of how this history was made.

What we can see is how the "fate of Tibet" was not some supposedly "inevitable tragedy," an inherent fault of the victim or the "manifest destiny" of an uncontrollably expanding Chinese imperium, but rather a result of the pungent combination of imperial blundering with failure of nerve of first the British empire and second its American and Indian successors. Always looming in the background were the self-deceiving fantasies of the successive empires' commercial greed—how much money each one thought it would be able to extract from the belly of the Chinese dragon after feeding her Tibet as a distracting sacrifice. Against this background, the people of principle, with the vision to see past personal desires and prejudices to find the humanity of their Tibetan counterparts, ranging from Sir Charles Bell and Hugh Richardson all the way to Joel McCleary, Charlie Rose, Nancy Pelosi, the author himself, and a number of others, stand out as the still undefeated exemplars of what is required to turn the tragedy around.

Complementing this vision of the outsiders' roles with the Tibetans' own perspectives are the memoirs of H. H. the Fourteenth Dalai Lama and the members of his family, and the *Portrait* of the Great Thirteenth Dalai Lama left us by the British plenipotentiary Sir Charles Bell (unfortunately, the Great Thirteenth himself did not leave us a memoir).

Finally there is a perspective that has not yet been generally factored in as a *political* perspective, because it may seem to come from a *spiritual* place beyond politics—namely the perspective of the *prophetic* speeches and writings of H. H. the Fourteenth Dalai Lama himself, as presented in his many speeches and his books, such as *Ethics for the New Millennium* and *Beyond Religion*. In those works, we can find the Tibetan challenge to the whole militarized world system—the residue of the last five centuries of colonialist imperialism, which is destroying not only Tibetans but also many other local peoples and even our entire little ball of earth and water, our cosmic planetary home. The Dalai Lama calls for a "twenty-first century without war," with conflicts settled nonviolently through dialogue; a "century of environmental restoration," with the industrial engines of consumerist greed tuned down to a nonpolluting level; and a "century of mutual understanding," beyond a "clash of civilizations," with the world religions and the world movement of secular humanism finding ways of mutual accommodation and a heartfelt embrace of pluralism.

And this is where we can discern the role of the central figure looming above Knaus's tale, the Dalai Lama himself (perhaps in both his concerned embodiments, but especially the present one!), who offers not only Tibet but also America, China, India, and the whole family of nations one viable way out of the potential doomsday we all face if we continue with the clash of "Great Powers." This way is the path of the *political* embrace of our inevitable interrelatedness, our life-and-death need of nonviolence, and our transformative turn to sincere dialogue with "enemies" as well as "friends."

In conclusion, a hearty welcome to this magnum opus, and may its skillful narrative and honest factual presentation create a forceful if implicit wake-up call that comes to fruition as soon as possible.

Jey Tsong Khapa Professor of Indo-Tibetan Studies, Columbia University;
President, Tibet House US; author of Why the Dalai Lama Matters
MAY 2012

In *The Tale of Genji* Murasaki Shikibu wrote, "The storyteller's own experience of men and things, whether good or ill—not only what he has passed through himself, but even events which he has only witnessed or been told of—has moved him to an emotion so passionate that he can no longer keep it shut up in his heart. Again and again something in his own life or in that around him will seem to the writer so important that he cannot bear to let it pass into oblivion. There must never come a time, he feels, when men do not know about it."

I have had the privilege of knowing and working with the Tibetans over the past half-century as they have fought and maintained the struggle for the right to live in their own country according to the beliefs that define their unique identity. Consequently I feel the need to record what I know of this history and the variable role that the United States government and people have played in preserving it. It is a chronicle of events, personalities, objectives, and politics—some noble and some self-serving—that have defined the role that the United States government and people with varying constancy have played and continue to play in the past and future of Tibet. It is the legend of a people, their leader, and the actions they have taken to preserve their homeland, their way of life, and their identity as an active presence in the contemporary world.

The history of America's contributions to the preservation of this unique culture attained enhanced relevance in 2008 from the spontaneous protests raised in Lhasa which spread and continue throughout Tibet protesting China's rule of their country and the absence of their exiled leader, whose honorific title "Kundun" means "the Presence." Beijing's relentless efforts to suppress these protests and its inflexibility in negotiations with the Dalai Lama's representatives offering a "Middle Way" aimed at a solution confirming the status of Tibet and its leader continue to chill prospects for resolving this centuries-old conflict.

That the Tibet issue nevertheless remains alive in the foreign policy portfolio of the United States—even as a policy of guilty default—is a testament to both its innate merit and the unique capacity of these people and their "turbulent priest" to attract and retain the better feelings of their fellow man throughout the troubled past century, in the present, and into the future. This book attempts to record this legend, with its claim upon the conscience of people of goodwill everywhere and the role America has played in preserving it, so that there "will never come a time when men do not know about it" and do what they can to ensure that these people and their way of life survive and continue to enrich our lives. The Dalai Lama's recent announcement of his intention to retire from active participation in the political affairs of his people reaffirms its current relevance. Meanwhile, Kundun, his Presence, and its legacy of participation remain.

ACKNOWLEDGMENTS

A half-century ago Tibet became an active matter of interest and concern on the international scene, when its leader, the Fourteenth Dalai Lama, fled his country to avoid complete subjugation by a repressive Chinese government. In the intervening years he and his people and their cause have not only survived but have become the subject of international interest and concern as they moved "beyond Shangri-La" to become contributing participants in the current world.

While writing this book I have had the privilege of being a research associate at the Fairbank Center for East Asian Research at Harvard University, whose distinguished scholars and authorities on China and United States involvement have been of great assistance to me. I am particularly indebted to Professor Roderick MacFarquhar for sharing his keen insights on the politics in China since the Mao government assumed control and in keeping me on track in recording Chinese actions as they affected Tibet. His associates, Merle Goldman, Ezra Vogel, Robert Ross, Arthur Holcombe, and Leonard van der Kuip, and William Kirby have all provided stimulating views on events and personalities in the political scene that has been unfolding in Beijing and Tibet over the past half-century. Holly Angell, Deirdre Chetham, and Jorge Espada have given me needed support. I am grateful to you all.

I have also had the benefit of perusing the papers of William Rockhill at the Lamont Library at Harvard, whose staff maintain them with a deserved sense of pride and provide ready and informed access to them. I am grateful for finding this same informed access at the FDR, Truman, and Kennedy libraries to the original papers of the presidents filed there. Ambassador Harry Barnes was similarly generous in sharing the conclusions of the mission on which he served, looking for a constructive solution to the Chinese occupation of Tibet. The ready access to President Nixon's conversations in the Oval Office with Dr. Kissinger which were available at the National Archives was a pleasing surprise.

I am also very grateful for the ready reception and assistance I received from the members of the United States Congress and their staffs who have worked with diligence and insight into supporting the Tibetans in their struggle for recognition. From Senator Helms to Senator Feinstein and from Congresswoman Pelosi to Congressman Wolf they have provided their weighty support to a conscientious balance in Washington. Senator Udall's readiness to obtain bipartisan support for my efforts to place a plaque at Camp Hale in his home state commemorating the Tibetans who were trained there and later died defending their country was very gratifying. I am particularly indebted to Congresswoman Pelosi's aide Jonathan Stivers and Senator Udall's aide Jennifer Barrett.

The Tibetan government-in-exile has provided me with ready access to its leaders, particularly the Dalai Lama's family, represented by Gyalo Thondup, his wife and children, and brothers Thubten Jigme Norbu and Lobsang Samten. I am grateful for the long friendship and confidences that Gyalo and his faithful friend the late Lhamo Tsering shared with me as they navigated through the many and at times conflicting demands that have been made on both of them jointly and separately. Having access to Lhamo Tsering's timely reports and compilations of the records of the operations conducted by his fellow countrymen against the Chinese occupation of their country and their efforts to find a lasting peace and an equitable accommodation between his people and their Chinese neighbors has been invaluable. This has been enriched and enhanced by a deep and lasting relationship with many of the younger generation who have served as interpreters and aides between the Tibetan leaders and their countrymen and the Americans who worked with them on common endeavors and enabled us to compile an accurate history of the events that were involved. Lodi Gyari and Bhuchung Tsering have been tireless and effective advocates of the Tibetan government-in-exile's efforts to reach a permanent agreement with their Chinese counterparts concerning regional autonomy within the scope of the Constitution of Tibet. Fortuitously, during the past decade that I have been writing this book, I have shared it with Lobsang Samten as he prepared himself at Harvard to serve his country, which he now does as prime minister of the

Tibetan government-in-exile. They have also been ready to expound on and explain to me the status of these negotiations over the past decade.

I am particularly indebted to Joel McCleary and Robert Thurman for having shared their recollections, documents, and photographs. These provide authoritative evidence of what they have done to carry out successfully the injunction of their Buddhist mentor, Geshe La, that "this is not the age for mountains, but for politics."

Throughout my work on Tibet I have had the support of my wife, known as "Miss Andy" to the many Tibetans we have known together and who have enriched both our lives. I have also had the privilege of having my children, Maggie, Holley, and John, share this interest and the way of life it represents. Thank you all.

CHAPTER ONE

Washington Discovers the Hidden Land

The Meeting at Wutai Mountain

In the summer of 1908 William Woodville Rockhill, Theodore Roosevelt's envoy to China, made a five-day journey by foot and mule train to a remote mountainous region west of Peking for America's first official contact with Tibet. It was a journey rich in symbolism and political significance. His destination was Wutai Mountain, a Buddhist shrine revered by both Tibetan and Chinese Buddhists. Rockhill was there to meet with a dispossessed Dalai Lama who was en route to Peking, where he had been summoned by the incumbent Manchu rulers anxious to guarantee his continued conformity to their waning authority over his country. This was the beginning of America's now century-old relationship with Tibet and its ruler. It is a history of coincidences and ironies.

The immediate coincidence was that the Dalai Lama, who had fled invading British troops four years earlier, was meeting with the one man in the American government who had unique knowledge of the history and culture of Tibet and appreciated the critical role that the Dalai Lama played in it. The irony was that Rockhill had conflicting drives and commitments. As a young man he had so keen an interest in Tibet that he taught himself the Tibetan language at the Bibliothèque National de France in Paris while attending France's Saint-Cyr Military Academy. Fifteen years later he confirmed this dedication when he resigned from the United

FIGURES 1 AND 2
William Woodville
Rockhill, the Tibetan
ethnographer.

States foreign service and made a trek to eastern Tibet in an unsuccessful attempt to reach Lhasa. This zeal was not untempered when he was welcomed back by the State Department five years later where he became the primary champion of the Open Door Policy to preclude the dismemberment of China. This stemmed from his work as a commissioner negotiating for indemnity for the victims of the Boxer Rebellion.

When Rockhill finally met with the Tibetan ruler in two sessions at the historic shrine of Wutaishan on June 19 and 21, 1908, he demonstrated his role as a diplomat apart from his zeal as an ethnographer.[1] In a breathless dispatch to an equally adventurous President Roosevelt, Rockhill said that the appearance of the Tibetan ruler at their first meeting took him "absolutely by surprise." He had imagined "a rather ascetic looking youth, bent by constantly sitting bow-legged on cushions, with a sallow complexion and a faraway meditative look." On the contrary, he had found "a man of thirty-three, with a very bright face, rather dark brown, a moustache and a small tuft of hair under his lower lip, whose eyes were large, rather prominent and obliquely set: his eyebrows rising slightly toward the temples gave him a rather narquois [Fr., cunning] expression. His mouth was large, his teeth white and perfect. His head was bare, and, as it had not been shaved for some days, it added to the general worldliness of his appearance."[2] The Dalai Lama, pleased with what he saw in his Tibetan-speaking interlocutor, asked him to return for a more substantive conversation two days later. His primary concern was the options he might have if he acquiesced in his hosts' requests that he return to Lhasa. He said he was most anxious to return to Tibet, "but that he would not be driven back there by the Chinese: he would go when he was ready, not before."

Although delighted with his advisory role, Rockhill, the equally careful diplomat, made it clear that there were limitations imposed by his position, and he "could only do certain things to oblige" the displaced sovereign. He optimistically assured him that the Sino-British-Tibetan agreement which had been signed in Calcutta the month before would bring new benefits to Tibet and "spoke to him most earnestly of the desirability for him to establish close trade relations with India and cultivate friendly relations with neighboring states, but especially with India, his closest neighbor." In response to the Dalai Lama's reference to "the remoteness of his country and the fact that it had no friends abroad," Rockhill reassured him that he was mistaken and "he and Tibet had many well-wishers in America and in other countries, who hoped to see him and his people prosperous, well and happy."

Rockhill concluded, "The Tale [Dalai] Lama seems to me a man of undoubted intelligence, open-minded, perhaps as the result of his misfortunes

FIGURE 3
William
Woodville
Rockhill, the
diplomat.

of the last four years, a very agreeable, kindly thoughtful host, and a personage of great dignity, though simple withal, quick-tempered, perhaps, but of a cheerful temperament." The never falsely modest Rockhill closed by saying, "[I] felt a deeper and more complete satisfaction with these two interviews with the mysterious potentate and incarnation of the god Shenrezig than would anyone who had not, like myself, given so many years of their life to Tibet. . . . It was all too extraordinary. I could not believe my ears and eyes."[3]

Rockhill received a reply from his equally fascinated correspondent, "a real Rooseveltian one." Although he belittled the letter,[4] he could only have expected that Roosevelt, with his enthusiasm for undeveloped frontiers, would have been excited by his representative's meeting with this exotic person. "Really," the exuberant TR had declared, "it is difficult to believe that it occurred. I congratulate you, and I congratulate the United States upon having the one diplomatic representative in the world to whom such an incident could happen."[5] His only question was how he might reciprocate the gifts that the Dalai Lama had sent him. He had sent the Pope a set of his books. Would this be appropriate for the Tibetan pope? He thought it "just possible" that the Pope might have glanced at them, but he doubted if Rockhill's new friend would do even that.[6]

Roosevelt shared Rockhill's report with his close friend, the British ambassador to Washington James Bryce, who thanked him for sharing this "first real glimpse of that mysterious personage that has perhaps been ever obtained by any Westerner capable of appreciating and describing the head of the oldest and strangest church in the world."[7] Bryce reported that Foreign Secretary Edward Grey had commented, "[If the Dalai Lama] will only believe that we have no designs upon Tibet and require nothing but a friendly attitude from Tibet in trade relations, he will not be disappointed and will find the result entirely satisfactory to himself and beneficial to Tibet."[8] This would seem a measured description of the policy that the British government had adopted toward Tibet in the aftermath of the criticism that had resulted from Younghusband's successful march to Lhasa four years earlier.

The Dalai Lama Comes to Peking

Two months after his meeting with Rockhill at Wutai Mountain, the Dalai Lama, "after much hesitation, and only after repeated peremptory representations from Peking,"[9] made his way to Peking. The Manchu government sent a special train to bring him to the Imperial City, where he was received with highest honors. The *Times* continued its censorious coverage of his presence, noting that the Dalai Lama was described by those who saw him as "lacking in intelligence and character. . . . There is no love lost between the Peking city officials and the followers of the ruler of Tibet. The head priest of the Dalai Lama has had several encounters with the officials, who are prone to call him uncomplimentary names to his face. 'Barbarian' is one of the least offensive of these."[10]

The *Times* may have been taking its cue from Whitehall's now restrained enthusiasm for Tibetan matters and the cold shoulder which the Empress Dowager's court was giving to its reluctant guest once it had him under its physical control in the capital. His imperial audience, scheduled to take place within a week after his arrival, was canceled when the Tibetan leader refused to comply with the court ceremonial, which included kneeling and kowtowing (touching the ground with his forehead). He had unsuccessfully argued that these signs of deference had not been required of his predecessor the Fifth Dalai Lama when he had visited the first Manchu emperor two and a half centuries before.[11] The Chinese Foreign Office then kept him in seclusion by requiring that Chinese officials would accompany any foreign representatives with whom he might wish to meet. (The current Dalai Lama is equally wary of the prospect of similar "Golden Isolation" if he were to accept the offer of the present-day successors of the Manchus to live in Beijing but not in Lhasa.)

The refugee Tibetan ruler resorted to sending an emissary to those foreign ambassadors whose advice and assistance he hoped might help him break out of his isolation. His choice of an envoy was another historical irony. It was the notorious Buryat Mongol Buddhist lama Agvan Dorzhiev. His activities in trying to solicit the support of the tsar for the Dalai Lama eight years earlier had been one of the triggering factors in the mounting of the Younghusband expedition, which had led to the Tibetan leader's exile. The Mongol monk had first turned to the Russian ambassador Ivan Korostovetz, but he had found no help there. Moscow's involvement in central Asian politics had greatly diminished after the disastrous shellacking Russia suffered in its encounter with the Japanese three years before. Rockhill reported that Korostovetz's advice was bleak: "The Dalai Lama had no choice but to submit to what the Chinese Government might decide upon. The time when Russia was concerned in advising or supporting eastern rulers was at [an] end; as a spiritual ruler Russia was greatly interested in the welfare of the Dalai Lama, as a temporal ruler he must obey China."[12]

When Dorzhiev said that since the Russians were refusing to advise him, he would have to turn to the British minister, Korostovetz discouraged any prospect of assistance from that quarter, saying that Sir John Jordan had told him that he could have no direct relations with the Tibetans. Questions concerning Tibet were to be settled with the Chinese government, the suzerain state as stipulated in the Russo-British Convention of 1907. The Russian minister could only suggest that Dorzhiev see Rockhill as "the representative of an absolutely disinterested power."[13]

When they met in Peking on October 24 Rockhill found Dorzhiev "a quiet, well-mannered man, impressionable, like all Mongols, and apparently but very little less ignorant of politics and the world in general than the Tibetans." He did not think he "was . . . more of an intriguer than any Asiatic would be when confronted for the first time" with someone like the Dalai Lama.[14] This was a surprising underestimation of Dorzhiev as both a man and a political player coming from an anthropologist with a cosmopolitan background and by then a seasoned diplomat. Rockhill didn't survive to witness the overthrow of the Romanov tsars and the succession of the Soviets as participants in the twentieth-century version of new Great Game of Asia. Dorzhiev, however, not only survived but was to be an active participant in these events over the coming three decades, something about which the United States government was to remain largely ignorant.

Although Dorzhiev must have been expecting encouraging counsel from the only American official who at that time had any knowledge of his adopted country, Rockhill was even more of a determined bystander than his Russian and British colleagues. This became apparent as they talked. The Mongol emissary opened with a bid for advice for the Dalai Lama, who he said was trying to decide whether he should return to Lhasa or remain in Peking until he learned of the reforms that the Chinese were planning for Tibet. He feared that the Chinese government intended to curtail the temporal power he and his predecessors had exercised long before the Manchus came to China.

Rockhill, whose mission as a diplomat was to preserve China's territorial integrity so that its faltering bureaucracy might patch together solutions that would prevent, or at least postpone, its collapse, gave him no encouragement. He bluntly told Dorzhiev, "Whatever may have been the sovereign rights of the Dalai Lama before the present dynasty came to the throne, his present position, like that of his predecessors since the middle of the eighteenth century, was that of a vassal prince whose duties, rights and prerogatives had been fixed by the succeeding emperors." He followed this dose of realpolitik with his opinion that the reforms which the Manchu government was reportedly planning were purely administrative in nature, that is, dividing the country into districts, as in China; reorganizing Tibet's military forces, currency, and education; introducing agricultural and stock-raising programs; and building roads. If these were the reforms contemplated, the American diplomat, who was anxious to see his Manchu hosts develop a more efficient administration within their own country, professed to see no objection the Dalai Lama could have to them. Furthermore, as a defender of Chinese sovereignty Rockhill concluded, "Military questions, relations with foreign states, additional questions (in some countries) were all imperial matters which could not be left to the various states [i.e., the Tibetans] to deal with independently."[15]

Although this was not the counsel he had hoped to take back to his principal, Dorzhiev said that the Dalai Lama "had absolutely no objection to raise against the extension of education in Tibet nor to military reforms." He solely feared Chinese encroachment on his temporal authority. He felt strongly on only two issues: that the Yellow Church which he headed should be maintained in all its honors and that he be given the right to send representations ("memorials") directly to the throne rather than through local or regional Manchu administrators. Rockhill responded with surprising optimism, saying he was "convinced" that the imperial government would do nothing to lessen the dignity of the Tibetan Church. He considered the Dalai Lama's wish to communicate directly with Peking "reasonable and in the interest of good government," but he advised that the Tibetan pontiff "ascertain informally how such a request would be received and act accordingly."[16]

Rockhill then dismissed the Dalai Lama's emissary with a reaffirmation of his advice that it was in the Dalai Lama's best interest to get back to Lhasa as soon as possible and "show the Chinese Government that he was sincerely favorable to all measures for the good of his country, as on this must depend the continuance of the Imperial favor and the granting to him of the favors he so much desired." The American diplomat took a far different tone in this report to TR than in his breathless and admiring dispatch three months earlier describing his first meeting with the Tibetan pontiff at Wutai Mountain. Now he reported that he gathered from this conversation with Dorzhiev that the Dalai Lama "cared very little, if at all, for anything which did not affect his personal privileges and prerogatives, that he separated entirely his cause from that of the people of Tibet, which he was willing to abandon entirely to the mercy of China."[17] The former Saint-Cyr officer did not countenance willful local monarchs, even exotic ones, who threatened the shaky authority of the government to which he was accredited and determined to support.

Following this bleak meeting of his representative with Rockhill, the humbled Tibetan was kept in splendid political isolation by his hosts, who then gave him an imperial banquet. The Empress Dowager celebrated her seventy-fifth birthday by conferring a new title on him, adding the ominously instructive words "Sincerely, Obedient, Reincarnation-helping" to his existing description as "Great, Virtuous, Self-existent Buddha of the West." The decree further delineated his status by ordering that he must "immediately return to Tibet . . . be reverentially submissive to the regulations of the Sovereign State, [and] induce the Western Barbarians [i.e., his people] to obey the laws and practice virtue."[18] The decree denied him the right to address his representations to the throne directly, but dictated that he must communicate through the Chinese resident in Lhasa, "who [would] memorialize for him," and "must respectfully await the decision." In response to the by then thoroughly demoralized Dalai Lama's request for advice on whether he should make one more attempt to obtain the right of direct communication in the letter of thanks he had been ordered to submit to the throne, Rockhill urged that he give up this battle. He counseled that he "saw absolutely no way out of the difficulty": "The Dalai Lama must submit to his sovereign's commands. He had received many honors, his relations with India had been satisfactorily arranged by China, the interests of the Yellow Church were safe. He must [now] take the bitter with the sweet." The only suggestion that the American diplomat could make was that "he should not delay too long complying with the wishes of the Chinese Government, as it might be misunderstood and lead to further complications."[19] Rockhill was sympathetic, but he obviously thought it was time for this fascinating, but stubbornly independent, subject to yield to the interests of the established order, especially one that the American diplomat was committed to preserving.

Rockhill, the ethnographer and historian, concluded with a clinical note: "The special interest to me is in that I have probably been a witness to the overthrow of the temporal power of the head of the Yellow Church, which curiously enough, I heard twenty years ago predicted in Tibet, where it was commonly said that the thirteenth Dalai Lama would be the last, and my client is the thirteenth."[20]

The Dalai Lama Leaves Peking

The Dalai Lama's stay in Peking and his first encounter with the United States were disappointing. Rockhill's letter to TR arrived in Washington at the same time that one cable from the Chinese Ministry of Foreign Affairs announced, "Heaven, inexorable and pitiless, has overwhelmed us with deep sorrow depriving us [of] our imperial parent, the departed Emperor of China," and another announced the "visit of a second affliction in the demise of Her Imperial Majesty, the Grand Empress Dowager."[21] Although the death of the unfortunate emperor, who had ended his days as a semiprisoner in the Imperial Palace, was of less consequence than that of his royal jailer, the successor Manchu government had little interest in dealing any further with their humiliated Tibetan visitor. He remained for the funeral ceremonies of the imperial persons and then left Peking on December 21, 1908.

CHAPTER TWO

The Dalai Lama's Long Journey Home

Despite his American mentor's frigid advice that he accept his admittedly poor situation and get back to Lhasa to deal with it without further delay, the Tibetan ruler chose to travel at a more leisurely pace. It was to be another year before he reached the capital from which he had fled five years earlier. Unlike the generally very favorable press outside of China that the present Dalai Lama enjoys, his predecessor was frequently derided, or at best patronized, by the English-language press of that time. The Peking *North China Daily News* correspondent covered his homeward journey in the same unfavorable light it had accorded his travel to Peking, highlighting the discourteous reception he received when he made his first stop at Kumbum monastery, the birthplace of the founder of the Yellow Hat sect of Tibetan Buddhism, of which the Dalai Lama is the head. The abbot at first refused to meet him, reportedly because he recalled the pontiff's prolonged stay the year before, with its consequent drain on the monastery's treasury. The reluctant host finally invited his superior to make a return visit despite the burden his stay would devolve upon the local farmers, who would be supplying the head of their church and object of their veneration and his sizable entourage with "straw, peas, fuel, sheep, bread, etc for so long a period." The reporter did note, "The Dalai Lama, shut off from all communication with the outside world save through his own followers, is not aware of the sufferings of the people through their [his staff's] oppression and leeches, but he left this district followed by many a curse and the hope that they will see his face no more."[1]

It wasn't until early spring that the Dalai Lama finally took leave of his hosts at Kumbum to begin his eight-month journey back to his capital. He was in no hurry to confront the new constraints on his political authority that he knew the Chinese were planning to impose. Before leaving Kumbum he sent a letter to Rockhill reaffirming an earlier request for contact and not to forget him.[2] Some months later Rockhill responded from his new post in St. Petersburg, assuring his depressed client, "I will remain always at the service of Your Holiness."[3] On November 11, 1909, Rockhill noted from his new post in St. Petersburg that the Dalai Lama's faithful aide, Dorzhiev, had arrived there.

The Dalai Lama's premonitions about the bleak prospects facing him in Lhasa turned out to be well founded. As he was making his way home in the late summer of 1909, the newly appointed Chinese resident in Tibet, Chao Erh-fang, began to implement the tightened administrative controls over the provinces on the eastern side of the Upper Yangtze, which were heavily populated by Tibetans.[4] Chao's well-equipped troops carried out these measures with a heavy hand, destroying a number of monasteries and provoking strong resistance from the Dalai Lama's people, which remains alive in this area a century later. The new Chinese overlord then sent an advance guard of two thousand men to Lhasa with orders to seize the Dalai Lama, who had finally reached his capital on Christmas Day 1909. According to Charles Bell, the Chinese plan was to capture the Tibetan pontiff and force him to affix his seal to the decrees imposing the new reforms while executing his ministers, on whom they had fixed a bounty of 1,000 rupees per head.[5]

In another historically ironic act the Dalai Lama decided to seek asylum in the territory of the British from whom he had fled six years earlier. Within two months of his arrival back in his capital the harried Tibetan was again in flight through the winter snows to the Indian border. The Manchu government had meanwhile deposed him for the second time, denouncing him as "an ungrateful, irreligious, obstreperous profligate who is tyrannical and so unacceptable to the Tibetans, and accordingly an unsuitable leader of the Tibetans."[6] The London *Times* was equally unsympathetic about the plight of one who "seemed to be disposed to emulate the exploits of the Wandering Jew," whose appearance in India was an "awkward complication in a situation already somewhat confused": "For most of the tribulations which have overtaken the Tibetans in recent years the Dalai Lama has been directly responsible, and the only excuse that can be made for him is that up to the time of his flight he was utterly unversed in worldly affairs and the prey of political adventurers."[7]

Although the government of India issued orders to maintain strict neutrality, the viceroy did invite him to Calcutta for a state visit, providing him with an escort of Bengal cavalry and a salute from a guard of honor. When they met, the dispossessed pontiff formally requested that his British host intervene on his behalf to urge the Chinese government to withdraw its military occupation of his capital and permit him to exercise the remnant governing powers that it had agreed to allow him.

After his formal meetings with the government of India, the Dalai Lama was taken on a tour of various factories and the Royal Zoo in Calcutta. He then returned to the West Bengal hill station of Darjeeling, where the government of India had rented a house called "Hillside."[8] This was to be the exiled pontiff's home and the seat of his government for the next two years. From there he sent futile appeals to his British hosts to intercede with the Chinese to permit him to return to Lhasa. The supportive British political officer Charles Bell, however, brought the disappointing news that the script-bound British government refused to intervene on his behalf with the beleaguered Chinese government.[9]

In another reversal for the Tibetan, his erstwhile supporter the Russian tsar responded to his appeal with a friendly but noncommittal reply, which was delivered not by a Russian emissary, but by Charles Bell. This final snub was one of the last acts of the Great Game for the control of Central Asia.

The responses to the two appeals for advice and assistance that he had sent to his American intermediary were equally discouraging. Since they had met in Peking Rockhill had lost neither his interest in the affairs of the Dalai Lama nor his conviction that the Tibetan ruler could find no solution to his problems outside the fraying authority of the Manchu Empire. For the past eighteen months the scholar diplomat had spent considerable time at his new post in the tsar's capital compiling a history of the relationship between the Dalai Lamas and the Manchu emperors over the past two and a half centuries.[10] In replying to the young ruler's request for how he could extricate himself from his exile and regain his former position in Lhasa, he drew upon this book, which he said he had written thinking his views on this subject might be of use to the Dalai Lama by making them known among foreigners and the Chinese.[11]

Rockhill assured the Dalai Lama that he had "been constantly thinking how peace and happiness could be permanently restored" to him, his church, and his people. The diplomat declared, "[I cannot] but think that the present unsatisfactory condition of the relations of Your Holiness and the Government of China is the result of a long standing misunderstanding, which could be dispelled by a full and frank discussion of the various questions in dispute." He recalled that the Tibetan ruler had in his "great wisdom" seen the "vast importance of direct discussions with China of matters affecting Tibet" and had requested the right to correspond directly with the throne, a privilege that "in [his] humble opinion" would be of mutual advantage to both parties. He pointed out, however, that the present relationship between Peking and the Tibetans was based on the laws imposed by Emperor Ch'ien Lung in 1793, after his armies were forced to intervene in Tibet to repel an invasion by the Nepalese Gurkhas occasioned by the intrigues of a renegade brother of the Panchen Lama. These laws empowered the emperor's residents in Lhasa, conferring with the Dalai Lama and the Panchen Lama, to take part in the administration of Tibet; denied the two Lamas the right to address the throne directly in memorials; and gave the residents control over border defenses and foreign intercourse and trade, effectively closing Tibet's borders. Rockhill found these laws "wise and in nowise oppressive, and had they always been equitably carried out, the country would certainly have enjoyed constant happiness." He conceded, "Unfortunately such has not been the case, and the officers of the Emperor posted in Tibet have not always had these laws before them, nor considered the rights of the Yellow Church and the people of Tibet; ignoring the wishes of the Emperor, they have made the sincerity of this affection for the Yellow Church and Tibet to be doubtful."[12]

This dedicated American supporter of Manchu authority, despite its warts, concluded with the clinching argument, "But Tibet must have good government and good government can be given it on the basis of existing laws of the Empire governing it, if they are honestly and impartially applied. *To attain this end close and friendly relations with China are absolutely necessary for Tibet is and must remain a portion of the Ta Ts'ing [Manchu] Empire for its own good, and because the Great Powers of the world deem it necessary for the prosperity of their own peoples*" (italics added). Although dollar diplomacy was to become a trademark of the Taft administration, it was already an ingredient in Rockhill's China policy. His admiration for the Dalai Lama and the country and culture he represented was always tempered by a prime regard for the mercantile interests of the American business community, which required a working relationship with those governing an impoverished China. This was graphically demonstrated in a letter that he sent to the Dalai Lama from his post in St. Petersburg in September 1910, expressing "great sorrow over the many hardships of every kind to which Your Holiness has been subjected in the past year, and I greatly rejoice that you have found a pleasant safe residence in Darjeeling among devoted members of the Yellow Church."

The Dalai Lama had little choice but to swallow Rockhill's views on the appropriate relations between his government and Peking. He did note in his reply that the fixed parameters of the relationship were embodied in stone pillars erected by the Chinese in Tibet recording the pledges of the ancient emperors and the Tibetan pontiffs "to help each other and not bring trouble," explaining, "If any one violates the oath he would be severely punished." For a man sitting in exile and dependent upon the hospitality of his former enemy, a return to his capital to rule under the loose governance of the emperor's resident administrators, but with the autonomy he had enjoyed prior to his two flights abroad, might well have seemed tolerable—as it might to his present-day successor.

It was to be the Tibetan ruler's lot to try his avuncular British host's forbearance for another several months, before unforeseen events in China would permit him to return to his capital to resume his former position with greater authority, which he was then to exercise for the next two decades. Meanwhile Washington was quite willing to defer to the benign patronage being accorded by the cousins.

On October 10, 1911, while the Dalai Lama looked on from his refuge in India, four battalions of the Chinese army mutinied against the Manchu governor general in the eastern Chinese city of Wuhan. After considerable maneuvering with both the Manchu rulers and the revolutionary forces centered around Sun Yat-sen, the former courtier Yuan Shih-kai assumed the office of president of the new republic on February 14, 1912, two days after the abdication of the last Manchu emperor, the young boy Pu Yi.

In the Dalai Lama's capital most of the Chinese garrison mutinied and then moved against the local Tibetans in Lhasa, provoking skirmishes with the ill-armed and untrained Tibetan army and their civilian supporters. The Dalai Lama and his ministers were now ready to fight those who were threatening their country and its religion. Bell cites the reply that the Lhasa authorities sent from their exile in India to a monastery in Tibet, requesting instructions on whether to attack a Chinese company which had arrived on its property: "If they are stronger than you, send them off with soft words. If you are stronger than they are, cut them off by the root."[13] This instruction, however, was never sent by the British telegraphers. Bell was furthermore directed to instruct the Dalai Lama to order his people to stop the fighting and to save the lives of the Chinese mutineers who were now pillaging the Tibetan countryside. The Dalai Lama, expressing bewilderment at what he considered a one-sided display of British neutrality, acquiesced, and the Tibetan government cooperated in the orderly deportation from Tibet of the Chinese resident and the commanding general with his bedraggled troops. The Tibetans even provided food and ponies for those too weak or ill to make their retreat into India, from where they were repatriated.[14] By the end of 1912 the last of the Chinese troops were out of Tibet, and the Dalai Lama returned in triumph to Lhasa in January 1913.

Following these events there was a stiffening of British policy concerning China's relationship with Tibet. On August 29, 1912, the British envoy presented a memorandum reviewing the situation in Tibet to the Chinese government. While recognizing Chinese suzerainty, but not its sovereignty, over Tibet, his note contended that Tibet should be permitted to manage its affairs without Chinese interference. The memorandum objected to the sending of another Chinese expedition then on the borders of Tibet and to the incorporation of Tibet as a province of the new Chinese Republic. It recommended a new Anglo-Chinese agreement as a condition of Britain's recognition of the Chinese Republic, and indicated that British interests might warrant the stationing of a British agent at Lhasa.

The local colonial press was at first slow to pick up these new policy nuances. In Calcutta the *Times of India* reported that Britain's new position was contradictory in recognizing China's suzerainty over Tibet yet condemning its right to use force to enforce its authority there. This was reiterated by the equally bewildered American consul in Chungking, who stated that the views expressed in the *Times* "coincided almost exactly" with his.[15]

The Simla Conference

Peking promptly reacted to these shifts in the diplomatic barometer. Yuan Shih-kai's government gave notice that it was not about to repudiate any of the claims made by its Manchu predecessors, rejecting British demands that Tibet not be incorporated into a province of the new republic.[16] After some months of argument, and prompted by concerns over Russian diplomatic successes in Mongolia, a recognition of its own relative weakness, and fear that the British would undertake direct negotiations with the Tibetans which would exclude them, Yuan's government agreed to negotiations on Tibet on the terms set by the British.[17] In October 1913 Ivan Chen, the Chinese representative, arrived at the Indian hill station of Simla to begin negotiations with Lonchen Shatra, a leading Tibetan minister, and Sir Henry McMahon, the British plenipotentiary, who was assisted by the Dalai Lama's new friend Charles Bell.

McMahon spent the next several months struggling to find a compromise between the Tibetan demand for acknowledgment of the independence they had recently reestablished by evicting the invading Chinese troops from Lhasa and the Chinese claims to sovereignty over Tibet, resting on claims dating back to the Mongol domination of Tibet seven centuries earlier. Under pressure from the British the Tibetans eventually accepted the face-saving concept of Chinese suzerainty over Tibet, but did not agree to the proposed description of Tibet as an integral part of China. McMahon finessed these entrenched and seemingly irreconcilable positions by not including the description in the main body of the agreement, instead tucking it into the proposed notes that were to accompany the final accord. The British diplomat then took on the even more intractable disagreement over the competing claims between the Tibetans and the Chinese over the frontier. The Chinese claimed a line within almost sixty miles from Lhasa which had no historic basis beyond the recent failed Chinese offensives. The Tibetans made claims to land over which they had not exercised jurisdiction on the eastern side of the Yangtze, but which was populated by large numbers of Tibetans who paid spiritual allegiance to the Dalai Lama. To bridge these competing claims McMahon devised the formula of Outer Tibet, which would include the area primarily west of the Yangtze, over which Lhasa had exercised historic jurisdiction, and Inner Tibet, comprising the area on the eastern side in which the population was mainly Tibetan by race and religion. Richardson describes the effect of the proposed split, which would have created Outer Tibet as "something like a self-governing dominion," while Inner Tibet "would have been the subject of peaceful contention in which the better or more attractive administration could be expected to win."[18] This "peaceful contention" persists a century later, as the Hu Jintao government rejects the Dalai Lama's Middle Way proposal for the governance of these areas.

The Chinese emissary opposed the Solomonic solution until the last minute, but along with the British and Tibetan plenipotentiaries he finally initialed the draft. His principals in Peking, however, promptly repudiated his action and refused to sign the Convention, which was formally signed by the British and Tibetan ministers on July 3, 1914. With the outbreak of the First World War later that month Britain had concerns overwhelming those of fixing Himalayan boundaries, and the issue of governance in the Tibetan areas along the Upper Yangtze remains unresolved today.

Throughout this interlude of British intervention the Dalai Lama was re-establishing his position in Lhasa. Soon after his triumphal return to his capital in June 1912 and "when it was seen that the former Chinese position there was completely lost,"[19] Yuan Shih-kai sent word expressing regret at the excesses committed by the Manchu regime that he had served and announcing that he was restoring the Dalai Lama's official rank. The Tibetan ruler undoubtedly took great pleasure in replying that he wanted no rank from the Chinese, and, in what the Tibetans regard as a formal declaration of independence,[20] declared that he had resumed the temporal and spiritual governance of his country.

Despite the slights and humiliations of the previous eight years, when Britain entered the First World War the Dalai Lama, in his newly restored position, offered a thousand Tibetan soldiers to fight on the British side. He did, as Bell noted, "rather pathetically, when offering these men, write that he could not send rifles with them."[21] The Tibetan pontiff's offers of friendship were reciprocated "in a spirit of grudging circumspection" by a then preoccupied British government.[22] Four young Tibetan boys "of good family" were trained at Rugby.[23] But London offered only minimal material assistance in the way of arms or training for the modest Tibetan army, which was confronting Chinese threats and military incursions along the Yangtze frontier. The Simla Conference, with its contested Inner and Outer Tibets, marked the postponement of London's active involvement in Tibetan affairs while Britain fought for its survival in trenches closer to home.

American Indifference

In the period following his restoration to power in Lhasa the Dalai Lama no longer had the comfort of his culturally empathetic, but politically stringent, American friend. When Rockhill submitted his pro forma resignation President Woodrow Wilson accepted it without appointing him to a new post, as he had hoped. In October 1913 Rockhill therefore left his post in Ankara to make a trip to China by way of Mongolia. In Urga he spoke with the Mongolian minister of foreign affairs, telling him of his "interest in Tibet" and adding, "[I advised] the Dalai Lama not to seek complete independence, etc, and let him draw his own conclusions on the applicability of my advice to his country."[24]

In Peking Rockhill accepted Yuan Shih-kai's offer to become his political advisor at a salary of U.S. $1,000 per month on the condition that he might reside in the United States. He had no illusions about the man or the government he had agreed to serve. Yuan as an efficient public official serving to prop up the decaying Manchu Empire was one thing. By 1914, however, his ambitions for power within the infant republic which he would later try to smother had become evident. But apparently Rockhill had hopes that he could exert a restraining influence on Yuan as the kind of strong man that this badly splintered replacement to the vanquished Manchu Empire needed. On December 8, 1914, however, William Rockhill died in Honolulu on his way back to China. With his death the Dalai Lama lost his last contact with America's first official who had an interest in Tibet.

Although some of Rockhill's successors as ambassadors to China were educators, none shared his scholarly interest in remote areas of the former empire. And Washington was preoccupied with the new power structure in the Pacific following a world war in which China had played an insignificant role.

At the local level, the American consul in Chungking, Carleton Baker, who had the responsibility of keeping a watching brief over events on China's western frontier (the area McMahon had designated Inner Tibet), filed voluminous reports on the Chinese government's efforts to subdue local Tibetan uprisings there. Although sympathetic to Peking's aims of exercising its ill-defined suzerain authority over its unruly subjects, he was professionally critical of the mismanagement of the military campaign its badly armed and supplied troops had waged.

Baker apparently received little response or guidance from either the State Department or the embassy in Peking on his reporting. Finally, the hardworking but unappreciated consul complained, "If the Department gives little or no indication as to the importance which attaches to reports which the consul submits from time to time, it is very difficult for him to know whether the painstaking efforts which he has put forth in obtaining material and working it up are appreciated or even desired. The foregoing observations are made with special reference to the reports of Thibet [sic] which have been sent from time to time as a result of careful investigation and painstaking work."[25] There is no record of any reassuring reply that the consul's efforts to keep Washington informed on events in Tibet were appreciated or encouraged.

Despite feeling that his reports were falling into a void, Baker continued to provide accounts on what he considered to be the feckless campaign that the Nationalist government was conducting in its efforts to preserve its nominal authority over the Tibetans in its western border area. The disgusted consul still defended the right of the Chinese government to exercise its authority over an area in which it was the nominal suzerain power. He pointed out, however, that this right carried with it the obligation to adopt forceful means if necessary to secure it—a responsibility that he accused Peking of shirking. Baker concluded, "Not only has China's program respecting Thibet been futile as regards immediate results, but the whole idea which China has in subduing the Thibetans and occupying this country is likely to be futile as regards the future. Thibet to the Chinese is a cold, barren, and inhospitable country which is not adapted in any way to their habits and mode of living and it is doubtful if even a successful conquest of Thibet by China would be worth the trouble and expense which this would necessarily involve."[26]

Baker noted that the British, with more familiarity with the scene, had apparently arrived at a parallel conclusion. He cited an article printed in 1913 in the *North China Herald* deploring the ineffective and futile Chinese effort to reestablish its authority over the Tibet border area. In its newly found regard for Tibet, this pro-British paper declared, "Tibet is a free country [whose people] breathe freely its pure mountain air." Unlike its earlier unfavorable assessment of the Dalai Lama and his rule, the paper now asserted, "There is no tyrant's rule or despot's lordship there. Its people are virile, brave and free." The writer added with apparent approval an unidentified quote which painted an idyllic picture of "the high mountains and wide plateaux which give them home and pasture . . . and a freedom very few nations enjoy . . . unencumbered by no regal laws and where no petulant government disturbs their tranquil lives, no magisterial authority breaks the monotony of their romantic existence." The journalist warned, "Disturb them [the Tibetans] and you disturb a man who loves his country, put them under law and bondage and you will meet with strong resistance. . . . [While] the new young Republic is now looking for new worlds to conquer [and] an outlet is needed for her vast millions [the Chinese should move slowly as] Tibet was made for the Tibetans and nobody else." From his end-of-the-line outpost the American consul found this article with its rediscovery of Tibet and its people "very convincing."

The Tibetans may well have had mixed feelings about their neglect by the Great Powers. Although Lhasa could not count on London's support to counter any moves by the Chinese to extend its authority over Tibet, the Tibetans were left comparatively free to take advantage of the vacuum in Chinese authority on the eastern side of the Upper Yangtze, in which more than half of the Tibetan population lived.

The new revolutionary government in Peking, however, was as unwilling to give up its claims to these border lands as its imperial predecessors had been. It consequently continued a desultory military campaign to impose its authority over this area which McMahon had proposed be delineated as Inner Tibet under Chinese suzerainty—but not sovereignty. These sporadic hostilities kept the area in a state of unrest. Ill-supported Chinese troops scrounged to maintain themselves in this remote area of mighty rivers, deep gorges, and high passes crossed by difficult trails but few roads that the American consul had vainly tried to call to Washington's attention. In 1917 an ambitious Chinese governor of one of these contested provinces, Sichuan, in an attempt to intimidate his rebellious subjects into total submission, intensified hostilities accompanied by "noisy threats and menacing gestures." This roused the British government to lift its ban temporarily and release a small amount of ammunition, which the Tibetans made effective use of to drive the Chinese back across the Yangtze River and move deep into the province of Sichuan. The British had also sent their consul Eric Teichman to broker a truce between the two forces contending along the border. The Tibetans were well on their way to making good their claim to Inner Tibet, but were unable to advance farther without additional arms, which the British refused to supply. The Chinese were therefore quite happy to accept a ceasefire in August 1918 which called for the Tibetans to withdraw to a line along the Upper Yangtze that was roughly the same as the historic Manchu border. The boundaries set and signed in the armistice were intended to be part of an overall agreement on the issues governing Peking's relations with Tibet, but it was never concluded. Although both sides tacitly agreed to accept the border as defined in the armistice, the status of these areas was to remain unresolved and the subject of continuing contention between the Dalai Lama and his supporters and the present rulers of China nine decades later.

CHAPTER THREE

Beyond the Horizon

For the next three decades the Dalai Lama and the affairs of his country were in international political limbo, particularly in the United States and with only occasional spurts of British interest. This seclusion from world politics had been foreshadowed by events at the Versailles Peace Conference.

When they arrived in Paris in 1919 the Chinese found themselves submerged in the horse-trading that was going on among the former allies. The immediate concern was the reallocation of the territories of the defeated German and Ottoman Empires, which meant a concentration on affairs closer to home than on what was happening in the successor to the Manchu state in China. For the American president the paramount issue was to ensure the activation of the League of Nations. He consequently felt the need to yield to the Japanese threat to walk out of the Conference unless they were granted continued control over the powerful economic and political concessions in China's Shantung peninsula, which they had obtained as a prize of war.

Within a week the deal was reported in all of the major Chinese newspapers, leading to demonstrations in Tiananmen Square on May 4, 1919, by students from Peking University, which spread throughout China and were to be a seminal event in the development of Chinese nationalism. The Chinese delegation refused to sign the Versailles Treaty and eventually made its separate peace with Germany in September 1919.

Although by this time the Chinese might well have been disillusioned by the action of the United States and its British colleagues, one of the principal members of the Chinese delegation, Wellington Koo, was apparently still willing—or perhaps encouraged—to engage in some diplomatic shopping. At the time that he and his colleagues were negotiating a separate armistice with the Germans, Koo informed the leader of the American delegation, Franklin Polk, that for some time his government had been considering a proposal made by England before the war that China consent to establish Tibet as an autonomous state to act as a buffer to protect the Indian frontier. According to the Chinese diplomat, his government was willing to acquiesce in such an arrangement if the British would sign a treaty promising to come to the aid of China if she were threatened by an unprovoked attack (presumably by Japan). Polk agreed that from the Chinese standpoint this might be a desirable arrangement, but suggested that Koo consult Washington on how President Wilson might view this proposal, as "he was tremendously interested in the Chinese-Japanese situation."[1]

There is no record that Wilson ever heard of this latest dangle by the Chinese government to use Tibet as trading stock. At the time it was made, he was on his final barnstorming tour of the United States in his futile effort to build public pressure on the Senate to ratify the Versailles Treaty, with its controversial covenant establishing the League of Nations. The president had a massive stroke on October 2, 1919, soon after his return to the White House, and his time as an effectively functioning president was over. He continued to direct his unsuccessful campaign for Senate ratification of the League from his sickbed. Concerns about relatively peripheral foreign issues such as his country's relationship with the splintered Chinese state and its shadowy administration of its remote frontier dependencies were not on his agenda. It was to be another forty years before a secretary of state was prepared to tell the Dalai Lama that the United States government believed that the principle of self-determination "should apply to the people of Tibet and that they should have the determining voice in their own political destiny."[2]

The British Patrons

For the next three decades Washington, a bystander in events concerning Tibet, deferred to its British colleagues to fill the vacuum left by the inability of the Chinese government to exercise its claim to authority there. Beginning in 1921 Charles Bell, the Dalai Lama's unofficial British mentor, counselor, and friend during his exile in Darjeeling a decade earlier, met regularly with the Dalai Lama to work out the details of the aid that Britain had decided to provide. This assistance was intended to give him increased capability to bolster the de facto autonomy he was exercising. China was given formal notice of this new policy in a memorandum dated August 26, 1921, which was given to Wellington Koo, who was then the Chinese Minister to London.[3] The memorandum noted that the Chinese had accepted the agreement, with the exception of the boundary clause negotiated at Simla, which provided for Tibetan autonomy under Chinese suzerainty. Accordingly Foreign Minister George Curzon informed Koo, "We regard ourselves as at liberty to deal with Tibet as an autonomous State, if necessary without any reference to China, to enter into closer relations with her, to send an officer to Lhasa from time to time and to give the Tibetans any reasonable assistance they might require in the development and protection of their country."[4]

By providing limited military aid and political support Britain would regain its presence in Tibet, which had been sidetracked by the war. London agreed to provide a modest amount of arms and ammunition and an inconspicuous program of training officers and men of the small but relatively effective developing Tibetan army that Tsarong Shape was developing. The aim was to create a regular professional army, an institution that Tibet had never had. On the civil side a telegraph line was constructed from the British outpost of Gyantse in southern Tibet to Lhasa, giving the Tibetans the means, albeit through British channels and thus under their surveillance, to communicate in a timely fashion with the outside world. In addition a British officer conducted a geological survey in central Tibet to locate exploitable mineral resources; assistance was provided for obtaining equipment to build a hydroelectric plant in Lhasa; a Sikkimese officer was sent to organize a small police force in the capital; and a small English school was opened in Gyantse "for the children of noble and middle-class Tibetan families."[5]

This modest nation-building program was intended to provide the Dalai Lama with the elementary tools to bring Tibet into contact with the modern world and served as tacit British support of the Tibetans' challenge to Chinese efforts to expand their Yangtze borders. It did not flourish. The Dalai Lama's role in Tibetan political life had been a central but practicably limited one, hedged by the traditions of an entrenched and powerful religious hierarchy whose members were committed to the preservation of their offices and way of life. Throughout the nineteenth century none of the Thirteenth Dalai Lama's predecessors had lived long after they reached their majority at age eighteen. The powerful monastery heads, with their determined isolationism, had meanwhile maintained their feudal domains, opposed to any interference by either foreign forces or ideas. They regarded a professional army of laymen, armed and trained by foreigners, as a threat to the controlling role they had established for themselves as the primary protectors of Tibet's traditional political and social structure.

One of the prime targets of the monastic establishment was D. D. Tsarong, the commander of the skeletal army, a post to which he had been appointed in recognition of his role in repelling a Chinese force pursuing the Dalai Lama when he fled to India in 1910.[6] Tsarong had become a great favorite of the Dalai Lama, who had approved his marriage into a family that was one of the pillars of the Lhasa lay nobility. A new modern army was therefore not only a threat in itself; under the leadership of a leading figure of the rival civil power structure it was doubly repellent to the monastic establishment and to be resisted. Tsarong had also become associated with the Sikkimese police officer Rai Bahadur Laden La, a Bell protégé who in 1923 organized a two-hundred-man police force in Lhasa. Despite the jealousy that quickly grew between Laden La's police and Tsarong's regular army, the two men became close friends and allies in the effort to bring modernization to Lhasa.

This all came to an abrupt end in 1924, when some of Tsarong's soldiers became resentful of the higher salaries being paid to Laden La's policemen. In the aftermath of considerable brouhaha among the various political factions in the Lhasa political and clerical establishment, Laden La returned to Sikkim in October 1924, leaving the police force in disarray. Tsarong and the officers of the army corps loyal to him were relieved of their commands shortly after. This attempt at nation building had failed, and the shadow presence of British support for an independent Tibetan identity apart from Peking that it implied was a collateral casualty.

So too the English school opened in 1923 at Gyantse by a modest but able schoolteacher, Frank Ludlow, teaching modern science and subjects, was regarded as a competitor to the monopoly on the solely religious education carried on by the monasteries. The school was a failure due to the reluctance of local families to send their sons there, lack of support from both the Lhasa government and Ludlow's superiors in Calcutta, and possibly the repercussions of the Laden La–Tsarong politicking in Lhasa. Its lasting achievement seems to have been that of introducing soccer to Tibet. When Ludlow's three-year contract expired it was not renewed, and the school closed. A geological survey and the introduction of modern machinery represented further threats to an established way of life and also went nowhere. All of these programs had some supporters, but they were primarily among the old ruling lay families who had neither the will nor the political strength to challenge the monastic establishment. Furthermore a long-standing dispute between the Lhasa government and the Panchen Lama, with whom the British had maintained a long relationship, spilled over into a popular feeling against the British and the reforms with which they were identified. All of these long-held convictions and sentiments combined to identify modernization with a foreign threat to the society and culture that had evolved in isolation in the high Himalayas. The Americans, who were to experience similar disappointments in nation building elsewhere several decades later, were disengaged onlookers in these events.

Against this background the agreement which the Dalai Lama had worked out with his British political godfather and friend Charles Bell represented a significant political gamble for the Tibetan ruler. Moreover he must have had conflicting emotions as he attempted to move his entrenched society into a new identity disruptive to key elements of both the culture he was committed to preserve and his own instincts and thought patterns instilled in his formative years. His years of exile abroad had educated him in the ways of an outside world that his constituents knew little about and with which even he must have felt some uneasiness. His partial moves toward modernization and ending Tibet's isolation, while faltering and inadequate, were therefore in their own way heroic. They were, however, not enough to overwhelm the ethos of his fellow countrymen. Their identity was defined by standing apart and resisting the outside world. This balancing act between the Dalai Lama's ambivalent acceptance of the necessary evil of modernization and his constituents' resistance to it, coupled with rumors of British involvement in coup plotting, seems to have come to a head in 1925. There was a definite waning of British influence in Tibet for the rest of that decade.

Although Bell understood and respected the Tibetans' resistance to change, he believed that Tibet must gradually come in contact with the rest of the world. With fortitude and some misgivings,[7] he therefore traded on the unique confidence that the Dalai Lama had placed in him to obtain his permission for a British reconnaissance party to climb Mt. Everest. George Leigh Mallory, who headed the party, died on the attempt in 1924, but he had opened the way for subsequent foreigners to intrude on Tibetan land. This dispensation did not extend to Lhasa, which became the target of adventurers using guile and disguises, some of whose attempts were successful and recorded in best-selling books in the 1920s.[8] The first Englishwoman to enter Lhasa was the wife of Colonel Leslie Weir, a political officer who spent two months there as part of an official mission in 1930. Although these expeditions and the posting of hardy public servants popularized the legend of Tibet as a remote and unique country, British political influence reached its apex in the years immediately following Bell's tour. For the remainder of the Dalai Lama's twelve-year reign Britain was not a major factor in Tibetan affairs or its international status.

The United States as Bystander

Throughout this period, as the United States drifted toward isolationism, Washington's primary interest in foreign affairs concerned events in Europe. Its ambivalent paternalism toward events in the declining Manchu Empire was submerged by the 1911 Revolution, then the greater concerns of the First World War, followed by chronic civil war and the increasing role of the Japanese throughout the Chinese mainland. It was quite prepared to defer to the British on matters affecting China's relationship with the Thirteenth Dalai Lama, no longer China's vassal, and his remote country.

As spectators of events in Tibet the American legation in Peking and consulates in Chungking and Kunming kept only watching briefs on the efforts of the new Chinese government to maintain its weak authority over the Dalai Lama and his people on both sides of the Yangtze. The truce which the British consul Eric Teichman brokered in 1918 further diminished whatever marginal sense of obligation the American consulates may have felt to provide detailed or even timely reporting on what was happening on the border as the Chinese government made fitful efforts to exercise the authority they continued to claim, but could not maintain, over the equally unyielding local Tibetans. A typical dispatch from the Chungking consulate in May 1921 reported a fresh outbreak of violence "at a place called Changtu . . . west of Batang," a principal Khampa town from which the leadership of the revolt in the 1950s originated.[9]

For the most part the consulates were dependent on sporadic contacts with the tenacious American missionaries working in these outposts. One of these, a medical missionary from Indiana, Albert Shelton, was particularly well placed to report on what was happening in the continuing efforts of the Manchus and their successors to impose their authority over the Tibetans in the disputed Yangtze border area. Shelton lived among the Khampa people in the Yangtze border town of Batang from 1908 until he was killed by bandits in 1922. He was so accepted by the Tibetans that in 1918 he was asked to mediate on their behalf with the Chinese forces who were unsuccessfully trying to impose their authority in this disputed area. His wife wrote, "[He] established a Christian home and reared a family among the people he had come to save. That is of itself a tremendous factor in the Christian conquest of a primitive people. He taught them that cleanliness is a part of godliness."

He was the first man to take a bathtub into Tibet; he introduced alfalfa there. Believing that music had charms to soothe the Tibetan breast, on his return from his first furlough in America he brought an organ with him, the first one ever carried into that country. He constructed a hospital at Batang with provision for fifty patients and capable of caring for as many more. "This hospital is of itself a monument of the man's trust, his industry, his foresight."[10] Shelton's contribution to their medical care more than their personal hygiene apparently endeared him to the Tibetans as he believed he had the Dalai Lama's permission to go to Lhasa to carry out his lifelong dream of opening a hospital there.[11] From 1908 to 1922 the consulate in Chengdu thus had a man very familiar with the local scene on the distant border had they chosen—or had the opportunity—to tap his knowledge.

The only professional U.S. intelligence report on conditions in Tibet during this period was the one prepared by the assistant military attaché at the Peking legation, Major John Magruder, on August 10, 1921.[12] It was based on a six-month trip starting in Kunming by pony pack train into the Tibetan areas in Yunnan. From there he proceeded north to Sichuan, west through the Tibetan Marches, "reentering Chinese territory" three weeks later, from where he made his way by foot, river boat, and finally rail to Peking, covering some of the same ground in the frontier area that Rockhill had traversed on his two unsuccessful attempts to make it to Lhasa thirty years before. Magruder was in many ways an American counterpart to the British frontier cadre. He was a Virginia gentleman, educated at the Virginia Military Institute, whose early service was in his country's colonial ward, the Philippines. Unlike his British colleagues who went to Tibet to perform substantive missions, Magruder traveled to Tibet solely as a professional observer.

Magruder's account reflected the limited purpose of his travel. It was written as a reconnaissance report and appraisal of conditions in an area of marginal interest to the United States except for the chronic military tension there, which threatened the durability of the new Chinese republic. It was the first made by an American official to the area. By 1921 the unsettled conditions in this remote region, with their potential for challenge to the still unestablished Chinese government and consequent international implications, had made the situation there of at least tactical interest to the legation. Today these areas are very much in the center of the Dalai Lama's Middle Way proposals to resolve the contested status of his country.

On his more limited forays Rockhill had confined his observations about the Tibetan people primarily to the way they lived, which he described with the zeal of a museum collector. No eating bowl, saddle, or tent had been too insignificant to escape his notice, but his comments on the character of the people were less detailed. Magruder, the military observer, was concerned with the governing structure and the temperament of the Tibetans on both sides of the unfixed frontier as indicators of the political durability of this contested area. He was struck by the lack of resentment against the "over-whelming control over every phase of life and human activity" exercised by the monasteries and their abbots. This he attributed to "there being no inde-pendent thought in Tibet": "So little intercourse has there been with the outer world that it has been simple for the lamas to maintain that ideal of fixed religious orders—status quo. It seems inconceivable to the western mind that here exists today such blatant religious tyranny without any rebellious movement to destroy it." Magruder noted philosophically, "Tibet does not suffer the evil of religion in politics—but is afflicted with a religion which controls or is its whole political structure. . . . [But] despite this condition which arrests all progress, it is a fact that the people are unconscious of any rights withheld. There is not the slightest stir of radicalism in Tibet—a situa-tion almost unique in the world today—and the people appear quite happy and contented with things as they are."

Magruder described the Tibetans as "lacking in a high moral sense." "But," he continued, "they do not impress me as being immoral. The women are not permiscuous [sic], and, except in villages like Batang where they have been contaminated by the Chinese, there is no prostitution. But if it may be said that cattle in the fields are immoral, then the Tibetans, who are almost as natural as flocks, are immoral. There seem to exist none of the nobler affections and sentiments between men and women, nor does one hear of jealousy." He believed it was this latter virtue which made both polygamy and polyandry "purely an economic question and not an ethical one."[13]

The military attaché was similarly accepting—if clinical—about practices that others might fault in the Tibetans' way of life. Although he found the Ti-betans "blindly devout" in the practice of their "stupefying religion," he noted, "The very nature of their faith lulls them into a state of laissez faire to the point of killing all missionary zeal [and therefore they are] not fanatics and not in any sense dangerous because of their religion unless goaded to the extreme." Similarly he wrote, "The Tibetans are much given to lying. . . . It is not mali-cious, but is simply a result of the oriental tendency to avoid fact." In general he found the Tibetans to be "children of nature": "[They have] all the lack of modesty of children and appear to obey their impulses as naturally as the cattle and sheep in their herds. . . . The men are generally big, upstanding healthy specimens, and the women strong and capable looking. Infant mortality was high, and therefore the Tibetans truly represented the survival of the fittest."

Magruder's evaluation of the Tibetan army was critical but generally favorable: "As in China, there is a confusion of authority between civil and military officials too complex for the western mind to grasp." While Magruder was making his survey of the eastern frontier area, Charles Bell was in Lhasa organizing the British program of providing military equipment and training to modernize the Tibetan army. It would be some years before the products of this modest program would have any demonstrable, and then only transitory, effect. What Magruder was reporting on was the existing army of roughly six thousand variously armed and trained men. He was told that there was some mountain artillery stationed in Lhasa, but none in the border area on which he was reporting. There were no technical services, nor did the army officials have any maps of the area they were defending. In any event, the "technical ideas of the officers [were] those of children." However, he found the morale of the troops was good, and the men evinced a "lively interest and pride" in the drills and exercises. "The discipline was not harsh, but seemed the result of cheerful obedience and the natural subordination of the Tibetan to his superiors." Besides, any disobedience would likely be treated with severe measures. He explained, "[The officers are chosen] from the higher class of people who have always been accustomed to respect from the lower classes, but intimacy with their men is quite to be expected in a country where even the slaves [sic] eat at the same table and live in the same quarters as their masters." He found the Tibetan to be a "good shot, . . . trained to use a rifle and waste no ammunition, . . . inured to the hardship of camp and trail," and accustomed to "the simplest normal ration in the world." He concluded that the Tibetan soldier would prove a worthy antagonist in his own country.

Contrary to the popular perception of the Tibetans as xenophobic and opposed to contact with the outside world, Magruder found, "The Tibetans are by nature most hospitable. . . . There was never the slightest evidence of anti-foreign sentiment, but on the contrary only the most marked interest and friendliness was shown by the inhabitants. The officials everywhere were most hospitable, eager to assist us at all times, and spared nothing to show us honor and courtesy." He concluded that his reception had convinced him "that in the future should Americans have occasion to enter Tibet for any proper purpose, they will be received with great courtesy."

Magruder's extensive survey of Tibet, which he filed with 154 accompanying photographs, was a pioneer effort. It was supplemented by more limited surveys and reports by the American consular officers stationed in western China, but was not matched until twenty years later, when Ilya Tolstoy and Brooke Dolan made their trip to Lhasa as officers of the Office of Strategic Services (oss) and from there across central and eastern Tibet to Peking. There is no record of how Magruder's report was received by his superiors at the legation in Peking. His services were obviously well regarded, as he was promoted from assistant to full attaché during the nine years he remained in China.[14] The power struggle among the warring factions which was beginning when Magruder arrived back in Peking in the summer of 1921 focused the attention of the legation on events within the heart of China rather than on what was happening on the western frontier and the other side of the headwaters of the Yangtze.

CHAPTER FOUR

The United States Sits Out

When John Magruder left his post as military attaché in 1930 after his ten-year tour, the American legation in Peking lost its China hand most knowledgeable about Tibet. The loss was probably not noted in Washington. Interest in China was then focused on the potential fragmentation of the Chinese mainland, threatened by the Japanese occupation of Manchuria and the struggle for military control and political supremacy by the forces of the Nationalist leader Chiang Kai-shek against both the growing Communist army under Mao Tse-tung and the troops of the perennial warlords.

Washington found no occasion to take note of events in Tibet until the Thirteenth Dalai Lama died in 1933, and then its attention was fleeting. Word of the pontiff's death came in a radiogram to Suydam Cutting, a wealthy financier in New York who traveled to remote areas of the world on behalf of various American museums. In 1930 he made his way into southern Tibet, but not all the way to Lhasa. He had, however, established an indirect relationship with the Dalai Lama, to whom he had sent two dachshunds and two Dalmatians.

The dogs did not survive the trip, although the Dalai Lama sent Cutting letters thanking him for them. He also asked Cutting to intercede with the United States government to permit his ministers to buy silver directly from the United States rather than through the Indian government, which had raised the import duty on the silver bars that the Tibetans required for trade. Although Cutting believed that "the ruler's scheme was decidedly impracticable," he discussed it with the State Department and thereby "did not deprive him of the satisfaction of hearing it had been presented to the American government." The well-connected Cutting had obtained an autographed photograph of President Hoover which the Dalai Lama accepted "with jubilation."[1]

Cutting used the Old Boy network to ask his friend Kermit Roosevelt to urge his kinsman FDR to write a condolence note. In sending his "Dear Franklin" request, Kermit suggested that FDR use what he said was the customary opening salutation "I trust that Your Holiness is well as due to Your Holiness' kindness, I am also well." He explained, "Of course the new Dalai Lama, although only a month old, is theoretically as aged as the hills."[2] This would seem to be an ultraorthodox reading concerning the unbroken continuity of Dalai Lamas, as the "new Dalai Lama" was officially "discovered" only five years later.

When FDR asked the State Department's advice on whether he should send such a message, Undersecretary William Phillips, a particularly protocol-conscious officer, recommended against it. He feared that the Chinese might "misinterpret" the president's action as interference in their sovereignty, to which the Dalai Lama was "theoretically, at least, subject"; that the British might take offense, given their "special position . . . in Tibetan affairs"; that such a message might arouse Soviet "suspicions of anything going on in Tibet"; and that the Japanese might claim such an action "concerning a functionary over whom the Chinese claim sovereignty [was] somewhat inconsistent with the non-recognition of Pu-yi as sovereign of Manchukuo. Besides, the Panchen Lama, who [the State Department] believe[d was] contesting the selection of the present Dalai Lama, might complain of such interference in Tibetan politics."

Phillips was acting on the advice of the Division of Far Eastern Affairs, which included one further objection: "The present Dalai Lama is an infant . . . and his government is noted for attempted intrigue and it is hard to tell what use they might make of the fact that the President of the United States took occasion to communicate directly with the Dalai Lama."[3] As it had been barely a month since the Thirteenth Dalai Lama died and several former Dalai Lamas had not been discovered for eighteen months or more after the death of their predecessor, the State Department would seem to have been premature in expressing concern about the misuse of an infant successor who didn't officially yet exist.

The president, however, accepted Phillips's reservations. In a letter to Cutting's intermediary Kermit Roosevelt, FDR's secretary wrote, "[The president] doubts the propriety of his writing [to the Dalai Lama], although he personally would love to do it."[4] The Old Boys had been trumped by the foreign service professionals.

Mao Appears on the Screen

Washington did take a transient interest in Tibet when Mao Tse-tung's forces made their Long March from Kiangsi to Yenan in 1934–35. The American legation and consulates seem to have been mainly concerned about the effect the passage of this ragged band and their clashes with Chiang Kai-shek's pursuing troops might have on the American missionaries in the areas through which they were passing. The political implications of the Communists' relocation of their capital to northern China were yet to be appreciated. The consulate in Kunming reported, "The Communists have had an easy time of it in Kweichow, as the provincial troops have done nothing but run away from them . . . and lost a large number of men in their retreat merely because they couldn't run fast enough."[5] This candid assessment of the quality of the Nationalist troops was seconded by the vice consul at Nanking, who reported that Chiang could not trust any of the generals who should be confronting Mao's forces in Sichuan. He quoted "a young Chinese military officer of rank, who was educated in the United States and Europe," as saying that "the provincial forces would take to the field and telegraph reports that they had engaged and exterminated large numbers of the Communists, when actually no fighting would occur."[6] Despite this bleak assessment the Nationalist officer did not believe that "the Communist bandits" constituted a serious menace to China as a whole. He said that "all of China, except Sichuan, Kweichow, and Yunnan, was now free of any serious danger from Communism, and even if the Communists should entrench themselves in Sichuan the rest of China had been saved and the 'remnant' Communists would be completely exterminated in two, three, four or five years."

Soon after the Nationalist officer's optimistic prediction the Communist forces made their way westward, passing within ten miles of Yunnanfu, from where the Gimo and Madame Chiang, who had been staying there, were forced to flee on the French railway toward Indochina. This turned out to be a diversion, as the main body of Mao's army was making its way to the relative safety of western Sichuan, where it turned north, heading for the Sichuan-Gansu border. It was there that the Tibetans had their first encounter with the Red Army. It was not a happy occasion for either party. The Red Army was traveling along the Chinese Tibetan border, the area of the Mantzu tribal people and the Tibetan nomads, through a vast swamp of high, wild grass growing in muck and pools of water. They began their slogging journey with skimpy rations of confiscated Tibetan green wheat and giant turnips and beets in late August, which is one of the rainiest and foggiest months of the year. Mao told Edgar Snow the turnips were so enormous that one would feed fifteen men.[7] They were, however, alien to Chinese stomachs and produced further misery. Without referring to this unfortunate side effect, Snow quotes Mao humorously saying, "This is our only foreign debt, and some day we must pay the Mantzu and the Tibetans for the provisions we were obliged to take from them."[8]

In October 1935 Mao finally led his depleted force into Shensi, where he settled down for the winter. A year later Chang Kuo-tao and Zhu De led their troops, which had split off during the Long March from the main force and settled in eastern Szechuan, across the formidable grasslands to join Mao at his stronghold. In September 1936 an obviously relieved consul in Kunming reported, "For the first time [since] the undersigned assumed charge of this post twenty-one months ago, the monthly political report will contain no communist information, all important red groups having migrated to other consular districts."[9]

Snow, who made the trek to Shensi in 1936 to interview Mao in his relocated headquarters, noted in his now classic *Red Star over China* that local inhabitants had taken to the mountains. "Only by capturing tribesmen could they [Mao's forces] find guides through the country." But the soldiers made friends of the locals: "Some of them are now students in the Communist Party School in Shensi, and will one day return to their land to tell the people the difference between 'Red' and 'White' Chinese." Ironically it was a young Khampa named Phuntsok Wanggyal, who was attending the Mongolian-Tibetan College attached to the Central Politics College of which Chiang Kai-shek was president, who was to found the Tibetan Communist Revolutionary Party three years later.[10]

The British Presence in Lhasa

During these years of what later proved to be seminal events in China with momentous consequences for Tibet, the British finally achieved the long-sought goal of establishing a permanent presence in Lhasa. With a modest support staff composed of a medical officer, a radio operator, and two clerks, Hugh Richardson, a visiting young political officer, remained there on a temporary basis until the British government turned the mission over to their Indian successors in 1947. Richardson wrote, "The Tibetan Government never questioned the status of the Mission, and this 'semi-permanent' representation at Lhasa was, therefore, an example of the advantage of falling in with the Central Asian tendency to avoid precise definitions."[11] The new Indian government valued Richardson's knowledge of Tibet, and he remained there as officer in charge of the successor Indian mission until 1950.[12]

Reportedly the British consolidated their position in Lhasa by "moderately large" payments to Tibetan officials, both lay and clerical. According to David McKay, "In the absence of any other effective policy weapon, payments to individual Tibetans became the central pillar of the cadres' [the frontiersmen] policy."[13] Richardson later criticized this policy, although he must have been one of the early executors, saying, "A good deal of money flowed into Tibet during the war years, but it fell into individual hands and did not do any good to the country."[14] Whatever the means, by the late 1930s the British had ensured that a modus vivendi prevailed which accommodated a British presence in a capital under the actual rule of a Tibetan sovereign whose authority the suzerain Chinese were in no position to challenge.

Eric Teichman, the British consular officer who twenty years earlier had negotiated the armistice containing the chronic border war between the Tibetans and the Chinese Nationalist successors to the Manchus and their claims to authority over Tibet, described this indeterminate but quiescent situation:

> The Lhasa Government, representing the dominion of the great monasteries and the Lama Church, still rule over autonomous Tibet; their eastern boundary remaining undefined and swinging to the east or west as the result of intermittent frontier wars. Lhasa-ruled Tibet, though nominally a part of China, has no official connection with its suzerain. Intercourse of a kind subsists, for the Tibetans must have their coarse brick tea, which comes from Szechuan. Apart from frontier skirmishing, no real hostility exists on either side. To the Tibetans the bonds of tradition, sentiment and faith which bound them formerly to the China of the Manchu Emperors, have never been completely severed; only the new manners, doctrines and ideas of modern China seem to them strange and incomprehensible. The Chinese, on their side, if they think about Tibet at all, adopt the attitude that the Tibetans are as errant children meriting chastisement and corrections which their masters are not for the moment in a position to inflict, and that the Dalai Lama and his ministers have been

but temporarily estranged through misunderstandings due to the intrigue of a foreign Power.[15]

American Views of Tibet

The United States government had few such specialists—or objectives—in Tibet during this period. After Magruder left Peking in 1930, there were few American foreign service officers with even the knowledge that he had gained on his five-months' survey of the Tibetan border area ten years earlier. Unlike the British "frontiersmen," their American colleagues on the China watch had no mission to establish a presence or take anything more than a passing interest in events in Tibet. In reporting on the death of the Thirteenth Dalai Lama the legation in Peking suggested that both sides might make concessions in the long-standing dispute over the boundary, but added, "China, however, is usually inept in dealing with outlying territories." The dispatch drafter did include a bit of unsourced local conjecture: "If Pu Yi should become an emperor to whom Inner Mongolia gave allegiance, Tibet might be interested as the Manchu emperors made Lamaism a state religion and as the Mongols are Lamaists."[16] The body of the dispatch, however, was devoted to a thoughtful analysis of the history and current unresolved issues involved in the Yangtze border area dispute, complete with a hand-drawn annotated map of the boundaries under dispute—as they remain seventy-seven years later.

In 1939 the American consul general in Calcutta, J. C. White, spent a month in southern Tibet. He was unable to go beyond Gyantse, where the British maintained one of the three trade marts accorded them in the treaty Younghusband had negotiated thirty-five years earlier. Basil Gould, who was then the British political officer in charge of relations with Tibet, made it very clear that he would not give permission for his American colleague to go even to Gyantse if he thought he had any intention of proceeding on to Lhasa.[17]

Washington's only other on-the-scene reports came from unofficial American travelers. The two principal ones were the gentlemen explorers Brooke Dolan and Suydam Cutting. Both came from a social class comfortable with the British Himalayan frontiersmen, but the two Americans' interest in Tibet was in its animals and culture rather than its politics, although they both had access to those within the Lhasa power structure. Dolan was a friend and correspondent of FDR's distant cousin Kermit Roosevelt, with whom he shared an interest in natural science. In 1931, at age twenty-three, having dropped out of Princeton in his junior year, he organized and led an expedition to western China and northeastern Tibet for the Philadelphia Academy of Natural Sciences. He brought back the first specimen of the giant panda to the United States. Dolan apparently did try to alert his government to what was happening in China during the time of his second trip. Although the territory in which he was hunting was considerably east of the site of Mao's Long March, Dolan informed the American consul in Nanking of "the danger which might be apprehended from the military operations . . . in progress in Szechuan Province between the National Government and the Communists."[18] Dolan was accompanied on this trip by "Junge" Schafer, a German zoologist. Although aware of his teammate's political views—he had been an early member of Himmler's ss and led an expedition to Tibet in 1938 sponsored by Himmler—they remained friends until the outbreak of the war.[19] It was these two trips, followed by his continued interest in Tibet and his friendship with the other two American gentlemen frontiersmen, Kermit Roosevelt and Cutting, that secured Dolan a berth on the oss mission led by another well-born explorer, Count Ilya Tolstoy, to Lhasa in 1942.

Cutting had made exploratory trips on behalf of various American museums to Ethiopia, Assam, Yunnan, Burma, and the Galapagos Islands. Unlike the lonely hunter Dolan, he had a more active curiosity in the political situation in these remote areas. His interest in Tibet began in 1930, when he was able to visit southern Tibet and began his correspondence with the Thirteenth Dalai Lama, seeking to visit Lhasa. Despite Cutting's letters and gifts, the Tibetan ruler did not send him the desired invitation, which he received from the regent two years after the Dalai Lama's death. Cutting finally made it to Lhasa in 1935 and again in 1937, when he was accompanied by his wife in response to an unprecedented invitation that included her. In addition to meeting with two of the four boys educated at Rugby, Cutting became well acquainted with the power brokers of the Tibetan capital, including Tsarong Shape, who, despite his removal from the high office he had once occupied, remained a man of political influence.

Although the State Department did not encourage his unofficial efforts to nurture at least a passing acquaintanceship between his government and the Tibetans, Cutting did keep its officers in the field informed on what was happening in Lhasa. In Calcutta J. C. White reported on a "casual" conversation he had with Cutting in 1937 following his second visit to Lhasa: "On the whole, the desire of the Government of Tibet remains, as formerly, not to increase contact with the rest of the world."[20] Cutting said he found the governing Council of Four "surprisingly well informed as to the outside world, who with other influential Tibetans expressed great interest in the Sino-Japanese hostilities . . . their sympathies [being] manifestly with Japan as they are afraid of the Chinese."[21]

Lhasa was at that time preoccupied with the ongoing search for the successor Dalai Lama. After paying ransom to the local Muslim warlord, Ma Pu-fang, the young boy from near the historic monastery of Kumbum in China's Qinghai province was taken to Lhasa, where he was enthroned on February 22, 1940. The Tibetan authorities carefully choreographed a ceremony which implicitly recognized, but did not officially confirm, the special status of both China and Britain in Tibetan affairs. A new era in Tibet had begun.

The United States government had been a bystander in this whole process. Its interest in Tibet at that time was largely defined by the romantic image of a forbidden kingdom of very special but largely unknowable people, which had been propagated by the box office success in 1937 of the film based on James Hilton's fanciful novel *Lost Horizon.* Ronald Colman played the role of a world-weary but idealistic British civil servant, Hugh Conway, a man of vision and character, similar to the image of George Mallory, the legendary British mountaineer last seen on his final ascent toward the peak of Mt. Everest in 1924. At the end of the film Conway is on his way back to find the hidden valley of Shangri-La, a refuge hidden in the Kunlun Mountains of western Tibet, whose inhabitants live in a monastery where the constraints of time and worldly pressures do not exist. At a time when Americans, like most of the Western world, were suffering from the anxieties of a crushing economic depression and the gathering prospect of world conflict, the movie had a special impact that would permanently color the West's, especially America's, perspective of Tibet as a country and a concept.

The film reviewer of the *New York Times* wrote, "[Although] Hilton objected to being classed as an 'escapist,' he admits that the idea for 'Lost Horizon' was germinated out of anxiety over the European situation and a desire to stage a conception of a world as far removed from this sort of thing as possible."[22] It was to be another decade before American policymakers began to discover the reality of Tibet and the mettle of its young ruler and support his efforts to lead his country and people beyond Shangri-La.

CHAPTER FIVE

Washington Discovers Tibet

Tibet was not to have the luxury of sitting out the war that was engulfing the world in 1939. Its new international relevance was a matter of geography rather than a political revelation. The Japanese occupation of eastern China had shut off the shipment of war supplies to Chiang Kai-shek's forces, and he was looking for alternate routes to obtain supplies from India. In early 1941 he gave orders to begin construction of a road from Sichuan through the contested Yangtze border area to India's North East Frontier Agency. The Tibetan government vigorously opposed the construction of the road, seeing it as a renewal of Chinese efforts to invade and occupy their country.

Initially the government of the Raj in Calcutta also objected to what seemed to be Chiang's intention to build this road without Tibetan consent, arguing that doing so would compromise the de facto independence of Tibet and its consequent value as a buffer state. After Pearl Harbor, however, London, the Raj, and the British legation in Peking were prepared to shelve such issues in the interest of getting supplies to their new Chinese ally to counter the rapidly advancing Japanese army in southeast Asia. The Raj therefore proposed to the Tibetan government that it permit the shipment of supplies provided by the United States through Tibet to China. In deference to Tibetan sensitivities, these supplies would be limited to those carried by pack animals on existing trade trails.

Although the Lhasa government wanted to continue its now firmly established relationship with Britain and India, it was unwilling to provide any new opening wedges, such as an international roadway, in its long-standing policy of discouraging foreign intrusions into Tibet, particularly from China.

News of the proposed supply route from India through the disputed areas of eastern Tibet roused Charles Bell out of his retirement at the Old Charming Inn in British Columbia to warn his former chiefs of the opposition they could expect from the Tibetans to such a project: "[The Tibetans] are Buddhists and in sympathy with the Japanese, whom they look on as fellow-Buddhists. . . . [They] dislike the Chinese, who have treated them very harshly . . . and therefore may probably object to the idea of a road through their territory to help their Chinese enemy against their Japanese friend." Bell did suggest that if the Chinese were to give Tibet "Dominion Status of the kind that Chiang Kai-shek asked Britain to give to India . . . the Tibetans might agree to the road being made, and help in making it."[1] The Foreign Office sarcastically agreed that "perhaps the way could be smoothed if the Chinese could be persuaded to issue off their own bat a self denying declaration about home rule for Tibet," but it too did not "see them doing this at anyone else's suggestion, for what is sauce for the Indian goose is not suitable diet for the Tibetan gander."[2]

Despite continued representations the Tibetan government refused to back down on its opposition to the road. In fact they became more explicit, saying they wished to keep out of the war with Japan.[3] The British ambassador to Peking and the government of India in Calcutta suggested stronger pressure be exerted on the Tibetans in the form of a withdrawal of the promise given in 1941 by the British government to guarantee their "practical autonomy." In addition to this political penalty, they proposed the prevention of the export into Tibet of the Chinese brick tea that is a staple of the Tibetan diet and the imposition of a blockade on the export of Tibetan wool. A Foreign Office minute endorsing this action noted, "[Although] it has been our policy to support the Tibetans' claim to independence, because we want Tibet as a buffer state, [we will support these measures] in the changed conditions of today [i.e., the need to get supplies to their new Chinese ally]." The British did insist, however, that any pronouncement of such threats should be accompanied by pressing "the Chinese Government to announce publicly their policy of non-interference with Tibetan affairs": "In other words that they should do what they are pressuring us to do over India and Burma, and guarantee Tibetan autonomy."[4] The India Office in London added its endorsement of demanding such a guarantee from the Chinese: "Apart from the real value of an assurance by the Chinese in facilitating Tibetan acquiescence in the road scheme, the request will show the Chinese Government that two can play at the game of asking the other side to abandon their domination over alien races."[5]

The Americans Enter the Great Game

This inconclusive discussion about tactics among the British policymakers and the diplomatic deadlock between Peking and Lhasa continued into the summer of 1942, when the United States government entered the scene with a proposal to send two Americans to Lhasa, the first American officials ever dispatched to Tibet. The senior officer was Count Ilya Tolstoy, the author's grandson,[6] and his companion was Lt. Brooke Dolan, who had been an explorer in Tibet ten years earlier. Both were officers of the newly formed Office of Strategic Services, and their mission was to "move across Tibet and make [their] way to Chungking, China, observing the attitudes of the people of Tibet; to seek allies and discover enemies; locate strategic targets and survey the territory as a possible field of activity."[7] A background analysis prepared by OSS headquarters in Washington concerning the impasse over the reluctance of the lamaist government to permit the use of its territory to transport supplies to the perennial Chinese enemy was candid and expansive in its conclusions. It described the Tibetan government as "reactionary, church-controlled and anti-foreign . . . afraid of Chinese aggression due to inroads in the past" but enduring the presence of a Chinese ambassador in Lhasa who was "tactless, hate[d] the Tibetans and [was] hated in return." It recommended, "Though it is realized that the construction of a road to China would take too long to satisfy present war needs, it is considered that such a road would be valuable in maintaining Asiatic peace in the future. Unless Tibet has a protector, she will be conquered by one of her stronger neighbors."[8]

The two OSS officers dispatched to carry out the reconnaissance found a ready welcome in New Delhi in August 1942, when they arrived to negotiate with their British hosts and the Tibetan government. Their old mutual friend Suydam Cutting, now a major with the United States Observer Group, was delighted to provide his advice and contacts on negotiating with the Tibetans. Their hosts, the British frontier officers, recognized and welcomed the two as kindred spirits—gentlemen and outdoorsmen, with a mission that might serve the long-term British interests in Tibet that they were devoting their careers and lives to promoting. All agreed that the chances of the Tibetan government permitting the two men to go across eastern Tibet to China were "very slim." Accordingly Tolstoy and Dolan included in their request for permission to visit Lhasa a promise that unless "invited" by the Tibetan government they would not attempt to proceed beyond Lhasa to China. When the Tibetans, after weeks of consideration, granted the invitation and accorded the two a friendly reception in Lhasa, Tolstoy attributed it to four factors: he carried a letter and relatively modest presents from President Roosevelt to the Dalai Lama; the government of India urged that their request be granted; the British resident officer in Lhasa gave the mission a push; and the Tibetan government had a "sincere desire to establish relations with the U.S.A."[9]

The British representative in Lhasa described the president's gifts as too insignificant to impress the Tibetans.[10] The eight-year-old Dalai Lama, however, regarded the gold watch that Tolstoy had bought at the last minute at a jewelry store in the Mayflower Hotel highly enough to wear it for the ensuing seven decades. As for the letter, at a reception at the Library of Congress on February 19, 2010, he admitted that he had been more interested in the gift and had ignored the letter, "which was more important." He said "he hadn't even known where it was": "It was only yesterday after 68 years that he had received from President Obama a copy of the 1942 letter." While it was an interesting piece of history, the long-buried letter was little more than an introduction of the two house guests. It could have given him little more than a sense that the Americans' interest in his country was one of temporary convenience.[11]

The two men set out for Lhasa in late September 1942, stopping for three weeks in Sikkim with the British political officer for Tibet, Basil Gould, who had "left behind" an officer to set up a "temporary" British residence in Lhasa five years earlier. The incumbent, Frank Ludlow, was on hand to act as their host when they reached the Tibetan capital on December 12, 1942. Ludlow had been headmaster of the ill-fated English school at Gyantse which had opened in 1923. It had closed in 1926 after little support from the parents of the boys and the opposition of local officials, and possibly as a casualty of the fallout from an inept venture at political intrigue in Lhasa politics by his colleagues. In the interim Ludlow had become a highly respected naturalist as a result of his extensive tours throughout western Tibet. He was Tolstoy's sort of man, and the OSS officer consulted him on all matters of procedure in his dealings with the Tibetan officials.

In addition to these ceremonial rounds, the two Americans were very much a part of the Lhasa social scene. Their host, Ludlow, reported that his Christmas party did not break up until midnight. "[The] American visitors were astonished at the natural cheerfulness of our little Lhasa lady friends."[12]

The Americans were highly sought-after guests at the round of parties with which the Lhasa government and noble families, led by the still socially prominent if somewhat politically eclipsed Tsarongs, celebrated the Tibetan New Year.[13] In contrast to these apparently more lusty parties, Ludlow carried out his representational duties more formally when entertaining the First Family of Lhasa. He reported that at his final party in April 1943 the Dalai Lama's mother, "a rather frigid person in the forties with a baby a few days old," came with her daughter and two elder brothers, her sister-in-law, and another lady who were all "possessed of puling infants a few days, or weeks old." As a "hardened bachelor" Ludlow found "the situation . . . at times somewhat embarrassing, especially when infant hunger demanded sustenance, and infant hygiene the attention of nursemaids."[14]

Tolstoy informed Ludlow of his orders to proceed to China, and he agreed that he should seek permission or an "invitation" from the Tibetan government to cross Tibet to reach his destination. It is unlikely that either the British or his Tibetan hosts were surprised by Tolstoy's request, which was granted "over considerable opposition from reactionary ecclesiastical elements." Tolstoy attributed this surprisingly favorable outcome to the "respect and admiration for the U.S.A. and President Roosevelt among Tibetan officials [which was] fairly general and obvious." He cited the letter from the president to the Dalai Lama, which "was warmly received as an omen of happy future relations": "[The Tibetans] realize that the U.S.A. will have a large share in formulating the future peace and freedom of small countries.[15] They hope further to be included among the small independent countries of the world and were therefore anxious to do the U.S.A. the favor—to them a very big favor, unprecedented in 22 years—of permitting foreigners to cross Tibet." There was a second reason beyond this more lofty one, Tolstoy noted: "We may have prejudiced a decision in our favor by calling on the leading monasteries depositing with the abbots presents of money as is customary when foreign officials visit Lhasa." The Count later sent a copy of the thanks for a donation to a large Tibetan monastery of approximately three thousand monks to General William J. Donovan, head of the OSS, saying, "We thought you might be amused by it."[16]

After a final audience with the Dalai Lama and the Tibetan cabinet the two Americans left Lhasa at the end of February 1943 and made their unprecedented journey across Tibet, arriving in Lanchou three months later. They had carried out the United States government's official ceremonial entrance into Tibetan history with style. Although there were no agreements signed or proclamations issued, the energetic Count and his partner may well have raised expectations of future American political support that were to go un-fulfilled. Prior to making his farewell calls Tolstoy had pointed out that the Tibetans had received him and Dolan as envoys of President Roosevelt, although "surprised at [their] low ranks."[17] He noted, "A new angle in our undertaking [has] developed as a result of the importance attached by the British to the interest of the United States in Tibet," and he asked if there was any interest in his undertaking further projects here before going on to China. No response to this bid has been found.

In response to the letter and gifts that the Dalai Lama had sent him FDR wrote, "The messages I have received lead me to believe that Your Holiness and the people of your Pontificate share with me and the people of the United States of America a feeling of reciprocal interest and good-will."[18] Although it was not a bid for a formal alliance and was addressed to the Tibetan ruler in his religious role, it was a step beyond the cautious correspondence with which Tolstoy had been dispatched to Tibet the previous summer. The Tibetans may have believed that they had another card to play in their bid for international recognition.

The only tangible remnants of the Tolstoy visit were three radio transmit-ters and six receivers sent in response to Tibetan hints at their desire to improve their capability to communicate with the outside world. These were dispatched after considerable bureaucratic carping and dithering by an un-sympathetic OSS station commander and some of his State Department and American military colleagues in New Delhi. It was finally resolved by General Joseph Stilwell, the American ambassador of the China-Burma-India theater, who, painfully aware of—and increasingly disdainful of—Chinese "suscep-tibilities," enthusiastically approved the furnishing of this equipment, which he thought would be a good thing and would "give them [the Chinese] a little soap."[19]

Even with this nod of approval from the theater commander, it took over a year to assemble and deliver the equipment. A grateful Dalai Lama and re-gent had sent President Roosevelt "two large silver tea pots, two large silver cups, four silver tea cups with lids, two silver bowls for chang (Tibetan beer), two large silver vessels with spout for chang, all richly engraved and the main designs gold plated and of Tibetan workmanship."[20]

Two British mission radio operators undertook the training of local Tibetan and later more technically oriented Indian and Sikkimese young men to operate the radios. Everything was ready to go, except that the generators sent with the transmitters did not produce enough electricity in the rarified air. A year later three 450-pound generators arrived by pack train in Lhasa.

When the equipment and trained operators were finally in place Tibet had the elements of a rudimentary operational communications network. When the Chinese invaded eastern Tibet in October 1950, however, the newly appointed local Tibetan governor chose not to deploy the additional stations and operators in his area. One of the few tangible legacies of Tolstoy's visit thus went unused when it was most needed.

One of Tolstoy's more characteristically activist ventures was an apparently self-initiated act of extracurricular diplomacy in which he may also have sandbagged his politically guileless British host, Frank Ludlow, into participating. In a letter to his superior, Sir Basil Gould, Ludlow slipped in the bombshell that in one of his final meetings in Lhasa Tolstoy had told the Tibetan Foreign Office that he had recommended to his government that Tibet should be represented at the Peace Conference. Tolstoy, he said, emphasized that he had taken this action entirely on his own initiative and he did not know what reception his proposal would receive.[21] Tolstoy might have been referring to the Pacific War Council, which was being convened in Washington that summer. Subsequent references in the British official files that summer and for the next several months, however, make it clear that both London and Calcutta believed—and were irked—that Tolstoy had breached good form and judgment by issuing an invitation to an event which at that stage of the war was only a hope and to which invitations were not to be freely issued.

The amiable Ludlow reported that when the Tibetans asked for his personal view of Tolstoy's proposal, he had said that his views were "very similar to Tolstoy's": "If the Tibetan Government desired that their case should be represented at the Conference, I would do all in my power to help."[22] On March 14, 1943, five days prior to Tolstoy's and Dolan's departure from Lhasa, the Tibetan Foreign Office representative, "with a sheaf of notes by his side" and with Ringang, one of the four boys educated at Rugby thirty years earlier, translating, informed the two OSS officers and their British host that the regent and the cabinet had considered Tolstoy's suggestion and thought it a "very excellent one and that Tibet should be represented at the Conference." The Tibetan diplomats asked that they be informed as to the manner in which their application for representation should be made, trusting that "the greatest secrecy would be observed, otherwise Chungking might forestall events by taking drastic action before the Conference assembled." The exhilarated Tibetans "went on to explain to Tolstoy and Dolan that Tibet owed her present independence entirely to Great Britain . . . and what the Tibetan Government wished to see was America backing up Great Britain in her efforts to maintain Tibet's independence."[23]

Ludlow's superiors in Calcutta and Gangtok did not share in this exultation over their representative's support for Tolstoy's initiative. An obviously irritated viceroy wrote London, "Unfortunately Ludlow, who otherwise has maintained our position during last year with some sense, committed himself to personal expression of opinion in support of this view, and I am taking steps to inform him of the wisdom of his action. Nor am I impressed by suggestions recently received from Gould and Richardson [Ludlow's intermediate superiors in Gangtok] that Tibet should be prompted to follow up contact made through these representatives of the President of the U.S.A. and send a letter impressing on [the] American Government their theory of independence." The viceroy starchily concluded, "American enlightenment in matters Tibetan may come in due course, but I would judge it unsound that we from here should attempt to hasten the process." He did concede, "Whether we are in a position to call [a] halt to Chinese ambitions in Tibet without parallel action with [the] Americans is a question raised in our official telegram and must, I would judge, depend on degree of pressure which it may be found necessary to apply to the Chinese."[24]

By the time the Raj officialdom reacted to the modest tempest that Tolstoy had stirred up he had left Lhasa and was well on his way to China. His amiable host Ludlow had retired from government service to pursue his lifelong interest in botany, which had always interested him more than politics. Calcutta eventually sent an indecisive cable to Lhasa, leaving it up to Ludlow's successor whether he should "cold shoulder the subject" of Tibetan participation in the Peace Conference or discount Ludlow's "well meant" comments as "entirely personal" and not those of the British government if his hosts raised the issue. This moderately restrained British reaction reflected the united resentment felt by the Foreign Office in London, the Raj in Calcutta, and the Chancery in Chungking toward their Chinese ally, whose actions had frustrated efforts to establish a supply route to China across Tibet. At a meeting of the Pacific War Council in Washington that summer Winston Churchill raised with Chiang Kai-shek's foreign minister, T. V. Soong, the "disturbing rumor . . . that China was massing troops on the borders of Tibet." The British Bulldog expressed the hope that the rumor was unfounded "because it would mean diverting forces away from the true enemy—Japan—and . . . he would regret to see the Chinese take offensive action against a neutral."[25] Soong "emphatically" denied that there was any truth to the rumor, but warned, "Tibet is not a separate nation; . . . it is a part of China and . . . eventually China may have to maintain her sovereignty, but they have no intentions of taking such action at the present time."[26]

Tolstoy's venture into lay diplomacy may have been made more forgivable by the pique that the British felt over Chiang's actions in thwarting the supply route and the saber rattling that Chiang was exhibiting along the Tibetan eastern border. The British, who had initially been huffily offended by Tolstoy's unguided missile diplomacy, ended up regarding it somewhat benignly. Both Whitehall and the Raj were in the process of reviewing Britain's policy toward Tibet, and this unsolicited support for action requiring a review of its international status would seem on a second look not unwelcome. A memorandum prepared jointly by the Foreign Office and the India Office at that time cited Chiang's renewed claims to the right to treat Tibet like any other Chinese province. It specified the potential problem this presented: "We have promised the Tibetan Government to support them in maintaining the practical *autonomy* of Tibet, which is of importance to the security of India and the tranquility of Indian's north-east frontier." The drafters noted that while it was desirable to avoid an open dispute with their wartime ally in Chungking, "discussions between [the British] and the Chinese Government regarding Tibet's status [were] probably inevitable." The British attitude in such discussions would note that while Britain recognized Chinese suzerainty over Tibet, it was on the "understanding that Tibet [was] regarded as autonomous."[27]

The memorandum concluded, "At a later stage it may prove necessary to add that: If the Chinese Government contemplates the withdrawal of Tibetan autonomy, His Majesty's Government and the Government of India must ask themselves whether in the changed circumstances of to-day it would be right for them to continue to recognise even a theoretical status of subservience for a people who desire to be free and have, in fact maintained their freedom for more than 30 years."

British questioning of their policy concerning the status of Tibet continued long after Tolstoy's proposal had been quietly shelved. A Foreign Office minute written the following year commenting on continuing efforts to find a "way of dealing with Tibet which would make Tibet's position stronger and at the same time spare [the British] continued friction with the Chinese" referenced Tolstoy's suggestion that the Tibetans might be represented at the Peace Conference. The Whitehall officer wrote that although their representative in Lhasa had seconded the suggestion, the viceroy had "stepped heavily" on it. He, however, granted, "Theoretically it would seem a good solution if the Tibetan question were taken up by some international body.

But the Chinese are not likely to agree and if we acted as intermediary the effect on Anglo-Chinese relations would be bad apart from the undesirable precedent which would be created for British colonial territories."[28] A reviewing officer found "the point about a precedent specially important": "If Tibet, why not Burma, etc.?"[29]

Despite these qualms over raising precedents that might prejudice imperial interests, both London and those who were to be the last representatives of the Raj in India agreed that Britain should staunchly defend by diplomatic means the Tibetans' right of autonomy. This support became moot after the war and the subsequent dismantling of the empire; the issue was revisited and jettisoned in 1950, when a new Chinese government carried out its threat to impose the authority over Tibet that Chiang had been unable to implement.

Washington Stays Aloof

There is no record in the OSS files that Tolstoy officially informed his superiors of his self-generated venture into international diplomacy, from which the Tibetans seem to have let their American guests and pliant British colleague off the hook. It seems unlikely that the British never raised Tolstoy's buccaneering excursion into international diplomacy with their American ally, or that Tolstoy's superiors never called him to account. Although Washington may never have been officially informed of the specific proposal that he had floated with the Tibetans in Lhasa, he had obviously made no secret of his views. On his outward-bound trip from Lhasa to China he apparently strongly expressed his opinion to his American consulate hosts in Lanzhou that the United States should support the Tibetans in dealings with the Chinese government. Commenting on these conversations, the American chargé in Chungking reported that the Chinese vice minister of foreign affairs complained that he had received reports that "Captain Tolstoy ... assured the Tibetans that the United States would support them in their desire to remain independent of China."[30] The British embassy in Washington also reported, "Colonel Tolstoi, who is known personally to at least one member of the Embassy here, was in Washington for some months last year and talked freely on these lines. . . . It is unfortunately a little optimistic to think these American missionaries for Tibetan independence have made much impression to date." The surprisingly sympathetic diplomat went on to say, "That is not to suggest that their ideas will not eventually percolate or that we should not encourage their good works."[31] It seems more likely, however, that Tolstoy's extracurricular diplomacy was discounted and consequently filed as another instance of excessive zeal, for which there was a certain tolerance granted in Washington for the young "can-do" agency.

The lack of follow-up from Washington to Tolstoy's initiative should have been a conditioning experience for those Tibetans who were prepared to look to their only somewhat committed British allies and their undependable new American friends for support in their efforts to resist incorporation into the Chinese state. The Lhasa government, however, did not neglect the observance of diplomatic niceties toward their suzerain claimant. When Chiang Kai-shek assumed the office of president of the Chinese Republic in late 1943, the Tibetan government sent a message of congratulation and had two "very large" gold medals, each with a large central diamond and turquoise stones, made for the Gimo and Madame Chiang. The British officer in Lhasa commented, "Actions of this kind weaken the foundation . . . of undertakings to render diplomatic support to Tibet vis-a-vis China."[32] The British were in no position, however, to urge the Tibetans to count on them as alternative protectors if they were to counsel the Tibetans to snub their persistent if ineffective would-be Chinese guardians.

When Tolstoy and Dolan returned to Washington in the summer of 1943, they prepared their final eighteen-volume report on their travels, which was to be the United States government's basic country guide to Tibet for the next two decades. The mission was a remarkable bargain in financial terms. Tolstoy's final accounting totaled $42,663.27.[33] He noted, "The present Tibetan Government is most unfavorably minded toward any opening of Tibet, and towards motor vehicles as 'modern and unTibetan.'" He had not broached the subject of a trans-Tibet motor road, writing, "We are not connected with the road project at all to the Tibetan mind."[34] After the Japanese cut off the Burma Road as a supply route to the battered Chinese Nationalist forces, however, Tolstoy revived the possibility of transporting supplies by pack animals through Tibet to China.[35]

In endorsing this proposal to the State Department, Tolstoy's chief, General William J. Donovan, admitted that the amount that could be transported by this means would be of "little material assistance to the armed forces in the China Theater, but it would be of great use in the OSS operations in China."[36] The Department's response was definitely unenthusiastic. It did, however, for the first time admit, "The possible importance of Tibet in relation to the United Nations is not to be disregarded. . . . It might be found desirable to make arrangements in due course, if feasible, for the purchase and shipment to the United States of Tibetan wool and possibly of other Tibetan products; . . . in exchange, the Tibetans would probably be glad to receive certain needed supplies of American medicines and other American products; and . . . eventually it might be considered expedient to endeavor to station an American representative in Tibet."[37] A few weeks later the Department apparently felt less kindly toward the whole project and advised General Donovan that it was "not prepared to undertake the coordination and participation of the Chinese and British authorities as suggested."[38]

The pack train route was never opened, and the flicker of American interest in Tibet aroused by the Tolstoy mission was shelved "for the duration." Later that year the War Production Board did approve the import quota for Tibetan wool that Tolstoy had argued for as an inducement to the Tibetans to approve the supply route.

CHAPTER SIX

A Small Part of the Bigger Picture

In the years immediately after the surrender of Japan in August 1945, Tibet disappeared again from Washington's political radar, lost among greater concerns about what was happening in China and the rest of the world. The Tibetans, however, had by this time begun to recognize more fully that their former isolation was a mixed blessing. Moreover they had become more conscious of the appeal of their unique identity and their ability to represent themselves.

The Tibetans had also correctly concluded that they were going to be on their own in determining their political future. There was considerable debate within the ecclesiastical and lay governing structure about whether and how to reaffirm and give substance to the autonomy they had quietly enjoyed for the past three decades. Their solution was imaginative, shrewd, and very Tibetan. They would send a victory congratulations mission to India and China.[1]

The nominally celebratory mission would provide cover for maintaining ties with the Chinese, which some of the Old Guard, particularly those in the monasteries, favored, while not foreclosing the increasingly distant support of the British for their independence. Such an umbrella might also permit the members of the delegation to negotiate with the Nationalist government to consolidate the de facto independence that Tibet had enjoyed for the past thirty-four years. The plan was for the delegation members to obtain an agreement which would recognize this status for

Tibet and then leave Peking to avoid the National Constitutional Assembly in which Chiang was anxious that they participate as delegates. If they hadn't finished their negotiations before the Assembly met, they were to attend as observers, not delegates, limiting their activities to lobbying for their positions. Fearing that the British might try to foil such bilateral negotiations, the Tibetans did not inform them of their plans, and when the British later learned of them Lhasa denied that they had any such intentions.

The Tibetan delegation's negotiating objectives were defined in a letter to Chiang Kai-shek which was drafted by the National Assembly outlining the parameters of the new relationship they wished to see established with Peking. The very precise letter began with a statement urging the Chinese government to "seek an [i.e., accept an] unrestrained relationship which has its precedent in the patron-preceptor relationship," which the Tibetan government would endeavor to reciprocate "as clearly intended by the religious and secular communities of Tibet." This was a face-saving position reminiscent of the advice given by the tradition-minded American ambassador William Rockhill to the previous Dalai Lama thirty-seven years before—but with a far different conclusion.

The letter went on to declare a considerably more expanded claim to Tibetan authority that reflected the changed power position that the Tibetan government had staked out in these intervening years: Tibet and "Greater Tibet," defined to include the contested eastern border regions, would "continue to maintain the independence of Tibet as a nation ruled by the successive Dalai Lamas through an authentic religious-political rule" with no interference from "the Chinese nor any other government." The restoration of the endowments and estates seized from the Buddhist monasteries and the reduction of the size of the security forces would secure "the well-being and safety of citizens in these border states." As for the able diplomat that Chiang had dispatched to reassert Chinese authority in Lhasa during the closing days of the war, they asked that he be withdrawn, honored "in an appropriate way, but not replaced." Future diplomatic discussions were to be "channeled through the resident Tibetan Mission in Nanking and by wireless." Should the need arise for Tibetan envoys to travel to China they would travel on Tibetan passports.

Finally, they declared, "If the [unspecified] adversaries leave Tibet . . . the only one nation which is dedicated to the well-being of humanity in the world unhampered and in peace and do not continue to hold those formerly seized territories, the nations of the world may not suffer disasters of war, famine and so on. . . . [This will] have great bearing on the stability of the

Chinese political system and will also render unnecessary the need for both China and Tibet to station large security forces along their respective borders."[2]

It was a remarkably brazen statement, hardly likely to receive a positive response from Chiang, who had no intention of yielding any part of the territory over which he was struggling to regain control. And it didn't. The victory congratulation mission found no one willing to negotiate a new relationship involving what amounted to the independence of Tibet. The members of the mission were maneuvered into attending the National Assembly by the vague promise that they could present their case for recognition of Tibet's unique independent status there. This opportunity never arose, and the mission spent several months touring China while vainly trying to find someone with whom to negotiate. The Chinese government, however, was able to exploit the mission's presence as evidence of Tibet's membership in the Chinese national family. After ducking out of town to avoid signing the final document drafted by the Assembly, which declared, "All present at the Assembly are subjects of the Chinese Kuomintang Government," the outmaneuvered mission returned to Lhasa in the spring of 1947.

The mission had accomplished little beyond going on record with their case with the increasingly beleaguered Nationalist government while incurring the generally patronizing contempt of their British escort officers, who sent deprecating reports to their superiors in New Delhi concerning the motivation, actions, and personal appearance of their charges.[3] But the Tibetans had crossed the pass from Shangri-La.

While the mission was being manipulated in Peking, the Tibetan government enjoyed a minor success in its campaign for international recognition. The Indian Council of World Affairs, under the guidance of Jawaharlal Nehru, decided to host a semiofficial conference of Asian countries in New Delhi in the spring of 1947, to which the Tibetans were invited to send a delegation. According to Goldstein, the British representative in Lhasa advised the Tibetan delegates that the conference would provide them the stage on which to demonstrate their de facto independence to their Asian neighbors.[4] Nehru obviously appreciated these implications when he included the Tibetans on the official guest list and refused to withdraw his invitation when the Chinese protested. This was a hint of the conflicted feelings he was to demonstrate in his relations with his northern neighbor. It was a mixture of proprietary regard for the Tibetans and their value as a buffer state of indeterminate status and allegiances even while recognizing the superior power position of China, which India was not prepared to challenge.

—

When the Tibetans arrived in New Delhi they refused the offer of money for their expenses which the Chinese ambassador tried to press upon them or to be part of the Chinese delegation. The Chinese ambassador did prevail upon his Indian hosts to repaint overnight a large map of Asia to blur the borders which showed Tibet as an independent country, but the Tibetans sat at a separate table behind their national flag, to all appearances as delegates from an independent country. The delegation met with Mahatma Gandhi and the Indian foreign minister, and headed back to Lhasa with a feeling of accomplishment. They went by way of Kalimpong, where they joined the hapless victory congratulation mission, which had been ordered to remain there while a serious struggle for power for the regency played out in Lhasa.

When both missions made it back to Lhasa that summer, this power struggle had culminated in the death, probably by poisoning, of Reting, the contender generally considered most sympathetic to the Chinese. The new Tibetan government was confronted with the immediate problem of determining what its policy should be toward the newly independent government of India, which was proclaimed on August 15, 1947. Their old friend Hugh Richardson, who was staying on as head of what was now the Indian mission in Lhasa, counseled the Tibetans to accept formally the same relationship with the new Indian government that they had enjoyed with its British predecessor. When he gave this advice, Richardson undoubtedly knew that his parent government had concluded that their Indian successors were designing a policy built on establishing a close relationship with China to provide leadership for Asia. He feared that unless the Tibetans accepted the equivocal but special status with the Raj, they would be left out in the cold with no ties to anyone in the international community but their unwanted Chinese patrons. This meant that the most the Tibetans could expect from New Delhi from now on was to act as a "benevolent spectator, ready at all times— should opportunity occur—to use their good offices to further a mutually satisfactory settlement between China and Tibet."[5]

The Tibetans, however, were inclined to use this occasion to negotiate with the new leadership in New Delhi for formal recognition of their status as an independent country and to bargain for the return of patches of the Tibetan border that the former British overlords had absorbed in the previous century. They solved this dilemma in a typically Tibetan way. They sent an official note of congratulations to the British governor general and Nehru on the transfer of power, but remained silent on accepting India as Britain's successor. This noncommittal action was followed by a note sent a month later making claims for the restoration of former Tibetan border territory.

They did not, however, raise any objection to the transfer of power at the trade agencies and missions in Gyantse, Gartok, Yatung, and Lhasa, where the new Indian national flag replaced the Union Jack. In a follow-up note sent a month later the Tibetans expressed their gratitude for Britain's intention to "consider any further maintenance of Tibet's *independence* [italics added] and common welfare as they have done so hitherto." To this notice that the Tibetans were not letting their old friends off the hook, they expressed the hope that His Majesty's government would support them in their request for the return of former Tibetan territories and in "trade relations affecting the general economic welfare of Tibet." It was a vain hope as the British Empire passed into history.[6]

Lhasa Looks to the United States

Undiscouraged by the failure of Tolstoy's superiors to come through with the invitation to a postwar peace conference that the OSS officer had held out as a prospect, the Tibetan government agreed upon a strategy to follow up on the channel to Washington opened by his visit three years earlier. They decided in the spring of 1946 to use the victory congratulations mission, then in New Delhi on its way to China, to proceed on to Washington to deliver congratulatory letters from the Dalai Lama, the Tibetan regent, and the Tibetan cabinet to President Truman, with accompanying appropriate ceremonial scarves and badges. All three letters made specific reference to the "good relations . . . between the Governments of the United States of America and Tibet," thereby reminding Washington of both Tibet's independent status and its desire to be treated as an ally. The American chargé in New Delhi, George Merrell, reported that in leaving these letters with him for transmittal to the president the mission made it clear that if Truman sent an official to Lhasa to convey replies to these letters "he would be given a cordial reception."[7]

When the Tibetans delivered the letters to the embassy in New Delhi Secretary of State General George Marshall was in China trying to persuade Chiang Kai-shek and the Communists to abide by the cease-fire he had badgered both parties into agreeing to while he tried to hold Chiang to his promise to convene a national assembly. By the time the State Department replied to the Tibetans' bid for recognition, Marshall had announced the failure of his mission and a full-scale civil war had begun in China. The Department had been quite aware of the "precarious position of the Nationalist Government" described by Merrell, but it was cautious about doing anything to tip the boat any further. It was therefore ready to second the War Department's bleak assessment of the military significance of Tibet and its conclusion,

"From the standpoint of Sino-American relations, no useful purpose would be served at the present time by action likely to raise the question of our official attitude with respect to the status of Tibet."[8]

The State Department did promise to prepare replies for the president's signature "which [could] be forwarded from Delhi by readily available means of communication, to the letters of the Dalai Lama." Apparently there were second thoughts that even a restrained response might ruffle Chiang's feathers, as no reply was ever sent.

Undeterred by the lack of response to its first overtures to Washington, Lhasa announced that Tsipon Shakabpa had been named to lead a mission promoting trade between Tibet and India, China, the United States, and Great Britain. Shakabpa was head of the Tibetan Mint and reportedly had a strong interest in accumulating sufficient gold reserves to back the paper currency printed by the government. The letter stated that Shakabpa would carry letters of introduction to the president and also to high officials with whom he would "have to discuss trade matters" and whose names he asked the American embassy in New Delhi to provide. Shakabpa was to be accompanied by L. Y. Pangdatshang, reportedly the richest trader in Tibet and the parent of the project. Both Suydam Cutting and Ilya Tolstoy had known these two men as part of the Tibetan inner circle on their visits there, so they might well have expected them to arrange reciprocal introductions to their American counterparts in the American establishment. The embassy, "in view of the Department's desire to avoid any action which may reflect on the Chinese claim to sovereignty over Tibet," cautiously addressed its reply to the Tibetan "Foreign Bureau" rather than to the "Foreign Office." They informed the Tibetans that a copy of their letter had been forwarded to the State Department "for such action as may be deemed appropriate" and assured them that the Department would be in a better position to advise them concerning the calls they wished to make. The embassy "hoped that these non-committal replies [would] leave the Department free to do as little or as much as it deem[ed] appropriate in looking after the visitors."[9]

Three weeks later the embassy sent a follow-up dispatch containing further details that they had gathered on the mission, primarily from A. J. Hopkinson, the British political officer who had been so caustic in his reports on the victory congratulations mission, which he had so grumpily escorted on its tour of India the previous year.[10] His previous assessment of its members as petty traders seems to have carried over to the present mission, which he suggested was motivated primarily by the desire to obtain gold and silver either to back Tibet's present paper currency or for personal gain. The embassy, however, stated that even if Shakabpa had some personal interest in the negotiations he hoped to carry on in Washington, he should be treated with the utmost courtesy and the Chinese embassy should not be permitted to interfere with this friendly contact. New Delhi recognized the State Department's strong desire not to offend the Chinese government by taking any action that they might interpret as a reflection on their sovereignty over Tibet, but they felt that the United States "should not throw away its unique opportunity to strengthen the friendly feelings which the Tibetans have exhibited."[11] The persistent embassy was apparently still smarting from the War Department's summary dismissal of the strategic importance of Tibet as a potentially useful site for defensive military operations in some future conflict. The drafter noted, "It would be interesting to know how many Army officers in 1935 would have taken seriously a prediction that ten years later a single aerial bomb could be utilized to demolish a city." The dispatch closed with a request for clarification of the current policy concerning the status of Tibet, an issue the embassy believed had been left ambiguous and warranted an update.

Two months later the State Department responded to the immediate issue of the embassy's request that the Tibetans be given a welcoming reception in Washington and the greater question of how it regarded the status of Tibet. It was not a time favorable to conceive a creative or radical shift in matters affecting China. This was particularly true concerning contingent issues such as the Nationalist government's political authority over what it claimed as part of its territory, which was being militarily contested elsewhere throughout the mainland.

It was an era of bold new initiatives such as the Truman Doctrine, under which the United States took over responsibility from the British for blocking the Communists from winning the civil war in Greece while promoting the Marshall Plan for revitalizing the war-torn European economy. However, without a similar wholesale solution to offer for the China situation, it was deemed politically expedient to do nothing to challenge the status of Chiang's faltering authority. The State Department ducked the embassy's bid for a review of its policy on Tibet, reaffirming, "China claims sovereignty over Tibet, and . . . this Government has never questioned that claim."[12]

Washington could therefore provide only an informal reception to the delegation. If they carried Tibetan passports, they should be issued visas as holders of passports from countries the United States did not recognize. In what appears to be a more accommodating mode, the State Department added that should the prospective delegation "apply for visas and should it appear that there exist technical grounds for denying them entry to the United

States, the Embassy should promptly apprise the Department of the attendant facts by telegraph; the Department may then in its discretion seek to make arrangements with the immigration authorities for necessary waivers." The mission should look to the Department of Commerce, not the State Department, as their official host. The cable ended with a general statement of various regulations governing the purchase of gold in the United States, but did not address the question of the motivation of those mission members who might be seeking it.

In January 1948 Shakabpa and Pangdatshang proceeded to China, where to all appearances they spent the next four months carrying out their mission of investigating trade prospects there. These men from the mountains, who Hopkinson had feared would be "babes in the wood," then executed a maneuver worthy of Talleyrand. The Chinese had provided the Tibetans with the foreign exchange they needed, with the understanding that they would use only Chinese passports if they proceeded elsewhere. Shakabpa and Pangdatshang, however, took the British minister in Nanking into their confidence, telling him of their plan to let the Chinese believe they had been persuaded to forgo their onward travel and compliantly return to Tibet. They asked him to grant them visas on their Tibetan passports, which they planned to use in proceeding on as planned to the United States and Britain. The sympathetic minister granted their request,[13] but his American counterpart was able to duck their request by pointing out that they first had to obtain exit visas from the Chinese, who would not grant them on their Tibetan documents. The nimble Tibetans thereupon obtained the exit visas on the Chinese passports they had used to travel to Peking, and then proceeded to Hong Kong, where they stashed their Chinese documents. There they hauled out their Tibetan passports and asked the American consul general for visas to make the long-planned visit to the United States which they had never intended to abandon. For reasons that have never been explained in official correspondence, the consul, despite the explicit instructions to the contrary that Washington had repeatedly sent since the issue was first raised, put the prized stamp on the Tibetan documents, where they have been used by the Dalai Lama's government as evidence of recognition of their independent status ever since.

Both the United States and British governments equivocated when the infuriated Chinese learned that they had been tricked and the Tibetans were not only carrying on with their missions abroad rather than returning to their isolated capital, but were also traveling on documents which challenged Peking's authority. When questioned, Washington simply denied that the visas had been placed on the Tibetan documents.[14] London apologized for the "technical error," which it promised would not to be repeated, then had to resort to another subterfuge. By the time the Tibetans were ready to travel to England after a long hot summer of more sparring with the Chinese embassy in Washington, the prized visa that the cooperative British embassy in Nanking had placed on their passports had expired. The British Passport Control Office told them that they would therefore have to travel on the documents used for stateless persons. The proud and indignant Tibetans announced that they had no intention of traveling on such status and were therefore canceling their visit. The British capitulated and came up with the face-saving formula of changing in ink the three-month limit to nine months on the original visa. The Chinese had made their point, and the two countries the Tibetans had sought as champions had backed away from any open challenge to the existing Chinese position in Tibet. But the men from the hills had documentary evidence that their national identity had been officially recognized by two of the world's most powerful countries.

The mission's visits to the United States and Britain were eventful ones. When they arrived in San Francisco on July 9, 1948, they were met by the British consul, with whom they held a press conference that received considerable attention in China, much to the annoyance of the Chiang government. In Chicago they were met by representatives of both the Chinese consulate and their host, the Department of Commerce. These dual reception committees also received them on their arrival in Union Station in Washington, giving notice that the Chinese embassy regarded the visitors as their charges and intended to stick with them throughout their stay in the United States. This immediately became an issue when Shakabpa asked his hosts to arrange an appointment for him and his delegation with President Truman. A diplomatic tempest followed when the Commerce Department informed the Chinese embassy that it felt obliged to grant the Tibetans this courtesy to reciprocate the hospitality that the Tibetan government had shown to the oss officers who visited Lhasa during the war. The Chinese ambassador and his equally adamant superiors in Nanking insisted that if such a meeting were to be held, it be initiated by his embassy on behalf of their subjects and that he accompany them. The equally resolute Tibetans refused to consider this, reminding their hosts that their government had received President Roosevelt's oss representatives without any involvement of the Chinese representative in 1942.

An exasperated State Department finally gave the Chinese minister a curt letter reaffirming that the United States government had no intention of acting in a manner that would call into question China's de jure sovereignty over

Tibet, but it was "faced with the practical problem caused by the presence in the U.S. of the Tibetan Mission which had not come at the behest of the U.S. Government but which must be received with the courtesy due to high-ranking representatives of far distant countries." The blunt note reminded the Chinese government, "[It] should appreciate that the fact that it exerts no *de facto* authority over Tibet is the root cause of the situation." Continuing with its candid observations, the note pointed out that if the press, which was showing considerable interest in the visit, should learn that the embassy had frustrated the Tibetans' wish to call on the president, it "would make the most of the situation to China's disadvantage." This was followed by an unusual threat: "Such a story might also be raised in light of self-determination which is a popular concept among the American people." The final argument was this: "[The] President has expressed a personal interest in greeting the Tibetans." Asking the Chinese ambassador to bring these points to the attention of the Chinese Foreign Office, the State Department note added, "[You] should emphasize that the U.S. Government does not wish to add a mite to Chinese current preoccupations, but we are confronted with a practical problem which discourtesy will not solve."[15]

This was surprisingly forthright language and what must have been one of the first intimations that the United States government might apply the principle of self-determination to the Tibetans—an action that was not taken, however, for another twelve years.[16] But the Chinese government in Nanking, with its back increasingly up against the wall, remained obdurate. The Tibetans were equally resolute, although Shakabpa did seem willing to consider a compromise package offered by the State Department. This would let the Chinese ambassador make the appointment with the president, to which he would accompany them, after which the Tibetans would be granted a separate meeting with Secretary Marshall, in which the Chinese would not be included. Ultimately Marshall met with the unaccompanied Tibetans on August 6, 1948; they presented him with photographs of the Dalai Lama and the regent, three letters, and a greeting scarf. Marshall "thanked them cordially for these gifts and expressed pleasure that they had come such a distance to visit the United States."[17]

In neither the meeting with Marshall nor the letters from the Dalai Lama, the regent, and the cabinet to the president did the Tibetans stray from what had been the advertised purpose of their mission, which was to "enquire about trade conditions for the export of yak's tails, fur and other trade goods from Tibet and the import of gold and silver bullion and machinery from the U.S." When Marshall asked whether the Tibetans had the dollars to make the purchases they desired, Shakabpa referred to the currency controls that the Indian government imposed on their exports and promised to prepare a letter outlining what assistance they required. The secretary said he would be pleased to receive such a letter and then presented Shakabpa with a gift for himself and a photograph he had inscribed to the Dalai Lama.

Apparently concluding that a private unescorted meeting with the president was not going to happen, Shakabpa then took his delegation to New York. There they enjoyed the public relations success denied them in Washington. Shakabpa and Pangdatshang renewed their acquaintanceship with Tolstoy and Cutting. Tolstoy arranged for them to meet with his fellow aristocrat, the ethnologist Prince Peter of Greece and Denmark, who was planning an anthropological trip to Tibet; with Lowell Thomas, who also expressed his wish to visit Tibet; and with General Dwight Eisenhower, who was then president of Columbia University.[18]

The State Department had meanwhile informed the Treasury Department that it saw no objection to permitting the Tibetans to purchase the 50,000 ounces of gold that they wanted for the purpose of stabilizing the Tibetan currency, as it did "not believe that such a sale would in any way constitute an impairment of the United States recognition of China's de jure sovereignty over Tibet."[19]

The Export-Import Bank, however, notified Shakabpa that there were "no funds available at the present time" for loans for currency stabilization purposes, but it did encourage him to provide more details concerning the machinery Tibet wanted to purchase, as the facilities of the Bank were available to "foreign governments and their agencies, foreign banks and enterprises" for such purposes. Shakabpa apparently did not pursue the possibility of obtaining a loan for the machinery, but after several months of wrangling he was able to obtain $250,000 from the Bank of India toward the $425,800 worth of gold that the Tibetans eventually had shipped to Calcutta and from there to Lhasa by pack animals. The source of the other $175,800 is not known.[20]

By the end of October the delegation was ready to leave for London, but they stayed a few extra days to witness the presidential election. Dewey's press agent turned down a request that the mission be allowed to observe the Election Night proceedings from the gallery of Republican national headquarters, explaining, "Since Mr. Dewey is practically president, they will have to be cleared by the FBI." Instead they were "fortunate indeed to witness the excitement of the re-election of Harry S. Truman at the Democratic Party campaign headquarters."[21] After sending their congratulations to the president, the Tibetans then set sail for England. Despite earlier intimations that they might expect a cool reception, they were received by Prime Minister Clement Attlee and the Lord Chamberlain on behalf of the ailing King George VI. Covering all bases, they called on Winston Churchill. Although none was in a position or disposed to take an active role in the affairs of Tibet, these symbols of remnant interest from the shattered British Empire were valued by the mission.

Shakabpa and Pangdatshang then returned to India with a justified sense of accomplishment. Although they hadn't been able to meet with Truman, who would be determining United States policy in the critical times they were to face soon, they had planted their cause firmly with him. His signed portrait along with the one that Secretary Marshall sent were tokens of the friendly regard in which their country was held in Washington and conversely of the decreasing solicitude there for the Chinese who claimed to be their sovereigns. Moreover they had obtained a modest loan and reestablished ties with those few Americans they knew, who in turn had introduced them to other members of the American establishment who were to become members of the new generation of "can-do" Cold Warriors. This surprisingly successful trip by these "babes in the woods" had moved official Washington one step closer toward taking Tibet seriously, not as a potential rocket-launching site, a romantic escape spot, or the preserve of gentlemen explorers, but as a factor to be taken into account in reconfiguring America's Far Eastern policy.

The United States Enters the Scene

When the Tibetan trade mission arrived back in Tibet in early
1949 the power structure among the world powers that had relegated Tibet to bystander status had changed drastically. Tibet was
going to be a player, albeit in a minor role, in the affairs of the outside world.

On January 21, 1949, the day Dean Acheson was sworn in to
replace his old boss George Marshall as secretary of state, Chiang
Kai-shek resigned as president of China and began his long withdrawal to Taiwan. Acheson noted, "We passed, I coming in, Chiang
going out."[1] Ten days later the Chinese Communist forces occupied Peking. Although the Tibetans had never regarded Chiang as
sympathetic to their defiant pursuit of independence, they soon
realized that they were going to confront new personalities with
the will and organized force capable of challenging them. Meanwhile Great Britain, India, and the United States, on whom Lhasa
had been able to look as committed, although passive, supporters
of Tibet's de facto independence, were reviewing their policies
concerning the new international power structure.

In April 1949 Washington responded to the recommendation
made by the New Delhi embassy three months earlier that it was
time to reconsider America's noncommittal policy toward Tibet
"in the light of changing conditions in Asia."[2] Ambassador Loy
Henderson followed this up with a proposal that if the Communists

succeeded in controlling all of China "or some equivalent far-reaching development takes place [the United States] should be prepared to treat Tibet as independent to all intents and purposes." The State Department weighed the pros and cons of regarding Tibet, which possessed a "relatively stable" government with "the stamina to withstand Communist infiltration," as an independent country rather than part of a China that had gone Communist. This seemed reasonable in view of the following: "The Chinese [Nationalist] Government cannot now assert—and there currently appears little likelihood that it ever again will be able to assert—effective de facto authority in Tibet. . . . [In addition the Tibetans] are now showing increasing interest in establishing trade and other relations with the outside world [and] it is to U.S. interest to see that these efforts are oriented to the West and not to the East."[3]

The "cons" began with the caveat that a decision to recognize Tibet involved not merely United States policy toward Tibet, but also its policy toward China. This would contradict "a basic principle of [America's] policy toward China [which] ha[d] been respect for China's territorial integrity." The drafter of the memorandum, Ruth E. Bacon of the State Department's Office of Far Eastern Affairs, declared, "[This policy] has retarded, while not entirely preventing, the gradual dismemberment of China and it helped China emerge from World War II with the status of a great power . . . and should not be abandoned unless it is clear that a permanent breakup of China is inevitable and that we have a substantial stake in Tibet." She added, "[It] would lessen the weight of our objections to current Soviet efforts to detach additional northern areas from China . . . and . . . might lead to intensified efforts on the part of the USSR to take Tibet into the Communist camp." In contrast to this dire possibility, if the United States "carried on toward Tibet much as at present, the Communists might be content to let the present situation ride." She added the further warning that if the United States was not in a position to give Tibet the necessary practical support, "because of its remoteness, [America] may in fact be pointing the way for Communist absorption of the area." In any event, "as a practical matter Tibet's importance both ideologically and strategically [was] very limited."

In summary, the State Department counseled a temporizing policy of "maintaining a friendly attitude toward Tibet in ways short of giving China cause for offense." This meant avoiding taking steps which would "clearly indicate that [the United States] regard[s] Tibet as independent," but "keeping . . . policy as flexible as possible by avoiding references to China's sovereignty or suzerainty . . . and by informing China of . . . proposed moves in connection with Tibet, rather than asking China's consent for them." If the Communists took over all of China and "an emigre National Government" continued to exist, the United States would be forced to decide whether it "should place emphasis on Tibet's independence by formally recognizing it and by sponsoring its application for membership in the UN or . . . avoid the matter of independence but maintain direct relations with Tibet without a public change of policy." Such a decision would be weighed against whether open recognition of independence "might stimulate Soviet activities to take over Tibet; [whether the United States had] the practical means to afford sufficient assistance to Tibet to make probable its continuance in a western alignment[;] and whether China's dismemberment [was] likely to be on a fairly permanent basis."

These recommendations to wait and see, keeping all options open, were compatible with the secretary's policy of waiting for the dust to settle concerning the drastically new and different power situation in the Far East. The activist embassy in New Delhi, however, forwarded a renewed appeal for taking action to establish some sort of contact with the government of Tibet. They argued, "If we make no effort to demonstrate a friendly interest in Tibet until a Communist dominated regime consolidates its hold on China, the impression will be created among the Tibetans that we were moved only by a desire to contain Communism and not to develop cordial relations with the Tibetan people."[4] Henderson's equally activist colleague in Moscow, Admiral Alan G. Kirk, sent his "full endorsement" of the embassy's proposal to establish some sort of contact with the government of Tibet, noting, "Although as New Delhi points out, Tibet is of little importance to the United States either economically or strategically, control of that vast Central Asian area by elements subject to the plans and policies of the Kremlin would have an adverse effect on the American position in Asia generally."[5] From the deserted capital of Nanking Ambassador John Leighton Stuart added his backing for sending a small mission to Lhasa that summer. He wrote, "[The] authority of the Canton Government [where the Nationalists had established a government after fleeing without a fight at the end of April] over Tibet [is] non-existent and we agree that any move with implications of recognition of the autonomous status of Tibet should be made before relations are established with the Chinese Communist Government."[6]

The only on-the-scene reporting from an American source on the situation in Lhasa that year came from the popular radio commentator Lowell Thomas. After considerable debate and correspondence the embassy and the State Department were unable to agree upon the composition, status, and duration of a temporary reporting team until it had grown too late in the season to send one to Lhasa.[7] Thomas, however, had no limitations, and he was on his way with his son to Tibet in early August 1949, two weeks after receiving an invitation arranged by Shakabpa, whom he had met in New York. The embassy in New Delhi observed that the Thomas invitation was an "outstanding exception" to the Tibetan government's policy of discouraging visits by foreign nonofficials. Although the embassy claimed that this exception was made "on the basis of friendly relations between this Mission and various Tibetan officials," it seems more likely that the politically aware Shakabpa had perceived on his own the influence that prominent journalists like Thomas had on American foreign policy.

The sage of the British frontier cadre, Hugh Richardson, who had remained as head of the Indian mission in Lhasa after the turnover, was there to meet Thomas and his son when they arrived in the early autumn. The old Tibet hand found the two sympathetic to Tibetan aspirations and acknowledged that Thomas Sr. had "obviously grasped the fact of Tibetan practical independence which ha[d] lately been underlined by the removal of the Chinese [Nationalist] Mission from Lhasa. But he appeared to know nothing of American policy toward Tibet and to be unaware that the State Department consider[ed] Tibet as part of China."[8] Richardson reported that in his initial meetings with Lhasa officials Thomas had been "excessively optimistic about Tibet's position, alleging that they were safe for ten years." But he added, "After I had explained to him the imminence of danger to Tibet, I hear that he became more cautious and more aware of the urgency of the position and that he promised to do all he could to enlist U.S. aid 'if it could be done in time.'" In the account of their discussions with Tibetan officials that he published following their return,[9] Lowell Thomas Jr. reported that they had taken a modest approach in responding to the Tibetan officials' appeals for aid, pleading that as unofficial visitors they could make no commitments on behalf of their government. The Thomases had not shown such caution, however, in their statements to the press on their arrival back in New York or in a private meeting later with Acheson. On October 25, 1949, the *New York Times* reported that the elder Thomas had suggested that the United States could aid the Tibetans by giving them more modern weapons and advising them on guerrilla warfare. In a meeting with Acheson the following February Thomas amplified his proposal, suggesting the United States send a military mission headed by a man like General Albert C. Wedemeyer to encourage the Tibetans to resist, arguing that their terrain was "admirably suited for guerrilla operations and Tibetan forces could put up strong resistance through such operations to any military force that could be sent to Tibet."[10]

Although the activist Thomas offered to lend his son to such a mission, Acheson temporized, citing the apparent reluctance of the Indians to be co-operative in any effort by outsiders to spur or support the Tibetans in challenging the Chinese and the possibility that any publicity concerning external support might move the Chinese to take preventive action.[11] By this time Acheson was fully aware of the complexities of all of the elements and factors in any action involving China. He hoped to preserve the option of eventually finding some mutually acceptable accommodation that might permit recognition of the Chinese Communist government and preclude an alliance by Mao with the Soviet government. But his wait-and-see tactic was dealt two massive blows. The first came that summer, when Mao endorsed Premier Zhou Enlai's policy slogan of the necessity "to lean to one side."[12] The second came when Mao went to Moscow to meet with Stalin ten weeks after he proclaimed the formal inauguration of the Chinese People's Republic on October 1, 1949. The subsequent formal treaty of alliance and assistance between these two Communist powers that was published three days before Acheson met with Thomas foreclosed the secretary's hopes of discouraging Mao from making common cause with the Soviet leader.

Acheson was well aware of the dynamite potential of arousing the new governors in Peking. He furthermore had to deal with increasingly vocal conservative domestic critics at home. They had reacted with bitter denunciations to the White Paper published the previous autumn, demanding that he explain why the administration should not be held responsible for the fall of the Nationalist government and also justify his refusal to support the use of overt military means to protect Taiwan. The administration was not inclined to come forth with any public gestures of support for the Tibetans that might provide ammunition to those charging it had contributed to the dismemberment of China.

Accordingly the State Department rejected two appeals from the by then very apprehensive Lhasa government. The first, in late November, asked Secretary Acheson to "consider extensive aid in regards [to] civil and military requirements and send a favorable reply at earliest possible opportunity."[13] Another two weeks later asked the United States for help in placing their "humble appeal" for admission to the United Nations.[14]

The Tibetan Foreign Bureau, by this time increasingly aware of the urgent need to attract international attention to Tibet's plight and of the value of personal diplomacy, also dispatched an invitation in early January 1950 to American Ambassador-at-large Philip Jessup to visit Lhasa. It was acting in response to an American commercial radio broadcast which Jessup had made the month before, in which he said that Asian nations "need[ed] U.S. assistance to stop the spread of Communism." The invitation stated that "Tibet ha[d] decided to oppose Commie aggression; they were planning to dispatch special missions abroad to ask for help and hoped that Jessup could include a visit to Tibet in his programme after reaching India."[15] They asked that he inform them how he would travel to Lhasa. Hugh Richardson, the British officer who was still acting as an advisor to the British mission in Lhasa, reported that the Tibetans had asked Heinrich Harrer, an Austrian mountaineer who had found refuge in Lhasa five years earlier, to supervise the construction of a temporary landing field for Jessup's plane.[16] It was not needed, as the United States government had no intention of making such dramatic gestures of assistance—nor in encouraging false hopes in Lhasa by dispatching the mission proposed by Thomas to encourage the Tibetans to undertake guerrilla operations to resist a threatened invasion by Mao's forces.

Passing the Buck

These midnight appeals from Lhasa did prompt a round of negotiations by State Department officers in Washington and New Delhi with their British counterparts. The sympathetic but cautious Americans were unsuccessful in persuading the British to take the lead in enlisting the Indians to lend both political and material support to encourage the Tibetans to defend themselves against China's occupation of their country. The Indian foreign minister told an embassy officer in New Delhi that the British high commissioner had shown him a draft reply to the Tibetans' request to send a mission to London seeking aid: "[The] British Government was giving consideration [to their request] in consultation with the Government of India." The foreign minister noted that this was a "neat way of passing the buck" and insisted the statement be removed. He declared that England still had responsibilities toward Tibet and that India had no intention of assuming all British responsibilities there.[17] The Americans and the British finally agreed that they should do nothing to "discourage the Tibetan authorities and that an effort should be made to give them moral encouragement even though it was not possible to extend material aid."[18] This precluded sending any sort of mission to Lhasa, which the British feared might "rock the boat" and cause the Chinese Communists to "assert sovereignty over Tibet sooner than they would otherwise do."[19] Ambassador Henderson expressed similar reservations about sending an official United States mission to Lhasa the following spring: "[Doing so might] mislead the Tibetans into believing we are prepared to aid them resist incursion [of] Chinese troops. It would be unfair for the U.S. to take any action which might encourage them [the Tibetans] to resist because of mistaken idea of help from the U.S."[20]

On December 30, 1949, the Indian government became the first member of the British Commonwealth to recognize the Chinese Communist government. Despite their reluctance to accept inheritance of Britain's former obligations to the Tibetans, the Indians were the ones who subsequently agreed to supply them with sufficient arms and ammunition for one brigade group for six months.

The Indian government provided this limited assistance despite the bleak assessment of their political officer in Sikkim, Harishwal Dayal, who had made an official mission to Lhasa to assess Tibetan needs and capabilities to deal with the threatened Chinese invasion. Although he believed the Tibetans would be unable to organize any resistance to such an invasion, Dayal did not recommend that his government advise the Tibetans not to attempt it. "In fact, he went so far as to say that if his Government adopted such a negative policy he would resign in order to avoid being placed in the invidious position of telling the Tibetans that the Indians, who for the past two decades ha[d] proclaimed themselves to be the best friends of Tibet, [were] unable to come to their assistance in their time of need."[21] Nehru apparently felt the same way when he agreed to provide the arms that the Tibetans had requested.

Shakabpa, who had been waiting in India to repeat his visit to Washington, graciously accepted the embassy's excuses for discouraging the Tibetans from sending a mission seeking aid at that time. In reporting this civil exchange the consul in Calcutta who delivered the message demonstrated fascination with the exotic image of the Tibetans coupled with a patronizing attitude of indulgence concerning their political sophistication.[22] Presumably the American diplomats followed the rationale provided by Washington: "Active or overt interest by non-Communist countries in Tibet at this time would tend to hasten or provoke Chi Communist action against [the] area whereas, in the absence of such action, the cost of full-scale Commie military expedition against Tibet in face of geographical and logistic difficulties might lead to indefinite delay [in] Commie military action, particularly if Tibetan military capacity to resist [is] quietly strengthened."[23] Shakabpa said that the Tibetans "recognized that they had made their effort to form closer ties with the U.S. too late."[24] He did express confidence that "in the end they could count on American friendship" and hinted that they might make a similar approach later.

Shakabpa would have been pleasantly shocked if he had known that Washington was then considering abandoning its policy of noninvolvement in favor of providing "comparatively little [i.e., small-scale] covert assistance in the form of specialized military instruction and supplies to the Tibetans, which might make a Chinese military expedition prohibitively costly, particularly if the Western States manifested no extraordinary interest in attempting to alter Tibet's international status."[25] The State Department laid out this policy in a memorandum given to the British embassy on June 15. The action it called for was not quite as bold as its language implied, inasmuch as it called for the Indian government to provide the actual military supplies and instruction for their use and for the British government to use its influence to persuade the Indians to take this action. The role of the United States was limited to providing the actual hardware if the Indians were unable to supply it from their stores. However, coming two weeks before the North Korean invasion of South Korea, which brought the Cold War directly to Asia, the proposed new initiative concerning Tibet indicated a stiffening of the Truman administration's policy toward China.

Washington's new resolve eventually came to naught. The British continued to stand aside from any involvement in supporting the Tibetans to resist the increasingly apparent Chinese intention to move into Tibet. The American embassy in New Delhi was therefore instructed in early August to proceed on its own to inform Shakabpa that the United States was prepared to assist his government in procuring military equipment and pay for it if Lhasa intended to oppose the Chinese. He was to follow the formula of first approaching the Indian government and informing them of Tibet's intentions to resist any moves by Mao's troops into Tibet and asking for the additional arms they would need to carry this out. If the Indian government was unwilling to supply them, he was to then ask for the government's "friendly cooperation by permitting passage of the aid it wanted to secure abroad."[26]

Ambassador Henderson then covered his flank by informing Nehru's senior foreign policy advisor, G. S. Bajpai, that in accordance with instructions from Washington he had informed Shakabpa that if Tibet should be invaded or was under threat of invasion, the United States would be willing to send a "certain amount of military equipment to Tibet if the Tibetan Government could arrange for the transit of such equipment across the countries through which it must pass in order to reach Tibet."[27] Bajpai thanked Henderson for his courtesy in informing him of the offer, but he believed it preferable that the Indian government take no action until or unless the Tibetans made a request for such support. He said that the Indian ambassador to Peking, K. M. Panikkar, had been instructed to deliver a stern warning to the Chinese government that, if China insisted on making an unprovoked attack on Tibet,

India might be compelled to revise its opinion of the peaceful intentions of China and "even take a different view re China's admission to the UN." Although in reporting this conversation Henderson expressed his doubt that the actual instruction had been couched in such strong terms, he was "convinced that Panikkar had been instructed to do his utmost to persuade Peiping not to invade Tibet."

The Mackiernan Episode

While this quadrilateral shadow boxing among the Americans, the Indians, the Tibetans, and the Chinese was going on, a more immediately dramatic event was taking place inside Tibet. In late April 1950 uninstructed or avaricious Tibetan border guards had shot and beheaded Douglas Mackiernan, an American vice consul, and two White Russians, who were members of a small party fleeing to India after escaping from Urumchi when the Communist Chinese took over Xinjiang. The American embassy had notified the Tibetan government in Lhasa of Mackiernan's plans, and the Dalai Lama's government had sent entry permits to several possible border posts. Unfortunately the permits intended for the outpost at which the Mackiernan party arrived had been delayed in transit. When the couriers from Lhasa carrying them belatedly showed up with the confirming documentation the border guards were thrown into appropriate consternation, fully aware of the punishment that was coming. The couriers escorted the two survivors, the American Frank Bessac and the White Russian Vasili Zvansov, to Lhasa. Their escorts carried with them the three bags containing the heads of Mackiernan and the two other Russians.

In the capital Bessac was received twice by the Dalai Lama, who gave him his blessing and autograph. Bessac in return presented him with the ten camels remaining from their caravan. The Tibetan pontiff promised that he would reward these animals for their services to Bessac and the other members of the ill-fated caravan by putting them in the special park he had for his animals, where they would have plenty to eat and no work to do for the rest of their lives. In response to a request from the American embassy in New Delhi for permission to send an official party to Lhasa to escort Bessac and Zvansov to India, however, the Tibetans made an urgent plea not to send such a party. They argued that they were better prepared by experience to handle the return of the survivors expeditiously without provoking any further Chinese allegations of "American designs on Tibet," especially when they were arranging talks with Mao.[28] Ambassador Henderson accepted the Tibetan offer, and Bessac and Zvansov rode Tibetan ponies through Jelep

Pass into Sikkim, where they were met in late August 1950 by embassy officials, who gave the Tibetan escort party 400cc of penicillin as a thank-you gift.

Before leaving Lhasa Bessac had attended the public lashing of the Tibetan border guards who had murdered Mackiernan and his two Russian associates, for whose graves outside the capital Zvansov had carved three white crosses. In response to a request from Bessac the Tibetans commuted the sentences of the leader of the border guards, who had been condemned to having his nose and ears cut off, lesser mutilation for two others, and fifty lashes for the other three guards. The new sentences were two hundred lashes each for the leader and the man who had fired the first shot, fifty lashes for the third man, and twenty-five each for the others. Bessac was invited to witness the punishment. He reported that he "watched and enjoyed the whole proceeding" and took photographs, which later appeared as illustrations for an article in *Life* magazine describing the whole episode, from the murder of his colleagues to the punishment of the perpetrators.[29] Surprisingly this whole unfortunate incident and inauspicious beginning did not have a lasting effect on Washington's new interest in Tibet or that of the American embassy in New Delhi.

It was against this backdrop that an anxious but frustrated Shakabpa had been vainly waiting in New Delhi for instructions from his government in Lhasa, which was beset by panic and dissension over how to meet the threatened invasion. Finally, in mid-October, he was joined in New Delhi by two representatives from Lhasa, sent under cover as a trade mission but with the real purpose of negotiating with both the Indians and the Chinese ambassador resident in New Delhi. By this time reports of Chinese military movements into Tibetan areas along the Yangtze River border were being repressed in Lhasa, while a divided government tried to agree on a strategy. Shakabpa was scheduled to meet with Ambassador Henderson on October 18, presumably to discuss the Indian response to the Tibetans' request for arms which the United States would provide. However, a member of his mission telephoned the embassy that day to cancel the appointment, saying they had received instructions to proceed immediately to Peking. Ten days later members of the delegation told the American consul general in Calcutta that in conversations with Nehru earlier in the month they had "obtained the impression that India would not help Tibet because of its relations with China." In view of the prime minister's attitude and their instructions to undertake negotiations with the Chinese, the Tibetans had not raised the question of whether India would object to Tibet's approaching other foreign powers if the Indian government declined to provide military aid.[30]

By this time the border probes by the Chinese army had become a formal invasion, and both Ambassador Henderson and the State Department in Washington agreed that any United States government expressions of "we told you so" or "now will you believe us" to Nehru could do much harm.[31] In response to Henderson's accordingly restrained expression of regret that China had decided to launch an invasion "in spite of Indian sensibilities re Tibet . . . and at time when the Tibet mission was preparing to depart for China for conversations," the chagrined Nehru agreed that the "U.S. could be most helpful by doing nothing and saying little just now." He feared that "announcements by the U.S. Government condemning China or supporting Tibet might lend a certain amount of credence to Peking's charges that the great powers has been intriguing in Tibet and had been exercising influence over India's Tibet policies."[32] Henderson quietly backed off, and the United States government temporarily retired from any further challenges to the Chinese move into Tibet.

Retreat at the United Nations

In Lhasa on November 17, 1950, the Tibetan cabinet invested the fifteen-year-old Dalai Lama with full authority as head of the Tibetan government and prepared its appeal to the United Nations to intercede on its behalf and restrain the Chinese. The document was a professional presentation based on a historical account of Tibet's "close and friendly relations between the Emperor of China and His Holiness the Dalai Lama . . . which was essentially spiritual with no political implications."[33]

> [Because Tibet is] devoted to the tenets of Buddhism and had eschewed the art of warfare . . . it had relied on its geographical configuration and non-involvement in the affairs of other nations, [although] there were times when Tibet had sought—but seldom received—the protection of the Chinese Emperor. The Chinese Revolution of 1911 which dethroned the last Manchurian Emperor had snapped the last of the sentimental and religious bonds that Tibet had with China. . . . [Furthermore] the slender ties that Tibet maintained with China after the 1911 Revolution became less justifiable when China underwent a further revolution and turned into a full-fledged Communist State . . . as there can be no kinship or sympathy between such divergent creeds as those espoused by China and Tibet.[34]

In forwarding this document the embassy said it believed the Indian government had helped the Tibetans draft the appeal.[35] Some of the more colorful references, such as "this sneak invasion" and "this unwarranted act of aggression [which] has not only disturbed the peace of Tibet, but is in complete disregard of a solemn assurance given by the Chinese to the Government of India," indicate that the Indian Ministry of External Affairs may have taken this opportunity to express its own indignation over the "deep disappointment" Nehru had expressed to Ambassador Henderson over Peking's behavior.[36]

The position that the United States took on Tibet's appeal was that of an active bystander. At the time that Henderson was being considerate of his host's sensitivities concerning his disillusionment over the peaceful intentions of his new neighbors in Peking, Washington was confronting the disastrous losses that the UN forces were suffering from surprise encounters with large concentrations of Chinese forces in northern Korea. On October 31 Russian MIGs first appeared over Korea, raising the prospect that what had begun as a localized police action could escalate into the Third World War.

Although the full extent of the dire predicament of the UN forces was not known throughout the United States government, those considering the appropriate response to Lhasa's appeal must have had some intimation of the bleak situation in Korea, which overshadowed all United States policy concerning Asia. In a strategy-drafting session on November 13 the State Department decided that the United States should follow the lead of India, the country that would be most directly affected if the Chinese occupied Tibet. They agreed it was unlikely that any action by the UN could influence the course of events if the Chinese were determined to carry out a military occupation of Tibet. But they suggested, "It might be possible to achieve a betterment of relations between India and the U.S. if this Government offers India support and cooperation without giving the Indians the impression that we are seeking to drive a wedge between them and the Chinese Communists."[37]

Ernest Gross, who had shepherded the UN resolution authorizing military action against the North Korean invasion the previous June, accordingly informed the Indian ambassador to the UN, Benegal Rau, that the United States would not take the initiative on the Tibet question. But he added, "In view of India's special interest in the matter, we would support any initiative India intended to take." Gross told Rau that he had heard that the Nationalist Chinese ambassador was considering bringing the question up at the Security Council, and Rau replied that this would be "quite unfortunate."[38] Two days later Washington instructed Gross to support a request from El Salvador that "the invasion of Tibet by foreign forces" be considered by the General Assembly:

[Although we doubt that the UN] could bring effective pressure on the Chi Commie Govt to withdraw or agree to respect Tibet's autonomy, nevertheless, we think that GA consideration of the problem may be of some value as propaganda in exposing Chi Commie actions.... [This propaganda advantage would lie] in a public debate demonstrating the aggressive tendencies of the CPR Govt and falsity of the position which seeks to justify its actions in Tibet by saying that imperialist powers threaten the country. This might aid us in the Korean situation and in hearings on the question of Formosa and air force bombings of the territory of China ... and assist in marshaling of world opinion against ChiComm aggressive actions in the Far East.[39]

Despite the lukewarm support the initiative received from India, the French and British delegations, and even their Central American neighbors, the El Salvadorans persisted in demanding that the Assembly consider the issue. Gross later recounted that this small, staunchly Catholic country had acted in response to the personal interest that Pope Pius XII had taken in the Tibetans' obtaining a hearing for their case by the international community and the consequent action taken by the Vatican to bring it about.[40] The UN General Committee, however, voted unanimously on November 24 to postpone consideration of the Tibetan appeal, basing its inaction largely on the assertion of the Indian representative that the latest note received by his government from the Chinese indicated that hope still existed for a peaceful settlement of its relationship with Tibet. Following the vote, Gross, who returned to the UN nine years later to present the Tibetans' appeal for condemnation of the Chinese occupation of their country, supported the postponement based on Rau's assurances. Nehru's foreign affairs advisor subsequently told Ambassador Henderson that Rau had provided a distorted justification of his instructions, which were to propose postponement because New Delhi believed that debate on the issue could only exacerbate bad feelings and perhaps jeopardize agreement "on more important issues." These issues did not include Tibet, about which Nehru's foreign policy advisor said there was only "faint hope" of that question being resolved by negotiations.[41]

By mid-December 1950 the Dalai Lama had fled his capital to take refuge in a monastery in southern Tibet a few miles from the border with Sikkim, where he was to remain with his entourage until the following summer. The Indians, along with the British and the Canadians, were then engaged in another effort to broker a cease-fire with the Chinese in Korea. Despite the still desperate situation of the UN forces in Korea, the American embassy in New Delhi sounded out the Indians on December 18 about reviving the Tibetan appeal to the UN.[42] Nehru's foreign affairs advisor temporized, saying that the Indian government would probably reexamine the whole problem of Tibet just as soon as it had done all it could in the matter of the cease-fire in Korea. The Chinese put an end to this one-sided bargaining the following month by rejecting the cease-fire proposal, and the Tibetans added the final bit of irony by failing to apply for the visas that they had been notified were waiting for them to enable them to present their case in New York.

One of the few developments favorable to the Tibetans that evolved out of this final joining of the Tibet issue—and it was to be of long-term rather than immediate use or comfort—was the review which the State Department conducted concerning its policy on the legal status of Tibet. This was done in response to a request made by the counselor of the British embassy in Washington on November 21, 1950, in the midst of the bargaining then going on in New York over whether to hear the Tibetan appeal. The motivation for this request for a statement of policy was not specified, but it could well have been that the British were looking for additional support in their efforts to wriggle out of supporting the Tibetans.

Oliver Clubb, head of the State Department's Office of China Affairs, however, offered his "personal opinion that the Tibet question should be given adequate consideration and pointed to the circumstance that climatic conditions were such that the Chinese forces could not expect easy going in Lhasa during the present winter." He added, "There was some reason to believe that the Tibetan incursion might have been mounted prior to the more recent actions which have caused the Chinese intervention in Korea to become a major matter and that it was probably unlikely that the Peiping regime would be inclined to despatch Liu Po-cheng's forces to Tibet in strength when danger threatened elsewhere . . . and that the Tibetans, if they did not feel they were being abandoned, might well add their resistance to that of the bitter winter and that the two factors could possibly hold back the Chinese advance for a time sufficient for other developments to occur which might bring changes into the picture."[43]

Clubb's colleague, the Department's legal advisor, also did not provide any reason to back away from the Tibetans. In one of the most complete reviews of United States policy concerning Tibet dating back to the 1911 Revolution in China, he noted that it did not appear "that the United States has ever taken an official public stand in respect to the legal position of Tibet." He went on to assert, "It is recognized universally that Tibet has exercised *de facto* autonomy from 1914 particularly, to the present date. . . . [Furthermore] the United States, which was one of the early supporters of the principle of self-determination of peoples, believes that the Tibetan people has the same inherent right as any other to have the determining voice in its political destiny. . . . It is believed further that, should developments warrant, consideration could be given to recognition of Tibet [as] an independent State."[44]

Although "developments" at that time did not lead to such formal recognition by the United States, recognition of the Tibetans' right of self-determination was a significant step forward in Tibet's claim to legal status apart from China. It was, however, to be another ten years before the United States was willing to announce formally and publicly this recognition, albeit then in a hedged manner.

CHAPTER EIGHT

Washington and Lhasa Regroup

In the bleak winter of 1951 Tibet and its legal status were of low priority to both its Indian neighbor and its intermittent patrons in London. When Ambassador Henderson briefed the Indian external affairs minister on the contents and conclusions of the State Department's legal advisor, the Indian diplomat thanked him for his courtesy but noted that his government "was at present so immersed in the problem of maintaining world peace that it was giving little thought to Tibet. In fact, he said, 'he did not recall that Tibet [or presumably the Dalai Lama's flight from his capital] was even mentioned during the recent Commonwealth Conference.' "[1] Similarly the Foreign Office gave the embassy in London its "informal view that the United Kingdom should support [but not initiate] any move on Tibet's behalf by India or another power but that the Tibetan problem was subordinate to larger issues and should not be raised at the moment."[2]

Washington got the message and on January 6, 1951, waded in on its own, stating, "Despite the lateness in time, the Department considers the matter [of a UN hearing of the Tibetan appeal] should not be permitted to go by default, particularly in light of the U.N. action re Korea [where American forces were taking a beating from the Chinese troops] and also the need for checking Chi Commie advances where feasible."[3] In a further reflection of this new derivative activism concerning Tibet, the American embassy was asked for its views on the effect on Tibetan resistance should the Dalai Lama, who had been sitting across the border in southern Tibet for the past month weighing his responsibilities and options, "flee to India and whether he would have any utility as a center of support [for] internal resistance [in the] event of a polit[ical] turnover in Lhasa." The State Department responded, "ChiCommie conquest of Tibet [in the] near future [is] probable unless new and unexpected factors appear but [we believe] every feasible effort should be made to hinder Commie occupation and give the case appropriate hearing in the UN." This newfound determination included an assurance: "[The] U.S. Government stands ready to extend some material assistance if appropriate means can be found for expression of Tibetan resistance to aggression."[4]

These reasons for abandoning previous decisions not to intervene in the Tibet situation were accompanied by reasons supporting a people recently found to deserve the right of self-determination. This was the administration that had fostered the Truman Doctrine, which declared, "We must assist free peoples to work out their own destinies in their own way." Washington was beginning to recognize the Tibetans' claim to merit such assistance. Moreover the drafters of that doctrine who were calling the shots on policy in Washington were all members of the activist generation of the Second World War. Dean Acheson had drafted the legal opinion in 1940 that FDR used to justify lending overage destroyers to a beleaguered England to keep the sea lanes open. Dean Rusk, who was in charge of Far Eastern affairs at the State Department, had served with Stilwell in the tough days of the China-Burma-India theater. Robert Lovett, who was General Marshall's protégé at the Defense Department, had been a responsible activist dating back to the First World War, when he was awarded the Navy Cross for flying British-made bombers to bomb naval bases inside Germany. They were quite prepared to match testosterone counts with those challenging their anti-Communist credentials.

In New Delhi Ambassador Henderson initially responded with some reserve to the State Department's invitation to inaugurate a more active policy in support of the Tibetans. Henderson had received his apprentice training as a diplomat in Soviet-controlled Latvia and in Moscow, where he had observed the workings of the Soviet system during Stalin's show trials in the 1930s. He was no stranger to controversy. His willingness to take on the popular wartime Soviet ambassador to Washington, Maxim Litvinov, and his open expressions of distrust in the Soviet system had caused him to be transferred from his post as head of the Department's East European desk to the Office of Near Eastern Affairs, where he was one of the architects of the Truman Doctrine. There the man who paradoxically later came to be known as "Mr. Diplomat" had again been relieved of his post because of his outspoken opposition to the creation of the state of Israel. He was in New Delhi because he had been hustled out of town to avoid being an issue in the presidential campaign of 1948.

Henderson wasn't one to avoid a difficult cause, but he was also not one to encourage others to take on a half-cocked one. He estimated, "Unless there is an immediate future indication that Tibet might receive moral as well as substantial military aid from abroad, the Dalai Lama might depart from [his] country and with his departure all effective resistance would probably collapse." He expressed his doubt that the Dalai Lama "would have any effectiveness as a center of support for internal resistance, if in India, and if the Chinese Communists control the Tibetan Government and country." In addition, the Indian government "would probably not permit him to direct resistance movements from India."[5]

He did believe that the Tibetans were owed a hearing at the UN, "where a cease-fire should be asked for and in the event Peking ignore[d] these actions, passage of a resolution condemning Communist China for using force in endeavoring to deprive Tibet of its long established autonomy."[6] He explained, "[I suggested these] comparatively mild steps in the hope they would appeal to the UN, particularly India, which we know does not desire to come to direct issue with Peking. At the same time in the absence of effective force by the UN or its members, they may serve to dramatize China's aggressive attitude towards Tibet in a world forum."

Henderson's statements of principle, coupled with a sober appraisal of Tibet's capability to defend itself, arrived in Washington at a time when more active measures were being considered to challenge Communist control of the mainland. A national intelligence estimate prepared on January 17, 1951, evaluated the vulnerabilities of the Chinese regime and the merits and consequences of various courses of action that the United States government might take to challenge them.[7] The estimators concluded that combining extensive support to anti-Communist forces already present on the mainland, landing revitalized and equipped Chinese Nationalist forces there, bombing industrial and economic capabilities in Chinese coastal cities, and continuing UN military operations in Korea, if applied in combination, would "imperil the regime. . . . They would [also,] however, create a grave danger of Soviet counter-reaction and would increase the danger of a global war."[8]

Throughout the early spring of 1951 the United Nations front in Korea fell into what Acheson described as "restless stability, disturbed by echoes of the irrepressible conflict in progress between Washington and Tokyo."[9] General

Douglas MacArthur had begun his public attacks on the administration's "muzzling" of his pursuit of more aggressive operations in Korea by taking actions against the China mainland. His public speeches after Truman relieved him of his command in April revived the "Who lost China?" outcry from the administration's conservative critics. The unfortunate Tibetans, discouraged by the cold shoulder that their appeal to the UN had received, were in the process of reluctantly entering into negotiations with the Chinese. The roseate Indian ambassador in Peking was reporting what he considered were acceptable terms being proposed by the Chinese: "[Eighty] per cent of the Tibetan monks have assented to the Chinese formula . . . which would authorize the Dalai Lama to retain both temporal and spiritual authority subject to Chinese suzerainty and Chinese responsibility for frontier defense. . . . The monks are convinced that neither their religion nor their property were endangered . . . [but] certain older and more reactionary monks are capable of being obstructive."[10]

Against this background the doughty Henderson, counter to established State Department practice, undertook on his own to support the beleaguered Dalai Lama, an action that was to have historic consequences. It was a reflection of the rich mix of personalities and instances of fortuity that were to characterize America's relationship with the Dalai Lama and his country from then on.

On March 29, 1951, the local *Time* correspondent, James Burke, brought Heinrich Harrer, whom he described as the "Austrian tutor of the Dalai Lama," to call on Henderson. Harrer was an Austrian mountaineer who had escaped from a British POW internment camp in India in 1944 and made his way to Lhasa after an arduous twenty-month trek with a fellow POW, Peter Aufschnaiter. There they were befriended by the influential Tsarong family and the mother and elder brother of the Dalai Lama. Through these connections, and by the force of their personalities and their technical skills, which they put to use in various public works projects, the two were able to fight off the automatic expulsion of foreigners who managed to get to Lhasa without official permission. The Dalai Lama had also been charmed by Harrer, whom he asked to tutor him on both world political affairs and the mechanics of some of his possessions, such as a motion picture camera. When the fifteen-year-old Dalai Lama decided to flee his capital Harrer also left Lhasa; he met up with the Tibetan ruler and stayed with him during the first months of the Dalai Lama's refuge in southern Tibet.[11]

It was in his role as a political tutor and unofficial political advisor that Harrer, perhaps prodded by the Dalai Lama's politically activist mother, made his presentation to the American ambassador. He described his young protégé as more intelligent and better informed regarding world affairs than any of his advisors, but very much in need of advice. Although "deeply conscious of the need for social and other reforms in Tibet," he had doubts about returning to Lhasa, but "some of the monks about him insist[ed] that he come to terms with Peking and do so." According to Harrer, the young ruler had grave misgivings about the Tibetan mission then en route to negotiate with the Chinese, fearing that even though his brother-in-law was a member of the negotiating party, they might yield to pressure.

The sympathetic but seasoned ambassador was "inclined to believe that Mr. Harrer [was] telling me the truth": "[I] was convinced that if the Dalai Lama goes back to Lhasa with his treasures both he and his treasures will eventually fall into the hands of the Chinese Communists." Moreover the government of India had thus far not promised to give him asylum. "It seems [therefore] that unless someone in whom the young man might have confidence should give him advice, he will fall into the Chinese Communist trap, or he will be in an extremely unenviable position in India." On his own initiative, therefore, Henderson "sent the Dalai Lama an unsigned message of advice written on paper purchased in India and bearing no indication of its origin." He specified that it was to be used in briefing the Dalai Lama, but not left with him.[12]

The Dalai Lama was to be told orally that the ambassador was sending a message to him. Henderson acknowledged that this whole undertaking involved "a considerable amount of risk": "But it is better for this risk to be taken than to see the Chinese Communists succeed by trickery in taking over Tibet and in gaining control of the Dalai Lama and his treasures." He did reassure the State Department that he had no "intention of following the practice in the future of going ahead in matters of this kind without proper authority," but he added, "This was one of the rare occasions when I should move forward fast, taking upon myself the entire responsibility for the consequences."

Henderson's letter, attributed to "a high foreign official who ha[d] recently visited Asia and who ha[d] sympathy for Tibet and deep concern for the welfare of His Holiness and His people," contained "the following earnest suggestions": "The Chinese Communists prefer to gain control through trickery rather than through force. . . . They therefore are anxious to persuade His Holiness to make an agreement which would allow them to establish a representative in Lhasa. [This] would serve only to speed up the seizing of all Tibet." He should not return to Lhasa while such a danger exists, but should leave Yatung (the Tibetan border town where he had sought refuge) for some foreign country such as Ceylon. "If His Holiness and His Household could not find safe asylum in Ceylon he could be certain of finding a refuge in one of the friendly countries, including the United States, in the Western Hemisphere. . . . It might also be useful for His Holiness immediately to send a mission to the United States where it would be prepared to make a direct appeal to the United Nations."[13]

When the Tibetan delegation, reluctantly making its way to Peking to negotiate with the Chinese, was delayed, Henderson took advantage of the "breathing spell" to suspend delivery of his proposed message until he received word from the State Department that it did not disapprove of his action. His belated concern for procedure turned out to be unwarranted, as the Department telegraphed its approval within a week, asking only that he delete the suggestion that the Tibetans send a delegation to the United Nations, as a recent survey of other countries had shown little support for an appeal on behalf of the Tibetans there.[14] Henderson also obtained the endorsement of his colleague in Ceylon, Joseph Satterthwaite, for his proposal that the Dalai Lama seek asylum there. His fellow ambassador wrote, "[You are] to be highly commended for the courageous course of action that you have taken . . . one that [I am] sure will have the full backing of the Department."[15] The director of the Department's Office of South Asian Affairs, Elbert Matthews, hastened to assure Satterthwaite of his "hope that Loy's project can be carried through . . . [as] it ha[d] full Departmental backing."[16]

Henderson remembered the fate of those whom the Stalinist system found in their way and was determined not to see the Dalai Lama become a similar helpless victim of Stalin's new partner in Peking. He was also fully mindful of the gross inequality of any contest between Mao's armies and any Tibetan military opposition.

Henderson wanted to preserve the Dalai Lama as a rallying point for opposition to further Chinese aggression in Asia, but he was above all a realist and had no use for quixotic gestures or making commitments that the United States could not keep. Henderson's initiative, and Washington's positive endorsement, marked the end of the United States government's reluctance to become involved in Tibetan affairs out of deference to its century-old regard for the territorial integrity of China and the beginning of a halting move as a principal player into the vacuum produced by the British and Indian withdrawal from involvement there.

Henderson's precedent-shattering letter was delivered to the Dalai Lama's representatives in northern India in mid-May 1951, beginning an involvement that was to persist with varying resolve through today. Ten days after it was delivered the Chinese unilaterally announced that the Tibetan delegation sent to negotiate Tibet's future had signed a seventeen-point "Agreement on Measures for the Peaceful Liberation of Tibet." The State Department's Office of Intelligence Research found the agreement "provide[d] further evidence of methods employed by International Communism aimed at achieving the political conquest of neighboring peoples under the guise of an altruistic 'anti-imperialist' movement."[17] In India the Dalai Lama's foreign secretary had been meeting with American embassy officers to sound out what support the Tibetans might expect if the talks broke down, as they anticipated would happen.

At that time Henderson's embassy was still working on the premise that the Tibetans—if assured of American interest in their situation—might be able to hold out against total capitulation to a Chinese military and political takeover of their country: "The Embassy remembers that the Department has in the past expressed the opinion that despite the lateness of the hour it does not believe that Tibet should be lost by default." It therefore proposed that the Department consider the removal or simplification of regulations on the import of Tibetan wool into the United States; study the possibility of developing a market for Tibetan products in the United States and of preemptive buying of strategic Tibetan products that might otherwise go to China; publish "in a proper form at a proper time" a statement with respect to its recognition of the autonomy of Tibet; further consider America's willingness to supply military assistance if Indian regulations and laws permit; and further support the Tibetan appeal to the UN. These actions were to be supplemented by more sustained contact with the Dalai Lama and the Tibetan situation through more frequent visits by American representatives to Kalimpong for liaison with the Dalai Lama's representatives and to support the area's only Tibetan newspaper, which was published there.[18]

Even before the State Department had an opportunity to respond to the embassy's appeals to take action to encourage the Tibetans not to cave in to a Chinese takeover of their country, Tsipon Shakabpa approached the embassy with a series of questions about what the Dalai Lama could expect in the way of support if he sought refuge abroad rather than yield to unacceptable Chinese demands.[19] Washington remembered Shakabpa as the canny and dogged man in charge of the trade mission that the Tibetans had sent to Washington in 1948 in a vain but generally respected effort to establish a more formal relationship with the United States government. For his part, Shakabpa must have recalled the equivocal treatment he received when Washington felt constrained by its ties to a fading Nationalist government from providing any significant substantive support to his mission. Now, two years later, he was ready with a list of specific questions which called for commitments by the United States to fish or cut bait:

Should Tibet appeal to the UN if their current negotiations broke down, and what could they expect in the way of help from Washington?

Would the United States approach the government of Ceylon on their behalf if the Dalai Lama decided to seek asylum there?

Would the United States be willing to grant asylum to the Dalai Lama and approximately a hundred followers and pay for their expenses? How would he be received? As a head of state?

Would the United States supply military and monetary assistance after the Dalai Lama left Tibet and the "time was ripe for enabling Tibetan groups to rise against Communist China"?

Would the United States establish an informal and covert representation in Kalimpong for liaison with Tibetan authorities?

Would the United States assist the Dalai Lama's eldest brother, Taktser Rinpoche, to go to the United States if he could not remain safely in India, where he had been forced to seek refuge because of his outspoken opposition to the Chinese Communists?[20]

In response, the supportive embassy suggested the Tibetans be encouraged to dispatch a delegation to the UN with a new appeal and approach the Ceylon government on their own, as an appeal "from one Buddhist country to another." Meanwhile the Tibetans should be reassured that the Dalai Lama would be received as an "eminent religious dignitary and head of the autonomous state of Tibet." With due Yankee restraint, Henderson hedged his proposed guarantee by specifying that the United States would decline wholly supporting an entourage but would consider what assistance might be given for the Tibetans to "live in a modest and dignified fashion." The embassy would send officers to Darjeeling and Kalimpong for "frequent queries of the situation" but could not establish official representation there. As for encouraging resistance, New Delhi recommended, "[The United States was] still prepared to provide military assistance providing it was practicable to ship it to Tibet without violating Indian laws . . . [and] to take action which might be effective in encouraging the Tibetan government to maintain [its] autonomy." Finally, Taktser Rinpoche (also known as Thubten Norbu) would be told that he was welcome to visit the United States if he was unable to remain in India.[21]

By the time Washington received the embassy's cable containing its recommendations on how to respond to Shakabpa's probes on what support the Dalai Lama might expect from the United States if the negotiators in Peking were forced to accept an agreement unfavorable to him and his country, the situation was no longer hypothetical. On May 27, 1951, Peking Radio had announced the conclusion (on May 23) of the Agreement of the Central People's Government and the Local Government of Tibet on Measures for the Peaceful Liberation of Tibet. The embassy chargé reported that he had gotten the impression from G. S. Bajpai, the Indian secretary of external affairs, that even his government "had been taken by surprise at the extent of the Tibetan capitulation." He wrote, "[Bajpai] had endeavored to gloss over the fact that his government was disappointed at the Tibetan failure to secure better terms and gave an unmistakable indication that India feels helpless in face of this development and will likely accept it without protest."[22]

The State Department's immediate reaction was to question whether the agreement had been "obtained through the threat of personal violence" against the members of the delegation or "was perhaps an arbitrary unilateral announcement of the Peiping regime: The Department believes Tibet should not be compelled by duress to accept violation of its autonomy and that the Tibetan people should enjoy certain rights of self-determination, commensurate with the autonomy Tibet has maintained since the Chinese revolution.... [Furthermore the] Department believes that the cause of world peace would be served if general support could be mustered for this point of view, and agrees with the Embassy that the U.S. itself should demonstrate its interest in the case in every practical political and economic way."[23]

Under this sturdy declaration the State Department accepted Henderson's recommendations to support the Tibetans, with a few exceptions. It was even less generous than the frugal ambassador in committing the United States government to provide for the expenses of the Dalai Lama should he leave Tibet, assuming that he could use the gold and silver that he reportedly brought with him for this purpose.[24]

Although agreeing to provide "limited assistance in terms of light arms depending upon political and military developments in Tibet proper, and also whether the Government of India's attitude would make such supply feasible," Washington carefully defined the conditions and limitations under which it would supply such support:

> The U.S. Government feels [such] aid could effectively be given only while there may be within Tibet political and military forces willing and

able to resist. Complete collapse within Tibet and offering of political campaign from outside would render the undertaking fruitless. [A] strong stand by the Tibetan Government against any clear aggression would encourage world support for its position, whereas surrender in Outer Tibet would almost certainly be followed by collapse of interest elsewhere. The U.S. is unwilling to commit itself to support any such undertaking from the outside, but if resistance is maintained in Tibet from the beginning it would contribute insofar as the attitude of the Government of India makes it possible.[25]

The State Department's summary of its position reflected not only its willingness to become involved in any challenge the Tibetans made to the Chinese but also its concerns about the resolve and unity of the Dalai Lama's government and his ability to commit it to such a challenge: "FYI although considering resistance would bear promise of fruits only if the Tibetan political organization can be caused to make [a] stand in Outer Tibet [that area west of the Yangtze,] we believe it important that the Dalai Lama not let himself come under the control of Peiping. The U.S. is sympathetic to the Tibetan position and will assist insofar as practicable but can help only if the Tibetans themselves make real effort and take firm stand."

These marching orders were consonant with the personality and personal ethic of Ambassador Henderson, who launched a round of diplomatic activity aimed at persuading the Dalai Lama to leave Tibet and go abroad, where he could become the center of an aggressive campaign to urge the Chinese to abandon their occupation of his country. The commitments made during that summer of 1951 were the basis for one of the major political action programs undertaken by the United States government during the Cold War and the continued, although at times sporadic, involvement of the country in the affairs of Tibet for the subsequent half century.

Shortly after Henderson dispatched an embassy officer with his unsigned letter urging the Dalai Lama to seek asylum abroad, his officers began a round of shuttle diplomacy between the embassy in New Delhi, the consulate in Calcutta, and the Tibetan representatives in the border towns of Darjeeling and Kalimpong. This unprecedented flurry of travel was undoubtedly noted by the Indian Central Intelligence Bureau, but the Indian government made no comment on it. It was not the first time that the ambassador had challenged his hosts. The year before he had created a considerable firestorm by his speech at the Indian Council on World Affairs, in which he criticized without naming them those who "shrank from close cooperation with the United States lest such cooperation create hostility toward them on the part of powerful forces of the world which feed on human poverty and suffering."[26] The ambassador was determined that the Dalai Lama not make any decisions out of ignorance of the willingness of the United States government to take action to preclude his being forced to return to Lhasa to serve as a puppet to the Chinese.

In Washington the ambassador's resolution and willingness to take bold action were matched by those calling the shots at the State Department. Dean Rusk, one of the principal Far East policymakers, later wrote, "The Korean War itself, with hundreds of thousands of Chinese 'volunteers' pouring across the Yalu and the mounting casualty lists of Americans as the war progressed, [had] stiffened the attitudes of many people in this country toward China, including my own."[27] When asked several years later what had motivated the United States government to undertake this activist policy of warnings and inducements to cause the Dalai Lama to seek refuge abroad, Rusk said he and his colleagues believed that "the young man might make a go of it" if he established himself abroad.[28] From there he could lobby his fellow Buddhists to support his claim for an independent Tibet. This action would dramatize Mao's true aggressive colors and serve as a warning to other Asian nations hoping to find an accommodation with the new rulers in Peking. In any event, it would serve the now solidified American purpose of "doing anything . . . to get in the way of the Chinese Communists." Rusk said that both his boss Dean Acheson and President Truman shared this view. Neither of them would have had a problem defending any tough action directed against the Chinese Communists at a time when they were being accused by their domestic opponents of having "lost" China by being "too soft" on Mao and his supporters.

In this climate Henderson directed the campaign to influence the debate that was going on in the monastery just across the border in southern Tibet. There the young Dalai Lama was being bombarded by conflicting advice about whether he could best serve his country by returning to his capital to find an accommodation with its new occupiers or by seeking refuge abroad to campaign against their presence. The pressure to flee came from a powerful group of his fellow countrymen and relatives in temporary residence across the border in India who were in direct and frequent contact with the band of rotating American officers mobilized by Henderson. These on-the-scene interlocutors included the Tibetan ruler's mother, who was in temporary refuge in Kalimpong and was a strong proponent of his flight, as she feared for his life if he returned to Lhasa. She had been joined by Phuntso

Tashi, who had been a member of the delegation that had "accepted" the detested Seventeen-Point Agreement that he was now urging his brother-in-law to disavow. The veteran negotiator Shakabpa and another of his trade mission colleagues from 1948, Surkhang Shape, were there, acting as couriers between the Americans and the Dalai Lama and his councilors one day's mule ride across the border.

The Austrian expatriate Heinrich Harrer was on hand, having returned from New Delhi after delivering the appeal to Henderson that had precipitated the American involvement. So too was another romantic personality, a young Scottish missionary, George Patterson, who had arrived in Calcutta a year earlier carrying an appeal from Topgay Pandatsang, one of the powerful Tibetan merchant lords who presided over an economically and militarily important fiefdom in the Kham area, east of the Yangtse. Patterson's Tibetan protector and sponsor was asking for food and medical supplies, which he pledged to use to resist an imminent Chinese invasion of Tibet. Pandatsang claimed to have learned of their plans after the Chinese attempted to commandeer his own scheme to carry out an insurrection against what he considered was an outmoded government in Lhasa. Although the American representatives declined to become involved in this rich Himalayan brew, they lost the opportunity to acquire what might well have been insight into the arcane complexities and allegiances of Tibetan politics. This lack of understanding of the mixed loyalties between and among the various Tibetan groups living on the eastern side of the Yangtze, who lived and operated in a fashion similar to the old Scottish clans, and their equivocal relationship with the central government in Lhasa, was to be an obstacle to a full appreciation of the Tibet situation which persists even today. The consulate in Calcutta did come to trust the integrity of the young Scot—and even more, to value his self-taught Tibetan-language abilities and firsthand knowledge of an area and people that they knew very little about.

By this time the young ruler's two elder brothers, Taktser Rinpoche, for whom the American consulate had succeeded in arranging a surreptitious flight from Calcutta, and Gyalo Thondup, for whom the State Department had interceded with his possessive host Chiang Kai-shek to permit him to leave Taiwan, were both in Washington. They were also enlisted by the Department to urge their brother to go abroad while he could.

In a last-minute effort to convince the conflicted Dalai Lama to flee, the New Delhi embassy dispatched Henderson's unsigned letter, which reached him in early July.[29]

It pledged that the United States government would issue a public statement supporting any disavowal of the Seventeen-Point Agreement
signed by his representatives in Peking and would support any new
appeal he might make to the United Nations.

It advised him to seek asylum in India, Thailand, or Ceylon so that he
might be closer to Tibet and thereby organize resistance to the Chinese, but promised that he could go to the United States "with some of
[his] followers" if he was unable to reside in any of those countries.

It promised that the United States would provide "light arms" and loans
of money if he was able "to keep up the resistance, spirit and morale of
the Tibetan people": "This is important if Tibet's autonomy is to be
maintained or regained in the event you should feel impelled to seek
asylum outside of Tibet."

Although the embassy would seem to have jumped the gun, on July 12 the
State Department reaffirmed orally essentially the same commitments to
Taktser Rinpoche to transmit to his brother. It went even further in declaring, "[The] U.S. Government believes that Tibet should not be compelled
by duress to accept violation of its autonomy and that the Tibetan people
should enjoy the rights [of] self-determination commensurate with autonomy
Tibet has had many years [which] . . . has consistently been [the] position
[of the] U.S."[30] It therefore promised:

"To indicate publicly its understanding of the position of the DL as head
of an autonomous Tibet."

"Similarly to endeavor other nations to take no action adverse [to the]
DL's position as head of an autonomous Tibet."

To support his request for asylum in Ceylon, pledging "appropriate support
from friends of Tibet in the U.S. for his family and entourage of a hundred 'or slightly more' in Ceylon: "It [is] our hope that among considerations DL wld have in selection wld be the political influence and
effect of the persons chosen."

The Department hedged the embassy's pledge to support any resistance
effort, declaring, "Resistance in Tibet must be viewed as a long range problem
limited by physical [and] political conditions in Tibet and in adjoining areas,
over which U.S. of course had no control." It did, however, add, "[We] made
clear to Taktser that our position [is] basic and longstanding and is not related to Chi Commie involvement in Korea and not to be affected by developments there." This was a significant pledge, as it was made at a time when

prospects for a settlement of the painful and increasingly politically unpopular Korean involvement were emerging.

Reports from Yatung that a resigned Dalai Lama was ready to yield to pressure from his conservative advisors to return to Lhasa to make the best deal he could with the Chinese precipitated a new flurry of efforts to persuade him to change his mind.[31] Copies of an unsigned letter addressed to him containing the pledges given to Taktser were shown to his mother and to Shakabpa in Kalimpong on July 14. A few days later another copy was taken personally to Yatung by Phuntso Tashi, and a similar unsigned copy was sent by the Maharajah of Sikkim's sister Kukula to her uncle, Tibetan Defense Minister Ragashar Shape.

By the time this last-minute appeal reached Ragashar he was already on the trail back to Lhasa with his sovereign. The somewhat perplexed minister sent word back that although it was still possible that the Dalai Lama might eventually go to India, he could not convince the Tibetan cabinet that the United States was really interested without a signed letter.[32] Leaving no possibility unexplored, Phuntso Tashi was dispatched over the mule trail to Yatung with copies of the letter and an accompanying surprise offer of a rescue plan worthy of Hollywood.[33] The plot called for the Dalai Lama to flee at night from his monastery refuge to avoid having to deal with the inevitable representations from his monastic supporters to return to Lhasa, and make his way "quietly" to India. If this was not feasible he should send a message requesting George Patterson, accompanied by Heinrich Harrer, to meet him at a rendezvous point inside Tibet; they would take him to safety in Bhutan. The United States had secured the agreement of the Bhutanese prime minister Jigme Dorje to provide refuge until he and his party could be flown by small planes from a tea plantation airstrip into permanent asylum. The details for this colorful plot of officially approved hijacking had been worked out primarily by Patterson, who by then was a skilled operator in the high backwoods. The worldly Scottish missionary said he grudgingly told Harrer, although he found him to be somewhat high-handed in trading upon his acceptance by the young ruler and his family, of the scheme because he needed his maps of the local terrain and his access to the pontifical household.

Patterson had vainly tried to make what could have been a substantive contribution to this scenario by pointing out that the references in these communications to the Dalai Lama as "head of an autonomous state" could lead to misunderstandings, as there was no word in the Tibetan lexicon that he knew and was using to translate the various commitments made to the Tibetans that distinguished between the concepts of autonomy, sovereignty, suzerainty, and independence.[34] No one in the State Department at the time seemed disturbed by these semantic distinctions, and the Tibetans undoubtedly heard what they wanted to hear.

By this time the Dalai Lama had met with Zhang Jingwu, who had stopped at Yatung on his way to take up his new post in the Tibetan capital as Chinese proconsul and executor of the Seventeen-Point Agreement. The teenage ruler had decided to make the best of what seemed to be a no-win situation. He and his entourage accordingly set out at a measured pace back to the capital from which he had fled eight months before. On August 1 Harrer informed the consulate that he had received letters from the Dalai Lama reporting the receipt of the unsigned messages with their promises of American aid if he sought asylum in India. The semicaptive Tibetan ruler had added that he hoped the United States government would not be angry with him. He had wished to go to the United States, but "had had bad luck with the lots."[35] He felt obligated to try to work out some accommodation with the occupiers.

The embassy in New Delhi had yielded to the Tibetans' demand for American promises in writing, and Henderson had sent a letter to his officers in Calcutta signed by him. There was now a written signed document promising, "[An] essential part of our cooperation would be a public announcement by the United States that it supports the position of Your Holiness as head of an autonomous Tibet. The United States would also support your return to Tibet at the earliest practicable moment as head of an autonomous and non-Communist country. . . . [This position is] fundamental and will not be affected by the developments in Korea or by the Chinese intervention in that area." The United States government would support him and a limited entourage abroad. The letter included a hedged pledge of material and assistance to support a resistance effort inside Tibet to be furnished "as feasible under existing political and practical conditions." In an after-hours meeting in the Calcutta consulate on September 30 the consul permitted another relative of the Sikkimese royal family, Yuthok Shape, to read and take notes on Henderson's signed letter before it was put back in the consulate's safe.[36] Yuthok was expected to transmit these qualified commitments to the Dalai Lama's representatives still across the border for transmittal to the young Tibetan ruler, who by this time was resignedly making his way back to Lhasa to find a modus vivendi with its new Chinese military and political overlords.

Four days earlier in Washington the State Department had met with the Dalai Lama's brother Gyalo Thondup, who had finally made his way there after an only partially voluntary prolonged stay in Taiwan. The increasingly anxious Department had reaffirmed its hedged position that the United States government recognized both the Republic of China's suzerainty over Tibet and Tibet's claim to de facto autonomy. Henderson's signed letter of pledges was shown to the Dalai Lama's mother on November 11. It would seem to be a pledge for a prospect rather than a deliverable commitment in view of her son's position as a gilded prisoner in his occupied capital.

These pledges remained part of a collection of open-ended commitments which the United States was to fulfill in whole or in part over the coming six decades. For the Tibetans it was rather like having a reassuring promissory note in a bank account to which they had limited access. By then it was early autumn 1951, and the only hope for the American project was that the Chinese had not successfully closed off all escape for the Dalai Lama if he found the situation unbearable upon his return to Lhasa.

It was time for the hard-charging Henderson to move along. His active opposition to the 1948 UN resolution that divided Palestine into Jewish and Arab states, which been a factor in his assignment "out of town" to India, was now fading history. Fortunately he was succeeded by an equally activist Chester Bowles. The former advertising magnate and congressman was not prepared to go so far as to endorse the proposal forwarded by the Calcutta consulate, which called for the United States to send planes to Lhasa to evacuate the Dalai Lama or provide arms and leadership to monks prepared to resist openly the Chinese occupation of their country. He was, however, quite prepared to have the "U.S. make at least one final effort by letter or oral message to encourage the DL to resist in ways best known to the Tib Govt."[37] He suggested that Taktser send a new letter to his brother, reaffirming the American commitments and "practical suggestions by Taktser whose knowledge of the situation in Lhasa should assist him in recommending steps to be taken in immediate future." He went on to suggest, "Although it may not be feasible, the Dalai Lama might for example make a pilgrimage to Buddhist shrines in Tibet from one of which he might escape southward to India." Ever the public relations professional, Bowles added, "[The State] Department might also send the DL small gifts such as the newest photographic equipment and colored film in which the DL is greatly interested. . . . [The] latter although small would represent tangible evidence to the DL of U.S. friendship and would have effect far out of proportion to their monetary value." Washington, equally responsive, prepared a letter affirming its "original position—full aid and assistance to [the Dalai Lama] when [he came] out," and stating that although it was not possible to fly into Lhasa for him, aid would be given to him in his flight if it was both necessary and feasible. A letter from Taktser, presumably relaying these assurances and the suggested gift for the Dalai Lama, was forwarded to Calcutta on November 25, 1951, confirming the opening of a new era in America's relations with Tibet.

It was new territory for both the Tibetans and the Americans. The Tibetans reluctantly accepted that they could no longer carry on their aloof existence as semidependent "grace and favor" appendages of the British, but must come to terms with a new force in Peking that had the capability of restoring its authority over their country and challenging its unique way of life. For the Americans it meant the dramatic replacement of a century-old policy dedicated to preservation of the territorial integrity of China in favor of an active contest with the new occupants of the Imperial City. The American commitments embodied in the documents sitting in the consulate safe in Calcutta were, however, to go uncalled for over the next eight years as the Tibetans struggled on their own to preserve their identity in Lhasa.

CHAPTER NINE

On the Sidelines

From Lhasa, where the Chinese were beginning the consolidation of their new authority, the Dalai Lama in the early part of the winter of 1952 sent a resigned response to the continuing pledges of support that Washington promised him if he reversed his decision to remain in Tibet. In a letter to his brother Taktser, who was then in contact with the State Department, the young ruler wrote that so far the Chinese had "given no open indication that they wanted to suddenly change matters in Tibet or injure the Tibetans." Under these circumstances, "since the Chinese were being correct and careful it seemed best to treat them in the same way, but the U.S. official friends should not feel vexed because of this, since Tibetan policy remained and would remain the same. He instructed Taktser to maintain contact with the Americans and not to allow misunderstanding or lack of confidence to develop between the United States and Tibet."[1]

Taktser accordingly met with Dean Rusk's successor, John Allison, who assured him of America's continuing "friendship and sympathy" and "explained his hope that the fall of Tibet to the Communists will resemble the tactics of Japanese judo experts who fall in order to rise again."[2] Taktser found Allison as gung-ho as his predecessor. Allison and the CIA had earlier discussed with him a proposal to intercept the Dalai Lama if he were to flee Lhasa and fly him and thirty of his supporters to safety outside Tibet.[3]

Their discussions had gotten down to such specifics as whether the ice on the lakes north or south of Lhasa was thick enough to land a plane. In deference to the Dalai Lama's stated wishes to try to make the best of his uncertain situation, however, Allison and his State Department and CIA colleagues all agreed that the United States government would make no public statements that might "invite undue attention to Tibet" at that time. When nothing occurred to substantiate these reports of incipient rebellion, the energized Washington establishment retreated to "watchful waiting."[4]

The Dalai Lama did seem to leave the door open in a message sent through the Crown Princess of Sikkim later that summer expressing his hope "that when the time [was] propitious for the real liberation of Tibet from the Chinese, the United States [would] find it feasible and possible to lend material aid and moral support to the Tibetan Government."[5] The message was delivered orally, and it may have reflected the aspirations of the messengers more than a bid for American support of a resistance movement against the Chinese. At the time there was nothing to support.

Washington's apparent willingness to become involved in an adventurous enterprise came from a combination of politics, personalities, and capabilities that underlay United States foreign policy in 1952 and continued to condition it for the next several years. Eisenhower was able to exploit the frustration generally felt throughout the country over the continuing stalemate in the Korean truce negotiations at Panmunjom. Since February 1950 Joseph McCarthy had been leading the anti-Communist crusade, which was highlighted by charges that the State Department had been infiltrated by Communists who were responsible for the "loss of China." By the time Eisenhower assumed office in 1953 congressional committees had already launched eleven different investigations of the Department.[6] Proposals and programs aimed at challenging the Chinese Communists would have therefore had a special claim to attention.

When Eisenhower subsequently made his promised trip to Korea he came back convinced that the situation was intolerable.[7] The choice was to negotiate an armistice that would mean abandoning North Korea to Communism or to continue to stand on a static front, accepting continuing casualties without achieving visible results. He found the latter alternative unacceptable. This left no choice but to accept a settlement that would anger his Republican Old Guard, who were arguing through MacArthur for him to threaten openly "to clear North Korea of enemy forces . . . through the atomic bombing of enemy military concentrations in North Korea and the sowing of fields of suitable radioactive materials . . . to close major lines of enemy supply and communication leading south from the Yalu." Eisenhower was "appalled at MacArthur's willingness—and that of so many others—to advocate the actual use of atomic weapons by the United States against Asian people only seven years after Hiroshima."[8] He was, however, willing to use the *threat* of an atomic arsenal as a tactic to induce the Chinese to accept a compromise solution in Korea and as the major deterrent against further aggression by the Soviets. Maintenance of such an arsenal, the actual use of which was unthinkable, was an expensive drain on America's resources. The stationing or use of American troops in the many potential trouble zones was unsustainable, but abdication to further Communist expansion was unacceptable. Defense expenditures had to be trimmed, but only to the point that the policy of containment remained credible.

One alternative that Eisenhower came to support vigorously was the development and use of a covert action capability that would permit the United States to continue to challenge Communist expansion without the commitment of large military forces. This capability was to become an accepted tool of American foreign policy. Eisenhower first made use of it in September 1953, when he gave the CIA approval to undertake with British Intelligence an operation to mount a coup to overthrow Iranian Prime Minister Mohammed Mossadegh. Operation Ajax was consequently launched, the troublesome old man was replaced, and the young shah Reza Pahlavi was restored to his throne. The apparent success of this relatively bloodless and inexpensive operation, directed by Theodore Roosevelt's grandson Kim Roosevelt, confirmed Ike's enthusiasm for the use of covert action as a weapon in the Cold War. When his brother Milton and his old friend Walter Bedell "Beetle" Smith, who was then undersecretary of state, convinced him the following year that Guatemala had "succumbed to Communism" under its democratically elected president, Jacobo Arbenz, Eisenhower again turned to the CIA to mount another covert operation to fix the problem. Although this operation did not go as smoothly as the Iranian coup, Arbenz, believing, probably correctly, that once Eisenhower had committed himself he would continue to undermine the Guatemalan government, finally capitulated.[9] At his first televised news conference, held on January 19, 1955, Eisenhower proudly proclaimed the elimination of the Arbenz regime as one of his proudest accomplishments.

There was thus a covert action capability—and a willingness to use it— that would have been available to the Tibetans had they developed a resistance movement that merited consideration. Between 1949 and 1952 the number of those engaged in covert action within the CIA increased tenfold, and the budget for these operations was twenty times greater than the budget for the Iranian coup.[10] Although Tibet would have then seemed an appropriate site in which to exercise these capabilities, the political situation there initially did not warrant it. For the five years following his return to Lhasa the Dalai Lama was engaged in an uneasy effort to find an accommodation with the Chinese that would check the occupation or at least make it less onerous on his people. There was also little or no organized resistance inside Tibet to challenge the new order being imposed there.

Gyalo Thondup and the Resistance

It was at this time that Gyalo Thondup arrived back on the scene and began his life's work of supporting the cause of his younger brother and his country. Thondup is an extraordinary and complex man of lively intellect, keen political sense, great charm, strong emotions, and driving dedication to his country and his brother. He is not one to suffer fools or opposition gladly. The Dalai Lama has described him as "the most fiercely patriotic" of his brothers, with a "very strong character and a tendency to be single-minded to the point of stubbornness." He has a strong attachment to his family and his fellow countrymen. The Dalai Lama said that it was Thondup who cried the most when their mother died: "I have seen him cry over the loss of men that he had sent off to fight in the resistance effort."[11] But Gyalo is no weeping Mossadegh taking refuge in his bed, but a passionate fighter who has devoted his life to finding an honorable solution that will preserve the institution of his brother and the identity of his country. His willingness to make what he believes are necessary compromises to achieve his goals has made him at times a preferred negotiating channel for the Chinese but also a subject of controversy among some of his brother's advisors and constituents. He was also the most skilled political operator I was to know and admire over the four decades that I served as a CIA political action officer.[12]

When Thondup arrived in the northern Indian town of Darjeeling in the summer of 1952 he was twenty-three years old. He went to this West Bengal border town, the summer residence of the Indian governor general and a companion town to the historic Tibetan trading post of Kalimpong, following an already colorful and richly varied career, which was to be a forerunner of the role he would play in the political life of his country. Born into a farm family in the northeastern Amdo territory of Qinghai province, he had learned early to preserve his Tibetan identity while living and operating in a

Chinese province governed by a Muslim warlord. One of his closest relatives was a senior cleric at the nearby Kumbum monastery, the birthplace of the founder of the Dalai Lama's sect, where his elder brother was later to become the abbot. Although Gyalo was never devoutly religious, he recognized early on the fundamental role that Buddhism plays in the identity of Tibet. He was raised as a farmer by his father, a horse trader used to bargaining and doing business with the Chinese, a necessary skill he imparted to his son. When Gyalo moved to Lhasa as a ten-year-old he received special instruction in Chinese from a Muslim who was a member of the regent's monastery, and he perfected his knowledge of the language and history of China by studying in the regent's library. This was in pursuance of his father's decision that he take charge of the family's land. The regent, with whom Gyalo's father became close after he became the head of Lhasa's First Family, was later involved in a power struggle that branded him as pro-Chinese. This later had some consequences for Gyalo among those with long memories of the Byzantine politics of Lhasa in those days. It seems doubtful, however, that the Chinese officials who have known and negotiated with him over the past half-century have ever regarded him as a pliable tool rather than a tough and skilled Tibetan advocate. Those of us who have worked with him over the years to oppose the Chinese domination of his homeland have never had any reason to doubt his primary and steadfast loyalty to his brother and his fellow Tibetans.

His mother recalled that it was only after her many long arguments against it, countered by his father's strong backing for it, that an eager Gyalo accepted the Chinese Nationalist government's offer to go to China to study in 1946.[13] Ironically he was following a historic precedent set by the Manchu emperors of educating the members of the Dalai Lama's family. He went to China as a teenager and became a personal protégé of Chiang Kai-shek and his wife, who treated him "like a son" and indulged him by providing him with a Jeep, with which he cut a wide swath as a young buck in Chungking. The Gimo told him that he feared the British influence in Tibet, but with a well-educated Gyalo advising the Dalai Lama he would feel that "China's back door" was safe, and he promised he would grant independence to Tibet at an unspecified date. The young Tibetan thus had a ringside seat at the events that led to Chiang's being forced to flee the mainland, and he recognized the role that corruption and inefficiency played in the collapse of his host's government. But years later, even after the problems that the Nationalist government made for the Tibetans at the United Nations and the Kuomintang machinations against him personally and among the Tibetan resistance, Gyalo still would not repudiate his regard for Chiang as a person.

As a political pro, he also has been willing to play the Taiwan card with China's present-day successors. This complex sense of fidelity coupled with his very pragmatic and outspoken conviction that any solution for Tibet must come out of negotiations with the Chinese who hold the cards, apparently caused Chiang's successors on the mainland to choose Gyalo for some years as the preferred agent for whatever maneuvers they were engaged in concerning the status of Tibet. He seems to have been sidelined in the chill imposed by the Hu Jintao regime in 2006, but he is busy at his retreat in Kalimpong, planning a new strategy to negotiate a way for him and his fellow exiles to retain their claim to their homeland. His prominence and freewheeling strategy have also earned him criticism from his more hard-nosed countrymen. Lodi Gyari, a protégé of Gyalo's who is now Dharamsala's primary negotiator with Beijing, says that the Dalai Lama, although at times impatient with his brother's stubborn and unilateral style of operating and negotiating—"He is a bit of [a] loose cannon"—professes not to share this distrust.[14]

When Gyalo finally took up residence in Darjeeling in 1952 it was after a long odyssey which began after he left Nanking in April 1949, before the capital fell to the Communists. He brought with him to India his new Chinese wife, Nancy, the daughter of a wealthy ex-army officer, Chu Shih-kuei, who had been one of Sun Yat-sen's supporters. His family, despite their pro-Chinese accommodation, were not pleased at his marrying a non-Tibetan, and the marriage did nothing to enhance his regard among the Old Guard in Lhasa.[15]

This was a time of seismic upheaval among the major powers and their leaders in East Asia and the United States. Gyalo was surveying these events and charting his future course of action from Kalimpong. It was there, in the autumn of 1949, that he received two messages from a surprising source. Zhu De, one of the progenitors of the new political order that was being established back in China, from which Gyalo had fled, was asking that the Tibetan government send a delegation to Peking to negotiate with the government he and Mao were forming. This chief of the People's Revolutionary Army stated that his government had no intention of invading Tibet, but would maintain the same relationship with the Tibetan government as its Nationalist predecessor had. Presumably he meant the semi-independent, ill-defined status that Chiang's government had accepted for want of means or opportunity to enforce a more rigid control structure.

Zhu De had been chosen to make this approach to Gyalo apparently because of the special relationship that Zhu had with Gyalo's father-in-law,

Chu Shih-kuei, which dated back to when they had been classmates and friends at the Whampoa Military Academy two decades earlier and was cemented in a dramatic event in the 1930s. Although this history was not a military secret, there is no record indicating that those within the United States government dealing with the China situation knew of the existence of—or at least the consequence of—this old tie between the two generals. Gyalo later told those of us who were working with him on Tibetan resistance and political matters in the late 1950s and 1960s of Zhu De's conciliatory approach, but not of the origin and basis of the Red Army chief's relationship with his father-in-law. Gyalo's son only recently recounted the origin of this apparently enduring friendship between these two unlikely soul mates. He cited an incident that occurred when he and his father visited China in 2003. One of their official guides on their tour through China, including the Tibetan inhabited provinces, volunteered his government's appreciation for "what [Chu] did for Zhu De in refusing Chiang Kai-shek's orders to have him executed seven decades ago."[16]

Gyalo said that he forwarded Zhu's approaches to his brother's officials in Lhasa, but "a befuddled, bewildered and incompetent government" there did not know how to respond, so nothing came of them. He remained in Kalimpong until April of the following year, 1950, when he set out on an unsuccessful self-initiated attempt to go to Peking to negotiate with the Chinese.[17] The British refused to give him a transit visa for Hong Kong when he tried to take on the mission himself. When he went to the Philippines hoping to get to Peking by way of Macao he was persuaded by old Kuomintang friends to go to Taiwan instead. There he and his family were to remain for the next sixteen months as well cared for, but increasingly unwilling, guests.

While Gyalo remained on Taiwan accepting the forced hospitality of the Gimo, his brother Taktser made representations to the State Department to bring him to the United States. He and his wife and daughter were eventually granted visas and spent the next five months in Washington. They were fully briefed by the State Department on the efforts that the United States had been making to persuade the Dalai Lama to seek asylum abroad, and his official hosts also offered him a full scholarship at Stanford in an effort to dissuade him from joining his brother in Tibet.[18]

However, Gyalo was not to be deterred from the sense of mission he had acquired in the five years he had been away from Lhasa. He once described the "incomprehensible experience" for an Amdo farm family such as his to become the First Family of Tibet as "like reaching Heaven."[19] Unlike his father, who seems to have enjoyed the perquisites that came with his son's new status more than the politics involved, Gyalo seems to have more fully taken on the obligations. He is also a born politician. The years that he spent in China under the driven and besieged Chiang were formative ones for Gyalo. He was indoctrinated by the legatees of Sun Yat-sen's Three Principles of People's Democracy, Livelihood, and Nationalism, while witnessing at the same time the disintegration of their government from a combination of inefficiency, maladministration, corruption, and popular fatigue. He became a man with a mission. He was determined to return to Lhasa to use any means to motivate what he now viewed as an equally outdated and increasingly irrelevant government there to inaugurate reforms that would checkmate the imminent Chinese absorption of the identity of his country and its people.

Gyalo therefore left his brother Taktser in Washington in February 1952 and returned to India. There he was reunited with his mother, sister, and younger brother, who decided to return to Lhasa with him to rejoin the Dalai Lama. He was going without his Chinese wife, as his mother was apparently still not reconciled to their marriage. Moreover the uncertain reception his wife could expect by both the new Chinese overlords and the Tibetan establishment did not augur well as the site for the birth of their second child, assuming she could have withstood the rigors of a midwinter journey to Lhasa. Gyalo left her in India and made his way with his remaining family over the Himalayas, following the route Younghusband had taken to the Tibetan capital in 1904. They were accompanied by the faithful Lhamo Tsering, his old buddy from their salad days in Nanking.[20] Lhamo Tsering's trip to Lhasa that winter was his introduction to what was to be his life's work as political confidante, soul mate, and alter ego to Gyalo.

Lhamo Tsering said in his memoir that Gyalo believed that he could provide leadership to young Tibetans who had a nationalist pride in their country with an accompanying loyalty to their religion.[21] The need was for immediate action to inaugurate reforms that would preempt those that the Chinese would soon impose and thereby consolidate their hold over the country. Gyalo therefore offered a reform plan to the Tibetan government, which was exercising a nervous authority at the sufferance of the two Chinese generals who had arrived to supervise the occupation. His plan, which represented a radical restructuring of the Tibetan polity, called for the following:

An inventory of the lands held by the three main monasteries and by government officials, which would be the basis for redistribution among limited individual holdings.
Public officials to be paid according to rank.

Debts owed by the people to the monasteries and the government to be validated and excessive debts forgiven.

The old system of excessive taxation to be replaced by a new, more equitable system.

The Dalai Lama's family to give up its estates and holdings outside of Lhasa, retaining only the traditional family estate in Lhasa.

Gyalo firmly believes that his family, including the Dalai Lama, approved these proposals, recognizing them as the only means of forestalling the more drastic measures that the Chinese would inevitably introduce into Tibet as they consolidated their occupational control.[22] The Tibetan government-appointed trustees of the family holdings, however, regarded Gyalo as a "lunatic." They asked him if he had no concern for his children, who would be deprived of their inheritance by such madness. The Dalai Lama's two prime ministers, Lobsang Tashi and Lukhangwa, approved of the strategy of initiating such reforms to forestall the imposition of more dire measures by the Chinese, but they cautioned Gyalo not to tell the other members of the cabinet, who might warn the Chinese of Gyalo's objective. But he said these old bureaucrats too eventually "thought blue" (i.e., were conservative) and decided against promoting the restructuring that Gyalo was advocating. In any event, the Chinese forced the Dalai Lama to cashier these shaky supporters of Gyalo's reforms, and Gyalo was feeling increasingly isolated.

Gyalo was also under personal pressure from the twin occupation generals, Chang Ching-wu, the chief administrator, and Chang Kuo-hua, the commander of the occupation troops. Although expressing their suspicions about Gyalo's having left his pregnant wife behind in India, they were intrigued when they heard of the governmental and land reforms that he was proposing. In an effort either to recruit a prize Tibetan and win a surprise political bonanza or to test this maverick's intentions, they began speaking about openly supporting him and the Dalai Lama to move against the nobility and the traditional government. Gyalo had no intention of becoming a Tibetan Quisling, collaborating in the occupation of his country, but he feared jeopardizing his brother's dicey political position if he refused their embrace. His dilemma was deepened when the Chinese urged him to go to Vienna that summer to represent the "new Tibet" at an international youth conference. After consultations with his increasingly politically savvy mother, but leaving the Dalai Lama unwitting so he could honestly plead ignorance of his brother's intentions, Gyalo told the Chinese that he was going to his estate in southern Tibet to carry out the reforms that he had already implemented on

FIGURE 4 Gyalo Thondup (left) and Lhamo Tsering en route to new lives in India.

the family's other estates. This was a mission they could heartily endorse for their presumed convert.

Gyalo said that he did take out some insurance by informing the Indian political officer in Lhasa of his plan to relocate in India. He was reassured by the response from Prime Minister Nehru, asking only where he planned to cross the border so that the appropriate Indian authorities might be alerted to admit him. The young political operator set off with the faithful Lhamo Tsering, taking the same route his brother was to follow into exile seven years later.

Soon after his arrival in India in the summer of 1952 Gyalo sent telegrams to Secretary Acheson and Chiang Kai-shek asking for their help in his work against the Chinese occupation of his country. When a nervous Indian government sent its political officer in Gangtok to demand copies of the cables and to warn him against carrying out any further political activities from Darjeeling, Gyalo reminded the officer of the promise he had received from Nehru, that he would be free to carry out his political activities if he came to India. Two months later Nehru's trusted intelligence chief, B. N. Mullik, went to Darjeeling and reassured Gyalo that the Indian prime minister was willing for him to carry out whatever political activities he considered useful as long as he kept Mullik's Central Intelligence Bureau informed. This was the beginning of Gyalo's long, at times tense, but ultimately mutually respectful association with Mullik and the CIB, its political boss, Nehru, and his successors. It was a rich mix of personalities: the Kashmiri Brahmin, his intelligence chief who was an untouchable, and the increasingly skilled young political operator from the Tibetan outback.

For the next few years events concerning Tibet went into a holding pattern. In Lhasa the Dalai Lama swallowed the Chinese demand that he dismiss his two prime ministers, who were resisting the commands of the occupation authorities. He was determined to make the best of a situation to which he saw no alternative, and such accommodation was generally accepted by the Lhasa establishment. Gyalo knew that most of the nobility were accepting payoffs from the Chinese, including his older sister and her husband, who sent their servants each month to receive their allotment of Chinese silver dollars from the occupation authorities.[23] The American consul in Calcutta cited the consulate's "long-standing friend," the Maharajah of Sikkim, when reporting, "[The nobility] are reconciled to the inevitability of change as they feel that even if the Chinese had not invaded Tibet, the present Dalai Lama would have pushed through reforms affecting their positions. . . . [They are] cooperating with the Chinese in the hope that they will be permitted to enjoy the benefits of their positions a little while longer."[24]

In early 1954 the twenty-year-old Dalai Lama accepted the invitation that the Chinese had been pressing on him to visit Peking. There he met with Mao in sessions at which Phuntsok Wanggyal, a Tibetan who had been recruited by the Chinese Communist forces as they crossed Tibetan territory two decades before, acted as his interpreter and became his friend.[25] At these sessions Mao spoke in conciliatory fashion, expressing his opinion that it was too early to implement all of the clauses of the Seventeen-Point Agreement, particularly the one imposing rule by the Chinese army over Tibet. Instead a Preparatory Committee would pace reform in Tibet to the wishes of the Tibetan people themselves.[26] The relieved young ruler decided, "The more [I] looked at Marxism, the more I liked it. . . . While unable to agree with its purely materialistic view of human existence, I felt it would be possible to work out a synthesis of Buddhism and pure Marxist doctrines that really would prove to be an effective way of conducting politics."[27]

Some of his illusions concerning Communism as it was being practiced in China under Mao began to wear thin as the Dalai Lama spent the next several months traveling throughout the country. It was on the evening before his return to Tibet that his final disenchantment occurred. Mao had summoned him to a surprise farewell meeting, which he began by offering what the young but increasingly seasoned Tibetan leader considered "excellent information" on how to govern, drawing on his constituents' opinions and then deciding on key issues. Mao reserved his rabbit punch for his final comments when he said, "Your attitude is good, you know, [but] religion is poison. Firstly it reduces the population, because monks and nuns must stay celibate, and secondly it neglects material progress."[28] The abruptly disillusioned Buddhist ruler recorded that he was "suddenly very afraid." Of Mao he thought, "You are the destroyer of the Dharma (the teachings of Buddha) after all." He could only explain Mao's misjudgment of his motivation for independence as due to misinterpretation of his strong interest in scientific matters and material progress.

This disillusionment with his host was preceded by a disturbingly awkward encounter with Nehru, whom he met for the first time when the Indian leader visited Peking during his stay there. This occurred at a state banquet at which Nehru graciously greeted all the guests to whom he was introduced, until the Dalai Lama was presented to him and he froze in silence. It was the young man from the hills who broke the ice by expressing his pleasure at finally meeting the man about whom he had heard so much. The usually urbane prime minister at last spoke, "but only in the most perfunctory manner." A follow-up meeting with the Indian ambassador was equally barren. It was obvious that the Indian government had no desire to associate publicly with this embarrassing prod to their conscience from over the border, particularly in the banquet halls of their neighbor's conqueror. The benign tolerance Nehru had directed his intelligence chief to extend to the activities in northern India of the Dalai Lama's brother Gyalo did not mean that he was going to jeopardize openly his high-priority pursuit of Mao as a partner in the policy of "peaceful coexistence" he was then ardently promoting.

By this time Gyalo had established himself, his family, and his faithful Sancho Panza, Lhamo Tsering, in Darjeeling and had begun a low-key effort to unite all Tibetans, from the old regime to the common people. Sitting in this historic border town across from the passes leading into Tibet, with very little money, the twenty-six-year-old demonstrated the abilities of the skilled political pro he was becoming. From the old Lhasa establishment he persuaded the politically adept former treasury official Tsipon Shakabpa, who had served as an intermediary between the United States government and the Dalai Lama the summer before, to remain in Kalimpong, along with another senior official, Yuthok Shape, who had also stayed behind when the Dalai Lama returned to Lhasa. Together with the Dalai Lama's trade representative in Kalimpong, Khenchug Lobsang Gyaltse, this informal organization became known as the "Jyin, Khen, Tsi Sum"—the Brother, Khenchug, and Tsipon Shakabpa. They held small meetings of twenty to thirty of their resident fellow countrymen to discuss events in Tibet and to organize delegations to New Delhi to lobby members of the Indian government and Parliament. In 1953 they expanded their activities to include raising funds to buy rice, oil, and other necessities for the Tibetan victims of the floods in the valleys of southern Tibet around Gyantse.

For these activities this rump protest group became known as the Tibetan Welfare Association, although these "welfare" activities were a one-time side project; the main effort was to publicize and mobilize opposition both inside Tibet and abroad to Chinese repressive actions in Tibet. It operated out of a back room off the kitchen of Gyalo's quarters in Darjeeling, which also housed the hand-operated printing presses used to print the literature urging Tibetans to resist the Chinese occupation. Two monks sent by the Dalai Lama's persistently anti-Chinese chamberlain, Phala Dronyerchemmo, prepared these pamphlets. They were later joined by four men who had fled Lhasa after the Chinese military administration demanded that the Tibetan government arrest them for writing and circulating letters from an organization called the Mimang (the People) protesting shortages and other abuses caused by the presence of the occupying troops.[29] These pamphlets were smuggled into Tibet through courier rat lines organized for this purpose and by the muleteers who were transporting the whisky Gyalo had been licensed by the Indian government to sell inside Tibet. This dispensation had been granted to him after the local Indian political officer, who had earlier warned him against engaging in political activities, notified Gyalo of his eligibility for this privilege. Apparently this was one of the perquisites of Gyalo's new status, which followed from the visit of the CIB chief in the fall of 1952.[30]

During this period Gyalo's Indian government contacts were interested only in the intelligence that he was able to provide from his home-grown sources. They had no interest in husbanding any resistance efforts. Similarly his links with the American consulate in Calcutta were primarily for keeping in touch. One officer who served in the consulate at that time said there was some talk of utilizing the continuing, if sporadic, cross-border trade into Tibet to smuggle ammunition in fruit tins, but this came to naught for want of any organization to utilize it. Meanwhile, despite New Delhi's cautioning against meeting with Gyalo "because it would be almost impossible to communicate with him in Calcutta or Darjeeling without arousing comment," the consul met with him when he went to Calcutta to accept what his sources were providing him.[31] This information supplemented what they learned concerning events primarily in Lhasa and southern Tibet from the family of the Crown Prince of Sikkim, who had close ties with the Tarings, Lhadings, and Ragashas, three of the prominent noble families in Lhasa. Intelligence concerning events in the Tibetan countryside, particularly in the volatile eastern border regions, was almost totally wanting. The Dalai Lama was sizing up his unwelcome hosts in his and their capitals, and Mao was promising a temporary reprieve in imposing his complete occupation of his guest's country. Both sides were on temporary hold.

CHAPTER TEN

The Stalemate Breaks

In late March 2004 a member of the Tibetan exile community sent an appeal for assistance in funding shelters for the veterans of the now nearly forgotten resistance effort that he and his country-men had carried out against the Chinese occupation of their coun-try. Addressed to the CIA officers he had known during the time they worked with him toward this objective, he based his request on the commitments made by the United States government al-most fifty years earlier. These obligations dated from 1956, which was a seminal year in the origin of the Tibetan revolt and the formal—and at that time very modest—involvement of the United States government in Tibetan affairs. This had taken place as China was consolidating its domestic control and emerging both as a world power and a new force within the Communist world, which was undergoing major upheavals.

In Tibet the Dalai Lama had made his way back to Lhasa from Peking in the spring of 1955, stopping en route at his birthplace, where his nervous Chinese hosts would not let him eat the food that his countrymen, including kinsmen, prepared for him. Despite his disillusioning final interview with the Chinese leader, the twenty-year-old Dalai Lama still "felt he [Mao] was a great leader and above all a sincere person." He was "convinced that so long as his [Mao's] officials in Tibet carried out his instructions, and provided he kept firm control of them, there was good reason to be optimistic."[1]

His Holiness's optimism and the relatively harmonious atmosphere between Lhasa and Peking were to be short-lived. The following year was a momentous one for events inside Tibet, for China's policies toward its reluctant ward, and for America's relationship with the Dalai Lama and his people. On June 27, 1956, the American consulate in Calcutta filed a roundup summary of the reports from local newspapers it had been receiving for several weeks of uprisings in Tibet.[2] According to this compilation, the first event had occurred in March in the Tibetan area along the upper Yangtze inhabited by the "wild nomadic tribes, the Goloks," where the Chinese had unsuccessfully attempted to impose their administration and confiscate the Goloks' arms. The rebellion then spread to the Lithang area, which is one of the principal centers of ethnic Tibet, primarily the naturally defiant Khampas. The consul concluded, "No neutral observer seriously believes the Khambas, Goloks and Litangas will be able to hold out indefinitely against the Chinese. They are short of ammunition and have no fresh sources of supply. While the present rebellion has delayed for a time the integration of this area into the Chinese system, there is no expectation this state of affairs can continue for more than six months to a year."[3] The prediction was to prove inaccurate within months, as the revolt spread throughout Tibet and the United States government became formally and materially involved in the affairs of the Dalai Lama and his people.

In Lhasa the Dalai Lama heard reports of the harsh methods being used by the Chinese to impose their "reforms" from the refugees arriving in increasing numbers from the Tibetan regions across the Yangtze. He noted that the Chinese in Lhasa were "carrying on as if nothing was amiss": "By not interfering with religion here in the capital, they were clearly hoping that I would be lulled into a false sense of security whilst they did as they pleased elsewhere."[4] The young ruler received another lesson in the limitations of Peking's benevolence when he requested that Phuntsok Wanggyal, who had been one of the principal founders of the Tibet Communist Party ten years earlier, and with whom he had developed a mutual trust and friendship, be posted to Tibet as the new Party secretary. After initially accepting his proposal, the Chinese authorities informed the Dalai Lama that his new friend wouldn't be coming to Lhasa, as he was a "dangerous man." This denunciation foreshadowed the eighteen years, from 1960 to 1978, that Phuntso spent in prison for espousing "local nationalism" in his native land.

The Dalai Lama sadly observed the decline in the honeymoon atmosphere as refugees from the Chinese forced "nationalization" in the eastern areas of Tibet, particularly among the Tibetan Khampas, began to arrive in Lhasa. Although opposed to the use of violence, he, as a Tibetan, noted sympathetically, "The Khampas, who were not used to outside interference, did not take kindly to Chinese methods; of all their possessions, the one that [they] valued above all others was their personal weapon."[5]

The Dalai Lama in India

On April 4, 1956, Nehru told his Parliament that the Chinese government had intervened to decline the invitation which the government of India, after considerable soul-searching, had issued to the Dalai Lama, the Panchen Lama, and a small group of their senior fellow Tibetan monks to attend the celebrations in the coming November to commemorate the 2,500th anniversary of the birth of Buddha. Peking had spoken for the two prelates, regretting that they would be too busy with the inauguration of the Preparatory Committee scheduled for that summer, and claimed that the Tibetan monks were too old to travel. They offered instead to send a delegation of eight other monks, five selected by the Chinese and three by the Indian government.

The Maharajah Kumar of Sikkim, who had delivered the invitations, told the American consulate that the Dalai Lama very much wanted to leave Tibet and asked if the United States would renew its assurances of finding asylum for him elsewhere and providing financial support to maintain him if he should escape to India. In a forthright response the Department of State authorized the consul to tell the Maharajah that "the United States was deeply sympathetic to the aspirations of the Tibetans to *independence* from the Chinese Communists and respected their right to maintain their own government and traditions; that if the Dalai Lama left Tibet, he should ask India for asylum; and that the United States would hope, in appropriate circumstances, to assist him in finding asylum in *some Asian country*."[6]

The Department advised that while it would support the Tibetan ruler's request for asylum, he should first seek help from India, since the "long range hopes of the Tibetan people" would require its help. The cable ended with the forthright statement "[The] cause of Tibet and of the Dalai Lama is very much in our minds and hearts and we assure the Dalai Lama that, under above circumstances, we will support him in his asylum requests." This pledge did not contain any reference to either the Maharajah's pitch for one thousand mixed rifles and machine guns to be delivered through Pakistan to the growing number of Tibetan resistance fighters in Kham or to the pro-posal to train ten Tibetans in Burma or Thailand in the use of artillery and anti-aircraft weapons.

One year later the Department's Historical Division included this pledge of political support in a compilation requested by the Office of Chinese Affairs on "United States policy concerning the legal status of Tibet."[7] This study concluded, however, that "nothing came of this approach [for support for an appeal by the Dalai Lama for asylum] . . . , and during the rest of the year there were no further developments of importance affecting United States policy with respect to Tibet."[8] The drafters were apparently not privy to the support for the resistance that had been initiated through other channels after a negative response was delivered to the Maharajah. These operations were to commit the United States government to involvement in the affairs of Tibet over the next decade and leave a legacy of engagement which remains today.

The Chinese, responding to what the Dalai Lama believes was the inter-vention of Nehru, reversed their decision and informed the Dalai Lama in early November 1956 that he was free to travel to India for the Buddhist con-vocation. But they warned him that there were "many reactionaries and spies in India, and should he try to do anything with them, he should realize that what happened in Hungary and Poland [would] happen in Tibet."[9]

The Tibetan leader, by then politically seasoned, accordingly set off with a small company of his advisors, but no Chinese warders, for India in late November. He planned to brief Nehru fully on the strictures that the Chi-nese had imposed on his political authority and his inability to intervene on behalf of his people against the harsh reforms and repressive measures being imposed on them in eastern Tibet. But when he presented a complete dos-sier of his efforts to accommodate to the Chinese rule which had been frus-trated by their actions, his delivery was apparently too long or too passionate and not what the Indian prime minister wanted to hear as "he appeared to lose concentration, as if he was about to nod off. He told his young visitor that he understood what he was saying, but went on somewhat impatiently, 'You must realize that India cannot support you.'" He furthermore rejected his visitor's appeal to remain in exile in India, saying, "You must go back to your country and try to work with the Chinese on the basis of the Seventeen Point Agreement."[10] He did promise that he would arrange for him to meet with the Chinese premier Zhou Enlai, who was arriving in New Delhi the next day.

Although the Dalai Lama says in his autobiography that Nehru's turn-down "was bad, but not unexpected news," his brother Gyalo Thondup is vehemently critical of his brother's gracious acceptance of what he says was a breach of bad faith. Gyalo had anticipated that if the Dalai Lama freely expressed his views in India, he would completely alienate the Chinese. Gyalo had therefore requested—and believes he received—a guarantee from Apa Pant, the Indian political officer in Sikkim, that his government would permit the Dalai Lama to remain in India and that Nehru would act as a mediator to persuade the Chinese to withdraw their troops from Tibet. He declares that Pant gave him complete assurances on both these points, promising Nehru's willingness to negotiate with the Chinese and that the Dalai Lama could have his choice of "maharajah's palaces" as a place of asylum if the negotiations turned out badly for the Tibetans.[11]

The Tibetan leader, however, found himself in the same position that his predecessors had suffered, and that he was destined to encounter repeatedly throughout the coming years: that of a pawn in an international chess game. New Delhi was the first stop on a six-nation tour of Asian capitals that his fellow star guest, the Chinese premier, was making to tout China as the principal advocate of "peaceful coexistence." Two years before, Nehru had sealed India's acceptance of China's autonomy over Tibet in an agreement with Zhou under this Chinese rubric.[12] In defending the agreement the Indian prime minister had said it was "proper, sensible, and creditable [and] not only politically correct, but absolutely correct." He added, "We have done nothing better in the field of foreign affairs during the last six years. . . . [The agreement] was good not only for our country but for the rest of Asia."[13]

To have the world's principal Buddhist leader flee his country in protest against its brutal occupation by China would serve neither Nehru's nor Zhou's purposes. For Nehru, it would provide his critics with damning evidence that his political ploy to neutralize the threat of the Chinese occupation of an alarmingly long stretch of India's northern border was ineffective. For Zhou, it would be a lousy kickoff to what he had expected to be a triumphal vindication of the image of China as a peaceful neighbor living in harmony with its fellow Asian nations.

An obviously concerned Nehru arranged for the Dalai Lama to meet with Zhou the following day. The Tibetan ruler found his "old friend just as [he] remembered him, full of charm, smiles and deceit."[14] But the Dalai Lama "did not respond to his artful manners and instead told him quite straightforwardly of [his] concern about how the Chinese authorities were behaving in eastern Tibet . . . and also pointed out the marked difference that he had noticed between the Indian Parliament and the Chinese system of government and the freedom of the people of India to express themselves as they really felt and to criticize the Government if they thought it necessary."

The Dalai Lama wrote, "As usual, Zhou listened carefully before replying with words that positively caressed the ear." He assured the skeptical Dalai Lama that things in China had "changed immeasurably for the better" since his visit there the year before, and then went on to warn that it would be a mistake for the Tibetan ruler to consider staying in India, as his country needed him. The Chinese premier also met with the Dalai Lama's two brothers, Gyalo Thondup and Taktser Rinpoche, who were "even more forthright" in rejecting his appeal that they too return to Lhasa. They privately called him "Chew and Lie."[15]

The Dalai Lama then set off on the pilgrimage to the principal Buddhist holy places for which he had come to India. At Bodh Gaya, where the Lord Buddha had attained Enlightenment, he received a message that Zhou was returning to New Delhi and wished to see him. When he arrived at Sarnath, where the Buddha preached his first sermon, he received a telegram from Zhang Jingwu, the Chinese military governor in Lhasa, requesting he return to Lhasa as "subversive reactionaries and imperialist reactionaries" were planning a revolt and his presence was urgently required there. The beleaguered but undaunted Tibetan returned to New Delhi, where he completed his religious obligations and then had another meeting with Zhou, who answered his complaints about the imposition of the proposed reforms in Tibet by reassuring him that Mao had already announced that no reforms would be introduced there for at least the next six years, and they could be postponed for another fifty years if necessary. (Mao did announce such a postponement of reforms in Tibet in a speech on February 27, 1957.) He then urged the Dalai Lama not to visit Kalimpong, which was "full of spies and reactionaries." Zhou undoubtedly was referring to Gyalo and Taktser, who had been so unreceptive to his pitch that they join their brother in Lhasa. He also may well have heard of the meetings that Gyalo had been having there with representatives of the incipient rebellion in eastern Tibet.[16]

When the Dalai Lama met with his host a few days later, Nehru reaffirmed that Tibet should expect no help from India and seconded Zhou's advice that he return to Lhasa without stopping in Kalimpong. The Indian Central Intelligence Bureau had undoubtedly kept him well informed on the resistance sentiment and planning that were growing in the two West Bengal frontier towns of Kalimpong and Darjeeling. But when the Taktser pressed him, the Indian prime minister resignedly backed off, saying, "India is a free country, after all. You would not be breaking any laws [if you stayed]."[17]

The young ruler therefore made his way to Kalimpong in February 1957. He occupied the same room in a house in which his predecessor had stayed during his exile in India almost a half-century before. There a solid family phalanx headed by his mother and all of his brothers urged him not to return to Tibet.

The United States Reenters the Scene

By this time Gyalo Thondup had arranged for six young Tibetans to be trained by the CIA on Saipan for missions inside Tibet, where they were to be parachuted to confirm reports on the growing resistance in the eastern border areas. Gyalo was responding to the appeals he had been receiving for some months by emissaries from the local resistance groups in the Amdo and Kham areas. He said that he had at first approached the Indian Central Intelligence Bureau director, B. N. Mullik, but found him willing only to train men to collect intelligence, not to supply military assistance to the resistance. When he then turned to his old patron Chiang Kai-shek, Chiang responded favorably. The Kuomintang, however, would not change its propaganda line that the Tibetans were rebelling in order to hasten Chiang's return to rule China rather than acknowledging that the Tibetan revolt was a home-grown movement.

When the CIA offered to train this pilot group, Gyalo reasoned that his people were resisting the Chinese on their own initiative. They were coming to him as the only Tibetan who had access to those who might supply the arms that would help them fight their unequal battle, and it was his duty to secure them. He further rationalized that in any event whatever the Chinese Nationalists might have provided would have come out of the American armory.[18] He therefore not only accepted the Americans' offer, but personally escorted the trainees to the river crossing into eastern Pakistan. From there they were exfiltrated, with his brother Taktser's personal manservant acting as interpreter, to the CIA training compound which had been established on an island in the Marianas.

Frank Wisner, who was then the CIA director of operations, insisted that all cables concerning these operations reflect that the mission of the men being trained was primarily to collect intelligence. Their reports would provide the basis for his determination whether the resistance forces seeking arms had the capability and justification for using them. Wisner was suffering deep remorse about the CIA's inability to provide support to the Hungarians who had revolted that summer with the expectation of receiving support from abroad. The officer who presented the cables for Wisner's signature suggested that Wisner may have wanted both to establish a record of his cautions and at the same time to warn Desmond FitzGerald not to move too quickly. FitzGerald was chief of the Far East Division, responsible for conducting these operations, and was known to be an activist officer.

But there was no doubt among the CIA officers planning these operations and training the Tibetans that these men were expected to be active participants, and not mere passive observers, should the insurgent operations to which they were being returned warrant arms to be supplied by air. The CIA officer who had designed and directed the training of these men noted that the two airdrops which were subsequently made to the resistance groups that they had been sent to assess and report on included a full insurgency armory of Enfield rifles, 57mm recoil-less rifles, 60mm mortars, and Bren and Sten machine guns, which the trainees had been taught to use.[19]

In early October 1957 the six Tibetan trainees were loaded on a B-17 Flying Fortress, piloted by a crew of Free Pole Second World War veterans. The Poles were vestiges of a previous commitment to a common cause, while providing a fig leaf of deniability as well as technical competence. On a path that minimized the air time over India, the trainees were flown into Tibet, thus beginning the first installment of the United States government's commitment to the Tibetan cause. The men were divided into two teams. One team of two men was dropped onto a sandbar of the Brahmaputra River south of Lhasa. The other team of four men was to be dropped into the resistance forces reported to be operating in the Kham area across the Yangtze in eastern Tibet.

Permission from the Dalai Lama

The primary mission of the two men dropped near the capital was to obtain the Dalai Lama's endorsement of the United States government's favorable response to his rebelling subjects' requests for arms. It was a daunting assignment. They were two young Khampas, Lithang Athar and Lithang Lhotse, known by their training names as Tom and Lou,[20] who had been part of a small pool of refugees living in Kalimpong, from which Gyalo Thondup had recruited them when the CIA indicated its willingness to train exploratory scouts. Neither came from a noble family or the traditionally rebellious local clans, but both were close friends of the leader of the other team, Lithang Wangdu (Walt). And Walt was the nephew of a wealthy local Lithang merchant, Gompo Tashi Andrutsang, who was to become the leader of the Tibetan resistance when it became organized in the following months as a national movement.

Through a combination of perseverance and serendipity Tom and Lou made their way to Lhasa, where they established contact with Gompo. At that time Gompo was in the initial stages of putting together the disparate elements of the members of the two dozen rival clans, monks, and common citizens into a national organization.[21] Because of his wealth and long-standing generous support of Buddhist institutions in Lhasa and at home in eastern Tibet, he was able to arrange for the two young men from his hometown to meet with the chief of the Dalai Lama's personal staff, Phala Dronyerchemmo, to relay their request for the pontiff's blessing for America to provide arms to his subjects. Although five years earlier Phala had been one of those who had urged his sovereign to accept the American offers to aid him in fleeing Tibet and seeking asylum abroad, he was not willing to ask him to violate his Buddhist vows and endorse a request for arms with which to kill people, even enemies. It was not a request that one could make to a Dalai Lama.

This did not mean that the Dalai Lama was unaware that his countrymen were receiving aid from the United States. Phala instructed Tom and Lou, "On concerned matters and clear replies you receive from India, you must report here. I have already reported about the two of you to His Holiness the Dalai Lama in great detail. His Holiness said, 'Since there are many people who come to meet me, except giving audience to you, I have no advice to give.'" Phala did give them His Holiness's *sungdu*, blessing cords with mantraized cords tied into them by a holy man, and a *jinten*, a blessed pill. Ecclesiastical ignorance of their mission had been maintained, but it hadn't been proscribed.[22]

The Tibetan ruler was not unsympathetic to his people's opposition to the destruction of a way of life based on the religious structure that he headed. But it was theologically impossible for him to give his personal blessing to the use of arms.[23] The two young men, having made two unsuccessful pitches to Phala, decided to move with Gompo Tashi to join with the growing insurgency, which by then had moved across the Yangtze River and controlled a considerable portion of central Tibet southeast of Lhasa. There were no more demands for blessings.

The Chushi Gangdruk

The remaining four graduates of this first training class had a more immediate mission. After dropping Tom and Lou, the plane headed east to deliver this second team. A thick cloud over the drop area forced abandonment of the first drop. On a second try a week later one member of the team froze at the door of the plane and had to be transported back to Dacca. The other three were dropped into the Lithang area, where the team leader had established contact with a group of the rebels fighting under the Khampa resistance banner, the Chushi Gangdruk. The name means "Four Rivers, Six Ranges." It refers to the major rivers—the Mekong, Salween, Yangtze, and Yalung—and the mountains of the Kham region, that were the breeding grounds of the resistance.

This seemingly auspicious beginning was augmented some weeks later when Dick, the radio operator, rejoined his teammates, bringing word from Gyalo that negotiations for arms drops were in the works. Unfortunately the messages that the team sent requesting these arms did not include the details necessary to pinpoint a drop zone to which they could be delivered. By the time messages sent repeatedly from CIA headquarters requesting these specific locations were received, the Chinese had moved into the area and killed all of the team members except for the leader, Walt.[24]

On June 16, 1958, the Chushi Gangdruk organization was reconstituted as the National Volunteer Defense Army in a ceremony at Trigu, in the Lhoka area south of Lhasa. The new name and the confirmation of Gompo as the organization's leader recognized the role that he had played in unifying the resistance and his understanding of the need to make it a national rather than a regional movement. The year before Gompo had organized a national collection drive for funds to build a golden throne for the Dalai Lama to use in public audiences. Over a hundred goldsmiths, engravers, painters, blacksmiths, welders, and other craftsmen spent several weeks preparing the throne to welcome the Dalai Lama upon his return from India.[25] During that time Gompo had remained in Lhasa while the resistance was being organized in his Khampa homeland. In addition to being at a geographical distance from the rebellion, Gompo was not one of the local clan chieftains running the war. Though a successful merchant and generous with his accumulated wealth, this man, who was to become the acknowledged leader of the resistance, initially was considered a nouveau riche outsider by both the traditional Lhasa aristocracy and the tribal leaders of eastern Tibet. Moreover he initially had no troops of his own to contribute. He was, however, highly regarded by the leaders and members of the three great monasteries of the Dalai Lama's sect, whose monks constituted half of the ground troops of the resistance. Furthermore he enjoyed access to Gyalo Thondup, the brother of the person that the force was dedicated to protect and the channel to the CIA and its promise of arms. He was therefore able to use the golden throne project as a vehicle to organize the previously loosely organized twenty-eight insurgent groups that eventually rallied to the flag of the National Volunteer Defense Army.

Shortly after the proclamation of the new organization and before the first arms drop was made, Gompo set off with a contingent force to attack the Chinese. Their objective was the government arsenal at Gaden Chokor, west of Lhasa. Before leaving the base area Gompo had complied with the request of the Chinese-controlled Tibetan government that he and his associates explain why they had left their homes and taken up arms. His reply could hardly have been expected to mollify those requesting it:

We stated that our movement [the Chushi Gangdruk] did not generate from any motives of disloyalty toward our government nor was it conceived in any spirit of lawlessness. Our sole objective was to resist and oust the Chinese who were oppressing our people. . . . Not only was personal safety at stake, but our national institutions and way of life were being extinguished slowly and cunningly. Individual freedom had become non-existent since the Chinese invasion and the communist doctrine was being barbarously enforced. Patriotic people felt there was nothing left to look for or live for. We were rebelling not from choice but from sheer compulsion.[26]

After issuing this political salvo the Chushi Gangdruk force had their first engagement with the Chinese People's Liberation Army. Gompo claimed the outcome of what turned into a fierce three-day battle was a victory for his forces; two hundred PLA soldiers were killed, compared to his loss of forty men killed and sixty-eight wounded, along with fifty mules killed.[27] At the Gaden armory they were able to persuade the initially reluctant officials to ignore the orders they had received from Lhasa not to release arms to the freedom fighters, and they obtained a significant haul of weapons and ammunition. They continued on their way, heading north, first to the military airfield at Damshung, north of Lhasa. From there Gompo led his forces in a series of engagements, in one of which he was wounded, across the mountainous and barren plains northeast of the capital to a region in eastern Tibet called Shopando. This was friendly territory, and Gompo was able to recruit a sizable number of reinforcements to replace and augment the losses from combat and by desertion in the ugly battles his forces had fought on the way. The plan was to control the area along the Sichuan-Lhasa highway over which the Chinese transported supplies to their troops in eastern Tibet.

By this time Tom had made his way to India, where he was being debriefed in anticipation of the arms drops that the CIA was planning to make to the resistance forces; it was now established that they were operating in central Tibet. His teammate, Lou, had remained at Gompo's headquarters in central Tibet and was there to receive, sort, and distribute these arms. There is some disagreement about when the drops were made. According to the records of Gyalo's assistant, adjutant, and records keeper, Lhamo Tsering, 403 Lee Enfield rifles (selected because they were of British manufacture and ones that the Tibetans were familiar with), sixty hand grenades, twenty machine guns, and 26,000 rounds of ammunition were delivered in two drops made in the summer and early winter of 1959. Tsering said that when the Dalai Lama fled from Lhasa in March 1959, the arms from the second drop had not been distributed.[28] Other Tibetans and American crew members told the author Kenneth Conboy that the drops were made in October and November of 1958, and that there was considerable bickering over both the number of arms available for distribution and the allegation that Tom and Lou had commandeered one parachute containing gold ingots.[29] The chute had actually contained a modest sum of rupees to pay message couriers.

These drops provided no immediate significant advantage to the resistance forces. They did mark the first steps toward the actual participation of the United States government and the American people in the affairs of Tibet. The existence of an active resistance effort inside Tibet had been confirmed. It was self-generated and composed of volunteers asking only for the arms that the two overflights had demonstrated the Americans could deliver. The question was whether the United States government was ready to make the political commitment to the Dalai Lama and his people that full involvement would entail.

CHAPTER ELEVEN

Promises Kept

In the first quarter of 1959 a rush of events forced the Dalai Lama and Washington into a series of policy decisions that were to have lasting implications for their relationship.

In the field the acknowledged leader of the resistance, Gompo Tashi, had organized an encouragingly large number of recruits in western Kham to conduct operations along the highway to Lhasa. After a series of fierce but inconclusive battles, Gompo moved farther north, where he had more success in recruiting volunteers but met with discouraging results in a series of unequal contests in which the Chinese prevailed by their control of the air. He therefore was in the process of leading a shift of his forces westward toward the area south of Lhasa.

In the capital the Dalai Lama had completed his final examinations and was granted the degree of *geshe* (doctor of Buddhist theology), which was celebrated with a great procession in February from the Jo-khang, the historic cathedral, to his summer residence. The procession was viewed by thousands of the citizens of Lhasa, now swollen by great numbers of refugees who had fled from the growing insurgency in the east. These events occurred at the end of the annual Monlam prayer festival, which had frequently been a volatile time in Lhasa. No one knew then that this was to be, as the Dalai Lama later recalled, "the last time the full pageantry of more than a thousand years of uninterrupted civilization [would be] on display."[1] A half-century later Beijing, forewarned by a continuing series of protests throughout Tibet over the absence of their leader, took extraordinary measures to forestall these observances.

On March 9, 1959, the Chinese announced that the twenty-four-year-old pontiff and head of state had accepted an invitation to a theatrical performance at the Chinese army compound. A growing crowd of already seething citizens surrounded the summer palace to prevent his going to what they feared would be captivity in the enemy stronghold. The concerned citizens began a series of demonstrations intended to keep him safely bottled up in his palace grounds with the members of his official cabinet. The young ruler and his staff remained secluded, fearful of showing any sympathy with their would-be protectors for fear of provoking the Chinese and prejudicing the negotiations they hoped to induce the Chinese governors to conduct with them.

This explosive stalemate prevailed for a week, during which the isolated pontiff had the company of his mother and siblings and the devoted and capable services of the head of his personal staff, Phala, all of whom were urging him to flee to India. His cabinet eventually came to believe that it was important for him to seek refuge nearby, inside Tibet, from where they could negotiate with the Chinese for his return under conditions that would guarantee his status, limited as it was. A series of divinations were held which all ended up with the challenging advice that he should remain in Tibet. By the night of March 17, after three days of escalating agitation from both his would-be protectors, who had taken over the palace grounds, and his increasingly incensed snubbed hosts, the oracle finally came through with the welcome message "Go! Go! Tonight!"[2] They went.

This was a reverse replay of the events eight years earlier, when the oracle had divined that he should return to Lhasa rather than seek refuge abroad. By 1959 the Dalai Lama and his faithful and astute political counselor Phala had learned from bitter experience that he might better serve both his religion and his people from outside Tibet rather than remaining a captive puppet. Ironically Peking's efforts to smother their unruly subject were to serve to emancipate him from the confines of presiding as a constrained head lama over a relatively politically insignificant Shangri-La to become an internationally respected religious and political leader—and a major foreign affairs embarrassment for Mao and his successors—for the next fifty years. Moreover, through his writing and teaching, Tibetan Buddhism was to become no longer an esoteric and exotic practice confined to remote mountain monasteries and isolated valleys but the shared religious practice and daily ethic of a sizable number of lay people throughout the world.

In the meantime Phala sent word to Gompo's National Volunteer Defense Army (the Chushi Gangdruk) headquarters to send a party to escort the Dalai Lama to a safe site in their operating area south of Lhasa. He had also taken out a bit of political insurance by sending a courier to inform the Indian consul general that His Holiness might be forced to leave Lhasa and seek asylum in India. Late on the night of March 17 the Dalai Lama left a votive scarf on the altar in his private chapel. Then, wearing a soldier's uniform and fur cap, carrying a rifle but not wearing his characteristic eyeglasses, he went with Phala, another senior abbot, his brother-in-law, and two soldiers out of the summer palace gate, telling the guards that they were making an inspection tour. They made their way undetected through the crowd of his would-be protectors to the bank of a tributary of the nearby Brahmaputra. Crossing in the traditional round birch and rawhide coracles, they were reunited with his mother, eldest sister, youngest brother, and two tutors, who were members of the party that had accompanied him to Yatung in 1950. With a skeleton bodyguard and four of his cabinet ministers who had made Phala's cut,[3] the escape party was met by thirty Khampa soldiers with ponies from Gompo's NVDA forces who had been dispatched in response to Phala's alert. They immediately set out for the guerrilla-held territory; they were joined a few days later by Tom and Lou, who used the radio they had dropped into Tibet to provide CIA headquarters with the first news of the Dalai Lama's flight and follow-up bulletins as the escape party made its way south.

At the White House, while the rest of the world was in the dark as to the whereabouts of the Dalai Lama, President Eisenhower was charting his flight based on the messages Tom was cranking out from his Second World War radio transmitter. At CIA headquarters arrangements were being completed to move a second group of young Tibetans then being trained at a site in tidewater Virginia to one at Camp Hale, the former home base of the United States Tenth Mountain Division in the Colorado Rockies. The new location would provide better facilities and far greater flexibility for training men in surroundings similar to those in which they would have to survive in their homeland. All the conditions that the United States government had set for its participation in the affairs of the Dalai Lama and his rebelling subjects were now present. The condition that he condone the use of force to support the rebellion had become moot when he accepted the services of members of the armed resistance to escort him on his escape journey to India.[4] He was seeking asylum abroad with the expectation that his fellow Buddhists in Asia would support him. A verified self-generated rebellion existed. The means of delivering support to the rebels existed. It was now up to the United States government to decide how far it would live up to its commitments.

In Washington the State Department spokesman Joseph Reap, citing sources considered "reliable," confirmed that "a revolt [was] in progress in Tibet." In response to a question, he said that he "assumed that Tibet [was] an independent country, but he would have to look into that."[5] On March 26 Allen Dulles, director of the CIA, briefed the National Security Council, saying, "[While the events in Lhasa] do not constitute any real threat to Peiping's control of the main town of Tibet, the Chinese Communists will certainly be obliged to face guerrilla operations by rebellious Tibetans." He noted, "[Chiang Kai-shek is] extremely anxious to do something to encourage the continuation of the uprising . . . [and] issued a pronunciamento today which went pretty far, but he does not have much influence in Tibet because in the past he himself has consistently opposed independence for Tibet."[6] The "pronunciamento" contained a surprisingly forthright pledge by the Gimo: "As soon as the puppet Communist regime on the mainland is overthrown and the people of Tibet are once again free to express their will, the [Nationalist] Government will assist the Tibetan people to realize their own aspirations in accordance with the principle of self-determination."[7]

Although the State Department spokesman said, "President Chiang's reiteration of his Government's respect for the political, social and religious autonomy of Tibet is most welcome at this time," the statement issued that afternoon by Christian Herter, acting for the terminally ill secretary of state John Foster Dulles, was less forthcoming. Herter expressed "shock at the ruthless suppression of human liberties in Tibet and the determined effort by the Chinese Communists to destroy the religion and culture of Tibet," but he was obviously unwilling to get into the issue of the legal status of Tibet. He confined himself to saying he was "saddened by the suffering of the Tibetan people": "We see in their resistance efforts one more heartening example of the indomitable spirit of man."[8] When pressed Read did go on to say that the United States had "never recognized or condoned the so-called 'agreement' [the Seventeen-Point Agreement signed by the Tibetan representatives in Peking in 1951] under which the Chinese Communists deprived the Tibetan people of the political autonomy which they had long enjoyed."[9] This backing and filling reflected the reserved position of the State Department at that time on the Tibet issue.[10]

The Chinese Nationalist government had pledged to do its best to aid "their brethren in Tibet to meet their urgent need for weapons and ammunition, communications equipment, medical supplies and military personnel,"[11] but the State Department avoided any reference to material support from the United States. This caution was in keeping with the advice of the Department's Indian wallahs, who warned against rousing Nehru's "almost pathological antipathy to Western, as distinct from communist 'colonialism'": "If Nehru came to believe, however unjustifiably, that the United States is attempting to exploit the Tibetan uprising primarily against the Peking government and only secondarily on behalf of the Tibetans themselves, it might make it easier for him to pretend that the uprising is not truly a popular one but only a maneuver in the cold war."[12] It was also a useful waffle which avoided taking a stand on the legal status of Tibet on which the Department had yet to come to terms.

On March 28 Peking finally took official notice of the uprising and announced the appointment of the Panchen Lama, with whom the Mao government had close ties, to replace the Dalai Lama, who they claimed was "under duress" by the rebels. It was the Chinese who roused the ire of the Indian prime minister, causing him to react strongly against Peking's charges that the Tibetan uprising was being led from India and that discussion of Tibetan affairs by the Indian Parliament would be "impolite and improper." Nehru recalled that Zhou Enlai had said in New Delhi two years earlier that Tibet was autonomous and that Mao intended that it remain so. He went on to describe India's strong ties with Tibet and declared, "Indian sympathies go out to the Tibetans."[13] Echoing Washington's policy of restraint Ambassador Ellsworth Bunker in New Delhi commented, "The progressive involvement of the Indian Government in a public controversy with the Chinese reinforced the Embassy view that the impact of the Tibetan revolt on the Indians will be greatest if it results from direct Indian experience in the absence of encouragement of revolt from the outside or interpretation by other nations."[14]

The generous welcome with which the Dalai Lama was subsequently received in India, accompanied by Peking's ham-handed charges that the Indian border town of Kalimpong was "the command center of the Tibetan rebellion," reinforced Washington's inclination to leave well enough alone. Nehru made the restrained comment that a "knowledgeable person had told him that there were more spies in Kalimpong than the rest of inhabitants" and "that all kinds of people had gone to Kalimpong" in various guises after the Communists took over China—"some as technical people, some as birdwatchers, some as journalists and some as just scenery advisers."[15]

The United States government continued to confine itself publicly to Herter's two noncommittal statements and one welcoming Chiang's statement that the Nationalist government would respect the political, social, and religious autonomy of Tibet. Ambassador Everett Drumright in Taipei was counseled not to endorse any "over-eager" exploitation efforts by the Nationalist government, "which would blur the spontaneous nature of the Tibetan uprising and lend credibility to Peiping's charges of GRC [Government of the Republic of China] instigation."[16]

Covert Participation

While Washington was able to take a public bye concerning these events, the Dalai Lama's departure from Tibet opened a whole new era of possibilities and commitments. Some were fulfilled by the United States government and others by their Indian hosts within the next few years. Some are still to be realized.

On the ground, however, there were situations within the resistance forces that required immediate decisions. The final message on April 2 from Tom, announcing the arrival of the Dalai Lama's party at the Indian border, contained an appeal for action that could not be ignored: "You must help us [as] soon as possible and send us weapons for 30,000 men by airplane. All Tibetans are suffering from the Chinese Communists."[17] Although there had been no commitment to deliver this quantity of arms, Tom and Lou had returned with the escort party to the rebel stronghold in the Lhoka Valley after they delivered their distinguished charge to the border. They were there to meet with the NVDA commander Gompo Tashi to provide the communications for receiving further airdrops for operations in the western Kham area among the resistance.

By this time the Chinese had brought in large numbers of troops and aircraft to crush this troublesome resistance a few days' march from the Tibetan capital. It was a massive effort, and by mid-April the Chinese had captured the major resistance bases between the Lhoka Valley south of Lhasa and the Indian border. With the Chinese in control of both the air and the ground there was no way of responding to Tom's appeal for assistance. Gompo records that his "commanders and freedom fighters alike deemed further resistance useless and [his] views and exhortations did not carry much weight with them."[18] He was forced to abandon the last attack, which he had persuaded two thousand of his men to carry out, after he and they had second thoughts: "What if the entire force is wiped out in this final battle, . . . only leaving us with a sorrowful memory?"[19] On April 29 Gompo and his men began handing over their weapons and ammunition to the Indian border authorities in exchange for the food and shelter they badly needed.

Plans were already in progress in Washington, however, to proceed with the ambitious program of providing assistance to the Tibetan insurgents

Gompo had left behind in eastern Tibet. On April 1, immediately before the Dalai Lama's arrival in India, Allen Dulles had informed President Eisenhower, "In light of the recent upsurge of Tibetan resistance and the flight of the Dalai Lama toward India, which have resulted in a complete break between the legitimate Tibetan authorities and the Chinese Communist government, plans are currently being made within existing policy authorizations."[20] The then chief of the CIA's Tibetan Task Force (known by his staff as "Slim") recalled that on the day the first message was received from Tom en route with the Dalai Lama's escape party, Desmond FitzGerald, the chief of Far East operations, called a meeting with his deputies, asking, "What next? Does the Agency cease any further support to the Tibetan resistance? what will happen to the resistance forces? what options do we have? what will happen to the resistance forces? will they be able to continue without our assistance? or is the effort futile at this point?"[21]

In response Slim delivered the following analysis and recommendations:[22]

Tibetan resistance forces, not CIA, had made the Dalai Lama's escape from Lhasa possible.

The gathering of primarily Khampas in Lhasa, which had provided a fortuitous cover for his escape, had been there for a religious holiday, not to foment a revolt at CIA's behest.

The resistance forces would continue to fight as best they could with or without CIA assistance, as they had been doing since 1956.

Abandoning support to the self-generated Tibetan resistance movement would validate the Chinese Communist charges that the United States was a "paper tiger" and earn the disdain of both America's friends in the "Free World" and its enemies and critics, such as the USSR and India.

The United States government should increase, not cancel, its assistance. The CIA had just begun to deliver supplies and teams into Tibet to join the already existing resistance there, so the Dalai Lama's departure need not be a signal that the resistance was folding.

He concluded with a projected schedule of monthly (full moon) airdrops of teams and supplies into the Kham and Amdo areas of eastern Tibet and a rhetorical flourish, quoting Jefferson's observation, "The tree of liberty must be refreshed from time to time with the blood of patriots and tyrants."

In addition to these tactical reasons for continuing the program there was the bureaucratic one of the immediate availability of the site to train the men who could provide the techniques and discipline of guerrilla warfare that the

FIGURE 5 Last roundup of the Tibetan Support Project alumni, October 2004.

home-grown guerrilla bands would need to survive. Camp Hale had been in operation for over a year; it was located south of Leadville, Colorado, at an altitude comparable to that of Tibet. The Tibetans who trained there called it Dumra, the Tibetan word for "garden." It was staffed by officers known to FitzGerald from earlier CIA paramilitary operations carried out in Asia. They had developed a unique sense of camaraderie with the Tibetans they had trained there and were eager to continue training more of their compatriots to carry out missions in support of a cause they had come to share.

A half-century later in this now deserted valley, on September 10, 2010, Senator Mark Udall presided at a ceremony attended by sixty of the surviving relatives of the over two hundred Tibetans trained in guerrilla warfare, two of the CIA trainers and the teenage Tibetans who had interpreted for them, the mayor of Leadville, and officials of the United States Park Service, who are now the custodians of the camp. The senator dedicated a plaque at the site, which reads:

> From 1958 to 1964, Camp Hale played an important role as a training site for Tibetan Freedom Fighters. Trained by the CIA, many of these brave men lost their lives in the struggle for freedom.
>
> They were the best and the bravest of their generation, and we wept together when they were killed fighting alongside their countrymen.
>
> This plaque is dedicated to their memory.

FIGURE 6 Senator Mark Udall giving a speech dedicating the memorial plaque at Camp Hale, Colorado, September 10, 2010.

Udall, who had a feel for the unique and intense bond that had developed between the trainers and these men from distant mountain valleys, concluded his dedicatory speech: "It is just so wonderful on this perfect, Colorado, early-autumn day—you can feel the connection between Tibet and Colorado—you can feel the connection between those who love the mountains and who know what the mountains have to offer."[23]

In 1959 this bond was not that apparent in Washington, but Slim knew how to make his case to his activist boss. As a young officer FitzGerald had served with General Stilwell in Burma, where he had gained a hearty appreciation for both the demands of irregular warfare and the fighting abilities of well-trained and -supplied Chinese forces. He was a dashing personality but a responsible man who knew the odds that were involved. He had been a close friend of Frank Wisner, the CIA operations chief who had been shattered over the failed support given to the Hungarians three years before. FitzGerald often reminded his officers that it "wasn't confetti they were dropping out of airplanes." The Tibetans, with their rugged spirit of self-reliance, appealed to him. He liked Slim's arguments and proceeded to obtain the permission of Allen Dulles and his deputy General Charles Cabell to proceed with the planning for continued support to the Tibetan resistance forces. Cabell was a senior Air Force officer whose ties with his old colleagues proved invaluable

FIGURE 7 The memorial plaque honoring the Tibetan Freedom Fighters, with two representatives of the men who trained at Camp Hale.

in obtaining both the approvals and the aircraft for the proposed drops. The CIA was ready to proceed.

On April 1 President Eisenhower gave his approval to the proposal drafted by Slim even as the Dalai Lama was completing the last leg of his flight into exile.[24] This entailed providing assistance to the Tibetan insurgents Gompo Tashi had left behind in eastern Tibet. It was sustained even after the bleak briefings that Dulles provided to the chairman of the Joint Chiefs of Staff, Nathan Twining, on April 23, when he reported on what had happened to Gompo and the resistance forces in central Tibet: "The resistance boys are badly trapped . . . [and have] been forced to the Indian border. The Chicoms waged a more effective war than we had anticipated and have more airpower than anticipated. They [the Tibetans] told us to postpone it [further operations] as they have lost the area where we were going." In response to Twining's question whether the resistance fighters were going to get out all right, Dulles clinically replied, "[I don't know] if the Indians will let them in and they won't be very much good to us in India."[25]

Three days later Dulles informed the National Security Council:

The patriots were severely beaten by the Chinese Communists and had been pressed into a relatively small area of Tibet. Their messages had a rather pathetic quality. The patriots had no food and ammunition and they were requesting our intercession with the Indian Government to permit their passage into India. . . . Of course we would do all that we

FIGURE 8 The author (second from left) with two old friends at the memorial plaque ceremony, September 10, 2010.

could to help them but it was a very difficult situation. The Chinese Communists had put on a very effective military showing. They were making very effective use of aircraft. It looked as though the rebel forces in the Khamba area had been pretty well knocked to pieces. The same was probably true of the rebel forces in the Lhasa area.[26]

Two weeks later Dulles informed the president that preparations were under way to carry out the delivery of the assistance to the surviving resistance in eastern Tibet that he had approved some weeks earlier, despite the "recent setback which befell the forces south of Lhasa following the flight of the Dalai Lama [which] . . . resulted in a delay . . . pending receipt of fuller information as to the continuing existence and location of active resistance forces." He assured the president, "Every effort is being make to identify and establish communications with such forces."[27]

The challenge, the technical capability to meet it, and the personalities to support it were all in place, and the program went on. It was not undertaken as a remnant Kipling holdover with either the Americans or the Tibetan political leaders prepared to fight to the last Tibetan for a glorious but hopeless cause. The rebels that Gompo Tashi had left behind in western Kham were committed but ill-equipped. They were asking only for the arms that would permit them to fight in an area in which they—and their suppliers—then believed they knew how to survive and take advantage of the vulnerability of the Chinese dependence on the two principal highways through the area to provide necessary supplies for their troops. The operational premise was that the Tibetans could survive the rigors of their native area and make it so expensive for Peking to provide these supplies that they would abandon the effort to consolidate their occupation in this remote plateau.

An analysis prepared at that time by the CIA's economic intelligence staff, titled "Logistical Problems of the Tibetan Campaign," provided reasonable validation of this premise. It concluded:

> The most serious vulnerability identified in this study is the limited capacity of the supply routes. The southern route from Lhasa to Ya-an [the proposed target of the resistance forces Gompo had left behind earlier that spring] is closed at present and would require a military campaign plus a period of construction before it could be used. The northern route from Lanchou is of limited capacity at best, and is subject to interdiction at several points between Golmo and Lhasa. Only a concentrated effort by the Chinese at keeping the road open will permit a sustained flow of supplies to Tibet.[28]

Gompo had two situations to deal with: finding useful occupation for the resistance forces that had fled to India with him when they were overwhelmed in the last battle in central Tibet and the even more immediate question of how to make use of the men he had recruited but left behind in western Kham.

One of the more ambitious covert paramilitary programs undertaken by the United States government during the Cold War was initiated at these meetings. The Indian government had accepted the remnant Tibetan resistance forces that straggled across the border with Gompo after the Chinese sweep through their former stronghold in central Tibet. Gompo suggested that these men might be utilized in a new effort to challenge Chinese occupation west of Lhasa. As a trader and pilgrim he had traveled through this area, and he particularly knew the Mustang peninsula of Nepal, in which there was a Tibetan enclave loyal to the Dalai Lama. Gompo furthermore had a good personal relationship with the area's ruling king of Lo, a man of Tibetan ancestry and Buddhist faith, which Gompo believed would ensure his acceptance of a transplanted resistance operating from his turf. Lhamo Tsering indicated his approval of the proposal, which meant that it had been endorsed by his principal, Gyalo Thondup, and the CIA agreed to seek approval for a pilot proposal to relocate to Nepal four hundred of Gompo's roughly three thousand dispossessed veterans, most of whom were resignedly working on road-building projects along the border.

The immediate problem was how to utilize the men Gompo had recruited and left behind in the area northeast of Lhasa. Gompo believed that if this group of willing but unorganized insurgents could be persuaded to break up into small guerrilla groups, conducting ambushes and raids along either of the two highways over which the Chinese supplied their troops in central Tibet, Mao might be persuaded that the price of occupying Tibet was too high.

This should have been a propitious time to try such a gamble. The Chinese leaders were having their own conference at Lushan that summer, debating the conduct and future direction of the Great Leap Forward launched by Mao the year before, which had begun to falter. This mass mobilization of the countryside, which shifted the direction of the Socialist revolution in China from the government bureaucracy to the Communist Party and away from the Soviet model of five-year plans, was to cause fundamental divisions among the leadership in Peking. The top military commander, Marshall Peng Dehuai, who resented the diversion of his troops to local agricultural projects and the emphasis on mass mobilization rather than building a Soviet-style, modernized, professional organization, was banished to the sidelines. Although the disastrous consequences of the Great Leap were not to become publicly apparent for another five years, Mao's government was vulnerable.[29]

Accordingly Eisenhower was convinced to approve proceeding with an all-out program of air support to the resistance forces still operating in the regions north and east of Lhasa. In September 1959 the first of over two dozen flights that dropped men and supplies to these forces was made. The last one, deep into the Kham area between the Mekong and Yangtze Rivers, was approved by the new president, John F. Kennedy, and made in March 1961. They were all valiant failures.[30]

It was a tragic ending to what had been one of the more skillfully executed technical and logistical covert operations of the Cold War. The willingness of the United States Air Force to lend its prized and relatively scarce C-130s; the provision of the tightly held overflight photography for producing maps to guide the pilots to previously uncharted areas; the innovative measures adopted by the air crews to find ways to carry extra fuel on these flights of unprecedented distance, altitude, and duration; the enthusiastic participation of the flight crews and parachute dispatch officers, who could hope at best only for lengthy imprisonment if the very real possibility of unforeseen hazards resulted in a crash or a forced landing—all bespoke a full determination to fulfill the commitment made to the Tibetans.

This was matched by the manner in which the material aspects of the operations were carried out. Those involved shared a sense of participation in the goals of the persons whose parachutes they were packing, and in preparing the pallets to ensure that the maximum amount of arms, ammunition, and supplies would reach them. Those planning these operations and training the men for their mission shared this same sense of identity.

The primary motivation for the policy support for these operations remained what Dean Rusk had identified earlier in the decade as "doing anything possible to get in the way of the Chinese." By 1959 there was the more pressing justification of providing substance to the Tibetans' claim for self-determination that the United States government was finally willing to support publicly. But for the Tibetans it was a noble failure which they accepted with remarkable resignation. Gompo Tashi expressed his disappointment that his colleagues had remained together in tribal groups rather than breaking into guerrilla bands, thereby providing vulnerable targets for the Chinese. But he too must have appreciated that it was both tradition and inhospitable terrain that had caused his fellow Khampas to band together rather than either hide or live off the land.

Lhamo Tsering, who had acted for his principal, Gyalo Thondup, in selecting the men who were trained by the CIA in Colorado and returned to Tibet to receive the arms drops and instruct the resistance forces on how to survive, could have resented the criticism that he and Thondup received for their role in this failed effort to sustain the resistance. Years later, however, he still thought it had been a worthwhile effort, and his only criticism was that the equipment that would have permitted the various rebel groups to communicate with each other, share intelligence, and coordinate their movements had not been provided.[31] This equipment had been withheld because it was feared that the rebels would not have observed proper communications security and thereby would have pinpointed their locations to the Chinese. In retrospect withholding this equipment now seems to have been a mistake, but the greater problem of persuading the resistance fighters to split into less vulnerable, smaller guerrilla units to live off a basically inhospitable countryside would still have remained. Here the fallacy in judgment was our unrealistic expectation that these people would abandon the only way of fighting that they had ever known and our underestimation of what the Chinese would and could commit to quash this challenge to their authority.

The United States government's fulfillment of one of the major commitments it had made to the Tibetans in support of their cause was a significant policy statement and an extraordinary technical achievement, but a tactical failure. Yet when those of us who had trained and dispatched the survivors of these unequal contests met them four decades later in India and Nepal, we were warmly greeted by them as their *ghegen* (teachers) who had tried to help them, but whose efforts had been unsuccessful against what the Chinese were prepared and able to launch against them.[32] As Buddhists they apparently were prepared to stress the value of our good intentions rather than dwell like Anglo-Saxons on the road to Hell that is paved with them. Like most human beings they find it difficult to admit that an enterprise in which they were engaged might be doomed, but they also have a stubborn single-mindedness that is being demonstrated again today by the survivors and descendants of these dedicated people who were willing to risk their lives to fight for the beliefs that define them.

CHAPTER TWELVE

Tibet on the International Scene

These paramilitary operations in support of the remnant Tibetan resistance were put into motion at the same time that the United States government was fulfilling—in part—the political commitments it had made to the Dalai Lama during the previous decade. These had originally been made with the objective of inducing him to leave Tibet and make his case to the international community. Although his departure from Lhasa had taken place according to his own script, Washington still considered it in its interest to honor those commitments.

The Eisenhower administration maintained its public posture of noninvolvement in the affairs of the Dalai Lama as he settled into his new position as a respected but politically sensitive permanent guest in India. Washington was prepared to ensure that his case, unlike the reserve accorded him nine years before, received proper notice by the UN and the world community—but within limits. It was an era of new objectives. When Washington first confronted the Tibet issue in 1950 it was in the context of the imminence of another world war, in which the free world might have to contest a united Communist world. The shibboleth of monolithic Communism dominated strategic planning.

By 1959 Mao was fulminating over what he considered the heresy of his Soviet partner Nikita Khrushchev for his diffident support in the crisis that the Chinese leader had created over Taiwan the year before. Khrushchev was compounding his perceived apostasy by not only cozying up to the Indians, whom the Chinese regarded as their partners in propounding peaceful coexistence in their Asian bailiwick, but also planning to travel to Washington to spread the new gospel he had appropriated as his own. Although the Russians couldn't be expected to endorse any statement by the UN to condemn China's actions in Tibet, their support of their Chinese ally could be expected to be relatively pro forma. For Washington "doing anything to stop the Chinese" was still fair game. It was to be another fifteen years before Nixon's discovery of the China card would result in the Tibetans being treated like embarrassing members of the family.

In 1959, however, there was little need for Washington to make any definitive pronouncements on the Dalai Lama's flight from his capital. From Washington's point of view things were proceeding nicely on their own. The State Department reported that although "official reaction lagged well behind press comment, the Australian, Malayan, Korean, Cambodian and Taiwan officials had condemned the Chinese actions and Japan's Prime Minister Kishi ha[d] made some cautiously critical comments."[1] In Burma leading English- and Burmese-language newspapers were taking the approach Washington hoped for, charging that the Chinese action against the Dalai Lama was an "attempt to suppress Buddhism by the forces of Communism." The *Nation*, Rangoon's leading English-language newspaper, considered close to the government, suggested, "The Government should seriously reconsider its neutralist policy."[2] Commenting on the events in Tibet, Vatican Radio welcomed a new ally, noting that "Islam and the religions of Asia had joined Christianity in opposing Communism."[3] In nearby Kathmandu the Congress Party, which had just won the country's general election, declared, "The tragic events in Tibet are an Asian parallel to the Hungarian annihilation."[4]

In Washington the Indian ambassador asked to "come in" to the State Department, where he declared that "the Indian feeling in this whole matter was perfectly clear, but that the Indian Government was trying not to raise any false hopes among the rebels. With regard to the effect in India of the present happenings in Tibet, the crux of the matter was the demonstration that the Chinese Communists were totalitarian fascists really... and that Indian leftist-liberals [including himself] [did not] object to the Communist economic system, but to their totalitarian methods.... [But] by and large, Indians tend to be a bit soft."[5] The counselor of the British embassy expressed an unusually forthright statement of support for the right of the Tibetans to a hearing at the United Nations, telling his State Department colleague that "since China had clearly repudiated the principle of autonomy, on which basis alone the U.K. had recognized Chinese suzerainty, the U.K. was no longer required to regard development in Tibet as an internal Chinese matter and would perceive no legal obstacle to United Nations consideration."[6] Unfortunately for the Tibetans, the counselor was apparently out ahead of his principals in London. There the Foreign Office continued to adhere to the legalistic noncommittal statement it had made while the Dalai Lama was in flight to India, that "the U.K. recognized Chinese suzerainty but only on the understanding that Tibet [was] regarded as autonomous." The Whitehall diplomats did add—off the record—that the Chinese action in Tibet had been one of "ruthless oppression and disregard for Tibetan autonomy and another example of Chinese Communist imperialism."[7]

While London's caution about endorsing the Tibetans' cause was based on a reluctance to offend Mao's government, Washington was hesitant to rush in and ruin a situation that, from their point of view, was developing nicely on its own. This required the United States to urge restraint on the Chinese Nationalists, who were anxious to exploit the Tibetan revolt and the Dalai Lama's flight to promote their proposed program of backing resistance throughout the China mainland. Although American Ambassador Drumright backed this program, he warned against any joint Tibetan-Nationalist activities "since the Tibetans [were] antagonistic to all Chinese regardless of their political affiliations."[8] The State Department noted, "Matters were now moving favorably, with Indian public opinion forcing Nehru and the Government of India into a more forthright position in support of Tibetan resistance . . . while reaction elsewhere among less committed countries in free Asia [was] also taking an encouragingly anti-Chinese Communist line": "[Therefore] it is not desirable that this trend be impaired by over-eager Government of the Republic of China (GRC) exploitation efforts, which would blur the spontaneous nature of the Tibetan uprising and lend credibility to Peiping's charges of GRC instigation."[9] Similarly the Department temporized when the Committee of the One Million sought support for an "American emergency committee for Free Tibet," sponsored by Lowell Thomas and Congressman Walter Judd.[10] This eagerness to embrace the Tibetan cause by Taiwan and its supportive China lobby was to be a mixed blessing for the next several decades.

Meanwhile the Eisenhower administration's game was to stay in the wings, taking no actions such as inviting the Dalai Lama to visit the United States, as urged by Senator Clifford Case.[11] It readily accepted the advice of its Democratic opponents, such as Averell Harriman and Chester Bowles, that the United States not be the first to rush toward recognition of a Tibetan government-in-exile should the Dalai Lama set up one or take actions that could give a "Cold War twist" to the situation. It also had not been ready prior to the Dalai Lama's flight from his capital to endorse publicly or, in this period before congressional oversight committees, to inform senators of the ongoing plans to utilize the turmoil in Tibet to support guerrilla activity against the Chinese Communists, as proposed by Senator Hubert Humphrey.[12]

Indian Ground Rules

According to the CIA, the Dalai Lama arrived in India in no mood for temporizing or equivocation.[13] When P. N. Menon, the Indian external affairs representative who was sent to welcome their new guest and to provide the code of conduct preferred by New Delhi for his stay, told him that Nehru suggested that internal autonomy, not independence, should be Tibet's goal, the Tibetan ruler responded sharply. He reminded Menon that he was now on India's doorstep as a refugee after following the prime minister's advice two years earlier and had returned to Tibet to work peacefully for wider autonomy. His Chinese overlords had not honored this reserved approach, but had continually pressured him to denounce the resistance movement and go to Peking, finally endangering his life and forcing him to escape. He and all Tibetans were now convinced that attempts at autonomy were useless. Tibetans were fighting and dying for complete freedom and independence, and he was determined to struggle for this goal no matter how long it took and regardless of the Indian government's attitude. The statement that he planned to issue upon his arrival in India proper was already drafted. It would note the spontaneity of the uprising in Lhasa, the Tibetans' denouncement of the Seventeen-Point Agreement, their peaceful approach to the Chinese Communists over the past years, his forced escape from Lhasa, the establishment of a Free Tibetan government during his exodus, and the fact that he was now in India to fight the Chinese Communists and to appeal to the free countries of the world for support of a Free Tibet. In response to Menon's urging that he not make such a categorical statement, the feisty Dalai Lama replied that he and his cabinet felt that if the Indian government would sustain a statement of support for autonomy only, and if his stay in India would be an embarrassment, they should not accept Indian asylum but persist in their goal of complete independence and find asylum elsewhere.

Menon's superiors in New Delhi were prepared to countenance greater freedom of expression and certainly wanted to avoid the opprobrium that would derive from appearing not to welcome their newly arrived guest. They asked only that he make no mention of the establishment of a Free Tibetan government or the contradictory letters exchanged under duress between his officials and the Chinese authorities during the last hectic days in Lhasa, or renounce the Seventeen-Point Agreement. This was in accordance with what the American embassy described as "the phlegmatic course being followed by the Indian Government, i.e., no hard-and-fast rule being followed; bridges will be crossed when reached," following the rubric enunciated by Nehru for a policy that would achieve a balance "between the sometimes contradictory factors of national security, the desire to have friendly relations with China, and strong feelings about Tibet [in that order]."[14]

In his statement upon arrival in India proper ten days later the Dalai Lama did not raise the issue of a Free Tibetan government. Nor did he specifically renounce the Seventeen-Point Agreement, but he did make it clear that it had been signed under duress and that it was the Chinese, not the Tibetans, who had repeatedly violated it. He made a pointed reference to the "strong desire for independence on the part of the Tibetan people . . . [which] throughout history has been asserted on numerous occasions." But he did not include a demand that India support such status. He stated "categorically that he had left Lhasa and Tibet and [gone] to India of his own free will" and had not been "abducted under duress," as Zhou Enlai had charged. As for his future plans, he needed time to "rest and reflect on recent events before making any decision."[15]

The Fourteenth Dalai Lama was now ready to work out the terms of his self-imposed exile, as his predecessor had been forced to do almost a half-century before. Although he too arrived as a vanquished ruler, dependent upon the hospitality of a host who would have preferred that he stay at home, this Dalai Lama had more assets which worked to his advantage in fixing the terms of his forced residence abroad. He enjoyed the measured respect of his fellow Asian Buddhists and the sympathetic regard among the general public of the non-Communist world, who saw him as another casualty of aggression by a totalitarian government. The Thirteenth Dalai Lama had slipped into India as a refugee, preceded by a press which had generally portrayed him as a somewhat retrograde Oriental autocrat. His successor was welcomed by an Indian honor guard after a dramatic flight covered by a generally sympathetic international and domestic Indian press. The world spotlight was on him—and his Indian host—and the manner in which he was received. While his predecessor had eventually earned the restrained respect of the American ambassador and his government, the United States had never extended any active support for him or his country. This Dalai Lama arrived in India with commitments from the United States to support both the political status of his country and his right to air his case abroad, and the uneasy but fortifying knowledge that the United States backed its commitment by active support to the resistance his people were conducting against Chinese occupation of their country. While the use of force which this support involved presented him with a moral dilemma, it could also provide him with a certain confidence in dealing with his pragmatic host, who he knew was undoubtedly also aware of America's support. The Dalai Lama had moved out of Shangri-La.

Accordingly, when the determined Tibetan pontiff met his host in the appropriately Kipling-like hill town of Mussoorie on April 24 they greeted each other warmly, with their palms together in the traditional Hindu style and an exchange of white scarves in accordance with Tibetan custom. Nehru had attempted to lay down the ground rules a few days earlier, when he responded to a question in Parliament about their new guest's political rights, "Political activities are not carried on from one country with regard to another."[16] For his part the Dalai Lama appeared to be following his host's advice to refrain from making public statements about controversial issues involving the status of his country. A White House briefing note on the meeting reported that the Dalai Lama's reorganization of his official staff indicated that he intended "to direct covert political activities from India."[17] This turned out to be an accurate forecast of his intention to function as the head of a government-in-exile, even though it might not receive Indian or international recognition.

With his able and politically canny brother Gyalo Thondup now at his side, the exiled ruler was able to organize a shadow government on the other side of the mountains from his homeland that has successfully operated for the past five decades through the interstices of the limitations imposed by both his hosts and the frequently schizoid objectives of the world powers. In 1959 this meant finding a modus vivendi with their Indian host. Nehru was an ardent nationalist who had reached his high office by successfully challenging another world power, so he had a natural empathy with rebels fighting to retain their identity. He was also a pragmatic politician. While his natural sympathies were with his Tibetan northern neighbors, who had also provided a useful buffer against a historic enemy, he was painfully aware of the sad state of India's defense capabilities and its inability to engage in any quixotic foreign challenges.

When Mao first sent his troops into Tibet earlier in the decade the Indian leader had told his intelligence chief, B. N. Mullik, that for a thousand years

China had never been able to subdue Tibet, and though the Tibetans had often given way to Chinese military pressure, he doubted they would succeed this time. He said that he was therefore "very keen that the morale of the Tibetans was kept up" and had sent Mullik to contact Gyalo Thondup when he took up residence and began his low-key opposition efforts in Darjeeling in 1952.[18] At that time he told Mullik to keep in touch with Gyalo and "all the other Tibetan refugees and help them in every way possible." This meant that Nehru was also able to keep an eye on and silently support Gyalo's activities as long as he did not promote anything that would compromise the Indian leader with the Chinese, with whom he was trying to peacefully coexist. Meanwhile he continued to enjoy his international reputation as a spokesman for the new Asia, living according to the Five Principles of Peaceful Coexistence, which he had authored. Continuance of this hospitality since 1959 has permitted the Dalai Lama and his people to be viewed and respected not as hopeless refugees and a burden, but as exponents of an active cause which has won them international support and respect for their Indian hosts.

The Tibetans have been aided in carrying out this balancing act of reconciling their continued existence as a political entity, resident in a sympathetic but nervous country, by the heavy-handed policies of the Chinese, who shanghaied the Five Principles for their own use. After his return from meeting with the Dalai Lama in Mussoorie, Nehru told a very sober Parliament that India was "greatly distressed" over China's use of force to suppress the legitimate feelings of the Tibetan people. He was obviously offended by the charges made by Premier Zhou before the Chinese National People's Congress on April 18, that the Dalai Lama had been abducted. Zhou had criticized "people abroad who express[ed] sympathy for the Tibetans but [did] not identify the sector of the Tibetan population with which they sympathize[d]," meaning the rebels opposing the Chinese-imposed reforms. He called on all "well-intentioned friends, namely those subscribing to the Five Principles, to demonstrate sympathy for the majority."[19] In response Nehru dismissed Peking's accusations that the Dalai Lama was under any kind of duress in India as "both unbecoming and entirely void of substance." He called on China to make good its repeated assurances of autonomy for Tibet, rejecting as absurd their contention that "upper-strata reactionaries" were solely responsible for the uprising. He noted that even official Chinese accounts showed that the revolt was of considerable magnitude, indicating that it must have been rooted "in a strong feeling of nationalism affecting all classes of society." "Any attempt to explain the situation by the use of rather worn-out words, phrases and slogans is seldom helpful," Nehru concluded.[20]

Washington Plays It Cool

While the Dalai Lama was testing the ground rules for his new abode the Eisenhower administration was formulating its public stand on his new status. In a discussion with the French ambassador, Assistant Secretary Walter Robertson, one of the State Department's most staunch anti–Chinese Communists, philosophically noted, "[It is] a tragedy of our time that modern man cannot rebel against modern artillery unless and until the army goes over to the people as had happened to some extent in Hungary." He did not discount such a thing happening in China, despite the fact that "the prospect had to be looked at in the long term and the Americans did not like to deal with long term problems": "If the non-Communist world stood firm long enough we would win. The death of Mao, for example, might have an important result. The only danger was that we would get weary as time went on."[21] (Robertson would undoubtedly have been astounded by the continuing support over the ensuing fifty years for the Tibetan cause by both Democrat and Republican administrations.)

In April 1959 a circular was sent to all posts on April 21 providing guidance concerning the Chinese suppression of the Tibetan revolt. American diplomats were told that they might comment at their discretion along the lines of the acting secretary's expression of the "deep shock that all Americans [felt] at the Chinese Communists' barbarous action in Tibet and [their] attempt to destroy the liberties of the Tibetan people." While the United States was "keenly alive to the plight of the Tibetan people and would support any feasible step to assist them, this was complicated by various factors. For example, any action regarding Tibet must take into account the wishes and views of various countries with particular concern with Tibet such as India." Similarly diplomats were told, "You should point out it is difficult to assess the desirability and practicability of United Nations action in the absence of knowledge of the wishes and plans of the Dalai Lama and other [unspecified] relevant factors including circumstances [also unspecified] then existing. The U.S. wishes to avoid the appearance of exploiting the situation for cold war purposes and feels any initiative in the matter would come more naturally from an Asian country."[22] This sensitivity, particularly about being vulnerable to Cold War considerations, made good political sense in not frightening off potential neutral allies. It also provided some leeway while

Washington explored the attitudes of both the Chinese Nationalist and British governments, each of which for different reasons could throw a wrench in the works. Furthermore it was a new era in the Cold War, heralded by the unprecedented visit that Soviet Premier Khrushchev was to make to Washington that summer to promote his newly found passion for peaceful coexistence, to the discomfiture of his increasingly fuming former allies in Peking.

Accordingly when the Dalai Lama, through his now on-the-scene principal political advisor, Gyalo Thondup, sent a request to the United States for recognition of his newly proclaimed Free Tibetan government, Washington temporized. Ambassador Bunker was authorized to deliver only an oral response to the Dalai Lama, assuring him of the "concern and sympathy of the U.S. Government and people with him and his people's courageous struggle" and that "developments in Tibet [had the president's] personal attention and that of the Secretary and other high officials." The State Department did inform the ambassador that it was considering steps to get the Tibetans a hearing at the UN and also to sound out "close friends, beginning with the United Kingdom and the Government of the Republic of China (which technically continues to claim suzerainty over Tibet) on the attitude they would take if the Dalai Lama requests recognition": "It seems to us that we could regard recognition as a practical measure only if it is believed that the request would meet with a warm response on the part of other nations, including Asian nations."[23]

It would appear, however, that those within the State Department responsible for Chinese affairs were prepared to be surprisingly supportive of the Dalai Lama's interest in seeking international recognition of Tibet as an independent state. On May 5, 1959, Assistant Secretary Robertson's staff forwarded a memorandum for their colleagues' approval dictating that if these proposed soundings were favorable and the Dalai Lama made a public appeal for recognition, the United States should consult "with other free world nations on an urgent basis to persuade them to respond favorably." If such cooperation was forthcoming the United States would extend its recognition. "The attitude of Indian and other uncommitted Asian states should be considered, but would not be decisive." They added, "We should seek to induce the Government of the Republic of China to join us, [or] at least not to challenge the validity of the U.S. and other free world recognition." If the responses were unfavorable, the United States would have to reassess the situation. "[But] if as a result of seeking international recognition for Tibetan independence the Dalai Lama should have to leave India, we should try to assist him to gain asylum in some other free world country, and, if appropriate, offer him asylum in the United States." This action would be accompanied by parallel soundings about support for any appeal that the Dalai Lama might make to the United Nations. If the Dalai Lama made such an appeal, the United States "should determine the most promising form of UN action and appropriate sponsorship." "Depending on developments, we should favor an invitation to the Dalai Lama to appear before the Security Council or General Assembly." Providing any support to the Dalai Lama's request for recognition of his government was shelved, but it was decided that the United States "should act to have the matter raised at the U.N.," again preferably with Asian sponsorship.[24]

The State Department's counterparts across the river at the Defense Department were more robust in their recommendations for action. On June 4 National Security Advisor Gordon Gray told the National Security Council that "there existed very strong feeling in some part of the DOD that [the] current U.S. 'hands off' policy with respect to Tibet required re-examination." The Defense Department filed three position papers urging, "The government should take positive action to denounce the Communist action as additional evidence of the inevitable course of international communism; concurrently openly proffer assistance to the Tibetans in every way possible in order to capitalize on the present [political] climate in Asia; and not accept the view of some who feel that it is wise for the West to refrain from action while the other Asians work out their own immediate destiny." They emphasized, "Inaction at this time by the West can be interpreted by the Asians as an indication of weakness, indifference and a lack of dynamic leadership."[25] The president did not support his former Pentagon colleagues, but deferred to the State Department.

The State Department's circumspection was reinforced by the unsurprising cool reaction Assistant Secretary Robertson received when he proposed to the Chinese Nationalist ambassador George Yeh, "It would help a great deal if the GRC could publicly renounce suzerainty over Tibet and recognize its independent status." Yeh cited constitutional reasons why this would be "virtually impossible," but agreed to refer the question to his superiors in Taipei. When he returned with a negative response five days later Robertson probed a little further, asking if it would embarrass the GRC if the United States recognized the Dalai Lama's government as independent. Yeh resignedly answered, "[The] United States must exercise leadership in these matters, and if it felt it must make a statement of this kind, it should of course do so."[26] In Taipei Yeh's boss told Ambassador Drumright that should the Dalai Lama proclaim a separate independent government, the GRC would be unable to give it open support: "About the best it could do in that contingency would be to provide covert moral support."[27]

Chiang Kai-shek's agnostic response was comparatively more forthcoming than the murmurings from the British cousins. Whitehall was still readjusting to Great Britain's reduced status; the once vast empire overseas was drastically shrinking in size and significance. Two years before, Prime Minister Anthony Eden had resigned after presiding over his country's humiliating forced withdrawal from Egypt. London was no place for the Dalai Lama to look to for support for any challenge he might want to make to either his Chinese occupiers or his Indian hosts.

The British were taking a bye on a situation that they had bequeathed to the Indians. This was confirmed that fall when Gyalo Thondup stopped in London on his way to New York to present the Tibetan appeal to the United Nations. One of those shepherding him through the British government and establishment was the well-known author and Himalayan ethnographer Marco Pallis, who also served his government as an intelligence agent. For some years he had been in contact with Gyalo, advising him that only the British government could help Tibet and that he should seek aid from London exclusively. Accordingly he arranged a meeting for Gyalo with the chief of MI-6, the external intelligence service whose agents had been keeping an eye on affairs in Tibet for the past century. The chief, Sir Richard White, asked Pallis to remain outside while he talked privately with Gyalo. He told Gyalo that Pallis's advice was "nonsense." The United Kingdom had abandoned responsibility for affairs east of Suez, and Gyalo was doing the right thing by looking to the Americans for support, as only they had the means to help the Tibetans.[28] When Her Majesty's intelligence chief advised Gyalo that any special relationship that Great Britain might have had with Tibet was now only history, he spoke for his colleagues in the Foreign and Commonwealth Relations Offices. They were most anxious to let Nehru carry the ball, a reserve shared to a certain extent by the new American ambassador to India Ellsworth Bunker.

Unlike his predecessor, Loy Henderson, who had taken the ball and run with it in promoting active support for the Dalai Lama and the Tibetans eight years before, Bunker seemed content with an observer role. This passivity toward intervention on behalf of the Dalai Lama stemmed from Bunker's view of his mission, which was primarily to preserve a close relationship with Nehru, whose self-appointed role as leader of a non-Communist alternative to Mao's emerging role in Asia he respected and supported. It was not based on any reluctance to engage in Big Power politics, as evident in his service eight years later as both LBJ's and Nixon's ambassador in South Vietnam, where he was one of the principal hawks supporting American intervention in that country. Neither was he hesitant to utilize his country's Cold War tools of covert action. He was also concerned that his intrusion would damage the personal rapport and consequent effectiveness that the Dalai Lama had reestablished with the prime minister. Moreover both the situation and the American policy objective in 1959 were different from those that Henderson had been dealing with in 1951. Then the objective had been to get the Dalai Lama out of Tibet—and India—to another, preferably Buddhist nation in Asia, from where he could launch an international appeal as a victim of Communist aggression. In 1959 it was to help him remain in India, where he would be on the conscience of both his host and the world in this latest chapter of the Cold War.[29]

By this time discussions in Washington had moved on to planning tactics for the international hearing the Tibetans were finally to have at the United Nations—this time with American support, albeit behind the scenes.

CHAPTER THIRTEEN

The United States Remains Involved

At his meeting with the international press on June 20, 1959, following his flight from Lhasa, the twenty-four-year-old Tibetan ruler belied his presumed inexperience in international politics by his adroit answer when asked if he considered himself and the cabinet ministers with him as a government-in-exile: "Wherever I am accompanied by my Government, the Tibetan people will recognize such as the Government of Tibet."[1] He thereby gave current meaning and political and moral vitality to the title Kundun that goes with his office. It means "the Presence," a quality and a status he demonstrated then and has maintained through today. The Indian Ministry of External Affairs announced the next day that it would not recognize the Dalai Lama as heading a "separate" government of Tibet operating in India. He and his people, however, without further joining the issue, have been able to find a formula to function as such for the past half-century. As a result India has received a positive response from the world community and understands the negative image it would create by appearing inhospitable to a beleaguered people and their widely respected leader. Moreover the Dalai Lama and his followers early on appreciated that their departure from Shangri-La and entrance into the world beyond would call for an extraordinary combination of creativity and patience as they established a niche of their own.

The State Department told Eisenhower that if the exiled leader requested formal recognition and a substantial number of nations granted it, this "would be a most helpful step from the free world point of view." Conversely, should the request not be well received, it "would be a severe setback."[2] When Washington took soundings beginning with the United Kingdom and the Republic of China, they discovered that neither of these "close friends" had any interest in granting such recognition. The Dalai Lama apparently accepted the same message from his hosts, and he and his rump government settled for the shadow but substantial status that they have successfully exploited ever since.

The terminally ill secretary of state John Foster Dulles, in forwarding a letter to Eisenhower from the Tibetan leader two months later, noted, "The Dalai Lama has already made it clear that he is no longer interested in autonomy for Tibet under the Chinese Communists (having twice tried this course with disastrous results) but is determined to work for Tibet's independence. This puts him in fundamental conflict with Nehru's policy on Tibet. If we do not now respond positively to the Dalai Lama's appeal for support, Nehru's policy may well prevail, which would mean the destruction of the Dalai Lama." He offered this solution:

> Although we are not now in a position to recognize the Dalai Lama as the head of an independent Tibetan state, we believe that we should convincingly assure him that he is regarded by the United States Government as the rightful leader of the Tibetan people in their struggle against oppression, and that to this end we are prepared to support him financially if he is forced to leave India and to help him find asylum elsewhere.... [Moreover] the Tibetans should be given a chance to present their grievances to the United Nations just as the Hungarian case was heard and we believe that the personal appearance of the Dalai Lama at the General Assembly would be beneficial.[3]

The State Department accordingly proposed that Eisenhower reply to the Dalai Lama with the following assurances:

> He is regarded by this Government as the rightful leader of the Tibetan people in their struggle . . . ; the United States continues unequivocally to oppose the admission of Communist China to the United Nations . . . ; his Government should have the full opportunity to present his case to world opinion and he should carefully consider the possibility of going to

the United Nations . . . after thorough preparation and further consultation with us; we agree to the desirability of his making a tour to selected national capitals from which he has reason to expect support; and if he is forced to leave India as a result of following our advice, we will assume the obligation to support him and an appropriate entourage, and will undertake to help him in finding asylum elsewhere.[4]

The president was not prepared to be as forthcoming as his diplomatic advisors, led by their still feisty chief. He requested that his response include a final paragraph advising that the Dalai Lama avoid or minimize any open break with Nehru; that it not suggest he go to the UN, "but simply note that he might conclude that the UN [was] his best course of action"; and "with regard to the item on assuming an obligation to support the Dalai Lama, this should be qualified or at least limited."[5] When this more restrained message was delivered orally, the Tibetans, possibly disappointed in its more qualified commitments and also mindful of the difficulty their colleagues had experienced eight years earlier in getting written confirmations of such commitments, were reportedly "unhappy." An unyielding Eisenhower nevertheless sent a brief signed letter to the Dalai Lama on July 9 confirming that the reflections that had "been successfully conveyed" to him were his "considered counsel on the problems,"[6] that is, they did not welcome further deliberation.

The Search for Sponsors

The Dalai Lama's unsuccessful bid for recognition of his government presaged the backstage reservations and maneuvering involved in obtaining a hearing for his case at the United Nations. Early on, the doughty Irish had expressed their willingness to champion the Tibetan cause there. The El Salvadoran foreign secretary reminded Washington that if the United States and Great Britain had supported his country's lonely appeal to the UN in 1950 on behalf of the Dalai Lama, the current situation in Tibet might have been avoided. But Washington was cagey about taking any action that might inhibit the "rising tide of indignation against the Chinese action in Tibet" that it saw in Asia or give credence to charges that it was exploiting the Tibet situation for Cold War purposes.[7]

When the State Department did begin its more active search for fellow supporters of the Tibetan case it met with a cool response from its usual Western allies. The British cousins were particularly disappointing. Although Prime Minister Harold Macmillan was by then seeking to reestablish the special relationship with Washington that had become a casualty of the Suez crisis two years earlier, the ties to the shattered remnants of the old empire still constrained his foreign policy. After considerable wriggling Foreign Minister Selwyn Lloyd told Secretary of State Christian Herter, "It would obviously be difficult for us not to support debate on Tibet in the General Assembly agenda, but if we did so we should be acting contrary to the line we had always taken on Article 2 of the UN Charter which proscribes intervention within the domestic jurisdiction of any state." He warned that it could open discussion even on segregation in the United States. He added a snide jab, saying that he "found it strange that an Irish Catholic country rather than the Tibetans' fellow Buddhist nations was taking the lead in sponsoring the resolution." He pointed out that inscription would be done against the preference of the Indians, and added, "Generally speaking . . . it is desirable not to interfere with Indian relationships with China. . . . If the white people interfere it will only bring India and China closer together."[8]

The British Foreign Office eventually agreed to vote for inscription of an item in general terms as long as it provided no benefit of the doubt about the legal status of Tibet, about which the United Kingdom wanted to remain uncommitted. The cousins, however, did pass on their reluctance to the Soviet UN ambassador. When he approached his British counterpart on this subject, Sir Pierson Dixon "made a quick decision to be completely frank" and told Vasiliy Kuznetsov that the United Kingdom did not favor the Tibetan item and had been seeking to discourage it, but that British public opinion was such that if the item were proposed they would have to support it.[9]

Meanwhile the United States had met with the Dalai Lama in India and assured him of its strong support for his appeal to the United Nations. The embassy officer did convey Washington's advice that the Tibetans base their appeal on seeking a condemnation of the Chinese for violating their human rights rather than charging them with aggression, which would raise the unsettled issue of the legal status of Tibet. He advised the Dalai Lama that Washington believed that he should consider taking his appeal to the UN in person, noting Nehru's reported assertion to the Dalai Lama that he was free to take any action he saw fit with respect to the UN. It would be difficult to see how the Indian government could refuse him readmission to India following such a trip.

When this statement of the Department's action was presented to the Dalai Lama he was adamant that the charge of Chinese aggression must be the basis of his appeal, as it had been in 1950. Any lesser charge would be a retreat. When his brother Gyalo Thondup arrived in New York in early October to present his brother's case to the UN he obediently reiterated this argument.

Their Irish and Malayan sponsors were finding it tough going to obtain any kind of hearing. The Tibetans' fellow Buddhist nations had not roused themselves to take up the cudgels on their behalf. The major Western nations, with the exception of the United States, which was remaining in the background for tactical reasons, were equally unenthusiastic. No one wanted to take on the issue of supporting the Tibetans' contested claim for independent status, which a resolution charging Chinese aggression would necessarily raise.

In New York the American delegation showed little enthusiasm for taking on the challenge of supporting the case for the Tibetans on any grounds. In Washington, however, Assistant Secretary J. Graham Parsons expressed "surprise that, despite the decisions reached at the highest level in this Government and the assurances which this Government has given to the Dalai Lama, USUN [the American delegation to the UN] should suggest that the Department seriously consider dropping the idea of inscription in the light of comments by the U.K. delegation."[10] Parsons's previous post had been as ambassador to Laos. His tour in that former colonial kingdom endangered by internal rivalries and increasing Communist subversive activity had prepared him to be sympathetic to persons facing similar threats to their survival. His boss, Undersecretary for Political Affairs Robert Murphy, had been the Department's, and more significantly Eisenhower's, top troubleshooter for the past decade. When Murphy took on the Tibetan cause it was noted throughout the national security establishment. Similarly when Murphy on his own hired Ernest Gross, a veteran of the aborted UN resolution in 1950, who later was UN Secretary General Dag Hammarskjold's personal counsel, this sent a message that Washington was serious about finding effective support for the Tibetans in New York.

Gyalo and Gross developed mutual respect for each other's abilities as negotiators and political operators. Gyalo, in accordance with his instructions from his brother and his Tibetan counselors, duly argued for an appeal which would condemn the Chinese aggression in Tibet. Anything less would represent a retreat from the aborted resolution from which the UN had walked away in 1950. Gross, however, was receiving briefings from the Irish and Malayan sponsors on the negative response they were receiving to a resolution condemning aggression, which would necessarily mean consideration of the issue of the legal status of Tibet. This was an issue on which there was no consensus, and many delegations wished to avoid it. As an old pro, Gross had taken his own soundings and recognized that if the Tibetans stuck by their demand for such a resolution they would lose their present appeal and prejudice future consideration of their case. As a lawyer, he also appreciated that Gyalo had to convince his principals that he had presented their case and was coming home with the best deal he could get and one which kept their case alive.

Gross therefore heard Gyalo out and then came up with a formula that would obtain a hearing and allow him to assure his brother and his advisors that their case had not been foreclosed. The general theme condemning the Tibetans' loss of their human rights should be "Our plea concerns not land, but people." After a rehashing of the impracticality of holding out for a debate involving Tibet's international status, Gyalo yielded. His able, well-educated interpreter Rinchen Sadutsang was a member of an Old Guard family. He could affirm to the expected critics in Lhasa that Gyalo had energetically presented the case and had settled for the best bargain he could get.

When Gross brought Gyalo to meet with USUN Ambassador Henry Cabot Lodge in New York two days later to plan strategy for presenting the Tibetan appeal, Lodge persuaded Gyalo that it would be unwise to seek an invitation for his brother to present his appeal in person. Gyalo seemed prepared to accept Lodge's argument that it was wise to "maintain the dignity of the Dalai Lama and keep him above the battle." He still argued against settling for a resolution condemning the Chinese for violating the human rights of the Tibetans rather than one charging the Chinese with aggression. He made the argument his principals had sent him to deliver, but Lodge concluded, "[He] recognizes the importance of not seeking action on a basis which would fail and could then be exploited by ChiComs and others against the Tibetans." Gyalo had apparently impressed the patrician ambassador, who reported that he was "struck by his deep sincerity and by his strong desire to do whatever circumstances here seem to require in the best interest of the Tibetan people."[11] This would not be the first time that Gyalo the realist, son of an Amdo horse trader and tutored by the arch survivor Chiang Kai-shek, would bargain and settle for the best that he could get for his people, who did not always appreciate his pragmatism.

The Tibetans had their hearing two weeks later, and all the participants performed as expected. The Irish and Malayan sponsors led off, paying deference to Indian sensitivities by expressing their sympathy for the victims of unusually devastating monsoon floods which had struck India that month. The Malayan ambassador reminded his fellow Asians that the Chinese had subscribed to the respect for human rights and freedom promised by the Bandung Declaration four years earlier, and took due note of the increased prospects for an improved international atmosphere produced by the recent meeting between Khrushchev and Eisenhower. His Irish cosponsor endorsed these arguments, adding a peculiarly Irish twist and a poke at both the British and Russians as wet blankets. He declared that his country's interest in Tibet reflected its heritage from the Irish revolutionary Michael Davitt, who was "rightly described in the Soviet Encyclopedia as a staunch fighter against colonial oppression," as demonstrated in his efforts to arouse public opinion against the British expedition to Lhasa in 1904. Soviet Ambassador Kuznetsov, after paying due deference to "the promising prospects of ending the cold war" promised by the joint communiqué issued by Chairman Khrushchev and President Eisenhower, proceeded to blast the "gross and intolerable intervention in the affairs of the People's Republic of China" which the current debate represented.[12]

Kuznetsov's expected diatribe was followed by one of the few surprising speeches of the debate, made by the Cuban foreign minister. At that time the Castro government had yet to ally itself with the USSR.[13] The foreign minister argued, "It will not hurt the great Chinese people to open negotiations with the Dalai Lama for a peace settlement and to recognize the right of the small Tibetan people to control their own destiny, but it will greatly help the world, including China."

This sympathetic plea for consideration of the Tibetans' appeal was in bleak contrast to the lack of support from their fellow Asian Buddhists. The only one that spoke, the Nepalese ambassador, was no help. He cited the "special kind of relationship that exists between China and Tibet," the "no longer desirable social status quo" in Tibet, and the consequent absence of any value in bringing the question of Tibet before the United Nations.

The former European colonial powers had similar inhibitions. After expressions of sympathy for the Tibetans, both the French and Belgian delegates abstained, citing Tibet's uncertain legal status as making it ineligible for action under Article 2 of the UN Charter.[14] Only the Dutch, now formally out of Indonesia, felt free to support the resolution.

America's position was firmly staked out by Ambassador Lodge, who apparently had overcome any misgivings about championing the case. He challenged those who would "frighten [members] out of discussing the matter by the use of strong words," declaring, "We have been asked to believe it is all right for Chinese Communists to kill Tibetans, but that it is a provocation for us to talk about it." He dismissed the arguments concerning the Assembly's competence under the Charter: "It has become established, for example, that inscription and then discussion of an agenda item do not constitute intervention in matters which lie essentially within domestic jurisdiction. Charges of very serious violations of human rights and fundamental freedoms in Tibet have been presented to this Assembly. The General Assembly is surely competent to express itself concerning such action and to appeal for the observance of liberty." After a lengthy review of history of Chinese actions which violated individual rights and threatened the entire culture of Tibet, the usually reserved Bostonian concluded with an eloquent peroration: "Among the purposes written in the Charter is that of 'promoting and encouraging respect for human rights and for fundamental freedoms for all without distinction as to race, sex, language, or religion.' We have an opportunity now to prove that those words mean what they say, and that neither thousands of miles of distance nor ingenious arguments nor violent words nor faintness of heart can deter us from our duty to a brave people in their time of agony. If they are not afraid to fight and die, let us at least not be afraid to speak the truth."

Among those apparently unmoved by Lodge's words was the British ambassador Sir Pierson Dixon, who waited until the last day of the debate to deliver his poisoned arrow of pious abstention. Britain would support the Tibetans' right to discussion of their plight, but not action to ameliorate it.

The Indian representative, the volatile Krishna Menon, was surprisingly moderate in his remarks. (Indian Foreign Secretary S. Dutt had promised the embassy in New Delhi that the Indian delegations would not indulge in strong words, then added, "[But you] never know what Krishna Menon will do, . . . [despite being] under very strict instructions in this case.")[15] Menon made it very clear that India was taking no position on the legal status of Tibet and that there was "no question of a Tibetan Government under the Dalai Lama functioning in India." However, India was interposing no objection to the Tibetans obtaining a full hearing for their charges of Chinese violations of their human rights. He quoted his prime minister on the Chinese reforms in Tibet: "Such a change can only take place effectively and with the least harm to the fabric, to those people concerned, if it is done by themselves. The moment a good thing is done by bad means that good thing becomes a bad thing." Menon then concluded that India would not support the resolution being offered because it did not seem to offer any constructive approach to reconciliation between the Tibetans and the Chinese, which was the only hope for a satisfactory solution to their differences.

The Byelorussian delegate spoke on the theme set by the Soviet delegate and echoed by his Ukrainian, Polish, and Hungarian counterparts. He cited the reforms being carried out by the Chinese in Tibet and decried any action that might impede the improvement of international tensions promised by Khrushchev's recent talks with Eisenhower. Then, on October 21, 1959, forty-five members of the Assembly voted for the final resolution:

> [The] fundamental human rights and freedoms of the people of Tibet, to which they like all others, are entitled include the right to civil and religious liberty for all without distinction. . . . [These rights] have been forcibly denied them. . . . [This Assembly,] deploring the effects of these events in increasing international tension and in embittering the relations between peoples at a time when earnest and positive efforts are being made by responsible leaders to reduce tension and improve international relations: 1. Affirms its belief that respect for the principles of the Charter of the United Nations and the Universal Declaration of Human Rights is essential for the evolution of a peaceful world order based on the rule of law; 2. Calls for respect for the fundamental human rights of the Tibetan people and for their distinctive cultural and religious life.

In addition to their Malayan sponsor, the Tibetans' Asian neighbors voting for the resolution included China (Taiwan), Japan, Laos, Pakistan, the Philippines, and Thailand and the two Commonwealth countries Australia and New Zealand. Their fellow Buddhists in Burma, Cambodia, and Ceylon abstained. Ceylon's action was ironic in view of the fact that it was the preferred place of asylum according to the plan offered the Dalai Lama by the United States government eight years before. As promised, the United Kingdom, India, France, and Belgium also abstained.

The initially unenthusiastic Ambassador Lodge had not only delivered, but he seemed to have found satisfaction in doing so. He reported to Secretary Herter, "We obtained maximum results on the Tibet Item . . . [which] confirms the wisdom of the strategy we adopted of permitting the Irish and the Malayans to take the lead. . . . [Thus] we were able to deny the USSR the handle it was always seeking in order to tag the U.S. with the responsibility of reviving the cold war and to convince others that the U.S. was not truly interested in peace. . . . [While it is] regrettable that our closest Allies, the U.K. and France, abstained, Dixon's unhelpful speech being separated from the colonial powers on issues of this sort also has compensations." Lodge noted that they had been able to block Dixon's maneuver, which was designed to adjourn debate without any action, by "immediately making known (in private) [America's] intention to oppose adjournment in the strongest possible way." He concluded, "We appeared clearly as a non-colonial power, which is always an attractive way to appear in the General Assembly and which we all too often are unable to do. I think you should also know that there was widespread distaste for the whole operation [presumably Dixon's foiled ploy]."[16]

Although the resolution did not provide the recognition of their country as an independent state that the Tibetans wanted, their cause had been noted. When the Tibetans first sought international recognition a decade earlier they had been regarded as somewhat exotic people from the mountains, best known for the production of yak hair used for Santa Claus beards. The UN was able then to sidetrack their appeal for help in resisting the Chinese moves to absorb their country. Now they had a claim to the continuing attention of the international community. Their spokesman, Gyalo Thondup, had won its respect, and he had developed a close working relationship with one of the world's most highly regarded international lawyers, a relationship that was to continue for the next forty years. He had also won the respect of the State Department, which gave him "much of the credit for success in the General Assembly due to the excellent preparatory work of his persuasive behind the scenes presentation of the Tibetan case [which] created a very favorable impression among many of the delegates."[17] He had established the Tibetan claim to an ongoing relationship with the United States government, and in a manner that would ensure the sustained hospitality and toleration of his brother's continuing claim on the international community from his country of asylum. The United States had fulfilled at least partially one of the commitments it had made to the Dalai Lama and his people when it sought to establish a relationship eight years earlier.

The Tibetans, however, had learned a valuable lesson regarding the limited support they could expect from supposedly like-minded nations. The Dalai Lama's initiative to develop his people's capacity for self-government dates from those days.

The Legal Status of Tibet and the Dalai Lama

Washington was only beginning to absorb the depth of the growing differences between Khrushchev and Mao that year and the effects this development would have on the dynamics of the international scene. Policy concerning Tibet then did not embrace attempts to play either the Russian or the Chinese card. Washington's decision to play a supporting rather than a sponsoring role in presenting the Tibetan case to the UN as a non–Cold War item and in a manner that would not offend the Dalai Lama's Indian hosts seemed tactically prudent. Although the UN resolution did not win the international recognition of Tibet as an independent country, Tibet now had an established role on the international scene.

A supportive Assistant Secretary Parsons noted that in connection with the Tibetans' UN appeal, the State Department had done a study concerning the question of America's recognition of Tibet's independence. It concluded that very few countries would follow America's lead:

> [Consequently] our recognition now would make the Dalai Lama the leader of a government-in-exile obviously dependent on the United States for political support. This would almost certainly damage the prestige and influence he now enjoys as one of Asia's revered leaders and would hamper his activities on behalf of the Tibetan people. Nevertheless, there remains the need for the United States to appear responsive to the Dalai Lama's appeal and take a stand conforming to our historic position as a supporter of the principle of self-determination of peoples. Unless the Tibetans are given some definite indication of our sympathy for their cause, there is the danger that the morale of the resistance movement will flag . . . and to ignore the Dalai Lama's appeal altogether might weaken his determination to keep pressing the Tibetan cause before the world and might damage the reputation of the United States as an upholder of international morality.[18]

Accordingly when Gyalo Thondup spoke with Robert Murphy in Washington, the undersecretary "indicated that great importance [was] attached to keeping the Tibetan situation before world public opinion."[19] Murphy suggested the Tibetan leader travel to other world capitals, especially neighboring Asian countries (despite the mixed support he had received from them at the UN). Murphy then told Thondup that the United States "traditionally stood for self-determination of peoples and believed this principle should apply to the Tibetans." Although Thondup "expressed appreciation for this stand," he may not have immediately realized the full implications of what he had just heard. (In informing the Chinese Nationalist ambassador of this decision the following week, Parsons said, "The United States had made a decision to go somewhat beyond its previous position with regard to Tibet, namely that it is an autonomous country under the suzerainty of China.")[20] In case Thondup missed the point, Murphy "reiterated the desire of the U.S. to support the principle [of] self-determination for the people of Tibet, in keeping with [America's] traditional belief that all peoples should have a determining voice in their future." Thondup, undoubtedly tutored by Gross on the significance of U.S. recognition of the applicability to Tibet of the term "self-determination," repeated it a few days later in a memorandum of their meeting: "The U.S. Government would take such measures as may be found necessary to enable the Tibetans to exercise that right." He then sent Murphy a copy of the memorandum. Murphy, undoubtedly amused by the old pro's pitch, sent word that "he regretted that he could not confirm all aspects of Mr Thondup's note." But he stated, "While it has been the historical position of the United States to consider Tibet an autonomous country under the suzerainty of China, the American people have also traditionally stood for the principle of self determination. The U.S. Government intends when a 'suitable opportunity presents itself' to make a public statement of such support." Thondup's embellishment committing the United States to take the necessary steps to support the Tibetans in exercising this right was not included in the statement, but the ball was now in play.[21]

Washington Delivers—In Part

The Tibetans had not pressed for an appearance by the Dalai Lama at the UN, so the issue of his political status was temporarily shelved. It was revived, however, when Eisenhower announced his itinerary for the tour to India that he had long wanted to make. The Dalai Lama immediately wrote Ambassador Bunker, stating that he could be in Delhi during the president's visit and would like to meet with him. When Bunker made a strong pitch for such a meeting Indian Foreign Secretary Dutt indicated with "unusual firmness that Nehru had already indicated that he did not want the issue raised with him."[22] Dutt argued that such a meeting would inject controversy and cloud the whole visit. Bunker, despite the strong arguments made by Washington for such an event, recommended that Eisenhower duck the issue. No meeting was arranged. One of Ike's closest Cold Warriors, C. D. Jackson, made a last-minute effort to persuade the White House to change its mind, offering full coverage of such a dramatic meeting in *Time* and *Life*. He was unsuccessful.[23]

The president was thus able to fulfill his boyhood ambition to see the Taj Mahal, but the Tibetans' hope of a meeting between their leader and an American president was not to be fulfilled for another three decades. The Dalai Lama remained in his refuge in northern India, but his representatives delivered a letter to the American embassy in New Delhi from the resistance leader Gompo Tashi, stating the intentions of the Tibetans to continue fighting for their freedom and asking for continued guidance and support. They also included a Khampa sword—"by which we fought our enemy who is the enemy of the world as well"—a charm box, and Tibetan clothing. In forwarding these reminders of America's other obligations, the embassy said that they "had accepted the letter and gifts and would acknowledge them orally and believed no further action was required."[24]

Although he was not to be accorded the public recognition that a meeting with the president would have brought, the Dalai Lama did have a signed letter from the American ambassador informing him formally of the United States government's position on Tibetan self-determination. Bunker was instructed to deliver the letter in advance of the president's arrival, but to make no mention of its existence until Washington announced it publicly, which it planned to do "as soon as it appear[ed] advisable following the President's trip to India."[25]

The formal announcement of this significant statement of United States policy came two months later. On February 29, 1960, it was released to the press in the form of an exchange of correspondence between the Dalai Lama and Secretary of State Herter. The Dalai Lama expressed his gratitude for the active support of the United States during the General Assembly's debate the previous autumn, and Herter thanked the Tibetan ruler for his letter and reaffirmed Murphy's pledge three months earlier: "As you know, while it has been the historical position of the United States to consider Tibet as an autonomous country under the suzerainty of China, the American people have also traditionally stood for the principle of self-determination. It is the belief of the United States Government that this principle should apply to the people of Tibet and that they should have the determining voice in their own political destiny." This has been the rubric under which both the White House and the State Department, intermittently, and Congress with more constant vigor, have supported the Tibetan leader and his cause ever since, thereby partially fulfilling one of the major commitments promised by Ambassador Henderson in his letter locked away eight years earlier in the American consulate safe in Calcutta.

By this time the Tibetans had come to realize both the promise contained in the term *self*-determination and their obligation to provide the substance involved. Today it is the Tibetans who are dramatically demonstrating what they have done—and are doing—to fulfill this obligation. And they are looking to the United States to maintain the support it pledged over a half century ago.

CHAPTER FOURTEEN

New Commitments, New Problems, New Solutions

The 1960s were the high-water mark of the tripartite relationship among the governments of India, the United States, and the Dalai Lama. A unique combination of events, personalities, and politics united these three in a common cause against China as Mao undertook programs with revolutionary potential for his own country and abroad. In this process the Tibetans consolidated their position as assets rather than wards in India and established the basis for a continuing claim by the Dalai Lama and his cause within the international community. It was not a neat process. The Americans, the Indians, and the Tibetans joined in a common effort, but each had different objectives. For a decade they worked together, not in perfect accord, but the end results consolidated the unique claim that the Tibetans and their leader had acquired and have maintained since then on the international conscience, thereby remaining active players rather than becoming historical footnotes.

The component elements of this alliance were forming at the time that the Dalai Lama sought asylum in India in 1959. Since 1957 Indian officials had been looking the other way on the exfiltration of Tibetans from India to be trained by the CIA and on the overflights by which they had been returned to their missions inside Tibet. They maintained this official blindness in the summer of 1960, when the CIA began to support a new resistance effort in western Tibet. This one employed the veterans from central and eastern Tibet led by Gompo Tashi, who had been forced to flee to India after the Chinese troops swept their operating area southeast of Lhasa following the Dalai Lama's flight. As a trader and pilgrim Gompo had made treks to western Tibet, where he had become acquainted with the Mustang area of Nepal, which juts into Tibet south of the main highway between Lhasa and Xinjiang. He had come to know the ruler of this remote kingdom, the Maharajah of Mustang, whose people shared a common religion and language with the Tibetans. Gompo argued that by establishing a base in this ideally located safe haven, the Tibetans could conduct raids across the border to harass the Chinese military traffic moving along their principal route of supply to their troops in Xinjiang. This would force them to divert troops from eastern Tibet and thereby reduce the pressure on the Tibetan insurgents still operating there. It was an appealing prospect to employ Mao's own classic formula of conducting guerrilla operations from a secure base. The area was remote enough that the control exercised by the Nepalese government from Kathmandu was negligible. Transplanting a force of foreign insurgents en bloc to establish a permanent base in a country with which it maintained friendly relations, however, was unpalatable to even the most gung-ho members of the New Frontier. The CIA task force chief therefore initially agreed to consider supporting a pilot group of four hundred, with the understanding that they would temporarily set up camp in the Mustang areas; from there they would move into Tibet to establish permanent operating bases from which to conduct operations against the Chinese.[1]

The final plan that evolved after further meetings with Gyalo Thondup and Lhamo Tsering called for a force of 2,100 veterans predominantly from the Kham and Amdo areas of eastern Tibet who had formed the Chushi Gangdruk, with a contingent from the Mimang movement of central Tibet.[2] They were to be quietly recruited in the border towns of India, Sikkim, and Bhutan, where many of them were working on road construction projects. They would move in groups of three hundred to Mustang; from there they would proceed into Tibet, where arms and equipment would be dropped to them and they could establish separate operating bases from which to attack their targets moving along the Lhasa-Xinjiang highway. It was to be a controlled, staggered operation, with each group moving to Mustang only after the preceding group was established inside Tibet so there would never be more than three hundred fighters in temporary residence at one time in Mustang.

As a plan it seemed sound and appealing. In practice it turned into a constant problem. It was predicated on the men being supplied and equipped by air only after they had established relatively secure drop sites inside Tibet.

There had been no problems on the earlier drops that were made to the sites in the east. Now that the c-130 aircraft were available, flights to these sites close to the border should have been a relatively routine procedure. Flight plans designed to make the air time over India a matter of minutes minimized the possibility of embarrassment to the equivocal Indians. And previous flights had penetrated far deeper into China without encountering hostile challenge.

Then, on May Day 1960, a u-2 flight was shot down over Russia. Washington's botched public reaction to the incident was followed by Khrushchev's storming out of the Paris Summit, which was to have been a prelude to an unprecedented visit by Eisenhower to Moscow and a continuation of the "Spirit of Camp David" born the previous autumn. A disappointed Ike ordered a stand-down on intelligence operations of a provocative nature. This included covert flights over sensitive areas, and developments in Mustang that summer placed operations there in this category.

Despite the potential problem of resupply airdrops it was decided that an initial phase of the operation would proceed. But instead of the planned covert relocation of a pilot group of four hundred men, 2,100 resistance veterans joined what became a well-publicized stampede by bus and train and on foot from their jobs on road gangs in the hill stations of India, Sikkim, and Bhutan to rejoin the battle. The alert Indian press covered "the mysterious exodus from Sikkim; Khampas leaving in hundreds."[3]

In Washington the cia demanded that Gyalo Thondup halt this unwanted spectacle, but he was unable to stop the stampede to Mustang. There the men were received by an autocratic Khampa leader, Gyen Yeshe, who had no intention of yielding his position as chief of this new force to a compatriot who was favored by the cia, Gyalo, and Dharamsala. This was one of our early exposures to both the strength and the internal frictions within the tribal society of Tibet. The stubborn, angry, and proud Gyen Yeshe was there at the end of a ragged chain of command, stuck with the responsibility of providing food and quarters to a disgruntled crew stranded in an area where such commodities were scarce and difficult to import. It was a grim winter that year in Mustang.

At a meeting at the White House on Election Day 1960 Eisenhower promised that if Nixon was elected, cia operations in Tibet would continue. This pledge implicitly included lifting the ban on overflights to supply them. However, Eisenhower could not speak for Kennedy.

The Eisenhower administration provided its final political endorsement of the Dalai Lama's cause in a meeting Secretary Herter held with Gyalo

Thondup on October 27, 1960, a week before the presidential election. Herter suggested that an effective way for the Tibetans to keep their issue alive would be for the Dalai Lama to travel to various countries as a great religious leader rather than as head of state.[4] Although this was only half the loaf that the Tibetans wanted, the meeting itself was the first time that a secretary of state had met with a Tibetan official since George Marshall overrode the objections of Chiang Kai-shek to meet with Tsipon Shakabpa on his trade mission to the United States twelve years earlier. It was also the last time for some years that Gyalo or his brother was to be received by an American official of this rank.

Gyalo could report back to his brother and his counselors in their mountain refuge with some sense of accomplishment about the results to date of his bargaining with the Americans. So far Washington was delivering on its promises. Material support was being provided to the Dalai Lama and his entourage, an obligation made less demanding because of the generous hospitality of his Indian hosts. The arms and training support to the Tibetan resistance begun two years earlier was continuing, despite the disappointing results of these efforts. Washington had ensured that the Tibetans had the opportunity to obtain at least a hearing for their cause at the United Nations. And it had moved another step toward keeping Secretary Loy Henderson's promise: "An essential part of our cooperation would be a public announcement by the United States that it supports Your Holiness as head of an autonomous Tibet . . . and . . . would also support your return to Tibet at the earliest practicable moment as head of an autonomous and non-Communist country."[5]

Washington had denied the Dalai Lama's request for formal recognition of his government-in-exile for two major tactical reasons. The principal concern was that such an action might force Nehru to ask His Holiness to vacate his strategically desirable base in India. The second reason was that the issue of Tibet had become entangled in the American domestic squabble promoted by the China lobby. Although some of the Tibetan leader's more worldly advisors recognized the hard facts of United States and international politics, others felt strongly that he should not travel to the United States unless he was assured that he would be received as a head of state. Consequently when Ernest Gross, acting at the behest of the National Security Council Special Group, arranged for him to be invited to visit the United States in the spring of 1960 as guest of the National Council of Christians and Jews, with the prospect of a half-hour meeting alone with Secretary Herter, his tradition-bound secular and monastic officials prevailed and he declined the invitation.

It was to be seven more years before the Tibetan pontiff made his first visit outside of India, and that was to Japan and Thailand, where he and his resigned officials settled for him to be received as a religious leader, but not as head of his well-established government-in-exile in northern India. This is the formula that has established him as a world figure while retaining a base on the other side of the mountains from his homeland, an arrangement that he and his hosts have come to regard as serving their mutual purposes for half a century.

CHAPTER FIFTEEN

A New Ballgame

The members of the new team that arrived in Washington in 1961 to take over foreign operations were as activist as their predecessors. Secretary of State Rusk had endorsed Ambassador Henderson's commitments of support to the cause of the Dalai Lama ten years earlier, when he was in charge of the Department's Far Eastern affairs. Rusk's deputy, Chester Bowles, promoted what Theodore Sorenson called "crusading commitments of the heart."[1] Averell Harriman, who had been troubleshooting for presidents since FDR, took Rusk's less prestigious former Far Eastern affairs post because it was where the action was. Roger Hilsman, who had led an oss guerrilla unit behind the lines in Burma, was director of the State Department's Office of Intelligence and Research. JFK had enlisted one of the Pentagon's more activist and intellectual senior officers, General Maxwell Taylor, to serve as his senior military advisor. Although their enthusiasm for covert intervention had been somewhat dampened by the ill-fated Bay of Pigs debacle in April, the president's Washington foreign policy team was still ready for action.

Two members of the team did not accept unconventional warfare as a foreign policy: Kennedy's Harvard tutor John Kenneth Galbraith, now his ambassador to India, and George Ball, who was Bowles's undersecretary of state. Galbraith and Ball had also been skeptics of the efficacy of the Allied bombing of Germany during the Second World War and Galbraith now sought to enlist Ball to oppose further support of the Tibetan resistance force in Nepal that had been on semihold for over a year. A few weeks before the Bay of Pigs operation the new administration had authorized an airdrop of supplies sufficient to arm seven companies of the festering insurgents at Mustang. On March 8, 1961, prior to Galbraith's appointment as ambassador, the drop was made to a zone inside Tibet across from the Mustang stronghold in Nepal.

The original plan called for these arms to be dropped to men who had established a chain of separate operating bases inside Tibet which would wean them away from their politically sensitive safe haven in Nepal. That did not happen. The men found no sites in this relatively desolate area of their homeland that they felt were sufficiently secure to permit them to relocate. The arms consequently were distributed to the waiting forces who had begun by late summer to make forays into Tibet, where they attacked Chinese army convoys moving along the Lhasa-Xinjiang highway and then retreated back to Mustang.

In October 1961 one of these raids was led by a man who had been trained by the CIA at Camp Hale in Colorado. They ambushed and killed all of the members of a Chinese army convoy moving along the target highway. The convoy commander carried a pouch that contained an intelligence gold mine. Among the 1,600 classified documents were twenty-nine issues of the Top Secret journals of the Political Department of the Chinese People's Liberation Army. These privileged documents had been circulated to regimental commanders and their superiors to use in counseling their troops on the problems of governance growing out of the economic failures and food shortages originating in Mao's Great Leap Forward campaign. They provided authoritative intelligence describing widespread hunger throughout China and the critically low morale resulting in defections by soldiers shaken by the plight of their relatives. On the basis of these documents the Pentagon dropped the People's Militia from its order of battle as part of China's military forces. The journals documented not only that this multimillion-man force was an empty asset but also that in some cases its members had participated in the uprisings against the government they had been formed to protect. The documents also contained privileged insights into Peking's external policies, including a sober appreciation of United States military strength, no expectation of Soviet aid, and no prospect that China would soon acquire its own nuclear weapons.[2]

Fortunately the Camp Hale alumnus appreciated what he and his men had captured, and the documents were forwarded to Darjeeling and hand-carried to CIA headquarters. There a proud Allen Dulles was able to lug the blood-stained pouch to one of his last appearances before the Special Group and spread its contents before his duly appreciative colleagues. Although no event could eradicate the ghost of that spring's disaster at the Bay of Pigs, this intelligence coup did help the veteran director to depart on a note of accomplishment from the scene that he had long dominated. It was probably one of the key factors in winning support for making a second airdrop to the men operating from Mustang, again with the understanding that they would find permanent sites inside Tibet from which to operate. This drop, made on December 10, 1961, provided arms to equip six more companies. It was made only after a final bitter exchange of correspondence between Ambassador Galbraith and the White House.

In biting prose Galbraith addressed a series of protests to his former bombing survey colleague George Ball, his former Harvard colleague and current national security advisor McGeorge Bundy, and his former pupil JFK, asking that they cancel plans to make the drop and cease providing support to the Mustang forces. Reminding his colleagues of the still sore wounds of the Bay of Pigs debacle and deprecating the value of the recent extraordinary intelligence haul, he argued, "The reasons for the operation," which in his view "were never sufficient," "have diminished in value and now depend in part, as in the case of Cuba, on the fact that men have been trained, action is under way and now must be continued and in part on intelligence yield." He noted, "It was once thought that the operations would keep the Chinese from consolidating their hold on Tibet. [But] of this there is not a chance. The operations cover a few square miles of an incredibly vast area. Finally, it is argued that by keeping alive the resistance, the Chinese aggression in Tibet is kept before world opinion. Again, the fact that this is confined to a few acres destroys this case."[3] The resolute ambassador had made these same points in a private message to the president three days earlier, assuring him he was "quite familiar with intelligence including [the] recent coup and other claimed results," and declaring, "[But] they offset neither risks [n]or diplomatic costs plus possible effects on current negotiations."[4]

A week later the unappeased ambassador sent one final appeal to JFK expressing his anger, which was "inevitably associated with the fact that [he took] seriously [America's] affairs here and [did] not kindly take to the brush-off." He would "deal with those responsible" and "was not without resources." He made the case that his strong feelings were fueled by the current situation in India. The objectionable defense minister Krishna Menon was under fire as the result of recent Chinese incursions along the Indian frontier, and Galbraith wanted to ensure that Menon was provided with no ammunition that would permit him to slither away with the excuse that these Chinese invasions were balanced by "the Americans who are just as aggressive as the Chinese." He ended by reminding the president that he had (apparently unsuccessfully) made his views clear to Kennedy's appropriate senior officers at the State Department: Averell Harriman, George Ball, and George McGhee. "With all vigor, let me stress that this is a matter on which one informed and politically experienced man can be right and a dozen wrong." He pointed out to his former student that on the occasion of the Bay of Pigs debacle the previous spring, he "had been the lone dissenter in face of the most extravagant promises of accomplishment": "I was right. The majority was wrong."[5]

Three decades later a mellower Galbraith admitted that he might have overreacted—"I frequently did"—but he still felt that it had been a mistake to continue these operations, which could have provided Menon with an out. Galbraith was engaged at the time in another unsuccessful effort to persuade Nehru not to back Menon's push to occupy the historic Portuguese enclave of Goa on India's southwest coast. He still recalled Menon as "an awful man" and felt great satisfaction that he had helped to contribute to the defense minister's eventual removal from office the following year.[6]

In the late fall of 1961, however, the dynamic ambassador was battling against the tide as the Tibetans were enjoying a short run of successes. On the resistance front they could point to the extraordinary intelligence haul documenting the vulnerabilities of their enemy. On the political front the Dalai Lama had reacted promptly to the message Gyalo brought back from his skirmishes at the UN of the need to demonstrate that what he and his country represented was not some quaint retrograde feudal relic that had no relevance in the contemporary world. This message reinforced the exiled ruler's strong belief that part of his mission as a twentieth-century Dalai Lama was to prepare his people to govern themselves. His successful relocation from Lhasa had produced both the opportunity and the obligation to produce this capability. Now established in the abandoned former British army cantonment of Dharamsala in the upper Kangra Valley and separated from his country by only a range of lesser peaks, the Dalai Lama gave his support to institutionalizing a modern form of government.[7] It is based on the principle and practice of the self-governance that he has spent his life in exile inculcating among his constituents.

He would later declare that if the Tibetans were permitted to return to Tibet and had an elected leader, then the institution of the Dalai Lama would no longer be relevant. He would be happy to live in semiretirement and let the institution die with him. In the face of the seemingly implacable refusal of the Chinese to come to an agreement that would permit him or the refugee community to return to Tibet, he has resignedly fulfilled his duties.

In August 2006 he said second-generation Tibetans living in exile in India would decide the issue "Who after me?"[8] This is what he believes he has been preparing them to do. The challenge that his leadership has provided in the six decades since he assumed the full powers of his office is being dramatically demonstrated in the continuing protests in Tibet against Beijing's efforts to supplant him. It was validated in the Diaspora Conference he convoked in November 2008 to deal with the present stalemate between his government-in-exile and China over the governance of Tibet.

On the diplomatic front the Tibetans scored a success in their claim for international recognition. On December 20, 1961, with fifty-six yeas, eleven nays, and twenty-nine abstentions, the UN General Assembly renewed "its call for the cessation of practices which deprive the Tibetan people of their fundamental human rights and freedoms, *including their right to self-determination.*" This endorsement (and a reminder of the pledge given by Secretary Herter to the Dalai Lama in 1960) won even the grudging vote of the British. This shift was apparently made on the orders of the new foreign secretary, Lord Home, who may well have wanted to rid his conscience of the guilt he had expressed the year before to Prime Minister Harold Macmillan about feeling forced to withhold support for the Irish-Malay resolution at the UN in 1959. This victory for the Tibetans came three weeks after Bowles, one of their prime champions, lost his powerful post as the State Department's number two officer. But the momentum that he helped build ultimately brought along Adlai Stevenson, a less ardent supporter of the Tibetans. Bowles was able to resume his support for the Tibetans when he returned to India as ambassador two years later.

1962: The Year of Changing Alliances

In 1962 there was a shift in India's regard for the whole issue of Tibet which had special implications for the Tibetan refugees living in India. On September 8 Chinese troops crossed Thagla Ridge, a mountain summit in Tibet opposite India's North East Frontier Agency. This move put them in position to attack one of the forty-five new Indian military outposts which Nehru and Defense Minister Menon had set up the year before to "plug the gap" in a systematic move to establish the McMahon Line as their recognized northern frontier. Nehru had adopted this policy in an effort to end the clashes which had begun three years before along this long contested frontier. He acted under the assumption that a war between China and India was "unthinkable."

But the "unthinkable" happened, and the Chinese troops came pouring over Thagla Ridge. In early October the Indian government, despite the heightening of the already poor odds their troops in the eastern frontier were facing, appointed the chief of the general staff, B. M. Kaul, to command the offensive to drive the Chinese back to north of the McMahon Line. Kaul, a man of great enthusiasm but limited field experience, saluted and set off to the front. After a survey of the potential battle area on one of the Himalayan ridges, to which he had to be carried by a Tibetan porter, he discerned the tactical absurdity of the proposed offensive and the almost total absence of the logistics to support it. He sent off a report describing the situation, but not including a proposal that the mission be abandoned. By then it was too late, as the Chinese were ready to move down and establish themselves in force in the disputed territory.

A week later a Chinese force of ten thousand seasoned veterans, acting under an order from Peking to "liquidate the invading Indian army," launched an overwhelming attack against the six thousand ill-armed Indians, many of them fighting in these alpine heights in summer uniforms. Within days the Chinese had captured all the posts of the forward line established by the Indians over the past months, and the members of the Indian Seventh Brigade were dead, wounded, captured, or in flight. The triumphant Chinese juggernaut, having dramatically established its superiority, then paused within India's North East Frontier Agency.

Despite the enormity of this disaster, Nehru could not back away from the wave of national unity that had swept over his frequently divided country. He did sack his friend, the unpopular Krishna Menon,[9] but the Indian papers reported that the Indian army was preparing an offensive to drive the Chinese forces out of the North East Frontier Agency. Unfortunately these reports were true. Although the Chinese again proposed negotiations, even the rarely inhibited American ambassador withheld his advice to accept this opportunity to back off. Galbraith later said, "Given the current state of Indian opinion and its nearly total divorce from military circumstance, this could not be considered and I did not suggest it. To have done so in that excited atmosphere would have been to lose credibility as a friend. Perhaps I should have so urged."[10] It is doubtful if anyone could have persuaded the Indians to save themselves from the inevitable disaster that occurred when, on November 14, the hapless Kaul resumed his offensive against his overwhelmingly militarily superior opponents.

Within four days a desperate Nehru stifled his reluctance to consort publicly with the American Cold Warriors and appealed to President Kennedy to send airplanes to ward off Chinese air attacks on New Delhi that his frantic but still militant constituents were convinced were imminent. The Indian prime minister had been informed earlier that month that his Russian friends, who had angered their Chinese comrades by not lending their full support to their ventures in the Himalayas some three years earlier, might now feel forced to withdraw the pending delivery of MiG aircraft to New Delhi. International bedfellows were changing alliances in the fashion of a French bedroom farce.

While Washington was watching the Russian ships carrying missiles to Cuba approach the quarantine line proclaimed by JFK, Chinese troops were pouring into the contested Himalayan frontier area to clear it of the outposts set up by Nehru to establish Indian authority there. Both the Russian and Indian leaders had acted on what turned out to be mistaken assumptions that they could get away with their bold moves. On October 28, however, Khrushchev blinked, and the Chinese felt only contempt for what they regarded as further evidence of the Russian premier's cowardice. After clearing the border area of the defiant Indian outposts they remained in place, ready to meet any further challenges from the Indians. When the balky Indians refused to either negotiate or yield, but ventured one more challenge, they were met with the full force of the seasoned Chinese troops, which sent them into a humiliating rout.

This forced the proud Indian prime minister to send off his plea to JFK for large-scale American aid and air intervention to counter the assumed threat to Assam and Bengal. Nehru was feeling very lonely. Khrushchev resented his belligerent Chinese comrades' actions in the Himalayas, which he believed were aimed at sabotaging his policy of peaceful coexistence. But during the missile crisis that he had precipitated he had felt it necessary to modify dramatically Russia's neutral position on the Sino-Indian border dispute. The suspension of negotiations on delivery of the Russian MIGs had made the Indian skies suddenly seem very vulnerable.

The Harriman Mission

Against this background of failed pretensions, false hopes, and near misses of cataclysm JFK responded to Nehru's request for assistance by sending a delegation of New Frontiersmen to assess the needs of his new client. Galbraith, who had been en route to Moscow, was ordered to return to his post in New Delhi immediately so that he might deliver messages to Nehru concerning the growing confrontation with Russia in the Caribbean. The ambassador was therefore on the scene as the conflict in the Himalayas heated up and "in consequence of this coincidence," he "had more independent authority than any modern ambassador has enjoyed in another country in wartime."[11] He was not reluctant to assume this authority. The White House informed him that his old Harvard colleague Carl Kaysen would be the highest official in Washington with any time for his problems. Kaysen and he "had long seen eye to eye on the need for less adventuresome, less militarily oriented foreign policy and [Galbraith] could [therefore] be sure that his support would be broadly sympathetic." Of the secretary of state he wrote, "[Dean Rusk,] most generously in light of our earlier acerbic correspondence and relations, confined himself throughout to expressions of warm confidence in my management. . . . [And] unlike other ambassadors, I had no independent military (or CIA) contingent with which to share power."[12]

The always confident ambassador was capable of self-examination: "In these weeks, I learned also the main temptation of such times; it is that one will come to enjoy war too much. Civilian administration is by discussion and consensus; military action is by information and command. The latter has a rewarding simplicity for all civilians and especially for anyone from the discursive traditions of academic life. This is why few men become as dangerously warlike as the academic figure who is plunged into military affairs."[13]

When the Chinese, having made their point, stopped their sweep across the border into Assam on November 21 and proposed a cease-fire, Galbraith abandoned his newfound role as a war commander and hastened to meet with Nehru to urge him to accept the Chinese offer. Galbraith understood that no Indian leader, particularly this proud Brahmin, could survive the humiliation of accepting outright this gesture of largesse from his now despised Chinese neighbors. The year before Nehru had told Secretary Herter that India could make minor revisions in the border, but nothing on the scale that the Chinese were demanding. Galbraith did believe, however, that the exhausted and defeated Indian prime minister found his advice to make a deal with the Chinese "shoemakers and laundrymen" far more compatible with the reality of Indian capability than yielding to the clamor which was sweeping across India for a revenge that would inevitably be both costly and probably unattainable.[14] Galbraith made his views public and was called "another Kennedy," meaning the president's father, who had been similarly denounced twenty-five years earlier as a Munich appeaser. He noted, however, that the public and parliamentary criticism over the debacle in NEFA quickly "dissolved in the deeper relief that the war was over" and his "own Indian nimbus remained undiminished."[15]

A NEW BALLGAME

—

Despite his halo, the ambassador was not permitted to enjoy the absence of aid and counsel from Washington. There, despite the preoccupations of a possible nuclear war, those keeping watch over affairs in the Indian subcontinent had managed to remain involved. Within three days after Khrushchev agreed to withdraw the Soviet missiles from Cuba, the United States had initiated an air shipment of military supplies to India "designed to reinforce Indian resistance on the border to the Chinese Communists."[16] These shipments, made "after deliberately waiting for the Prime Minister's request," included 40,000 antipersonnel mines; 1 million rounds of .30 caliber ammunition; 200 .30 caliber machine guns; 54 81-millimeter mortars; 100,000 rounds of 81-millimeter ammunition; 500 Army Navy portable radios (ANPRC); and 250 Army Navy ground radios (ANGRC). Washington also made unsuccessful attempts to get Pakistan to seek better relations with India; publicly stated that the United States recognized the McMahon Line as the international border between India and Tibet; and increased its flow to India of intelligence concerning Communist China.

On November 10 CIA Director John McCone had met with Secretary Rusk to raise the question of whether the objective of freeing Tibet from Chinese Communist occupation adopted in 1958 and the plans developed pursuant to this policy remained valid. He had stated that he raised this question in view of the objections by Secretary Harriman and Ambassador Galbraith, which "restrained and frustrated long-range plans developed to support this policy . . . because of the weight given to these viewpoints."[17] A message sent by McGeorge Bundy to Galbraith a week later indicates that active contingency planning by the CIA had not been ruled out. The two airdrops made the previous year to supply the Tibetan resistance forces operating out of Mustang, both of them over the objections of Galbraith and one of them following the Bay of Pigs disaster, were indications that the Kennedy administration had not abandoned unconventional warfare as an operational foreign policy tool.

However, JFK had obviously learned the potential perils and limitations of such operations, and he was exercising a tight hold on proposals being made at that time by Chiang Kai-shek to use American airplanes to launch teams in a Nationalist effort to return to power on the mainland. But according to Dean Rusk, JFK had no interest at that time in making any changes in the United States policy of opposition to the Mao regime.[18] He was quite ready to welcome his new Indian ally in this containment effort and to take advantage of the dramatic shift in political atmosphere and alliances in New Delhi. A State Department analysis of the situation in early November had noted the political advantages the United States would obtain "if the dispute were quiescent but unresolved along a de facto border not too humiliating to the Indians." The advantages which the drafter had cited were that the United States "would be less likely to hear the Indians plead the Chinese case in the United Nations, and elsewhere neutralist nations would find it harder to act in concert, and neither the USSR nor Communist China would find it so easy to have the best of both worlds and appear the friend of both neutralists and Communists."[19]

The unilateral cease-fire proclaimed by the victorious Chinese on November 20 released JFK from having to respond immediately to the frantic pleas sent by Nehru the day before. The beleaguered prime minister had asked the United States to dispatch twelve squadrons of supersonic all-weather fighters manned by American personnel "to assist the Indian Air Force in air battles with the Chinese air force over Indian areas" and to train Indian pilots to fly the two squadrons of B-47 bombers that he was also requesting to "neutralise Chinese bases and airfields."[20]

Kennedy held a strategy session with his top political and military advisors, who all agreed that the United States should provide a ready response to Nehru's request for help. Secretary of Defense Robert McNamara urged that the first move be to find out what the real situation was: "If we were to put our prestige and resources at risk, we must find out the score." A week before, Washington and London had signed a memorandum of understanding concerning the Indian conflict, and Rusk queried "whether strategic and technical advice shouldn't come from the U.K. in the first instance." He readily acceded, however, to McNamara's concern that such advice might not come soon enough and that the United States "needed to get some C-130 aircraft on the way while [they] were making a more systematic evaluation." Rusk again urged that "the U.K. take the lead on such a mission, with the U.S. participating if desirable": The more we got in front the more we could push Moscow toward Peiping." Kennedy decided on immediate action. The United States would get a mission off to Delhi, send some C-130s, take care of C-119 spare parts, and push the British to get the Commonwealth involved. "There was some discussion of the desirability of using Tibetan guerrillas,"[21] and the meeting ended with JFK ordering the State Department to bring Senator Stuart Symington, but not the full congressional committees, up to date.

The United States was engaging in a shadowy latter-day replay of the Great Game. Not to do so would deny Washington a unique opportunity to develop closer ties with Nehru, a key spokesman of the uncommitted world in the Cold War. It would also reopen the field to the Russians to renew their efforts to cultivate a position of influence with the Indians that they had been forced by the missile crisis to suspend. But the objective was to do this without arousing the anger of the Pakistanis, who viewed the troubles of their neighbor and traditional enemy with equal amounts of satisfaction and concern. Washington's immediate goal was to determine the extent of India's needs and the manner in which they should be resolved.

Accordingly on November 21 a mission left Washington headed by Averell Harriman, whose decision to accept the less prestigious post of assistant secretary of state for Far Eastern affairs—"where the action was"—seemed vindicated. The other members of the mission traveling on the converted c-130 included Bundy's deputy, Carl Kaysen; the Pentagon's assistant secretary for international security affairs, Paul Nitze; the State Department's intelligence chief, Roger Hilsman; the cia's Desmond FitzGerald; and lesser spear carriers. In Washington Robert Komer, another Harvard "intellocrat" later called "Blowtorch Bob" because of his zeal in pursuing any program under his authority, would be monitoring and providing policy guidance for the mission.

Hilsman noted that in the discussions en route a hawkish Kaysen "very much" favored a war over the Chinese incursions into Indian-held territory. Nitze, with whom Harriman "by and large" agreed, argued for a period of de facto cease-fire during which the Indians could build up their strength and the United States could make moves toward settlement of the Pakistani-Indian dispute over Kashmir. When the mission arrived in New Delhi Galbraith whisked them to a somewhat anticlimactic meeting with Nehru. According to Hilsman's account, Nehru appeared to be embarrassed and ill-at-ease. When they arrived he introduced them to the British political economist Barbara Ward, with whom Nehru said he had been having an interesting half hour discussing the "fantastic changes" that had taken place in the villages of India since her visit there three years earlier. This was a surprisingly low-key introduction to a conversation in which the prime minister, who three days earlier had sent off a panicked plea for help, now took "a general attitude of extreme embarrassment." Hilsman attributed Nehru's apparent chagrin to "the failure of his policy of courting the Communist Bloc and reluctance to admit that he had been wrong and now had to ask for American aid." He found Nehru's general attitude was that of a "very tired, and somewhat overwrought man" and his welcome "not warm, but *pro forma*, withdrawn, very limited."[22]

Following this disappointingly tepid reception by the man to whom they had traveled eighteen hours to offer aid, the principals adjourned to the embassy for cocktails and a Thanksgiving dinner, after which they discussed their schedule for the next two or three days and the attitude of Pakistan toward their mission. Galbraith argued "what [they] all believe[d]": "A settlement of the Kashmir issue is fundamental to the problem before us."[23]

During the following days, while the other mission principals met with their counterparts within the Ministries of Defense and External Affairs to determine the dimensions of the United States military and political commitment, Desmond FitzGerald, who had been joined by his Near East affairs counterpart James Critchfield, met with the Indians and Tibetans involved in the covert challenge to the Chinese. Critchfield had flown from Europe to join the party after being told by the CIA's chief of operations, Richard Helms, to link up with the Harriman mission, as it was the "hottest ticket in town." Helms, who shared Critchfield's lineage of intelligence rather than the covert action side of the CIA, represented by FitzGerald, felt more comfortable having his old OSS colleague on the scene. Certainly Ambassador Galbraith did. He said he enlisted Critchfield to keep watch over FitzGerald, whom he regarded as "a dangerous man." Four decades later Galbraith, at age ninety-six, with his characteristic cackle recounted his satisfaction at having been able to monitor FitzGerald's activities while he was in New Delhi. As FitzGerald's spear carrier on the Harriman mission, I sat through several lively verbal sparring sessions between him and Critchfield.[24]

These personal differences did not, however, prevent the two CIA barons from utilizing their individual contacts and assets to develop a substantial program of covert support involving Tibetans to challenge Chinese control and activities in Tibet. FitzGerald was chief of the Far Eastern Division, which by then had been training and providing active support, albeit with disappointing results so far, to the Tibetans in their resistance efforts inside their homeland and in taking their case to the United Nations for the past three years. He was in bureaucratic charge of both the real estate in Colorado where training of the Tibetan resistance fighters was conducted and the bases in Southeast Asia from which the air support missions flew. He therefore was able to offer these facilities to develop new intelligence nets inside Tibet and to renew support to the guerrillas operating from Nepal to continue harassing raids inside Tibet. Critchfield and his staff officers in place in India were in contact with Nehru's intelligence chief, B. N. Mullik, the man whom Critchfield had the previous December informed of the airdrops by which the Agency had supplied the underused potential insurgents in Nepal. The CIA's support to the Tibetans thereby became a shared responsibility in a new, never completely happy or neat, but workable division of labor between the two Agency components. Even the skeptical ambassador learned to live with it.

During the mission's stay in New Delhi Harriman had four meetings with Nehru in which the now much calmer Indian prime minister indicated that he would make some temporizing reply to the Chinese cease-fire offer within the next few days. However, he seemed to feel no sense of urgency as he thought the Chinese "wanted to make a deal." In the meantime he planned to raise various objections to the Chinese. Harriman and Galbraith both emphasized the need for the Indians "to make a reasonable counter offer to put the onus on the Chinese who at the moment look[ed] reasonable and this advantage had to be taken away from them." Nitze did add that in "his preliminary view it would take at least until the end of next year for the Indians to get into a good military position." Nehru, who only ten days earlier had sent his frenetic request to JFK for American planes to protect his cities from Chinese air attacks, now discounted the need for any urgent action as "he did not believe the ChiComs would attack at least for some months." In response to Harriman's ploy that he had heard that the Russians had definitely declined to provide the promised MiG aircraft, the determinedly impassive Nehru replied that the governor's information was outdated. Khrushchev, he said, had "recently assured the Indian Ambassador a MIG factory would be delivered in a couple of years and in the meantime the few MiGs under discussion would be delivered in ample time for training purposes." Nehru similarly dismissed Harriman's strong expression of the need to take action to improve India-Pakistan relations "to calm [President] Ayub and Paks from their emotional binge against India and the U.S. and their [corresponding] pro-China [binge] and disinterest in addressing the long term problem of defense of the subcontinent." After initially rejecting any negotiations over Kashmir and considerable airing of historic and present grievances, the proud Kashmiri Brahmin Nehru finally agreed that, if Ayub were willing, he would join in starting negotiations, preferably on the ministerial level.[25]

Harriman then went to Karachi to tackle the ancillary objective of his mission, which was to use this opportunity to encourage a settlement of the always potentially explosive dispute between India and Pakistan over Kashmir. The governor had earned his spurs as a tough negotiator as a wartime ambassador dealing with Stalin and in the postwar battles within his own political party in unsuccessful efforts to be its standard-bearer. But even "the Crocodile," as he was known by his hard-driven but admiring colleagues at the State Department, could not find the magic solution to this ancient feud.

CHAPTER SIXTEEN

The United States and India as Allies

On December 10, 1962, JFK signed an action memorandum calling for emergency military aid to India of up to $60 million, with the understanding that the United Kingdom and the Commonwealth would provide a like amount. The previous day he had dispatched a letter slightly edited to exclude what his usually not overly shy ambassador objected to as "just a suggestion of ex cathedra preachiness" in its emphasis on "the necessity to find a solution to the Kashmir problem." (Galbraith had warned, "In studying Nehru as no one before in history, I know with great certainty what will anger him and arouse his resistance to no purpose.")[1] Satisfied with the addition of the words "yet, as you of course know better than anyone" to the sentence "effective defense against the Chinese requires that available resources be concentrated to this end," Galbraith delivered the letter. It retained JFK's feeling "that far more effective defense against the Chinese is possible if the issues which divide India and Pakistan, the most important of which is Kashmir, are resolved."[2]

When JFK and the British prime minister met in Nassau ten days later to negotiate their respective responsibilities for delivering the aid they had contracted to provide, Macmillan grumbled, "What worries me is that, as so often before, we support the people who are troublesome, such as Nehru and Krishna Menon, and abandon people who support us." He was "sure it would be dangerous if [they] let Ayub feel [they were] abandoning him. The equal danger was that India would be overrun." A memorandum of their conversation summarized: "Nehru, he feared, might be a bit more uppish now that the Chinese have gone away. Macmillan liked the idea that we start slowly and not go ahead building up armies of the people who for 12 years or more have attacked us, have trumpeted the benefits of being non-aligned, have helped build up the neutralist Afro-Asian Bloc, and who have been . . . contemptuous—like a camel looking down his nose at you."[3]

After these ventings of shared frustration the two leaders agreed to send a mission to India the following month to assess the need for air defense assistance, while continuing to pressure both Nehru and Ayub to reach a settlement over Kashmir. In the following months the United States delivered the emergency arms assistance to which it was committed, and the Indians were eventually able to use the arms provided by the Americans and British to create or convert eight mountain divisions. Kennedy tried his personal touch to move Nehru forward on a Kashmir settlement, writing him "with the private thought," "President Ayub is in a weaker position in his own country than you are and Pakistan is the lesser power. By these tokens it is harder for him to take the first step toward you than you toward him. I too have repeatedly been forced to accept that more is required of great powers than of others. It is always the weaker who must seem unyielding."[4]

But Nehru, the Kashmiri Brahmin by both lineage and politics, was not able to make such a gesture. Washington's dream of using this new era in American-Indian relations to effect not only a settlement of one of South Asia's longest disputes but to arrive at a deeper relationship with Nehru himself did not happen. This is not surprising. Nehru's ego had taken a brutal shellacking. His vaunted alternative to the Cold War in Asia of peaceful coexistence with China was shattered when Mao's troops flooded into the North East Frontier Agency. He had had to swallow the ultimate humiliation of accepting (while not acknowledging) a cease-fire offer in order to avert total disaster. It must have been particularly galling that the offer came from Zhou Enlai, the man he had touted as his fellow guarantor of peaceful coexistence in Asia and that Zhou termed what had been viewed in India as an imminent catastrophe an "unfortunate border conflict." The proud prime minister could take little comfort from his Asian neighbors, who demonstrated a disappointingly mixed bag of reactions to the Sino-Indian conflict. Six of them—Australia, South Korea, New Zealand, the Philippines, Thailand, and South Vietnam—were "strongly for India"; Japan, Malaya, and Nepal were "moderately for India"; Afghanistan, Burma, Ceylon, Indonesia, and Laos were "generally neutral"; and Cambodia was "moderately" and Pakistan "strongly" for China.[5] Moreover the Indian leader had been forced to turn for help not only to the United States, the Cold War's strongest protagonist, but also to his country's former colonial masters. It was to be an era of new alliances, produced by necessity.

While a milestone in American-Indian diplomatic relations had not been fully achieved, the American presence in India, particularly in the intelligence field, found a new welcome. Nehru, ever the practical politician, had kept watch over events in the vast Tibetan plateau on his northern border, hoping to exert a benign influence in a situation he was unable to do anything about militarily. Ten years earlier he had sent Mullik, director of the Central Intelligence Bureau, to establish the ground rules under which Gyalo Thondup was permitted asylum in Darjeeling, from which he ran his rudimentary intelligence rat lines to and from Lhasa. When the Chinese troops crossed into NEFA Mullik had volunteered to resign as CIB director and organize a popular resistance movement in Assam.[6] The unilateral Chinese ceasefire had negated such an immediate endeavor, but Mullik's proposal and Nehru's readiness to entertain it bespoke the new hospitable climate for unconventional operations.

James Critchfield, the chief of the CIA's Near Eastern operations, had established a privileged relationship with Mullik the year before, when he briefed him on the overflights into Tibet to supply the Agency-supported Tibetan guerrillas. Although Mullik was aware that these flights were taking place, Critchfield's show of willingness to take him into his confidence had produced a bond favorable for shared ventures in the new operating climate. The CIB now became a joint participant in the opposition to the Chinese occupation of Tibet. Both the CIA and the CIB had established relations with and shared confidence in Gyalo Thondup, who would be the pivotal man for recruiting his fellow countrymen for what now became a tripartite endeavor.

Although he never became a fan of covert operations, Ambassador Galbraith came to accept them as assets that the Indians might use in their defense. They were not likely to cause any significant diplomatic flap if exposed in the prevailing united anti-Chinese political atmosphere in India, especially if they were being carried out with the cooperation of the host intelligence service. He was also apparently willing to accept the division of labor that Critchfield and the man he considered "dangerous," Desmond FitzGerald, had worked out with the CIB concerning the use of their respective territorial holdings and assets.[7]

Galbraith was willing to make fuller use of these intelligence assets as part of the assistance package that he had to offer his hosts for their protection. But he had not become a convert to the Tibetan cause. When the annual debate about further appeals to the United Nations was being considered the following spring, the obdurate ambassador sent off a particularly harsh recommendation that the United States end its support for further UN consideration of the Tibet case. He declared:

> We have no reason at this time to feel particularly gentle toward the Chinese or sanguine about their intentions. We would certainly be much happier if they were not in Tibet. But we regard the Tibetan operation in the UN as signifying in the main the traditionalists' love for familiar issues with just the least suggestion of failure of imagination. Whatever happens we know and the world knows that these worthy monks are not going back. And there is the further sad possibility that even had the Communists never come in their day was over. So we don't really keep the issue before the world. What we do is identify ourselves with a transparent and somewhat artless plot.[8]

Joint Operations

By midsummer 1963 Galbraith had turned over his post to Chester Bowles and was now free, as JFK had chided him earlier that spring, "to become a critic rather than an executor of [American] policy."[9] Bowles did not share either his predecessor's distrust of covert operations or his measured regard for the Tibetans and their cause. The year before, when he was undersecretary of state, Bowles had written his friend Adlai Stevenson to urge him to find some way to maintain the UN's focus on the Tibet issue.[10] At the CIA Director John McCone, although he had little of his predecessor's innate zest for covert operations, was quite prepared to see the Agency's resources and contacts used as long as his fellow National Security Council members were aboard. In the case of American support to India, he gave his colleagues his pragmatic views on endorsing aid to neutrals: "The Pakistanis are critical,[11] but we must recognize the importance of the Indians. If they joined the Chinese we would have no free South Asia. The Pakistanis are struggling against the Indians and the Afghans. They will use or attempt to exploit our power. Our interest is to make a strong sub-continent. We will use the country that can help further that aim. We have used India lately. We do not like their present leadership, but we can use them. . . . We cannot settle all disputes, but we want to keep them free from the Communists."[12]

McCone's measured view included maintaining Agency support to the covert operations that the Indians were now prepared to undertake involving Tibet and the Tibetans, who had become assets rather than wards of their Indian hosts. The CIB would be a partner in the ongoing operations that the CIA had been conducting and the new programs that they would develop together. No longer would CIA officers have to play the game of meeting with their Tibetan contacts in Calcutta, New Delhi, Darjeeling, Kalimpong, and even in Nepal, without acknowledging these actions to the CIB, who they knew were monitoring their moves wherever they could. In Washington the agreed new division of labor, assets, and programs between the Agency's Far East and Near East Divisions, which would be carried out by their respective officers in the field, produced a more civil bureaucratic atmosphere. This was reflected in the development and conduct of several activities involving Tibet:

Ongoing operations utilizing the resistance forces operating from the Mustang area of Nepal targeted against Chinese troop and supply movements across the Lhasa-Xinjiang highway in Tibet.

Training and support of the new Indian border force, headquartered at Chakrata, another former British army cantonment in the Himalayan foothills.

A new Indian covert air support base in Orissa, south of Calcutta, to support Indian border forces and operations.

The new program of intelligence collection to be carried out on the ground in Tibet by the 125 Tibetans being trained at the Far East Division site in Colorado at Camp Hale and who would be dispatched on their assignments by the CIB.

A program of political action: a major one of supporting offices in New York, London, and Geneva to represent the political activities of the Dalai Lama in the international community; another to train young Tibetans to support both the intelligence operations being conducted with the Indians and the Dalai Lama's unilateral political activities abroad;[13] and the establishment of a Tibet House in New Delhi to collect and house a gallery of Tibetan religious art paintings, which were then being scattered into private hands in India and Hong Kong. Nehru's daughter demonstrated India's new acceptance of their Tibetan residents by attending the opening and eventually assuming the maintenance of this institution dedicated to preserving and proclaiming the unique culture of their Tibetan guests. This institution continues to serve this dual cultural and political purpose today.

On the scene in India the CIB quickly accommodated to the division of direction, control, and funding between those projects and activities. The newly created Joint Operations Center in New Delhi monitored and directed the operations being conducted by the resistance veterans from their headquarters at Mustang. The operations by the 125 men being trained at Camp Hale for intelligence missions directed at identifying and supporting small-scale resistance inside Tibet were also determined by the Joint Operations Center.

The newly established Special Frontier Force (SFF), which was an Indian creation, would remain under the command and policy control of CIB Director Mullik. The CIA's role would be restricted to providing training and arms support, a relationship with which the Indians, CIA, and American embassy all felt comfortable. Within the CIA, the Near East Division would have the primary responsibility for this support. The relationship that Critchfield had established with Mullik and the CIA's proposal to undertake its mission with a handful of officers, in contrast with the Pentagon's usually much larger military contingent and attendant publicity, reassured all hands. This formula, by which the Indians called the shots, was followed in the training and equipping of the support which the CIA provided to India's covert air capability.

My Indian colleague's regard for the Tibetans was shared by the senior CIB officer who had assumed control of these operations, a Kashmiri Brahmin named Ramji Kao. Immaculately groomed and erect in posture, Kao had the mien and manner of a Sandhurst officer. He also had an admirable sense of personal responsibility and regard for the Tibetans. He later admitted that in dealing with the Tibetans he had committed the "cardinal sin" of the professional intelligence officer by "falling in love with his agents." The honeymoon years of the new relationship between the CIA and the CIB were a remarkable cooperative enterprise and a privileged operational experience that I rarely duplicated in subsequent decades as an operations officer.

Mustang

By the time the Joint Operations Center assumed direction of the two thousand resistance veterans lodged at Mustang it was an available capability, but it was also a chronic operational headache. It had been plagued since shortly after its inception by its inability to relocate inside Tibet, as its original operating plan called for. An unsettled command structure and challenging and uncertain logistical support further vitiated this force of dedicated resistance fighters and turned Mustang into a breeding ground of frustration.

In late 1960 twenty-seven of the leaders from the resistance veterans who had made their way to Mustang were selected as company commanders by Gyalo Thondup and the CIA and flown on a "black" flight to the CIA's Far East Division training camp in Colorado. Four of these men, including Lobsang Chamba, the man designated by Gyalo and the CIA (but not by Gyen Yeshe, who had established and was commanding the Mustang encampment) to be the commander of the Mustang operations, were parachuted back into Tibet on the initial arms and ammunition supply drop made to the Mustang force the following spring. Those arms and the Camp Hale alumni were safely retrieved and brought back to the encampment in Nepal.

At Mustang the issue of Gyen Yeshe's relinquishing his command was not directly joined, as a snag in the expected return of the remaining potential company commanders presented a more immediate problem. The plan called for them to be returned from Colorado by air to East Pakistan, from where they had been exfiltrated six months before, and then make their way overland through west Bengal to Mustang. But President Ayub Khan, piqued by the economic aid and the sale of a sizable number of tanks to his mortal Indian enemies, retaliated by closing the East Pakistan border to any more covert crossings. This stalemate was overcome later that summer as a fortuitous outcome of a candlelight dinner at Mount Vernon honoring Ayub. Allen Dulles took the Pakistani president, under the spell of Jackie Kennedy's "magic" hospitality, on an after-dinner stroll along the Potomac and persuaded him to reopen his border to permit the stranded Tibetans to cross one more time. By August 1961 the remaining leaders had been returned by air to East Pakistan and made their way across the now well-worn exfiltration route across the Teesta River into India; from there they traveled over the same trails they had used when they had rushed to volunteer at Mustang the summer before.

Once reassembled, the Mustang forces had accepted the fait accompli of Gyen Yeshe's assumption of authority, and an uneasy command situation prevailed. Autumn through spring was the optimum time for the insurgents to make their way across the streams and rivers between their Mustang stronghold and their targets moving along the Lhasa-Xinjiang highway. In September 1961 seven men found the area inside Tibet along the border area across from Mustang devoid of population, having been declared off-limits to herders by the Chinese. They were able to attack a small army post and kill a small number of Chinese soldiers before returning to Mustang. Then in October, one of the Camp Hale alumni led a party of forty guerrillas on the raid that resulted in an attack on a Chinese army caravan whose commander was carrying a pouch containing 1,600 classified documents. This intelligence gold mine, containing privileged insights on both Chinese military capabilities and domestic political problems within China, provided welcome justification for overriding Ambassador Galbraith's vehement opposition to a second drop of arms and ammunition. Another raid was made across the border inside Tibet, and the arms were retrieved and carried back into Nepal without incident. But over half of the men were still unarmed, and there was no inclination in Washington to approve further drops until the operations were permanently moved out of Nepal into Tibet.

In the summer of 1963 three of my colleagues and I met in a safe house in the hills above Darjeeling with Gyen Yeshe and five of his company commanders, all of them Hale alumni, including the Agency's protégé, Lobsang Chamba, who seemed reconciled to having lost out as chief to Gyen Yeshe. We were there to work out a solution that would end the stalemate over their refusal to leave their safe haven in Nepal and relocate inside Tibet. This last effort to turn what had become a wasting capability and political headache into an asset was a failure. In several long days of discussion, interrupted by extended periods in which Gyen Yeshe withdrew to pray, he and his commanders made their case, citing the problems of leaving a natural safe haven in Nepal to establish permanent sites in Tibet in an area that provided little natural protection. Besides, fewer than half of their men had been supplied with arms by the two drops that had been made. We cited the increasing political problems of their continuing presence in Nepal and Washington's reluctance to make any more drops that would encourage their continued location there. They made a strong case, but we had no flexibility in our negotiating instructions. The Tibetans finally came up with a compromise, which they offered to return to Mustang to present to their men for approval. They would consolidate into seven groups, four operating inside Tibet, while three would operate from Nepal.[14] After a final session of good cheer and a generous consumption of beer and exchange of gifts, we parted. I received a basket of dried yak tails, which the donors described as a special Tibetan delicacy. I noted that they declined to share their offering with me, and have subsequently wondered if it was a subtle, if pungent, bit of silent revenge for what they knew was going to be an unworkable solution to our operational problems.

It was no great surprise when Gyen Yeshe and the four other commanders reported that upon their return to Mustang they had not been able to find suitable relocation sites inside Tibet. They promised, however, to continue sending extended reconnaissance and raiding parties from Mustang to harass Chinese forces moving along the Lhasa-Xinjiang highway. This they did. According to Lhamo Tsering, these operations forced the Chinese to use a longer route north of the target highway to supply their forces in western Tibet.[15] But the Mustang capability which the CIA and the Tibetans brought to the Joint Operations Center was more a problem than an asset, one which the Indians were inclined to defer to the CIA to deal with.

The whole problem of command, control, and mission of the Mustang force was highlighted by a peripheral incident of Himalayan melodrama in the summer of 1964. It starred George Patterson, the Scottish missionary who had first appeared on the American screen of Tibetan events in 1950, when he approached the American consulate in Calcutta seeking support for his Khampa protectors in their efforts to resist Chinese occupation of their homeland along the Yangtze frontier. The CIA officers who had dealt with Patterson found him a "bit of a romantic" but "a direct, honest and decent person," and had used his language capabilities and contacts in the negotiations to persuade the Dalai Lama to flee Lhasa and seek asylum in India. Patterson stayed on in India for another decade as a British correspondent, until he was forced to leave after several disagreements with the Indian government. Now he was back to again take up the cudgels on behalf of the Tibetans, whose strengths he admired and whose weaknesses he recognized but was willing to overlook, fearing these people were destined to be consigned to oblivion. His present goal was to get sympathetic viewers abroad to take note of them on their television screens and persuade their governments to support their cause.

Accompanied by a British producer and a Tibetan cameraman, Patterson made contact with one of Gyen Yeshe's commanders who was conducting raids on Chinese targets inside Tibet from a site sixty miles and many mountain valleys from Mustang. He had little difficulty convincing the commander and his men that the Dalai Lama's cause would be well served if they would conduct an ambush on a Chinese convoy moving along the Lhasa-Xinjiang highway, which he would film and get shown on international television. The commander did send a courier to seek Gyen Yeshe's approval to stage this event, but by the time he reached Mustang it was already too late to cancel the fifteen-minute ambush in which four trucks were destroyed or disabled and eight Chinese soldiers were killed—and photographed. The Tibetans had one casualty, a fifty-two-year-old Khampa who somehow made his way back to the guerrilla base three days after he had been left for dead at the ambush site.

When Gyen Yeshe eventually notified the Joint Operations Center of the event some days later it was met with due expletives, threatened recriminations, and concern that the Chinese, and certainly the Nepalese, would take retaliatory action once the spectacle appeared on international television. Fortuitously various complications caused it not to be broadcast for three years, but there was no dodging the fact that Mustang was far from a reliably controlled capability.

By this time the Indians had the makings of a more responsive and controlled capability over which they had unilateral command in the newly organized Special Frontier Force. This force was being trained and armed in northern India, but the Indians were not yet ready to see the Mustang force, already in place on the northern frontier, disbanded, even with all its problems. Washington and even the embassy, now under Chester Bowles's command, were similarly reluctant to abandon a capability in being, troublesome and contentious as it was. The Americans did urge that Gyen Yeshe, who seemed to answer to no one's command, be replaced. This presented problems for Gyalo Thondup, who had appointed Gyen Yeshe to his command. He had done this in response to the request of the grand old man of the Tibetan resistance, Gompo Tashi, who had just died. Thondup was fully aware of the consequences that would come from stirring the pot of tribal loyalties that Gyen Yeshe's removal would provoke. In any event, all sides agreed that Gyen Yeshe's complaint that fewer than half his men were armed was a legitimate concern. The command problem was again shoved under the rug, and a third airdrop of arms and ammunition was made in May 1965, this time in Nepal and with Indian support.

For the next three years the Joint Center applied a variety of remedies to keep the Mustang force patched together. In 1966 the Center sent the deceptively mild-mannered but fundamentally tough perennial negotiator Lhamo Tsering to Mustang to arbitrate a growing dispute between a group of officers, most of them Camp Hale alumni, and the increasingly self-isolated Gyen Yeshe.[16] The complainants were disgruntled over the high-handed manner in which the old monk shared neither his decisions nor funds with those he believed had been corrupted by alien ways. Lhamo Tsering quieted this storm by establishing a finance department for the receipt and disbursement of funds. He also came back deeply impressed by the paradox presented by the surprising discipline of what was a well-trained and organized force, but one without a justifiable mission to demonstrate it. The photographs that he brought back caused the Center to share his enthusiasm and renew its efforts to find gainful employment for what was obviously a capability going to waste—and to seed.

Within a few months, however, Gyen Yeshe reverted to his tribal chieftain form, dismissing the finance department and issuing his edicts from his self-imposed isolation. In 1968 the Center sent Wangdu Gyatotsang to Mustang to act as Gyen Yeshe's deputy. Wangdu had been dropped by the CIA into Kham in 1957. As a veteran of the firefights into which he had landed, and also as a member of a family which had early on participated in the resistance, his credentials and personality qualified him to challenge the stagnation and disaffection that had become endemic under Gyen Yeshe's misrule. Soon after his arrival in Mustang the activist Wangdu organized a training center and began sending groups to carry out harassing operations against the increasing Chinese military presence in western Tibet—and, if possible, to establish permanent bases inside Tibet according to the original operational plan. But the Center soon realized that the Chinese had committed sufficient forces to this area so that ordering the Mustang units to carry out guerrilla actions against them would be futile and irresponsible. Instead they were directed to infiltrate throughout the area to collect intelligence and build an underground, recognizing that it would be a modest one, given the limited number of inhabitants in this remote area of the Himalayan plateau. Lhamo Tsering later claimed that the intelligence collected by these small bands, which was relayed to the Joint Center by five radio teams located just across the border in Tibet, provided intelligence on Chinese military activities along a 350-mile front.[17]

There was, however, little support left for the difficult child at Mustang by its CIA parents, its Indian stepparents, or even its godfathers at Dharamsala, who had delegated the burden of directing and supporting this difficult capability to an increasingly absent Gyalo Thondup. He in turn had passed this responsibility on to the already much burdened Lhamo Tsering. In Washington the project's strongest supporter, Desmond FitzGerald, had died playing tennis with the British ambassador on a sultry August day in 1967. The report card of his more reserved Near East counterpart James Critchfield to the NSC oversight committee noted that the program's "achievements inside Tibet were minimal—outside more substantial." Critchfield added, a somewhat debatable comment, "The Tibetans by nature did not appear to be congenitally inclined toward conspiratorial proficiency."[18] The Indian partners by this time had their own paramilitary capability for challenging the Chinese, the SFF, which had been training and was equipped with CIA support at its site in northern India. It was a ready capability unencumbered by the personality, command, and mission problems that were plaguing the Mustang operations. The Indians therefore continued to play their passive role concerning the Mustang force and deferred to their American and Tibetan partners to close down their difficult creature.

In early 1969 the CIA notified Gyalo Thondup that it was withdrawing its support for the Mustang operations. He was asked to draw up a plan that would permit an orderly withdrawal, dispersal, and resettlement of the Mustang force over a three-year period, which was later extended. The language used in the termination notice sounds clinically reasonable. The actual disengagement from operations involving the lives and aspirations of a dedicated group of men was both untidy and painful. It ended with the tragic death of the unyielding Wangdu on the Indian-Nepali border, the seven-year imprisonment in Kathmandu of Lhamo Tsering and six of the Mustang veterans, the-self imposed exile of the embittered and generally shunned Gyen Yeshe, and a mixed regard by the Tibetans for their withdrawing American supporters.

Value judgments on operations involving the loss of lives are not simple. The Tibetans paid their dues to their Indian hosts, but they were heavy ones. The conduct of these and other trilateral (India, United States, and Tibet) operations as a joint enterprise had collateral value in consolidating the new relationship between the United States and India, particularly at a time when the renewed hostilities between India and Pakistan in Kashmir and LBJ's freeze on plans for rearming the Indian army threatened to chill it. Whether they were worth the costs will always be debatable.

The Tibetans Fight—But Not in Tibet

A serious breach of the terms of Gyalo's original agreement came in 1971, when the Indians unilaterally decided to use the Tibetans in their operations to "liberate" East Pakistan. Uban's audacious action evoked surprisingly little controversy or opposition among the Tibetan members of Establishment 22 who were being sent off to fight their host's war in a country that had been helpful to them in the past rather than against the common enemy they had been enlisted to fight. A few members recalled that it was a poor way to repay the Pakistanis for their hospitality in permitting them to cross their borders covertly en route to training and operational missions abroad. The Tibetan political officer of Establishment 22, Jampa Kalden, did go to Dharamsala to confirm that the Tibetan government-in-exile approved Uban's proposed mission for them. He came back with word that the Security Department of the government-in-exile, which was in nominal charge of the Tibetan component of Establishment 22, had not given a formal order, but rather tacit approval, that they comply with Uban's use (misuse?) of their services. Sonam Palden, a member of one of the surgical teams that served with Establishment 22 in East Pakistan, recalls that the Dharamsala officials said, "If the Indians send 1,000 soldiers to Bangladesh, the Tibetans should send four," a Tibetan dodge for saying "Send the minimum number that you have to." Generally the members of Establishment 22 were ready to go. Their government had agreed that they should comply with Uban's command, and they couldn't let Dharamsala lose face. Besides, there was a "we'll show these Indians that we Tibetans can fight" mentality.[19]

The three thousand Tibetans who consequently fought in East Pakistan in November and December acquitted themselves well. They took particular pride in having rescued the Tibeto-Burman royal family, the Chakmas, from the troops that were on their way to murder them when the Tibetans took control of the Chittagong Hill Tract in which the family and their lands were located. They subsequently took part in the victory parade through Chittagong, were rewarded for their gallantry, and were given anonymous credit for their contribution by their commandant, General Uban, in his book, appropriately called *The Phantoms of Chittagong*.[20] They had lost fifty of their fellow Tibetans but gained berths in the now established Special Frontier Force, in which they still serve as part of India's border defense. Gyalo Thondup claims that his original agreement with CIB Director Mullik in 1962 stipulated that the Tibetans he recruited for this force would be used only inside Tibet and not for border defense or in other areas.[21]

The End of an Era

In any event the always uneasy, unwritten common understanding between the United States, India, and Pakistan, which had permitted Tibetan operations against China over the past decade, became a casualty when Kissinger and his boss decided in early 1970 that it was in America's interest to begin seeking an accommodation with China. All of the old equations underlying the United States government's efforts twenty years earlier to persuade the Dalai Lama to flee his country as part of the goal of "doing anything to get in the way of the Chinese" was turned upside down when Kissinger flew to Peking in July 1971 to arrange for Nixon to visit the former enemy capital the following winter.[22] That this initiative was arranged through India's even more traditional enemy, Pakistani President Yahya Khan, who was then engaged in an offensive to suppress dissident elements in East Pakistan, doubled the irony. Politics had again made strange bedfellows.

CHAPTER SEVENTEEN

The United States Disengages

It is a common belief wisdom among Tibetans and some foreign policy commentators that the CIA and the Defense Department were acting at the behest of Henry Kissinger, seeking to ingratiate himself with the Chinese, when the United States withdrew its support for the Tibetans' military efforts to regain control of their country. But the chronology of actual events contradicts this assumption. During their visit to Peking in 1975 Kissinger and his client, President Ford, did make a point of disowning any United States government political sponsorship of the Tibetans. But by then the untidy process of dismantling the Tibetan guerrilla force at Mustang had been in process for several years for primarily operational rather than geopolitical reasons.

By 1968 it had been concluded that, after repeated tries in response to continuous prodding, the Mustang force was not going to be able to relocate inside Tibet. Nor were the cross-border forays against increasingly effective Chinese forces by an aging guerrilla force justifiable. Gyalo Thondup was accordingly requested to prepare a three-year plan for the dismantling and resettlement of this force, which had lost both its reason for existence and its constituency. India's interest in such a capability was by then being served by the Special Frontier Force, which was under its unilateral command. The Tibetans continued to be frustrated by their inability to solve the increasingly pernicious command problems among the tribal leadership at Mustang. The original CIA Far East Division godfathers had been nudged aside by their Near East Division counterparts, who had less proprietary enthusiasm for supporting an operation fathered by the late Desmond FitzGerald. He, in any event, would not have approved an unjustifiable expenditure of lives.

These decisions were therefore already in play in November when the lame-duck Johnson administration, with President-elect Nixon's blessing (and prior to Kissinger's appointment as his special assistant), accepted a Chinese offer to resume the stalemated talks looking for reconciliation between their two countries, which had been going on in Warsaw since 1955. Donald Anderson, who had acted as aide and interpreter for these talks, categorically denies that the subject of American support to the Tibetan resistance was ever raised.[1] Both Ambassador Winston Lord and Ambassador John Holdridge, who prepared the briefing books for Kissinger's and Nixon's subsequent "polo"[2] visits to Peking and sat in on the meetings with the Chinese leaders which superseded the Warsaw talks, said that the United States government's past or present involvement in Tibetan affairs was not a "significant" issue in these talks.[3] Holdridge said that other, more delicate matters were being raised, and both sides were trying to avoid controversial subjects.[4]

Two years before Kissinger and Nixon made it to Peking a resigned but mildly bitter Gyalo Thondup had initiated plans for the withdrawal and resettlement of the 1,800 displaced veterans in Mustang who had lost the mission and occupation that had dominated a significant portion of their adult lives. These men had looked to Gyalo and consequently felt personally let down by him as they were being forced to make new lives in a foreign country with the vanishing prospect of ever returning home. It had been up to him and Lhamo Tsering to devise a program that would disperse and resettle this potentially volatile group of disappointed, unemployed warriors. Their original plan, calling for the men to be shifted in groups of five hundred for three years to the Indian Special Frontier Force, had not panned out. Only a small number had joined their fellow countrymen at the SFF encampment in India. The bulk of the force therefore had to be resettled in Nepal. This turned into an untidy but active process, cobbled together between 1969 and 1974 among the beleaguered Gyalo Thondup and the faithful Lhamo Tsering, an initially purportedly cooperative but increasingly difficult Nepalese government, a reluctant but somewhat resigned and divided Tibetan command at Mustang, and a helpful United Nations High Commission for Refugees.

The untidy and painful process began in 1969, when Gyalo Thondup dispatched three of his Cornell-trained interns under Lhamo Tsering's supervision to Nepal shortly after receiving notice that the Mustang operations were to be terminated. They arrived with twelve looms, which were to be used to establish a Tibetan carpet-weaving industry first manned by the now-unemployed guerrilla warriors. They also were to work with the Mustang commanders in setting up the farms that were to be established in the northern border region around Mustang. The weaving projects moved ahead, but the relocation farms took some time to get moving. The first site, near Dhaulagiri, soon had to be relocated farther south, away from the border. This move was made in response to Nepalese government demands acting under Chinese pressure to ensure that none of these relocated warriors would be tempted to reconvert their plowshares back into swords and resume raids into their homeland. There was also considerable debate among the various camps as to who would resettle, where, and with whom, dating back to old parochial loyalties and unresolved rivalries that had nibbled at the unity of the resistance movement from its inception. This internal dissension was further exacerbated when the tempestuous Gyen Yeshi refused to accept his dismissal as commander of the original force and led a rump group of his townsmen to set up a rival camp south of Mustang. All this slowed the relocation process until 1972. At that time an Austrian named Roman Kohaut, who enjoyed the confidence of the Nepalese government and had a keen knowledge of Chinese sensitivities and vulnerabilities, began a particularly productive tenure in getting these projects set up and operating. Kohaut was apparently acting at the urging of Nepali King Birendra, who did not share his late father's special feeling for the Tibetans and who may also have been more responsive to Chinese pressure.[5]

This combination of UN support, Nepalese interest in getting the Tibetans out of the Mustang peninsula, and Dharamsala's acceptance of the inevitable dismantling of the force resulted in a flurry of new projects employing the former guerrillas and their dependents, including forty-two orphans who were legacies of the Mustang occupation. By this time the twelve hand looms which Gyalo had sent in 1969 had been used to establish carpet and handicraft weaving centers in nearby Pokhara and in Bodinath. After early lean years they developed into a relatively flourishing Tibetan carpet-weaving industry. Another group of entrepreneurs set up and ran the Annapurna Hotel in Pokhara. Others developed a transport business running buses and trucks between Pokhara and Kathmandu. Some drove taxis in Kathmandu.

These projects were all overseen by the steadfast Lhamo Tsering on frequent visits to Nepal during the five years of the dispersal, for which he was poorly rewarded by the Nepalese government. In March 1974 he was arrested by the Nepalese military at, ironically, one of the projects of the peaceful reconstruction process—the veteran-owned Annapurna Hotel in Pokhara. He had gone there to urge the Mustang command to cooperate with the Nepalese demand that they surrender their arms. He was taken to Kathmandu, where he remained in prison for the next seven years. During those years the Nepalese government put the body of the Mustang commander Wangdu, who had been killed while trying to escape into India, on display in a Kathmandu public park. It also began a Nepalese government campaign to portray the Mustang veterans as phony warriors living at a resort-like camp. This was capped by a public show trial in 1979 of Lhamo Tsering and six other jailed Mustang veterans. These included the hero of the ambush who provided the documents that are still considered one of the great hauls of American intelligence. The defendants were all found guilty and sentenced to continued imprisonment in Kathmandu, where they were to remain for seven years.[6]

While Lhamo Tsering was sitting in jail Gyalo Thondup was contacted in Hong Kong by representatives of Deng Xiaoping's post-Mao government looking to find a political solution to the Tibet situation. In March 1979 Gyalo made the first of his twenty-odd trips to Peking over the next twenty-five years. Looking on from Nepal, the king and his government apparently got the message that it was both timely and politically acceptable to close this tragic chapter on the Tibetans' efforts to resist Chinese occupation of their homeland. In 1981 Birendra accordingly responded to an appeal from the Dalai Lama and put Lhamo Tsering and his fellow jail mates on his birthday amnesty list. Lhamo Tsering returned to Dharamsala, where he spent the remaining eighteen years of his life preserving the resistance records and resolving the recurring resettlement problems of the veterans of the Mustang and earlier resistance operations.[7] He was not working as a scribe, but as a participant in demonstrating his countrymen's continuing efforts to prove to the free world Tibet's worthiness as a member.

Political Withdrawal

Reporting to President Nixon on his success in arranging a visit to Peking in February 1972, Kissinger warned, "The process we have now started will send enormous shock waves around the world. It may panic the Soviet Union into sharp hostility. It could shake Japan loose from its heavily American moorings. It will cause a violent upheaval in Taiwan. It will have [a] major impact on our other Asian allies, such as Korea and Thailand. It will increase the already substantial hostility in India." He concluded, "For Asia and for the world we need to demonstrate that we are enlarging the scope of our diplomacy in a way that, far from harming the interests of other countries, should instead prove useful to them. Our dealings, both with the Chinese and others, will require reliability, precision, finesse. If we can master this process, we will have made a revolution."[8]

One of the earliest indications that the Tibetans were to be collateral political casualties of this "revolution" was the postponement of the belated visit by the Dalai Lama to the United States, which had been scheduled for 1970. The working-level officers of the State Department were not privy to the elaborate secret maneuvers that Kissinger was engaged in to finagle an invitation for Nixon to visit Peking. Open moves, such as policy reviews and the easing of restrictions on trade with China at the president's direction, however, made it clear that the possibility for rapprochement with one of America's former prime enemies was being considered. Accordingly when the Dalai Lama's representative inquired about the possibility of his principal having an appointment with the president during a proposed visit, the State Department sent a memorandum to the White House: "[This visit] would be particularly inopportune at a time when we are hoping to develop a useful dialogue with Peking. . . . We are opposed to a visit and believe we should make every effort to forestall it."[9]

The Department's proposed telegram to New Delhi recommending forestalling tactics was too bleak for even those in the White House looking to "make a revolution within the new relationship." General Alexander Haig, the deputy assistant to the president for national security affairs, asked the Department to revise its telegram to make it "somewhat less negative" while retaining the essential guidelines: that the visit occur in 1971 (after the UN General Assembly was over); that it be a private visit; and that the Dalai Lama "would not expect to see officials higher than [UN] Ambassador [Charles] Yost or Under Secretary [Alexis] Johnson: The Dalai Lama and his entourage would be given to understand that we would not expect the question of the political status of Tibet to come up, and if it did, we would go no further than to repeat our present position" (presumably backing undefined self-determination for Tibet).[10]

The embassy in New Delhi apparently thought it appropriate that this genteel snub be delivered personally to Gyalo Thondup, who was still the principal person handling his brother's political relations with the world outside Dharamsala. Accordingly an embassy officer was dispatched on April 22, 1970, to travel the now well-worn path to Darjeeling. It had been nearly two decades since his predecessors had traveled this route to urge the Dalai

Lama to leave Tibet and present his cause to the international community, assuring him that should he go to the United States he would be received there as a "great religious leader and as leader of an autonomous state."[11] Now, however, Thondup was told such a trip would "not be convenient," and "should his future visit eventuate" he would be limited to meeting with officials no higher than senior State Department officials. Furthermore it was "expected that the issue of Tibet's political status would not arise." Thondup "outwardly at least took the message with good grace," providing "in his suave manner" the face-saving rationale that the Dharamsala leadership had merely been considering the possibility of the Dalai Lama's making such a trip. He closed the meeting with the "remark that he was fully aware of the desirability of the U.S. Government developing a dialogue with Peking, but he hoped [the Americans] would keep Tibetan aspirations in mind." The embassy officer "assured him this was the case."[12]

The Tibetans, however, were not quite ready to let Washington off the hook. The following month the Dalai Lama sent a representative to the embassy in New Delhi to revisit the cancellation of the proposed visit, arguing that Washington had misunderstood the Dalai Lama's purpose in traveling to the United States. The emissary contended that because Gyalo had been traveling and was therefore not fully up to date on his brother's plans and intentions, he was not in a position to make it clear that His Holiness's sole purpose in traveling to the United States at this time was for "widening his perspectives on Western philosophy, religion and culture." It would be a purely private and nonpolitical visit. He did not plan to visit Washington, and furthermore, if Washington wished him to avoid the UN, "he would have nothing to do with it." He had planned to travel to Western Europe afterward but felt that the whole program of educating himself on the thought and ways of the West was so interrelated that if the American portion was cancelled the European portion would also have to be scrubbed. These "detoxification" arguments failed to persuade Washington to reconsider its position.[13]

In December 1970 Ernest Gross, who had been acting as the Tibetans' political advisor for over a decade, having shepherded their three successful appeals to the UN and advised them on the drafting of their constitution, renewed their request that the Dalai Lama be permitted to visit the United States in 1971 "solely for the purposes of educational and cultural exchange." Gross explained that the visit would include seminars at the Century Club, where Columbia University had arranged for prominent philosophers, theologians, and educators to participate, and meetings and exhibits at the Asia Society and the Museum of Natural History, which had been scheduled for the visit in

1970. He expressed the "wish to avoid a repetition of last year's unfortunate sequence of events in which the time and effort of many interested and responsible scholars and institutions were frustrated in a wholly unexpected manner by the advice to defer the proposed visit."[14] Gross's effort to resurrect the similar "non-official," but silently officially subsidized first visit by the Dalai Lama to the United States, which had been aborted ten years earlier, when the Tibetans refused to permit him to travel unless he was received as a head of state, was again frustrated. On March 1, 1971, the State Department and the White House initially agreed on the visit, albeit with some foot dragging and reservations.[15] Undersecretary Johnson well knew that his former colleague and old friend Ernie Gross was acting within the original game plan and guidelines under which he had been retained by the United States government a decade earlier to represent the Tibetans and keep their cause alive within the international community. Three months later these guidelines became dramatically outdated when Kissinger made his "secret" trip to Peking.

On July 22, 1971, Secretary of State William Rogers met in the Oval Office with the president and Dr. Kissinger to plan strategy for the new relationship with China that had evolved as a result of Kissinger's "revolutionary" trip. At this meeting the United States government's relationship with the Tibetans in the new era was briefly raised and summarily consigned to limbo.[16] It was Rogers—who had belatedly been made a member of the team—who raised the problem of the Dalai Lama's scheduled visit the next spring and volunteered to take charge of postponing it. The president and Kissinger accepted his offer without discussion. They also accepted his offer to have the United States Information Agency shelve the film on the Chinese occupation of Tibet that they had ready for release. As Kissinger commented, "It [the film] won't do us much good at this point." On December 26 the New York Times reported that the USIA had "conceded" that there was little likelihood, if any, that the thirteen-minute film Man from a Missing Land, portraying the takeover of Tibet and the Dalai Lama's subsequent flight to India, would be released in the near future.

The following month Undersecretary Johnson informed the hosts for the Dalai Lama's repeatedly postponed visit, "[Because] a visit this spring would inevitably have significant political overtones in view of the President's [forthcoming] visit to China . . . we have concluded that a visit should be deferred until next year."[17] In recommending this action Assistant Secretary of State Green wrote, "The Dalai Lama may be somewhat irritated at this further postponement but we believe that understanding the sensitivities involved he will accept it quietly and in good grace."[18] The Tibetans had no choice but to take this latest blow to their political status "with good grace," but the feeling of desertion still rankles among some political champions, such as Gyalo Thondup. The "postponement" turned out to last eight years.

Rogers's and his colleagues' readiness to abandon the Tibetans as they climbed aboard the move to rapprochement with Peking reflected a new era among the State Department's China hands. In their eyes, theirs was not an unprincipled position. Green said, "The Tibet issue was a real problem, because both the Beijing and Taiwan governments regarded it as part of China, something the U.S. had never contested. The U.S. didn't want to make an issue of this as there was nothing that we could do to help the Tibetans except by improving our relations with the Chinese Communists so that we might be in a position to exert pressure on them to moderate their policies toward the Tibetans." He admitted that this was "perhaps a rationalization": "We were sympathetic toward the Tibetans, but unable to do anything practicable about improving their situation. We also did not want to get involved in challenging Beijing over the issue of independence and create another major issue such as the one over Taiwan." He recalled, "No one wanted a repeat of the Li Mi situation."[19] Green's China hand colleague, David Osborn, the consul general in Hong Kong, agreed, writing at the time, "[It] seems an appropriate time to reconsider our position on the Tibet question as a whole. We will, of course, want to continue our interest in the humanitarian aspects of the Tibetan problem but we should consider dropping or discouraging its political exploitation on the assumption that it is an essentially futile exercise."[20]

While this shuffling of policy positions within the State Department was taking place the embassy in New Delhi reported that the "second secretary" of the Dalai Lama's bureau there, Lodi Gyari, had informed them that he had been in contact with the local *Novosti* correspondent, Vladimir Simonov.[21] Gyari said Simonov had approached him to offer his support and advice in forming and staffing the international political support group that Gyari was organizing, and he had arranged for Simonov to meet with the Dalai Lama. The Tibetan pontiff told the Russian that although he was a Communist and he himself was a Buddhist, "they could respect each other as humans," provided the Communists "[did] not hit [the Tibetans]." He had given Simonov no commitment for cooperation, however, and later instructed Gyari that none be given for the present, although the contacts could continue. Gyari said that the Dalai Lama was "fascinated by these offers of Russian support, but was suspicious that any organization formed with their support would end up as a 'Soviet puppet.'" The Dalai Lama must have been intrigued by—and consequently wary of—this latter-day replay of the Great Game the Russians had conducted with his predecessor a half-century before. The Tibetans believed that while the Soviets might support the establishment of a Free Tibet, they might jettison the Dalai Lama when it suited their purposes. Gyari, who was then beginning his long career as a representative of his principal's cause, may well have been passing along a very Tibetan diplomatic suggestion when he added, "The United States country would, of course, not think of such a breach of trust."[22]

Peripheral References

Prior to his first "secret" visit to Peking in July 1971,[23] Kissinger prepared a scope paper outlining his approach to, objectives for, and expectations from this "revolutionary" event. He acknowledged that the summit meeting between Nixon and the Chinese leaders that he was going to China to arrange would "constitute spectacular proof of China's having arrived at great power status, [and] would also gratify the 'Middle Kingdom' instincts which the Chinese leaders of today unquestionably share with their predecessors." He predicted, "They will treat the President's visit—and for that matter, my own—as being in the nature of a foreign 'imperialist' barbarian bringing tribute from the fringes of world society to those who are truly at the center of the true culture, and derive a great sense of personal, national and ideological pride thereby." He did expect the Chinese to be prepared to pay a price for this new status and occasion, recalling, "In Imperial times those who brought tribute to Peking were customarily rewarded with gifts which exceeded the original tribute in value."[24]

> Within this framework, I will want [and presumably demand]:
> —Indications firm enough to be taken as assurances that the Chinese will use their influence on the North Vietnamese to move them toward a peaceful and acceptable settlement of the Vietnam war.
> —A Sino-U.S. *modus vivendi* on the Taiwan situation which will permit our relations with Peking to develop while we at the same time retain our diplomatic ties and mutual defense treaty with the ROC.
> —Continuation of Sino-U.S. relations in some format amounting to direct contacts in which matters of mutual interest can be discussed, e.g. arms control, expanded trade and travel, reduction in tensions in East and Southeast Asia, etc. This could include sending a U.S. representative to Peking to work out details of a summit.
> —An appreciation by the Chinese of how they view the Soviet role in world affairs and how this relates to Soviet military capabilities.

Briefing congressional leaders following the disclosure of Kissinger's trip, Nixon stated that it had been his belief for many years that any structure of international relationships that would make a more stable and enduring peace in the world "must include the constructive participation of China and its talented and energetic 750 million people": "Thus a major goal from the outset of my Administration has been to launch a serious dialogue with Peking."[25]

This agenda had no place for issues such as Tibet, to which there were to be only peripheral references in the negotiations that followed. In his scope paper Kissinger wrote, "It is not the policy of the U.S. to stir up anti-Chinese sentiment in India," a significant shift in objectives from those prevailing when the United States government began its relationship with the Tibetans two decades earlier.

At their initial meeting in Peking on July 9, 1971, Zhou Enlai did raise the question of possible CIA or Pentagon involvement in the activities of the Taiwan Independence Movement (TIM) in conducting anti-PRC demonstrations at the UN in New York. Kissinger admitted that one of the TIM leaders, Peng Meng-min, had been a student of his fifteen years ago, but that neither he nor the CIA had anything to do with Peng or the TIM. He expanded, "There is an exaggerated opinion in the minds of people in many parts of the world about the abilities of the CIA. The only two countries where there have been revolutions in Asia in the last ten years [were] where we had no CIA: Indonesia [the Agency's abortive coup attempt against Sukarno had occurred thirteen years before] and Cambodia. For your part you might call these revolutions 'counter revolutions.' There was no CIA [involvement,] unbelievable as that may sound to you." When Zhou reaffirmed that he attached "importance to Kissinger's assertion that the U.S. Government and President [did] not and [would] not support the so-called Independence Movement of Taiwan," Kissinger wriggled a bit, saying, "[I cannot] absolutely exclude, again speaking totally frankly, that some office does something unauthorized sometimes." He declared, "If the President and Chairman Mao come to an understanding, then it's my job to enforce the bureaucracy" and reasserted that there would be no support for the TIM.[26]

When Kissinger returned to Peking three months later to make the final arrangements for Nixon's visit, Zhou, apparently prompted by anti-PRC demonstrations at the UN, again raised the subject of possible CIA backing of the TIM. Zhou was not prepared to let Kissinger off with a promise to investigate any evidence of such involvement that Zhou provided. He complained, "They [the CIA] have activities throughout the world. . . . People throughout the world are most unhappy about [the CIA] and that is why they are not welcome. Because after the second World War, the U.S. is taking a hand in all kinds of affairs throughout the world and this organization had a role to play. . . . The CIA thought they had the right to look into everything. The result of this is causing disharmony in the world." Zhou did observe, "It is possible that [American intelligence] activities in the China mainland are comparatively less but not perhaps nonexistent." This seems to have been a surprisingly delicate reproach for the well-publicized CIA involvement in resistance efforts in Tibet and elsewhere on the mainland.

In response Kissinger sputtered, "I am not sure it's in our interest to reassure you completely but I will. First, you said, what will CIA agents do if they don't make revolution somewhere? Most write long, incomprehensible reports and [do] not make revolution. They are mostly from Yale and they don't have the people [to conduct revolutions.]" Zhou responded that the "reports" that Kissinger referred to were in fact "intelligence": "While you use the word revolution, we say subversion." This prompted Kissinger to affirm, "It's not our policy to subvert the government of the People's Republic of China or its policy." Zhou then cited his escape from a plot to assassinate him on his way to the Bandung Conference in 1955 by fortuitously changing his flight reservations at the last minute. He delicately implicated—without directly accusing—the CIA and the Chinese Nationalist government as the ones responsible for planning his demise. "Such adventurous acts are not a good practice, regardless of the motives behind it, whether it is revolutionary or of a saboteur nature. I say these not as superfluous words but to explain how people of the world think of the CIA. As for we ourselves, we are not very much excited by the CIA. Maybe indirectly. I didn't know Dr. Kissinger was the chairman of the committee."[27] Zhou the mandarin was diplomatically warning that he would from now on hold his new interlocutor personally responsible for any future covert meddling in the Middle Kingdom.

The other issue that touched indirectly on the Tibetans was the India-Pakistan War, which was then moving toward a crisis. By the time Peking accepted Nixon's offer to send an emissary to China, Pakistani President Yahya Khan, who was acting as go-between in setting up this "revolutionary" diplomatic event, had embarked on the ill-fated invasion of East Pakistan to suppress the growing move to independence there. Kissinger notes in his memoirs that he and Nixon "faced a dilemma":

> The United States could not condone a brutal military suppression in which thousands of civilians were killed and from which millions fled from East Pakistan to India for safety. There was no doubt about the strong-arm

tactics of the Pakistani military. But Pakistan was our sole channel to China; once it was closed off it would take months to make alternative arrangements.[28] The issue hit Washington, moreover, in the midst of another of the cyclic upheavals over Vietnam. A massive campaign of disobedience was planned for May 1. To some of our critics our silence over Pakistan—the reason for which we could not explain—became another symptom of the general moral insensitivity of their government. They could not accept that it might be torn between conflicting imperatives; some had a vested interest in undermining their government's standing on whatever issue came to hand in the belief that this would collapse our effort in Vietnam. The Administration reacted in the same ungenerous spirit; there was some merit in the charge of moral insensitivity. Nixon ordered our Consul General [whose staff had signed a petition of protest over Washington's inaction] transferred from Dacca; he ridiculed Keating [the ambassador in New Delhi] for "having been taken over by the Indians." A tragic victim of the war in Vietnam was the possibility of rational debate over foreign policy.[29]

It was against this backdrop that Zhou charged, "[The] turmoil in East Pakistan in a very great way is due to India." Noting that "the so-called Government of Bangla Desh set up its headquarters in India," he asked, "Isn't this subversion of the Pakistani Government?"[30] When his guest protested, "The Prime Minister doesn't think we [the United States] are cooperating with this, does he?," Zhou did not hasten to reassure him. He said merely, "[I] would not like to draw a conclusion on that at present, but simply wanted to point out the phenomenon. We cannot but pay attention to this." Kissinger declared that the United States government had not given any military assistance of any kind to India since 1965: "And if India takes military action in East Pakistan we would strongly and publicly disapprove of it." There is no indication that India's use of the Tibetan members of the Special Frontier Force trained and equipped by the CIA as part of the successful guerrilla forces in East Pakistan was discussed. As it seems unlikely that Zhou was demonstrating unusual sensitivity toward his guest, and equally unlikely that the Chinese were unaware of the Tibetans' role as the "phantoms of Chittagong," this reticence remains unexplained.

In a skull session in the Oval Office on August 11, 1971, Kissinger reported that he had breakfasted with an old friend, a professor of Chinese history at Harvard. He said that this man, presumably John King Fairbank, "a left wing Democrat and a friend of Ted Kennedy, very much support[ed]" the initiative to normalize relations with China. The professor had warned, "[If you don't] play the Pakistan thing right [presumably the question whether to recognize the new government in Dacca] the Chinese will go up the wall. . . . They will see it as an example of the principle of self-determination being established and fear [we] may use it for Taiwan and Tibet."[31]

In late November Kissinger did give Huang Hua, the recently arrived Chinese representative to the United Nations, a once-over-lightly briefing on the extent and scope of the Indian army units and guerrilla forces then conducting operations in East Pakistan, including the ongoing operations in Chittagong: "As I remember, two Indian brigades are attacking in this area. The Indians claim they are guerrillas, and the Pakistanis claim they are Indian troops. Whoever they are, it is either the Indian Army or the best-equipped guerrilla force that has appeared in recent years."[32] If Kissinger knew that these forces contained a sizable number of Tibetans belonging to the Special Frontier Force trained and equipped by the CIA, he did not share this information with the ambassador.

As part of another *tour d'horizon* briefing which Kissinger was giving Huang Hua a year later he slipped in, apropos of nothing, "We have some very sensitive intelligence information in which a very senior Indian official made the following comment: 'China should not forget that the Tibetan question has not been resolved and that dissident movements in this vast plateau are still numerous. The refugees we have welcomed from these icy and inhospitable highlands adjust poorly to the heat of the large tropical valleys of India.' This is an extremely sensitive comment of a very high Indian official." The apparently perplexed Chinese ambassador's only comment was "That is like the language of a writer."[33] Kissinger provided no further elaboration or discussion.

In a preparatory briefing session prior to his trip to the Imperial City Nixon asked Kissinger what he should say if his Chinese hosts asked what position the United States government was taking on the recognition of the new state of Bangladesh. Kissinger readily endorsed Nixon's inclination to say it was premature to talk about the issue. He counseled that at this point the Chinese "would take violent exception to such action by the U.S. Government because of the parallels between Tibet and Manchukuo."[34]

It was becoming increasingly apparent that the tripartite alliance of the previous decade among the Americans and the Tibetans and their Indian hosts was a thing of the past. A month later Nixon was being toasted at dinner in Peking by Zhou Enlai for "reaching the Great Wall and becoming a great man." This was the feat Mao had challenged his fellow Communists to achieve in a poem written when they were passing through Tibetan territory on their way to the North four decades earlier.[35] Nixon had met with both Mao and Zhou and had made a point of shaking hands with Zhou in an effort to cauterize this long-standing grievance, dating from John Foster Dulles's publicized refusal to do so at the Geneva conference eighteen years before. Nixon admitted to Zhou that "at that time his views were similar to those of Mr. Dulles, but the world ha[d] changed since then."[36]

In further evidence of this new world, Richard Fecteau, a CIA officer who had been captured in an unsuccessful effort to rescue a Chinese agent dispatched to collect intelligence on the Chinese Communist forces in Manchuria in 1952, was released in advance of Nixon's visit.[37] Upon Nixon's return to Washington, the National Zoological Park in Washington sent two musk oxen to Peking in exchange for the two pandas that the Chinese were sending as a gesture of friendship. In June Congressmen Hale Boggs and Gerald Ford led a delegation on behalf of the House of Representatives "to learn as much as possible about China . . . and to contribute to better relations between [the] two countries, an objective not only mutually advantageous to the Chinese and American peoples, but also contributory to the relaxation of tensions throughout Asia and the world." They toured Canton, Shanghai, Peking, and Shenyang on China's East Coast, but no towns or cities in western China, except those on the way to the Great Wall, and none in the Chinese interior or Tibet. Boggs and Ford were impressed by the general economic well-being of the Chinese people and their apparent willingness to accept the absence of political liberty as the price of attaining these material benefits. They reported, "We did not detect nor did we sense any real dissent."[38]

The following February Kissinger added Hanoi to his precedent-shattering visits to former enemy capitals. He went there in an effort to expedite the implementation of the recently signed peace accord in Paris, which he and Nixon hoped would provide an acceptable way out of the Vietnam War. In an assessment of Hanoi's motives in a meeting requested by Kissinger, the CIA's Vietnam pundit George Carver noted that the North Vietnamese would derive the same satisfaction that his Chinese hosts had enjoyed by "having the barbarian chiefs come to pay tribute to the celestial emperor at the seat of civilization."[39] Although Kissinger was willing to make the journey to this new Communist Imperial City, the peace he sought was not to be had—at least for another two years.

Meanwhile Washington and Peking were consolidating their new relationship by establishing liaison offices in each other's capitals. On July 6, 1973, Nixon assured the newly appointed Chinese representative, Huang Zen, that any agreement the United States made with Leonid Brezhnev, the general secretary of the Communist Party of the Soviet Union, would not be "in derogation of [America's] relations with China." He also instructed Kissinger to make the point in a press briefing that an attack on China (presumably by the USSR) would endanger international peace and security. He explained, "We had determined on the basis of the security interests of the U.S. that the PRC should be free, independent and secure."[40] These tectonic shifts in the world order made the Tibetans even more irrelevant to the realpolitik interests of their former sponsors.

It wasn't until the summer of 1974 that the Chinese government formally raised the subject of Tibet and its relationship with the United States. On July 30 the counselor of the PRC's Liaison Office called on his counterpart at the State Department with a copy of a publication from the Office of Tibet, located at 801 Second Avenue in New York. The Chinese diplomat complained that this office described itself as the "representative organization of the Dalai Lama," and the publication contained "slanders towards the People's Republic of China and the Chinese people." He therefore was under instruction to say that this situation was "absolutely intolerable" and to "demand an explanation and measures to abolish the so-called Office of Tibet." Oscar Armstrong, the director of the Department's office in charge of liaison with the Chinese, said he had no immediate comment but would get back to the Chinese diplomat when he had more information on the subject. After five more minutes of "casual and amiable conversation," the protesting Chinese diplomat departed.[41]

The Office of Tibet had been operating since the Dalai Lama's government set it up eleven years earlier, with the guidance of Ernest Gross, as part of the program to keep the Tibetan cause alive within the international community. It had been most recently operating under the direction of a very able younger member of the Dalai Lama's new government, Phuntso Thonden, who in addition to working the UN circuit and the New York cultural and educational community had overseen the establishment of the first Tibetan restaurant in New York.

Washington made a modest effort to accommodate its difficult new ally's demand by sending Ernest Gross to ask Gyalo Thondup to close the office. Thondup had recently received the final payment of the monthly subsidy which the United States government had been paying for the maintenance of the Dalai Lama since 1959. He considered Washington's asking him to close the New York office to be the final act of betrayal by his former patrons. Thonden recalls that Gyalo "blew up" like the signature dish of the upper East Side restaurant where they were holding their meeting, a soup called "bombing Shanghai" which exploded when hot rice was poured into it. He told Gross, who had little heart for the message he was delivering, "You can put Mr Thondup in jail, but we are not going to close down."[42]

After Gross's unsuccessful effort to persuade the Tibetans to close the office, Washington was apparently prepared to rest on the argument that there was no legal way to force their former wards to terminate an enterprise it had helped to create and maintain. The Chinese government, now under Deng Xiaoping, revived the complaint a year later, three days prior to a visit by Secretary of State Kissinger, issuing a statement denouncing the United States government's "connivance at and support to the Tibetan traitors' activities in the United States." In a conversation with Assistant Secretary Philip Habib, Kissinger said, "The Chinese are screaming about the Tibetan thing. . . . I know we are brilliant but why was that necessary?"[43] Habib reminded Kissinger that he had been informed that the Chinese had revived their protest after refusing to accept the State Department's response that there were no legal grounds to force the Tibetans to close the office. The testy secretary replied, "I don't get to look at every paper that comes up here." The two then decided it "would be best to duck this issue." Habib suggested, "We [should] try to slide it off, but we should say nothing if they [the Chinese] will let it lie. . . . We have before accepted that Tibet is under Chinese control but that isn't acceptable to them now. Our relationship with the Dalai Lama makes it hard. We are phasing out of that now though."[44]

Accordingly the State Department spokesman announced the next day that the Chinese complaint "was apparently based on a misunderstanding of the American political system," adding, "None of our policies has a premise that Tibet is not part of China."[45] In a briefing paper prepared for Kissinger's use on the trip he was making to Peking, Winston Lord wrote, "[The] Chinese may interpret our carefully-worded statement as meaning that the U.S. recognizes Tibet as part of China. We need not argue that interpretation, but before explicitly accepting it [we] should consider its implications for our relations with India."[46]

Deng was apparently ready to give Washington a pass on the issue of Tibet. He made the point in a conversation on November 3, 1974, with George H. W. Bush, who was then chief of the American Liaison Office in Peking, that India "posed no military threat to China": "The only avenue of attack lies across Tibet, which has a vast land area and extremely thin air." He recalled "passing through a corner of Tibet on the Long March": "You simply cannot get used to the thin air. In climbing every step is a trial."[47] Deng had almost the same dialogue with Kissinger later that month. He seemed determined to emphasize the strategic insignificance of Tibet, again claiming that it had no air, a point the secretary deflected with a bit of heavy humor about the danger of drinking mai tai in such a place.[48]

Disavowal

In briefing his new boss on his first trip to Peking as president, Kissinger warned Gerald Ford, "Our relationship with China has cooled." He attributed this to "the initial impact of Watergate [Nixon had resigned on August 9, 1974] and the first instances of Congressional hobbling of Executive authority in foreign affairs; the fading authority of Zhou Enlai, the chief architect of the American opening; [America's] goofs in sending a high-level Ambassador to Taiwan and opening two new Chinese Nationalist consulates in the U.S. shortly after [his] November 1973 trip to Peking and its positive communiqués which included a reasonable Chinese formulation on Taiwan."[49] Kissinger also admitted, "[My] going to China in November 1974 right from your summit meeting and the SALT breakthrough with Brezhnev in Vladivostok probably raised Chinese historical and ideological hackles."[50]

Kissinger had good reason to lower Ford's expectations of a warm welcome or any major diplomatic achievements in Peking. On a visit there in October 1975 to plan for his boss's forthcoming trip Kissinger had received a chilly reception and a scornful denunciation by Deng of the policy of détente as one of weakness and the Helsinki Accords produced by the European "Insecurity" Conference, "with their smell of Munich in 1938." Furthermore the dramatic photographs distributed worldwide of the American helicopters evacuating the ambassador and his remnant staff from the roof of the American embassy in Saigon that spring documented the events that further depreciated the international prestige of the prospective visitors. Ford also had good reasons prompted by domestic politics to have second thoughts about the trip. Ronald Reagan, who was threatening to challenge Ford for the Republican nomination, was denouncing both détente and Ford's continued relations with Peking at the expense of Taiwan. Senator Barry Goldwater suggested that if Ford was going to visit Peking he also should visit Taipei, and threatened to switch his support to Reagan in the coming election if Ford visited China. But there was no good way for Ford to climb down without admitting the bankruptcy of what had been one of the showpieces of his predecessor's foreign policy.

So the show went on the road, but Ford was carrying a very empty bag of offerings to his host Deng Xiaoping and his moribund senior principals. When Kissinger met with Mao during his October visit to obtain this invitation to the Middle Kingdom for Ford, the chairman, after announcing that he "had already received an invitation from God," had said he "would be going to Heaven soon." However, Mao was plainly still very much occupied and involved in the affairs of the world he was leaving behind. He bluntly pointed out, "Yesterday, during your quarrel with the Vice Premier [Deng], you said the U.S. asked nothing of China and China asked nothing of the U.S. As I see it, this [is] partially right and partially wrong. The small issue is Taiwan, the big issue is the world." After a fit of coughing, Mao asked, "If neither side had anything to ask from the other, why would you be coming to Beijing?[51] Why would we want to receive you and the President?"[52]

After considerable small delays and quibbling over timing and the usual approved communiqué Kissinger and Ford were finally permitted to go to Beijing in early December. The political climate in both capitals did not augur well for any sort of latter-day Entente Cordiale. Kissinger had arrived back in Washington after his unpromising planning visit in time for the Halloween Massacre. In this major cabinet shuffle, he had been relieved of his dual role in foreign policy. Although Kissinger retained his position as secretary of state, Brent Scowcroft was given his other post of national security advisor, with its daily direct access to the president.

In Beijing Mao had meanwhile become engaged in a campaign against Deng's domestic policies, which undermined the authority of the man he had anointed to fill the mediator role that the ailing Zhou Enlai was no longer able to carry out. The American visitors appear either to have been unaware of or to have chosen to ignore the convolutions between the Gang of Four, led by Mao's wife, and the supporters of Deng, who were attempting to restore some political equilibrium to a China struggling to emerge from the final upheavals of the Cultural Revolution. This seeming disregard for the events which had been convulsing the political, economic, and social life of China for the past decade was apparent in the planning and briefing papers for the meetings of both Nixon and Ford with the Chinese leaders. It seems strange for these latter-day Talleyrands not to have at least attempted to exert some leverage from the vulnerability of Mao and his chief aides that in many ways equaled the political disadvantage the American leaders felt they were suffering from in December 1975.

When this conclave of politically and physically ailing leaders grudgingly took place in December 1975 it was with a minimum of expectations on both sides. Ford was granted an audience with Mao, which opened with some heavy lifting concerning Kissinger's intervention in Mao's "invitation from

God." Mao objected that Kissinger, "an atheist," was "undermining [Mao's] relations with God" by urging him to reject this invitation. After a perfunctory *tour d'horizon* discussion of events on the Iberian peninsula and Angola, Mao said, "Good," then called in the photographers to record the historic event. The official New China News Agency issued a press release describing the meeting: "After shaking hands with each of the American guests, Chairman Mao had earnest and significant discussions with President Ford on wide-ranging issues in a friendly atmosphere."[53]

In their lengthier conversations Deng and Ford talked past each other on a final settlement of the Taiwan issue. Deng maintained his position that this was an issue that "belong[ed] to the internal affairs of China" and brushed aside Ford's reaffirmation that any solution should be a peaceful one. "In his conversation with the Doctor [Kissinger] Chairman Mao mentioned five years, ten years, 20 years, 100 years, while the Doctor continued stressing the point that 'you had mentioned 100 years' [Laughter]. So I think that is about all for that question."[54]

A rather perfunctory exchange between Deng and Ford on the merits of increased trade and educational, cultural, and scientific exchanges was followed by Deng's report on and Ford's expression of appreciation for Chinese efforts to locate and return the ashes of Americans whose planes had been downed over China and to determine the status of other American MIAs. Kissinger offered to intervene in the process of obtaining the release of computers which the Chinese wanted. Deng then observed that the solving of such specific issues, while leaving some unresolved, "[would] not be of great effect to [their] general relations." The transcript notes that at this remark "the Chinese all laugh[ed]."

Disavowal of the Tibetans

In this atmosphere of forced amiability and mutual reassurances Deng then said, "There are also many small issues . . . between us that remain unresolved . . . for instance, the question of the Dalai Lama having set up a small office in your country. And during my discussions with some of your visitors, I said that was like chicken feathers and onion skin. [Laughter] Do you have such an expression?" George Bush joined the locker room exchange, replying, "We have an impolite one." It is not clear that Deng understood Bush's earthy reference, but he went on to explain, "In Chinese it means something of very little weight. Feathers are very light."

President Ford then intervened: "Let me assure you, Mr Vice Premier, that we oppose and do not support any [United States] governmental action as far as Tibet is concerned." Deng was not quite ready to let Ford off the hook, replying, "Things might be easier if you refused them visas." In response to Ford's reiteration that the granting of visas to the Tibetans staffing the Office of Tibet and the members of their visiting dance troupes had been done privately, Deng, with a spit into his spittoon, dismissed the issue, saying, "It is not so important." Kissinger then entered the exchange with one of his heavy humor sallies intended to lighten tensions: "When they [the Tibetans] become Communists, then we will have a legal basis to refuse them visas."

But Deng hadn't finished his lecture: "[The] Palace of Culture of Various Nationalities, which I pointed out to you in the car and which your daughter visited, was built for the Dalai Lama. And in 1959 [1954?], when the Dalai Lama came to Peking, he stayed there for one period. After he went back to Tibet he staged a rebellion and left, fled the country. At that time actually it was possible for us to have stopped him leaving the country. It was entirely within our capacity to stop him from leaving. But Chairman Mao said it is better to let him go. [The Chinese all laugh.]" No one questioned whether their laughter was provoked by this rewrite of history or the chairman's casual dismissal of a troublesome priest. Deng finished by describing the progress made in Tibet, where the standard of living under Chinese control was much higher than before and "in comparison to other areas of China [could not] be considered very low." Having made his case and staked out his position on past and present American actions concerning Tibet, Deng declared, "[These are] all the bilateral issues we can think of."

Ford agreed that the bilateral and international issues had been covered in depth, but he then inexplicably apparently felt compelled to say, "We do not approve of the actions that the Indians are taking as far as Tibet is concerned." Without pinning Ford down as to which "actions" he was referring to, Deng dismissed the subject, claiming, "We do not pay much attention to that because it is of no use. And to put it in more explicit terms, the Dalai Lama is now a burden on India. [The Chinese laugh.] If he should want to come back to Tibet, we might even welcome him back for a short visit. And perhaps he can see what changes have been wrought by the serfs that he had so cruelly ruled." This provoked another exchange of heavy humor between the two. To Ford's observation "I do not think you want to relieve India of any extra burdens than it has," Deng agreed, "Let them carry it for 100 years. We will think about it after that. The Dalai Lama must be in his 30's, at the most 40. He was very young at that [?] time. He might still live another 60 years to 100. So let India carry that burden for another 60 years at least."

Finally, in response to Deng's claims to the advances being made in Tibet in the Dalai Lama's absence, Ford reaffirmed that "he should stay in India." With this snapping of the towels in the club locker room, the executive branch of the United States government disavowed a quarter of a century's ties with the Tibetans and a decade of collaboration with the Indians.

Although Ford's repudiation of the Tibetans in an effort to appease the Chinese might have seemed tactically adroit, it was out of step with history as it was unfolding at that time. The American president had gone to Beijing knowing that Deng was piqued by his having signed the Helsinki Accords at the Conference on Security and Cooperation in Europe that past summer. The leaders of thirty-three other states, including Brezhnev, had also signed. Ironically Brezhnev's expectation of receiving favorable publicity for agreeing to the final settlement of the postwar boundaries was being fulfilled, but was also producing an unwanted bounty. The Helsinki Accords became a manifesto of the dissident and liberal movement, spawning a great revival of support for human rights and opposition to Communism, and the Helsinki watch groups established under the Accords kept opposition alive throughout the Soviet Union. The aging and disunited Chinese leaders were well aware—and highly critical—of the resistance potential their former Communist ally was courting. Ford's jettisoning of the Tibetans, while providing comfortable reassurance for the Chinese decision not to take any needless risks with regard to human rights, was not to provide lasting respite from this troublesome priest and his people.

The Dalai Lama Takes Stock

As the year 1975 ended the Dalai Lama must have been painfully aware that he, his people, and their country were standing alone. His principal patrons, who had greeted his flight from Lhasa sixteen years earlier with huzzahs, were now reluctant to receive him in their capitals, and supporting his subjects so they could militarily challenge the government that had forced them into exile no longer served their purposes. Three United Nations resolutions sympathetic to their cause passed during the previous decade had bolstered his country's international status but still left him and his people guests in their neighbor's country.

"When the going gets tough the tough get going" is an apt description of the Dalai Lama's personality and consequent response. He could take satisfaction that the actions he had initiated soon after his arrival in exile sixteen years before to conceive and promote self-government among his followers were now embedded in a substantive political structure. He also realized that, although he deplored violence and the use of arms, his constituency included significant numbers who were willing to risk their lives to fight for him and the way of life he personified—and their actions had won important support within the international community. He also acknowledged that a substantial portion of the resistance effort had been led and composed of Tibetans from outside what now constituted the Tibetan Autonomous Region. Any political settlement with their Chinese occupiers must take account of and include these people. This was the basic premise of the "Middle Way" proposal launched at Strasbourg three years later.

There was a more immediate premium to be derived as a side effect from the snubbing by his former principal sponsor. It obliged the Dalai Lama to acquire new supporters. He and his people were no longer America's protégés, but free, in fact forced to seek wider patronage. Their involuntary new status, while immediately disturbing, did leave potential new benefactors free to support the Tibetan leader and his cause without being vulnerable to accusations that they had become America's lackeys. As for the Dalai Lama, this imposed "freedom" obliged him to become an even more active participant in the worldly affairs of his people. By then he was forty years old and had spent over half his life confronting and largely succeeding in establishing Tibet's unique claim on the conscience of the international community. He was no longer the mythical high priest of a remote mountain kingdom presiding over a quaint populace of chanting monks and herdsmen, but the very present leader of a people and a way of life whose preservation presented an international obligation for which he was developing the reputation, the means, and the right to claim on his own. Kundun, "the Presence," had moved onto the world stage.

This new concatenation of political forces and its implications for the Tibetans was compounded by the dramatic events occurring on the Chinese political scene, which was reeling from the upheaval of the Cultural Revolution and the passing of the Old Guard. Zhou Enlai died in January 1976, and the sidelining of his hoped-for successor, Deng Xiaoping, was followed by the suppression of the mourning ceremonies in Tiananmen Square for Zhou, which had been converted into a protest against Deng's exclusion. One of Mao's last acts was to approve the banishment of Deng. Then, on September 9, despite the mantras spoken by millions for so many years, the Supreme Head died. It was to be the beginning of a new era with new challenges for achieving a peaceful settlement of the future of Tibet, which continues to elude closure four decades later.

CHAPTER EIGHTEEN

Rescue from Limbo

The Tibetans, though not officially disowned, were initially treated
like embarrassing relatives by the team that was elected to replace Ford and his Chinese-courting secretary of state. Soon
after he arrived in the White House Carter ordered his national
security staff to undertake a crash review of the commitments
the previous occupants had made to the Chinese. This review,
according to Patrick Tyler, was ordered after Secretary of State
Cyrus Vance was forced to admit his ignorance on a nationwide
TV talk show of a reported pledge made by Nixon and Kissinger to the Chinese to normalize relations during Nixon's second term.[1]

Mike Oksenberg, of the national security staff, and Richard
Holbrooke, the assistant secretary of state for East Asian and Pacific affairs, immediately devoted themselves to reviewing the
scattered records of secret diplomacy. They had been the subject
of a custody fight among the lawyers for the Nixon estate, the
Watergate prosecutors, the National Archives, and the files that
the recently retired Ford had taken home to Michigan. Oksenberg
flew to Ann Arbor, where Ford gave him a transcript of his conversation with Mao in 1975, in which he committed the United States
to breaking relations with Taiwan as part of the normalization
formula. Oksenberg consequently recommended that the president

authorize Secretary Vance to reaffirm these assurances to the Chinese. His boss, National Security Advisor Zbigniew Brzezinski, endorsed the recommendation, and Carter approved it and forwarded it to his annoyed secretary of state. Vance admonished Brzezinski not to make policy recommendations without clearing them first with him, and normalization was put on hold. This was the beginning of a contest between Vance and Brzezinski, a replay of the Kissinger-Rogers duel over authority, policy, and style concerning when and how to play the China and Soviet cards.

The Tibetans got lost temporarily in the shuffle of Washington's search for a new relationship with Beijing. This was ironic in light of the heightened emphasis on human rights in American foreign policy that had been heralded as one of the hallmarks of the new administration. Samuel Huntington recalled that at a meeting in 1976 with a small group of academicians headed by Brzezinski, who were supporting Carter's campaign, Carter asked for their help in preparing speeches on three subjects that were of particular interest to him stemming from his personal background and experience as an engineer, in nuclear weapons; as a peanut farmer, in global food problems; and as a social activist, in human rights.[2] Huntington wrote the requested speech on human rights, which Carter gave during the campaign at a B'nai B'rith national convention on September 8, 1976. Carter charged that President Ford and his advisors had "rationalized that there [was] little room for morality in foreign affairs and that [the United States] must put self-interest above principle."[3] This produced a vehement rebuttal at the time from Ford, who might well later have reason to accuse his successor of a certain shading as far as the Chinese were concerned. While taking a strong stand against human rights violations in the Soviet Union, the Carter White House was disposed to give Deng Xiaoping a pass in the interests of reaching an accommodation as he struggled to return from the political exile to which the dying Mao had consigned him. This tolerance left little room or inclination among the new team to revive interest in the Tibetans, whom Ford and Kissinger had gone out of their way to renounce.

The tricky problem of how the United States was to disengage from its past allegiance and continuing commitments to the Nationalist government on Taiwan provided a further complication in supporting the Tibetans and the associated issue of their contested political status. The new working relationship between the American and Chinese intelligence services added another factor to the equation. Reviving old associations with the Tibetans and reminders of past American support to their efforts to resist Chinese control of their country did not fit in the new political landscape.

The Dalai Lama Goes to Washington

When the Tibetans tested the attitude of the new White House occupants toward their cause they received a cool response. In October 1977 Tenzin Tethong, the Dalai Lama's personal representative in the United States, wrote the State Department from the Office of Tibet in New York, which had survived Beijing's demands for its closure, to inquire if it would be possible for the Dalai Lama to make his long postponed visit to the United States. By this time Secretary Vance had made what turned out to be an unproductive trip to Beijing. The new administration, however, was still interested in developing its own relationship with Deng Xiaoping, who was then engaged in reestablishing his position of authority. On October 23 the *New York Times* reported that a "source close to the issue said that the State Department was hoping that the [Tibetan] inquiry would be withdrawn because the Department did not feel the time was appropriate for a visit [from the Dalai Lama] but did not want to give a formal negative reply." This time the Tibetans let Washington off the hook by not publicly pressing the issue, and the brush-off went unpublicized.[4]

It was another two years before Washington found it acceptable for the Dalai Lama to make his long postponed first visit to the United States. On September 3, 1979, the forty-four-year-old Tibetan arrived at Kennedy International Airport to spend what the *New York Times* reported to be "49 days in the United States advancing the cause of an independent Tibet."[5] Although a week later the *Times'* headline was "The Dalai Lama Talks about Religion, Not Politics, on a 2-Day Visit to Washington," the Tibetan leader was able to reinstate his claim to both official and private attention during those seven weeks. This development was the consequence of one of those fortuitous combinations of persons located in positions to promote the cause of the Dalai Lama and his people which have helped the cause to survive as an issue in American foreign relations ever since.

The Geshe La Group

The person most immediately responsible for getting the Dalai Lama into the United States in 1979 was a young North Carolinian named Joel Mc-Cleary. While an undergraduate at Harvard, he and a fellow student interested in Zen Buddhism, Joshua Cutler, were introduced by Robert Thurman to Geshe Wangyal.[6] Geshe La was a Kalmyk monk whom the Dalai Lama's mother had sent to the American consulate in Calcutta in 1951 to enlist help in her unsuccessful efforts to persuade the Dalai Lama to leave Tibet rather than rule under the Chinese. Geshe La had subsequently emigrated to the United States, where he formed his own monastery in Freewood Acres, New Jersey. There Thurman, having left Harvard, studied under him to become a Buddhist monk. The persistent Thurman subsequently persuaded his spiritual mentor to take him to Dharamsala to continue his training under the Dalai Lama, who ordained him as a Buddhist monk in 1965.[7] Thurman later returned to the United States, married, and left the monkhood to return to Harvard, where he passed McCleary along to Geshe La. During this same period another Harvard dropout, Jeffrey Hopkins, had become "hooked" on Buddhism and spent six years on and off in Geshe La's monastery studying the Tibetan language and Buddhist scriptures. Consequently this third member of the Thurman-McCleary circuit acted as interpreter for the Dalai Lama when he made his first visit to the United States in 1979. He performed this service for the next ten years when the Tibetan pontiff traveled abroad. To all three, the worldly wise Geshe La, who knew what it was like for religious persons to live under a Stalinist regime, had given the same advice, "This is not the age for mountains, but for politics," an adage he practiced himself.[8] In the late 1950s and early 1960s he frequently went to Washington to assist in the instruction of members of the Tibetan resistance that the CIA was training and dropping into Tibet and to translate the messages they transmitted from there using the telecodes that he had devised.[9]

In 1979 McCleary was in the best position to implement Geshe La's advice to focus on politics, not mountains. Two years before, at age twenty-eight, he had become the youngest Democratic Party national treasurer, and as a protégé of Hamilton Jordan he was deputy assistant to the president for political affairs under Jimmy Carter. Throughout his successful involvement in high-level American politics McCleary had retained his deep interest in Buddhism as taught and practiced by Geshe La and their supreme mentor, the Dalai Lama. In 1979 he was able to bring together his participation in these two disparate realms to enable the Tibetan leader to make his long-delayed first visit to the United States. The Dalai Lama needed a visa, and there was little interest within either the State Department or the White House in granting it. McCleary stepped in. Thurman recalls sitting in McCleary's White House office and hearing him make a pitch to Secretary Vance to override both his own colleagues within the Department and his White House boss Brzezinski, who was reluctant to offend the Chinese he was courting.[10] McCleary prevailed. Some years later his fellow Geshe La

FIGURE 9 Geshe Wangyal, early tutor and emissary to the young Dalai Lama and mentor of the Geshe La group of supporters and advisors to the Dalai Lama in exile.

FIGURE 10 The Dalai Lama visits his old friend Geshe Wangyal at his monastery at Freewood Acres, New Jersey, in 1979.

alumnus Jeffrey Hopkins described with great relish how McCleary orchestrated the grant.[11] He had Hopkins, an advocate and the potential interpreter for the Dalai Lama, come to his White House office after first alerting Jordan to what he was seeking. McCleary's close relationship with Jordan was well known around the White House, so when he and Hopkins met with the National Security Council staff and Brzezinski stuck his head in the door as they were presenting their case for granting the visa, it was approved with little discussion. Brzezinski's only qualification was that the visit not take place within the next three to six months, as the relationship with Beijing was somewhat tense at that time. He may well have wanted to put some distance between the administration and this visit, which was sure to displease Deng so soon after his twenty-one-gun salute on the White House South Lawn earlier that year. He also may have been reluctant to roil the waters in the current policy debate within the State Department over how to react to the arrest and conviction of China's most well-known human rights advocate, Wei Jingsheng.

The Dalai Lama spent seven weeks touring the United States in autumn that year, at times overlapping with what the New York Times characterized as "the more triumphal tour" of Pope John Paul II. They both delivered the "same message of love, friendship and peace."[12] The Tibetan leader was able to pursue his interest in science and the relation between meditation and health in meetings with Glenn Seaborg, Jonas Salk, and others, but he generally skirted political issues in his public appearances, particularly at Constitution Hall in Washington, for which his patron McCleary received "some heat" in the White House for sitting on the stage with him. McCleary left the White House shortly after but felt that what he had done had been in "the best spirit of Jimmy Carter." Three decades later he considers getting the Dalai Lama into the country "the most important act" of his life.[13]

Another of McCleary's lasting contributions to the cause of the people of the mountains dates from this visit. As part of his White House domestic political duties he had gone to Wilmington, North Carolina, to speak at the local Democratic Party Institute as a guest of Charlie Rose, the United States congressman from that district. Following the meeting, the two had a layover at the airport as they waited for thunderstorms to clear so they could fly back to Washington. McCleary told Rose about the advice Geshe La had given him to involve himself in the politics of the Tibetan cause at the present time of crisis for Tibetan Buddhism. He expressed his disappointment at Carter's decision to promote normalization of relations with China with no regard for the consequences for the Tibetans. He asked Rose if he would be interested in arranging a reception for the Dalai Lama on Capitol Hill when

FIGURE 11 The Dalai Lama speaking from the podium at Constitution Hall, Washington, D.C., 1979.

he went to Washington. They both joked that it would be a low-cost affair as the guest of honor neither drank liquor nor ate meat.

As a relative newcomer to Congress, with membership only on the Agriculture Committee, Rose was interested in undertaking a new project that would permit him to exercise his own keen political talent and skills. As a liberal, he felt a sense of identity with the Dalai Lama as an underdog. He also knew that although he and Jesse Helms, the senior senator from his state, were from opposite ends of the political spectrum, Helms's increasingly well-publicized support of the Tibetan leader would appeal to Rose's conservative constituents, who might otherwise question his interest in so remote a cause. There was also less danger that the State Department would feel constrained to take notice of a low-profile congressman from the Agriculture Committee sponsoring such an event. Rose therefore arranged for the reception to be held following a lunch sponsored by Senator Charles Percy and Helms of the Foreign Relations Committee. It was a success. The Dalai Lama met and was photographed with several congressmen. This event launched him and his cause within Congress, which has continued to be the Tibetans' major source of support within the United States government.

Rose attributes the bipartisan appeal that the Dalai Lama and the Tibetan cause have retained to date in Congress to several factors. The first is the charisma of the Dalai Lama and his ability to transmit it in one-on-one meetings. "He's even better than Bill Clinton, who is the master at this. His story of the plight of his people is compelling." Rose acknowledged the admiration that he and other members of Congress have for the hospitality shown by the In-

FIGURE 12 The Dalai Lama flanked by his two sponsors, Congressman Charlie Rose on his left and Joel McCleary on his right, 1979.

dian government to the over 100,000 Tibetan refugees they have welcomed. "Can you imagine our Congress doing that?" He believes that Buddhism has appeal for liberals, as a "science of the mind providing mental discipline over actions." For conservatives, such as Jesse Helms, who were disappointed at what they thought was abandonment of Taiwan, the cause of the Dalai Lama as a victim of Chinese Communism was appealing. Finally, he noted that Tibet's cause brings the support of Hollywood stars such as Richard Gere, which provides an "added punch" for United States congressmen looking for votes.[14]

In Rose's case he responded to the appeal by letting his office run with the Tibet issue, backing whatever initiative they devised. Keith Pitts, who became another congressional staff champion for the Tibetans some years later, described his amazement when he began working as an intern in Rose's office and found files on the Dalai Lama and the Tibet situation in the drawer of his boss, a congressman from the Bible Belt of eastern North Carolina. Eventually Rose brought in another intern, Michele Bohana, and gave her a desk in his office to work on the Tibet campaign until the Tibetans established their own office in Washington. The indefatigable and able Rose and Pitts, who became his legislative assistant, became a team along with Bohana that promoted the Tibetan cause on the Hill for the next decade, and in Bohana's case through today. McCleary's representations to Rose during that rainstorm in North Carolina in the early Carter days have paid lasting dividends.

FIGURE 13 The Dalai Lama lunches with congressional supporters: (from left) Senator Jesse Helms (R.-N.C.), Senator Claiborne Pell (D.-R.I.), Congressman Dante Fascell (D-Fla.), and Congressman Ben Gilman (R.-N.Y.).

Benign Indifference

The White House's discomfort over McCleary's appearance on the stage of Constitution Hall with the Dalai Lama at an event it had made possible was characteristic of the schizoid policy concerning Tibet and the Tibetans during the latter days of the Carter administration. The Tibetans became even more irrelevant to the concerns of their successors during the first half of the 1980s. President Ronald Reagan placed higher value on maintaining the unresolved right of the United States to sell arms to its old allies on Taiwan than in cultivating the "strategic association" with Beijing created by Kissinger. He had no interest in taking up quixotic causes or acquiring unnecessary irritants to Deng.

Meanwhile there seemed to have been a shift in Chinese tactics toward the Tibetans, which initially made it seem less necessary for outside parties to take up the cudgels on their behalf. After reasserting his position as China's paramount leader in 1978, Deng Xiaoping instituted a new policy of "natural acculturation" to replace forced assimilation of minority groups in China. For the Tibetans this meant the release of former Tibetan landlords and aristocrats whose properties had been confiscated during the Cultural Revolution and of twelve Tibetan "enemies" involved in the uprising in 1959, including two of the resistance fighters trained by the CIA who had been captured eighteen years before. Looking to the wider political scene Beijing contacted the Dalai Lama's older brother, Gyalo Thondup, who had been living in Hong Kong since his withdrawal five years before from active involvement in the declining resistance activities he had helped his people organize and the internal and international political affairs of his brother.

Gyalo was summoned to Beijing, where on March 1, 1979, he met with Ulanfu, the director of the United Front Department, who escorted him eleven days later to meet with China's paramount leader. Deng told Gyalo that he was prepared to discuss all the Tibetan grievances as long as the Tibetans did not demand independence and separation from China. Gyalo said that he considered Deng "a very straightforward man who sincerely wanted to find a solution to the Tibetan problem which was very much a live issue at that time."[15] He told Deng that, although he was in Beijing at the invitation of the Chinese and with the permission of the Dalai Lama to hear what the Chinese had to offer, he had no authority to negotiate on specific terms. He did go on to make three "personal requests." He asked that Deng open Tibet to Tibetans who had been living in exile since 1959 to reunite with their families, travel around the country, and do business there. Deng gave the order permitting such rights that same day. The paramount leader was also responsive to Gyalo's request to be allowed to send Tibetan-language teachers from India to Tibet to teach Tibetans living there who had been without instruction in their native tongue for the past two decades. He grandly suggested that Gyalo send one thousand rather than the five or ten such teachers he had modestly requested. Finally, Deng pledged to extend the same largesse in his response to Gyalo third's request, that he personally look after the Panchen Lama, whose status in Beijing was still equivocal a year after his release from eighteen years in prison. He made the further offer to permit Gyalo to send his own people to Tibet to see for themselves what the situation was there. Gyalo accordingly set forth to hold Deng and his associates to these roseate readings of prospects for a peaceful settlement between their respective constituents. This has so far proven to be a thirty-year disappointment: Deng has died and Gyalo is now eighty-four years old, and his colleagues have recently thrown in the towel again for a respite in this marathon of negotiations. But both parties are tireless so far.

In August 1979 the first of these delegations, which included Gyalo's brother Lobsang Samten and his brother-in-law Phuntsok Tashi Takla, went to China. They were followed the next year by two delegations, one headed by the Dalai Lama's sister. These delegations were permitted to travel throughout Tibet, including the Kham and Amdo regions of Qinghai, Sichuan, Gansu, and Yunnan, where they were mobbed by their countrymen. They ended in Lhasa, where again tumultuous crowds pressed to meet them. This seemed confirmation that any final solution must both encompass these areas and include Kundun, "the Presence."

Deng's willingness to allow the visitors into these provinces in which Tibetans are significant populations seemed to indicate his recognition that any settlement of the Tibet situation would have to include them. Lodi Gyari says that early on the Dalai Lama recognized this as a geopolitical fact when he declared in 1973 that he could make no agreement with Beijing that did not include the Tibetan areas outside the Tibet Autonomous Region.[16]

But Beijing curtailed the tours of the two later delegations and canceled all further visits. The officials, however, apparently recognized that these popular manifestations of support for representatives of the Dalai Lama's regime demonstrated the failure of the Communist Party structure; the Chinese cadres governing Tibet not only denied the Dalai Lama's presence but compounded the excesses committed during the Cultural Revolution. On May 22, 1980, Hu Yaobang, a reformer and Deng supporter, arrived in Lhasa to announce a new six-point policy for the governing of Tibet. The key provisions called for Tibet to be given full rights to exercise (undefined) regional autonomy; a three-year moratorium on taxes and requirements to meet state purchase quotas to permit recuperation from the programs that had caused serious crop and livestock losses; introduction of a flexible economic policy suited to Tibet's special conditions; use of a greater part of the state subsidy for the development of agriculture and animal husbandry; development of Tibetan culture, language, and education following socialist orientation; and implementation of the Party's policy on minority cadres and promotion of unity between Chinese and Tibetan cadres. The commune system, which had been imposed with ruinous results, was to be disbanded and the communal property divided among the members. The Chinese cadres who had imposed and administered these programs over the past two decades were to be retired and replaced by Tibetan cadres. Hu proposed that within the coming three years Tibetan cadres should constitute two-thirds of the governing structure of Tibet. Chinese cadres under fifty would be required to learn Tibetan and be able to read Tibetan papers and documents. Although Hu did not specifically mention the Chinese military occupation forces, presumably his directives would apply to them.

Had Hu's entire program been carried out, it could have produced a change in the governing climate and structure of Tibet. As it was, there was a noticeable rise in the number of Tibetans serving as administrative cadres and a new air of hope within the Dalai Lama's constituency. In March 1981 the Tibetan leader sent Deng Xiaoping what Tsering Shakya describes as a "most conciliatory letter, " affirming his "belief in the Communist ideology" and expressing his "pleasure and applause for Comrade Hu Yaobang's efforts to make every possible attempt to right the wrongs by frankly admitting the past mistakes." He reaffirmed his support when Hu was reelected Party secretary a year later, expressing the hope that he would "one day be able to meet with him."[17]

It was a new era in China's policy on Tibet, but one with limitations. Hu spelled these out when Gyalo Thondup went to Beijing to meet with him three months later. The Dalai Lama should not raise old grievances about Chinese suppression in Tibet following the rebellion in 1959, but take note of the new era of reforms that the Chinese were introducing there. The Chinese government "sincerely welcomed" the Dalai Lama and his followers to "return to the motherland. The Dalai Lama might visit Tibet as often as he liked, but he should not live or hold any position in Tibet, leaving its administration to the younger Tibetans who were already there and performing well." He would be appointed a vice chairman of the National People's Congress and presumably live in Beijing while they worked out their temporal relationship. Deng and Hu had taken full note of the near riots and emotional outpouring of worshipful regard precipitated by the visit of the delegations representing the Dalai Lama to Lhasa in 1979 and 1980. Although they were more liberal than their predecessors, both Deng and Hu may well have appreciated the implications of the Dalai Lama's presence in Tibet, something which could constitute an unwanted alternative and challenge to their control there. The Dalai Lama was to be an observer—but not a direct participant in the governing of his country.

Three decades later Deng's present successors seem equally chary of the challenge if they were to permit him or his successor to return to Lhasa. Deng's prescription of a figurehead Dalai Lama resident in Beijing was not acceptable to large numbers of the Tibetan leader's constituency. Many of them were members of the Tibetan diaspora, who were now stranded abroad. They had been members of the resistance which had been composed and led primarily by those living in the Tibetan regions on the eastern side of the

Yangtze. One of the significant achievements that the Tibetan resistance movement had cobbled together with great difficulty was a unified effort that attenuated the tribal, cultural, and political difficulties that have existed between Lhasa and the outlanders from across the Yangtze throughout Tibet's history. The cornerstone of this agreement was their united dedication to the restoration of the Dalai Lama to govern from his historical capital. The tumultuous receptions accorded to the delegations composed of members of his family and exile government in 1979 and 1980 demonstrated that loyalty to the Tibetan leader both as a person and in his role as revered sovereign. The British had been unsuccessful seventy years earlier in persuading the forebears of the present governors of Beijing to resolve the problem of these topographically divided governments. Deng was similarly reluctant to tamper with any solution that might imply a loosening of control over this considerable area. He was unwilling to move beyond a formula that left Beijing in unchallenged political control over all of Tibet and the Dalai Lama an absentee figurehead living in a respected—but safely controlled—exile in Beijing. The lines of engagement had been set.

Deng's restricted agenda was reaffirmed a year later, in 1982, when a three-man delegation went to Beijing to take over the negotiations that the Chinese had conducted solely with Gyalo Thondup. The delegation consisted of a senior official of the Dharamsala government; the Dalai Lama's brother-in-law P.T., who was well known in Beijing as a seasoned negotiator; and Lodi Gyari, the son of a Khampa resistance leader and a former leader of the exile Tibetan Youth Congress. Thondup said that he had asked at this time to be relieved of his role as "the postman," carrying proposals between Dharamsala and Beijing. He had felt, apparently with some reason, that in Dharamsala he was incurring a certain amount of jealousy and suspicion about whether he was adequately defending the interests of the Dalai Lama and his constituents. Similarly, he said, "sometimes even the Chinese Government might have felt he wasn't correctly transmitting their position to the Dalai Lama."[18] Consequently he had yielded his role as the primary intermediary to those who had been chosen as representatives of the wider interests and demands of the diaspora and to move the negotiations beyond the cozy channel preferred by Beijing.

Despite the restrictive framework that Hu had mandated, the three men had carried two new proposals spelling out the conditions which would permit the Dalai Lama to return to China to serve all of his constituents, those who had fled Tibet with him and those who stayed behind but had remained loyal to him as their spiritual and temporal ruler. The concept of Tibet was defined to include all Tibetan-inhabited areas, that is, Cholka-sum, U-Tsang, the traditional area of central Tibet, and Kham and Amdo, which included portions of the western Chinese provinces of Sichuan, Qinghai, Gansu, and Yunnan, the historic areas of contention and where resistance to Communist policies and rule had originated a quarter of a century earlier. Although the proposal did not specify the governance of what would be a newly unified Tibet, it did foreshadow the issue of recognition by Beijing of a united Tibetan identity. The second proposal was that the newly defined Tibet should be given the same special status as Hong Kong and Taiwan.

Gyalo claims that it was he who first raised the unification issue with Hu Yaobang, who said that he had not heard this proposal from any Tibetan before and was quite "open-minded" about it.[19] In subsequent negotiations, however, Deng and Hu had dismissed these proposals, presumably counting on their less restrictive regimen in Tibet and the expanded cadre of Tibetans to carry it out to dissipate the need to accommodate such irredentist demands. They were similarly unresponsive to the Dalai Lama's announcement in February 1983 that he hoped to visit China in 1985 "if the present trend of improving the situation in Tibet continued."[20]

In 1984 the political climate and Chinese governing attitude in Tibet again changed, from an emphasis on reform in governing styles and policies to a program of economic development. The leadership was counting on improvement in their material well-being causing a diminution of the Tibetans' devotion and allegiance to the Dalai Lama and the demand for his return to authority in Lhasa. This emphasis on economic well-being was accompanied by a relaxation of religious suppression and the replacement of Chinese cadres by Tibetans, making the mid-1980s one of the more relaxed and hopeful eras in Sino-Tibetan relations.

The full impact of the removal of restrictions on the migration of non-Tibetans into Tibet and the transformation of the economy, which would further dilute the Dalai Lama's constituency and influence, had not become fully apparent. As for the political establishment in the United States, it was occupied with more immediate concerns, such as the unwinding Iran-contra imbroglio, dealing with a new USSR as Gorbachev introduced his policies of "openness" and "restructuring," and Reagan's promotion of his "Star Wars" Strategic Defense Initiative. In Washington's big picture there was little incentive or apparent reason to take critical note of the long-term implications of the seemingly more benign—but what proved to be ultimately more corrosive—events that were occurring on the Top of the World.

By 1987, however, the Dalai Lama and his advisors at Dharamsala had come to realize that they were facing a return to the state of political irrelevance and diplomatic limbo that they had been in before Deng took up their situation and then dropped it when they hadn't acceded to his formula of a benevolent protectorate minus the Dalai Lama. They decided it was time to move their case from the rapidly drying bilateral channel with Beijing to the international community. Accordingly when the Dalai Lama visited the European Parliament the following year, he amplified the five-point proposal "for resolving the issue of Tibet" he had made in Washington in September 1987. The key addition was the specification that Tibet, composed of Cholka-sum, U-Tsang, Kham, and Amdo should become "a self-governing democratic entity, in association with China."[21] Lodi Gyari, who had carried the original proposals, said that he had slept with them under his pillow when visiting his mother, fearing that, as a veteran Khampa resistance fighter, she would resent them as an abandonment of the fight for independence. When the proposals became public she reacted with the expected indignation at what she and many of her kinsmen regarded as a sell-out, while the Chinese government denounced them as inadequate acknowledgment of their authority.

The vitality of the Tibetans' sense of unique identity and way of life, and the zeal to preserve it and the person who embodies it, is matched by the intransigence of their occupiers. This has defined the confrontation that has kept this remote country and people on the international stage a half-century after they and their cause were consigned to history.

CHAPTER NINETEEN

America Rediscovers Tibet

While the Chinese were consolidating their control of Tibet in the first half of the 1980s with a show of more benign political policies and negotiations with the Dalai Lama, albeit ones in which they set the conditions, their former champion on the White House staff renewed his campaign to establish their political future. In 1986 Joel McCleary dumped his post–White House involvement as a professional political counselor in the swampy intrigues of Panamanian politics to put his political skills into practice on behalf of the Tibetans. He traveled to Russia, China, Japan, South Africa, and India, including ten days in Dharamsala, to study how the Tibet situation was perceived by the governments and general public of these countries and within the Tibetan communities in India and abroad. His study was intended to be a general guide for the Dalai Lama's use when he visited the United States that autumn.

McCleary's findings were not encouraging. The Tibetan government-in-exile at Dharamsala was in a state of depression. Moreover there was strong dissatisfaction among a significant number of the diaspora who regarded the exile government as interested only in the future of traditional central Tibet, to the exclusion of their interests and those of other Tibetan minorities from areas east of the Yangtze. This concerned principally the Khampas and Amdos, who had constituted a majority of the resistance forces two decades earlier. Abroad there was a general tendency to view the Tibetan situation as unfortunate, even tragic, but probably condemned to remain stagnant. Although McCleary found the Dalai Lama to be a tough-minded politician, capable of dealing with his domestic and international demands, his constituents were without unity of purpose or a clear sense of direction.

McCleary's keen judgments were the result of his years as a Democratic Party campaigner and a White House insider, seasoned, or perhaps seared, by maneuvering through the international political arena, tempered and balanced by his Buddhist insights into both the limits and capabilities of his fellow man, combined with his own humanist nature. His findings were incorporated in a 165-page study which is a classic in political analysis and substantive recommendations for action.[1] He cited fifteen critical problems confronting the Tibetan exile community on which the various factions generally agree—except for the basic one on negotiations with the People's Republic of China. The Chinese government says it is willing to negotiate on all issues other than Tibetan independence, and the exiles find it impossible to discuss anything but total independence. Anything less arouses fears that Kham and Amdo will be "sold out" for some compromise on central Tibet. But Beijing's current program of population transfers to Tibet makes it vital that the Tibetan government-in-exile engage Beijing in meaningful negotiations "for no other reason than to buy time on this issue." According to McCleary, "The problem before the Tibetan exile community in the next three years is not independence. The problem is slowing, stopping or reversing the population transfer."[2]

McCleary took on the problems on which the diaspora generally agreed and the sensitive issue of the geographical boundaries of the Dalai Lama's constituency. He made forty-three detailed recommendations for the overall strategy, organizational structure, operating philosophy, and mobilization of a campaign to confront them. The political realist asked those organizing the campaign to "stop dreaming about internal problems causing the PRC to crumble and get to the negotiating table." He stated that there was no coordinated international communications or lobbying effort with a message that was unified and defined. "People like to support causes in which their actions can have some positive effect. People like to win." Consequently the Dalai Lama's message must counter three negative images: that "Tibetans are a backward, superstitious people who have benefited by the Chinese occupation; that Tibetan Buddhism is a strange, primitive form of cultism; and that the Tibetan cause, while worthy, is a hopeless one." McCleary wrote, "Even your best friends in Congress have no idea what your practical objectives are. They write legislation asking the Chinese to negotiate with you, but they have no idea what you are going to negotiate."[3]

The seasoned political insider noted, "The Executive Branch does not control foreign policy. The Congress is a force unto itself, and therein lies a great opportunity for you. The objective is to win Administration neutrality. The Administration can never openly support the Tibetan cause. The most that you can hope for is that they will not oppose Congressional action or, if Congress does pass legislation favorable to Tibet, they will not impede its implementation."

McCleary delivered his prescient and comprehensive blueprint for action at a propitious time for its implementation. Several events, situations, and personalities came together to make 1987 the year that galvanized both American and international support for the Dalai Lama and the Tibetans that persists today. A network of congressional staff aides that began with volunteers and interns working from a desk in Congressman Charlie Rose's office eight years before had mushroomed. They had kept alive the interest generated by the Dalai Lama's first visit. The bipartisan Congressional Human Rights Caucus, chaired by Democrat Tom Lantos of California and Republican John Porter of Illinois, was available to provide an appropriate forum for the Tibetan ruler to enlist the congressional support that McCleary prescribed as essential for the survival of his cause.[4]

Lantos had become interested in the plight of the Tibetans while on a trip with his wife to India and Nepal the year before, when they visited several Tibetan refugee camps. As a Holocaust survivor who had escaped from a Nazi slave labor camp and survived the last years of the war acting as a clandestine courier in Budapest for Raoul Wallenberg, he had a ready empathy with the displaced Tibetans. He came back to Washington convinced that Congress had to take some action to improve their situation and that the Dalai Lama needed to plead their cause publicly in Washington. He accordingly invited him to appear before the Human Rights Caucus to make his case. The Dalai Lama used his appearance before a formal session of the Caucus on September 21, 1987, to present his "five point peace proposal,"[5] calling for the transformation of the whole of Tibet into a zone of peace, where the Tibetans would enjoy self-rule and the Chinese would discontinue their population-transfer policy, protect Tibet's environment, and abandon the use of Tibet for production of nuclear weapons and the dumping of nuclear waste and start "earnest" negotiations on the future status of Tibet. It was a program that appealed to a sympathetic Congress. A congressional bipartisan combination of infrequent bedfellows, such as Senators Claiborne Pell

FIGURE 14 The Dalai Lama and Congressman Tom Lantos express their mutual respect, September 1987.

and Jesse Helms, joined by their counterparts in the House, sent a letter to China's prime minister, Zhao Ziyang, endorsing the Dalai Lama's proposal as a "historic step towards resolving the important question of Tibet and alleviating the suffering of the Tibetan people."[6]

Although neither the American nor the international press accorded the Caucus event or the Dalai Lama's proposal much attention,[7] the Chinese embassy in Washington had early on been aware of the implications of the Dalai Lama's making a public political statement before a congressional audience. Three weeks before the event, the Chinese had demanded that the United States government "take measures to prevent him from engaging in any political activities in the United States against the interests of China." The State Department, which had little interest in reviving discussion of the Tibet issue, reassured the Chinese that the Tibetan ruler was visiting the United States as a "private person" and that he would not be officially received by the United States government—at least by its executive branch. After the Dalai Lama's speech on Capitol Hill Beijing angrily protested, contending that the United States had allowed him to intrude into internal Chinese affairs. Ironically the Chinese gave the Dalai Lama's first public address to a congressional body the publicity it had failed to attract in the United

States. Chinese TV broadcast clips of the event as part of a campaign to portray the Dalai Lama's "intent to split the motherland."[8]

This all might have evaporated as a transient one-up for the Tibetans except for the demonstrations and riots that broke out in Lhasa a week later. On September 27, 1987, monks from one of Lhasa's oldest monasteries marched through the central marketplace of Lhasa near Tibet's most sacred Buddhist shrine shouting "Tibet wants independence" and waving a traditional flag depicting the mountains and lions of Tibet. Chinese security forces suppressed the demonstration, beating and arresting most of the monks. Two young American tourists, one a lawyer, the other a physician, who had gone to the aid of the demonstrators were detained.[9] Four days later monks from another of Lhasa's principal monasteries staged a second demonstration. This one turned violent when the Chinese police lost control and began firing into a crowd of demonstrators who had burst into the police station and released the detained monks and their supporters. Between eight and ten Tibetans were killed, and the world press carried accounts from foreigners who had witnessed the Chinese actions. Tibet was back on the world screen.

For the United States Congress these events validated its growing interest and readiness to support the Dalai Lama's cause. Both Pell and Helms were ready in the Senate to support any sympathetic resolutions that their dedicated aides offered them. The Senate had begun public TV broadcasts of its proceedings, and Helms made full use of this forum to put his fellow senators on public record in support of the Tibetans. On October 6 the North Carolina senator held up a photograph which had been printed in that morning's *Washington Post* of a Tibetan holding in his arms his badly wounded young son, who had been injured in the protests. Helms dared anyone to vote against the legislation he was offering, which condemned the Chinese for their actions in Tibet. This legislation, which was part of the authorization act providing the State Department's funding for the coming two years, required President Reagan to certify that China was making progress in resolving human rights issues in Tibet before the United States proceeded with any new sale of arms or weapons technology to China. Helms had no problem enlisting sponsors; members of both parties wanted to be counted as condemning the Chinese actions in Tibet. Senator Robert Byrd, who was presiding, stopped the clock at 14 minutes 59 seconds so that the one missing senator could be located. Jay Rockefeller soon after rushed in, was informed about the crisis for which he had been summoned, and cast the vote that made Senate approval of the amendment unanimous.

The State Department took immediate objection to both the conclusions and the remedies offered by the Senate. One official was quoted by the *New York Times* as saying that any possible benefits of the Senate action for the Tibetan people were "insufficient to outweigh the almost certain damage to the U.S.-China bilateral relationship."[10] Only one week earlier the Department had issued a twenty-four-page report to Congress on the treatment of minorities in China which had taken a generally upbeat tone on Tibet. The report cited the efforts that had been made by the Chinese leadership to ease tensions in Tibet and begin economic and other changes. It concluded, "Beijing has stressed its commitment to preserve Tibet's unique cultural, linguistic and religious traditions in an effort to strengthen social stability."[11]

In testimony before the House Foreign Affairs Committee on October 13 Secretary of State George Shultz did acknowledge human rights violations in Tibet: "We deplore it, and we don't make any bones about it." His deputy assistant for East Asian and Pacific affairs, Stapleton Roy, was more defensive when he addressed a joint hearing of two House foreign affairs subcommittees the next day. He took strong issue with the view expressed by some congressmen that the State Department was reacting "in a spineless fashion" to recent events in Lhasa. Roy, an old China hand born to missionary parents, said that he "didn't think it advance[d] human rights for the State Department and the Congress to be in a position of trying to see who can be holier than the other on the issue of standing up for human rights." In this context he resurrected William Rockhill's trips to Tibet a century earlier: "The historical record on this, I believe is clear. The first American who attempted to reach Tibet back when it was a closed and distant region in the Himalayas, in 1889, was an American diplomat attached to our mission in Peking, who spoke Chinese, some Tibetan, and who spent many months trying to penetrate into Lhasa."[12] He then cited an edited version of Rockhill's dismissive dealings with the Dalai Lama a half-century earlier as certification of the Department's seniority and capability for handling (primarily abstaining from) affairs concerning Tibet. Roy went on to delineate the limits within United States policy governing this involvement: "When the Dalai Lama states, as he did in his remarks to the Congressional Human Rights Caucus, that fundamental human rights and democratic freedoms must be respected in Tibet, the administration is in full agreement with him. . . . [But when he] assumes a political status and advances a political program for Tibet, which we consider part of China, the U.S. Government cannot support him." He specified that the Dalai Lama's proposed five-point peace program that he had announced at the Congressional Human Rights Caucus ten days prior to the Lhasa demonstrations was "a political program advanced by a man who is the head of a government in exile which neither the United States Government nor any other government recognize[d]."[13] Members of the committee from both parties took strong exception to this restriction on the role of the Dalai Lama to that of a religious leader speaking out for the human rights of his people but not a political leader proposing a program to secure these rights. Lantos characterized it as a "phony dichotomy."

Despite this vigorous opposition by the State Department to what it considered an intrusion on its turf, those holding the power of the purse eventually prevailed, and those conducting foreign affairs had to listen if they wanted their paychecks. The provisions on Tibet, buried in the Foreign Relations Authorization Act signed by Reagan on December 22, 1987, were the first moves by the United States Congress to assume a meaningful voice in the formation and execution of policy toward Tibet. It has subsequently never relinquished this role. In addition to the proviso imposing conditions on future arms sales to China, there was a significant statement of policy contained in one sentence: "Beginning October 7, 1950 the Chinese Communist army invaded and occupied Tibet." This language, which implied that China had moved against an independent country, was crafted by William Triplett, a member of Senator Helms's staff. Triplett said that he had wanted to "get the Chinese Communists" and "settle some scores" with them ever since he was a member of an American military intelligence group which was monitoring the offenses committed by the Chinese in Tibet during Mao's Cultural Revolution twenty years earlier.[14]

The act also provided humanitarian assistance for the Tibetan refugees and established fifteen scholarships for Tibetan students and professionals to study at American institutions of higher learning. These two provisions were the contribution of Chairman Pell. His staff assistant Mary Beth Markey said that although Pell was fascinated with the interest that the Dalai Lama shared with him in paranormal phenomena, his concerns for the Tibetans and the consequent legislative actions on their behalf were very much of this world.[15]

Cleopatra's Nose

It was at this time that Congress consolidated its position as the initiator of United States government action and policy concerning Tibet. Amit Pandya, one of the participating congressional aides, cites this development as a classic case of Pascal's "Cleopatra's nose" phenomenon: "Cleopatra's nose, had it been shorter, the whole face of the world would have been changed."

In this case the activating conjunction of persons and events in 1987 was the Dalai Lama's appearance on Capitol Hill, the demonstrations and violent Chinese response in Lhasa, and the presence of several key senators and congressmen with a network of sympathetic aides.

The patriarch of this network, Charlie Rose, in addition to providing office space to an intern organizing a grassroots movement for the Tibetans, had enlisted his pal from across the aisle, Ben Gilman. Gilman had met the Dalai Lama when he visited Washington in 1984, and he had become one of his most faithful supporters. He also employed in his office an aide named Paul Berkowitz, who had become one of the pioneer Tibetan supporters on the Hill, a cause that he still doggedly pursues today. As a young student dissatisfied with his college courses in philosophy, Berkowitz had moved from England to India in 1977, ending up in Dharamsala, where he became a convert to both Buddhism and the political cause of the Tibetans.

Berkowitz went to work for Gilman in 1983. Gilman represented a district in which over 60 percent of the voters were Democrats, so Berkowitz's family credentials—his mother worked for Bella Abzug and his father was a staunch Jewish liberal—were a plus, even though Gilman was a Republican. Berkowitz had cut his teeth on legislative action by working to establish the House Select Committee on Hunger. In the process he learned how to work the Congress, primarily through peer-group aides. They draft the various bills and know how to tuck controversial provisions into large legislative acts, where they receive less scrutiny. He urged the neophyte Tibetan lobbyists in Washington to work through the congressional process rather than waste their time trying to influence a disinterested State Department or an amorphous general public. He also began bombarding his old friends in the Dalai Lama's government in India on the need to open an office in Washington targeted at Congress. Organizing Tibetan dance troupes and cultural events was useful, he advised, but mobilizing the abundant but unorganized sympathy for their cause among the congressmen was critical.[16] Berkowitz undertook to organize and mobilize this support and became the gadfly of this cause for the next three decades, earning the admiration and gratitude of those who sympathized with his objectives and the annoyance of those who objected to his goals, his methods, his zeal—and his occasional successes.

The objective of the "Tibet Mafia" on the Hill was to amplify and solidify the statement of congressional policy and support that had been inserted in that session's authorization act. On the Senate side Helms's aide Bill Triplett, the author of the language in the act stating that China had "invaded and occupied Tibet," had enlisted his boss to make this statement of policy even stronger and, more important, a matter of record. But it was Pell as chairman of the Senate Foreign Relations Committee who had to take the initiative. This was no problem. By this time Senator Daniel Patrick Moynihan had been brought aboard by both his colleague Pell and Moynihan's daughter Maura, who maintained a picket post in front of the Chinese embassy in Washington protesting the Chinese actions in Tibet.[17] Stephen Rickard, who had become Moynihan's legislative assistant in 1989 and thereby a member of the Tibet Mafia, noted that Moynihan's addition to the senatorial roster supporting the Tibetans was particularly useful as he was able to attract bipartisan support because of his background as a Democrat who had served a Republican president (Nixon) as ambassador to India.[18] Ironically it was Peter Galbraith, Pell's legislative aide, who was assigned the task of shepherding this resolution through Congress. It is not known whether he consulted his father, the ambassador to India, John Kenneth Galbraith, and whether the colorful ambassador had mellowed in his views on things Tibetan by then.

Because it was to be part of a money bill it had to be initiated in the House. Therefore Galbraith brought the draft resolution, with a strong statement of support for the Tibetans, to Pandya, who was the legislative aide to Congressman Howard Birman, the chairman of the House international operations subcommittee.[19] There he found another ready ally. Pandya had begun his career as an immigration lawyer, and through his work had become involved with Human Rights Watch and thereby the Tibetans. With Galbraith's approval, he rewrote the draft resolution to strengthen the language, which is how it appeared tucked in the authorization act enacted on October 28, 1991, as Public Law 102-138. It represented the most complete and forthright statement of congressional policy concerning Tibet on which subsequent legislation and sparring with the State Department and the White House in support of the Tibetans continue through today.

Section 355 of the law, entitled "China's Illegal Control of Tibet," stated, "[It is] the sense of Congress that"

1. Tibet, including the four western provinces of China containing Tibetan populations, "is an occupied country under the established principles of international law."
2. Tibet's "true representatives are the Dalai Lama and the Tibetan Government in exile as recognized by the Tibetan people."

FIGURE 15 The Dalai Lama with the "Tibet Mafia" on Capitol Hill. Left to right: Peter Galbraith, senior policy advisor, Senate Foreign Relations Committee; Paul Berkowitz, aide to Congressman Ben Gilman (R.-N.Y.); Mary Beth Markey, Senate foreign relations staff; Keith Pitts, aide to Congressman Charlie Rose (D.-N.C.); Sandy Mason, protocol aide, Senate foreign relations staff.

3. Tibet "has maintained throughout its history a distinctive and sovereign national, cultural, and religious identity separate from that of China."

4. "Historical evidence of this separate identity may be found in Chinese archival documents and traditional dynastic histories, in United States recognition of Tibetan neutrality during World War II and the fact that a number of countries including the United States, Mongolia, Bhutan, Sikkim, Nepal, India, Japan, Great Britain and Russia recognized Tibet as an independent nation or dealt with Tibet independently of any Chinese government."

5. "In 1949–1950 China launched an armed invasion of Tibet in contravention of international law."

6. "It is the policy of the United States to oppose aggression and other illegal uses of force by one country against the sovereignty of another as a manner of acquiring territory, and to condemn violations of international law, including the illegal occupation of one country by another."

CHAPTER 19

—

7. "Numerous United States declarations since the Chinese invasion have recognized Tibet's right to self-determination and the illegality of China's occupation of Tibet."

Those who provided the funds for the salaries and expenses of the American diplomatic establishment thus gave notice of how they wanted the money spent as far as this particular area of foreign policy was concerned. There is no record whether President George H. W. Bush signed the bill willingly or resignedly rather than engage in an unappealing public contest, but he did sign it.

Accompanying these measures promoting a more active policy of long-term support for the Tibetans, Congress enacted legislation providing for their more immediate relief. One of the most substantive acts of support was sponsored by Congressman Barney Frank, who was able to insert legislation in the Legal Immigration Act of 1990 providing one thousand immigrant visas in the three fiscal years beginning in 1991 for "qualified displaced Tibetans." When asked what prompted him to sponsor this legislation, Frank said that he had initially become interested in the Tibetans not because of a spiritual affinity—although he is a Jew, he is "not particularly religious," nor is he "a member of the Dalai Lama cult," nor had he seen *Lost Horizon*—but because of his position as chairman of the House Immigration Committee. "Here were deserving people who despite their mistreatment had retained a certain admirable personal gentleness, and they deserved to be helped." Also, like Charlie Rose, he was impressed with the unselfish action of the Indian government, a fellow democracy, which despite the many demands on its limited resources had been a generous host to the Tibetans, an act the United States government was morally obligated to match. In short, "it just seemed the right thing to do."[20] On April 16, 1992, the first of one thousand Tibetans who had been chosen by a combination of a lottery and interviews conducted by the Tibetan government at Dharamsala arrived in the United States, where they have managed to make good lives for themselves without losing their Tibetan identity in the American melting pot.

Cleopatra's Nose Grows Longer

Bush's signature on the authorization act which incorporated the will of Congress marked a new era in official support from both ends of Constitution Avenue for the Tibetans. The contributing elements were the continuing chill in United States–China relations following the Tiananmen Square massacre two years earlier, the awarding of the Nobel Peace Prize to the

Dalai Lama in December 1989, and the continuing and growing support for the Dalai Lama and his people within both houses of Congress, which had reached a new high with the "Ceremony to Welcome His Holiness the Dalai Lama of Tibet with Members of the Congress Assembled in the U.S. Capitol Rotunda" on April 18, 1991. This widely publicized ceremony was preceded by the first meeting between the Dalai Lama and a United States president, George H. W. Bush, who received him in the White House, albeit in the private quarters, on April 16, 1991.

The Tiananmen Chill

This enhanced joint regard for Tibet and the Dalai Lama by both Congress and the White House was a collateral beneficiary of the events that began on the night of June 3, 1989, when Chinese troops moved into Beijing's Tiananmen Square to quell student protests demanding the right of free expression and a more open society. The number of participants in these demonstrations, which had started two months earlier at the memorial service for Hu Yaobang, whom the students regarded as their spokesman for these rights, had grown from an initial thirty thousand to over a million. They erected a statue of the Goddess of Democracy, twenty-one feet tall, as a challenge to the Communist Party. By this time the world press was focused on this extraordinary event, and the sight of Chinese tanks mowing down unarmed students was appearing on TV screens and in newspapers throughout the world. Two days later Chinese troops fired on the apartments housing American embassy officers and their dependents, and Secretary of State James Baker made plans for a full evacuation of the 1,400 Americans in Beijing and the more than 8,000 Americans living in the rest of China.[21]

This was not the China that Bush had hoped to deal with when he traveled to Beijing during his first month in office only four months earlier. Then Deng had assured him that he and the two men whom he was grooming to succeed him, Zhao Ziyang and Li Peng, viewed Russia's "encirclement" strategy as their greatest threat, and it had seemed that the strong relationship initiated by Nixon to which Bush had contributed as the chief of the American Liaison Office was secure. When the former president and architect of the "opening to China" called him the morning after the attacks to urge him to "take a look at the long haul," Bush assured Nixon that was his inclination and intention.

By the end of June a united Congress had passed comprehensive sanctions legislation, including a ban on arms shipments, by a vote of 418 to 0. When Nixon, still eager to be involved, visited Beijing that autumn he had bluntly told his hosts at a formal banquet, "The fact is that many in the United States, including friends of China, believe that the crackdown was excessive and unjustified."[22] In a private session Deng told Nixon that it would have to be the United States that took the initiative in putting the past behind it, because only the strong United States, in contrast to the weak China, "the victim," could take the first step. "Don't ever expect China to beg the United States to lift the [congressional] sanctions," Deng insisted. "If they lasted 100 years, the Chinese would not do that."[23] Deng was in no mood—or perhaps position—to respond favorably to any advice from Washington on how China was governing Tibet.

This rupture in the "opening to China" took place as the whole structure of the Cold War world was collapsing. Communist regimes in Czechoslovakia, Poland, and Hungary toppled one after another, climaxing in November with the fall of the Berlin Wall. In December 1989 Winston Lord, the author of many of the documents supporting the initial opening to China, the chronicler of the negotiations that made it happen, and Reagan's ambassador to Beijing, unleashed an attack on the White House policy of attempting to find an accommodation with Deng and his government.[24] He argued that it was time to "shelve the double standard" of holding Gorbachev's Russia to the Helsinki Accords on human rights, while muting protests over human rights abuses in China.

Against this background Congress found ready support when it nominated the Dalai Lama for the Nobel Peace Prize. The award ceremony in Oslo on December 11, 1989, provided him the occasion to expand on his concept of transforming Tibet into a Zone of Peace, which had been the substance of the five-point peace proposal he had made to the Congressional Human Rights Caucus two years earlier. While this did not enhance his favor in Beijing, it further increased his stature and status in Washington.

Formation of the International Campaign

Another chip that fell into place at this time was the formal organization of the international campaign advocated by McCleary in his strategy paper. When the Dalai Lama made his visit in September 1987 a small group of the Washington hands began meeting in the law offices of Lloyd Cutler, who had been Jimmy Carter's legal counsel. At that time Cutler had a young associate, a specialist in international law, Michael van Walt, in his firm. Van Walt's field of expertise as well as his cosmopolitan background proved to be a great asset to the Tibetans in organizing and launching their campaign to consolidate international political support for their cause. Cutler made it clear that his firm received no compensation for what he termed van Walt's "extracurricular" activities. Furthermore, he said, he was no Dalai Lama "groupie," noting that on the one occasion they had met he found the Tibetan "unimpressive, a man in sandals and a robe, lacking only a green eye shade to appear to be a bookkeeper, and missing the 'real presence' of men like Mugabe and Nkrumah."[25] Cutler may have found it prudent to disassociate himself personally from the activities van Walt carried on from his office. However, the planning sessions and briefings given by van Walt and the author John Avedon and the Dalai Lama's fledgling diplomatic representatives in connection with the Tibetan leader's visit to Washington were greatly enhanced by having taken place under Cutler's widely respected roof.

The International Campaign for Tibet was formally established in early 1988. John Ackerly, one of the two Americans imprisoned in Lhasa the year before, became its first president, a post he held for the next two decades. It was based on the blueprint that was part of the organizational proposal Joel McCleary had submitted to the Dalai Lama some months before, but it was launched without his participation or that of his fellow members of the Geshe La group, Robert Thurman and Jeffrey Hopkins. Their absence may have reflected the ambivalence which members of the Dalai Lama's government-in-exile felt toward outsiders, especially collateral descendants of the "Mongol" influence. These three Americans had inherited a lineage through Geshe La's identification with his spiritual alma mater, the "pro-Mongol" Drepung monastery. So too, while the Dalai Lama's semijoking remarks that McCleary, Thurman, and Hopkins were incarnations of the Mongols who had helped put him in power when he was the Fifth Dalai Lama enhanced their prestige, it also made them objects of envy. They were highly regarded and their support for the cause was appreciated, but they were not exempt from these centuries-old grudges and jealousies. This did not, however, preclude their continuing to serve as effective advocates for the Dalai Lama's campaign for his people. In any event, McCleary believes His Holiness has always had a warm spot for his Mongol forebears and teachers and for the constituency still loyal to him in Mongolia. McCleary continues to be an honored advisor and financial supporter. Thurman similarly remains on the International Campaign advisory board while proceeding independently with his objective of preserving the culture of Tibet by founding the now well-established Tibet House and consciously keeping it apart from the Tibetan political campaigns. Hopkins remains a respected Tibetan scholar at the University of Virginia.

FIGURE 16 Robert Thurman (top row) and Joel McCleary (seated to left) visit with Tibetan friends at their monastery in Tibet, 1992.

The Congressional Ceremony in the Capitol Rotunda

The indefatigable Charlie Rose had been using all of his well-established friendships on both sides of the congressional aisle as well as his key position as chairman of the House Administration Committee, which made him the donor of various much sought-after perks for use as trading stock, to consolidate the special regard that the Dalai Lama had acquired on Capitol Hill in his appearance there in 1987. He had first tried to persuade Speaker of the House Tom Foley to convene a joint session of Congress which the Dalai Lama would address when he made his next visit to Washington in the spring of 1991. Foley had no problem with this, but the State Department was strongly opposed and moved to block it by scheduling an invitation to the Nicaraguan president Violeta Chamorro at the same time. The compromise was that Chamorro made the joint address to Congress, and the Dalai Lama was honored at an unprecedented ceremony of welcome in the Capitol Rotunda on April 18, 1991. In a demonstration of bipartisan support, the delegation that escorted the Tibetan leader to the Rotunda was composed of Senate Majority Leader George Mitchell, Senate Minority Leader Robert Dole, Speaker Foley, House Majority Leader Richard Gephardt, House Minority Leader Robert Michel, and his most faithful supporter in Congress, Charlie Rose.

Foley "welcomed to the Capitol of the United States the spiritual and temporal leader of six million Tibetans, the embodiment of compassion of fourteen million Buddhists, a world-renowned champion of human rights and dignity, a statesman of international repute, His Holiness, the fourteenth Dalai Lama."

George Mitchell said, "[It is] truly fitting that a man who has become a preeminent symbol of the struggle for human rights should today speak in this building, the U.S. Capitol, which we Americans proudly regard as the preeminent symbol of freedom in the world."

Mitchell's Republican counterpart Robert Dole gave one of the more rousing welcomes: "Today, together, let us reaffirm this message loud and clear. As His Holiness and the people of Tibet go forward on their own great journey, we are with them. We, the people of the United States, the Congress of the United States—we stand with them, and we want the People's Republic of China to hear this message. We stand with them!"

Richard Gephardt cited the "revolutionary changes" that had taken place in the past few years: "Dictators have died, Marxism is dying. And freedom has never been more alive. From Latin America to Eastern Europe citizens have pounded open their prison doors, and millions have eagerly passed through these portals to freedom and democracy. At virtually no time in our history has the power of the people been so powerful. Surely China cannot be much longer immune from these changes."

Gephardt's Republican counterpart Robert Michel recalled that on a previous visit the Dalai Lama had said, "Politics is necessary as an instrument to solve human problems. In itself it is not bad; it is necessary. However, if politics are practiced by bad persons out of cunning and lacking the right motivation, then of course it becomes bad." In this context Michel said, "This emphasis on personal responsibility for political action is one that was understood by the leaders whose statues grace this rotunda—George Washington, Abraham Lincoln, Thomas Jefferson, Martin Luther King Jr., Roger Williams. They all understood the necessity to bring to civil discourse the right motivation of which the Dalai speaks." He ended with the hope that "the memory of what Lincoln, Washington, and others have done will inspire him and his people as they carry on their struggle for freedom."[26]

Charlie Rose appropriately had the closing words. He took note of what Congress had done in the four years since the Dalai Lama's previous visit to the United States: "passing resolutions supporting the Tibetan people in their struggle for self-determination, providing funds for refugee assistance, [and] for a Tibet language section at the Voice of America which had begun broadcasting into Tibet the previous month, and introducing legislation linking U.S.-China policy to improvement of human rights conditions in Tibet." He referred to the "historic and commendable meeting" President Bush had held with the Dalai Lama. He warned that in the past China had increased oppression in Tibet in retaliation against such statements of support for their cause. "And so I ask my friends in the Congress and I ask the President of the United States and I ask the press to help us keep a watchful eye on the actions in Tibet and warn the [Chinese] government." He concluded, "This place is a symbol of freedom, and this holy man who says he is just a simple monk, a man of compassion and insight, who teaches peace and patience, and love for each other, has come to this shrine of America and asks that we stand up for what we are, for what our destiny has been, and see that the light of freedom shines in Tibet." Whereupon the ceremony was concluded.

Meeting with the President

It was one of those uniquely Washington ironies that this unprecedented convocation of bipartisan support for the Tibetans on Capitol Hill was scooped by the fullest demonstration of support the Tibetans had ever received from the previously nonresponsive White House. Two days before the congressional event Bush had become the first American president to meet personally with the Dalai Lama. He and his national security advisor Brent Scowcroft had been taking a beating from Congress and conservative critics for the White House's nonconfrontational policy toward Beijing after Tiananmen, and they were quite willing to move to the more hard-nosed public position that their NSC specialist on China, Douglas Paal, was promoting. Paal said that he also met little resistance from the State Department when he worked with the president's cousin Elsie Walker, a longtime vigorous Tibetan supporter, to obtain the president's agreement to meet with the Dalai Lama in the White House. Although John Avedon and the director of the International Campaign for Tibet, Lodi Gyari, were pushing for a meeting in the Oval Office, which would be a first such event and a heady signal of acceptance, Paal found the Dalai Lama quite relaxed about the locale. In any event they were all delighted when the meeting actually took place in the private quarters of the White House with only Barbara Bush, General Scowcroft, Paal, and Millie the dog sitting in. After presenting a full explanation of Chinese occupation policies in his homeland, the Tibetan leader deplored the stalemate in negotiations between his representatives and the Beijing authorities that had set in since Tiananmen. This apparently caught the special attention of the president, and he took the Dalai Lama off with Scowcroft for a private session, where Paal says the trio limited their discussions to spiritual matters, and no political affairs.[27]

Whatever its substance, the meeting was not listed on Bush's public schedule, but it was acknowledged by the White House press secretary, Marlin Fitzwater. In response to a question whether the Dalai Lama's visit had implications for United States–China relations, Fitzwater dodged, saying that the Dalai Lama was invited "as the religious leader of his country" and that the president met "all the time" with various religious leaders from "various countries at various levels." An unidentified "senior Bush administration official" said, "Of course we have heard from the Chinese on this, and of course they would prefer no meeting. But the Dalai Lama is a leader in human rights, a religious leader and the President wants to meet with him."[28]

CHAPTER TWENTY

Collateral Diplomacy

Throughout the remainder of the Bush I administration Congress maintained its pressure on the State Department and the White House to urge the Chinese government to negotiate with the Dalai Lama. By this time the Voice of America, in response to congressional legislation, had established a Tibet Service and was broadcasting a daily half-hour program in Tibetan. Although Beijing had turned down as "inappropriate at this time" a request from Senators Claiborne Pell and David Boren to visit China and Tibet in the spring of 1992, it did permit the indomitable Gyalo Thondup to resume his shuttle diplomacy between Hong Kong, Dharamsala, and Beijing in his continuing efforts to find a formula for the status and governance of Tibet that both his brother's government and Deng Xiaoping could agree upon.

When Desaix Anderson, representing the State Department, appeared before the Senate Foreign Relations Committee on July 28, 1992, for a hearing on "U.S. and Chinese policies toward occupied Tibet" he received a gentlemanly but rigorous hazing from skeptical senators.[1] While expressing appropriate regret at the recent Chinese action denying the request of two of the senators to visit Tibet, Anderson presented a moderately optimistic appraisal of the Chinese economic development program in Tibet, concluding, "There does not appear to be a conscious Chinese Government policy now of attempting to sinicize Tibet." He noted that

Secretary Baker and other senior American officials had consistently expressed the government's concern about the situation in Tibet, most recently during the secretary's visit to Beijing the previous November, when he "made clear [America's] concern for those imprisoned in Tibet for political reasons." He ended his presentation with the hope that "the Chinese leadership will actively seek progress in its dialogue with the Dalai Lama's elder brother . . . and that these talks could result in an agreement for increased Tibetan participation in the governing of Tibetan affairs."

Pell responded with a reminder that the "wonderful idea" for the VOA broadcasts to Tibet which Anderson had endorsed had come from Congress, "but it had been opposed by the administration." Anderson quickly responded, "Let me thank you for that suggestion. We followed up on it." After genial laughter Pell started off with a zinger: Had the State Department given any thought to opening an American presence in Lhasa, such as a consular agency? When Anderson pled the shortage of funds for creating such a presence there, Pell reminded him that Congress always had the fallback position of being able to earmark specific funds for such a consulate. The veteran foreign service officer rejoined, "We're familiar with that practice," and the subject was dropped.

After an inconclusive exchange with Senator Paul Simon, who took exception to the Department's acceptance of autonomy rather than independence as a worthy goal for the Tibetans, Senator Moynihan argued that the self-determination for Tibet called for in the resolutions passed by the UN in the 1961 and 1965 referred to independence. The dogged senator, a former ambassador to India, explained that the term "self-determination" carried a historic meaning dating back to its originator, Woodrow Wilson: "Self-determination anticipates exactly the kind of situation you have in Tibet, and the Congress has said we want that to be an independent country. I wish you could come up and say well, we don't agree with you. That's what the Secretary of State's job is, if he doesn't agree, to say so, but to recognize that our views are different. For example, when you praise—and you did, sir—the PRC's policy of reopening monasteries, our view is that these are not their monasteries to reopen, much less to have closed. I don't know how better to say it." Another dialectical exchange followed. The genial but persistent senator was determined to win acknowledgment that self-determination is intended to lead to independence. The equally courtly Mississippi-born diplomat defended the State Department's position that "self determination is not equatable necessarily with independence." Anderson did concede Moynihan's conclusion that "under normal circumstances" self-determination is intended to lead to independence, but stipulated,

"[It] would depend on the circumstances." Moynihan graciously predicted, "You'll go far, Anderson."[2]

Anderson then argued that since 1980 the Chinese had permitted the Tibetans to resume their culture by reopening the monasteries and allowing a greater practice of religious freedom. In response Senator Paul Sarbanes forced him to admit that since 1987 the Chinese had swung the other way: "When it became a question of advocacy of independence they cracked down on it." Anderson acknowledged, "Cracking down on political expression is reprehensible, but the underlying policy of allowing the Tibetan culture to flourish I think has continued." Sarbanes summarized, "What you are really saying is that it's reprehensible . . . but you are not willing to do anything about it. This is what happened," he concluded, "when the Chinese denied Senators Pell and Boren the right to visit China. The Department protested but did nothing further, and the Chinese got the sense that nothing was going to happen." Anderson responded that the Chinese had reversed themselves and made it clear that they would welcome the senators' visit. He acknowledged, "[That] doesn't overcome the original problem but at least they recognized they had made a mistake." This civilized exchange ending in a stalemate provided the Tibetans with a clear picture of the limits to any support they might expect from the State Department, despite the president's protocol-snubbing gesture in meeting with the Dalai Lama. It also gave them a clear guide on where to look for more forthcoming official support in Washington under the Bush administration.

The New Administration

By the time of the presidential election in November 1992 Lodi Gyari, now director of the International Campaign for Tibet, was well ensconced as the resident Tibetan spokesman in Washington for his people's cause. Lodi was one of the new generation of political operators created by the Tibetan diaspora. He was a *rinpoche*, a title given to Tibetan spiritual masters. Although he was not a protégé of Geshe La, he agreed with him that this "was not the age for the mountains, but for politics." As the son of a tribal leader, Lodi had ridden as a young man with his aunt, who led a group of her kinsmen and fellow Khampas in resistance activities against the Chinese. He had followed them into exile in India, where he had become a protégé of Gyalo Thondup. By 1977 he had given up his religious vocation and become president of the Tibetan Youth Congress (TYC), which was conducting political agitation in the form of a hunger strike and demonstrations against the Chinese embassy in New Delhi in support of Tibetan independence. He took it upon himself to petition directly the newly elected leaders of the Indian Janata Party to support TYC demands. To his surprise they agreed, and this first public support by members of the Indian government resulted in the successful termination of the TYC's hunger strike. The Tibetans' ardent supporter among the Indian opposition parties, Acharya Kripalani, had publicly offered orange juice to the strikers, and it seemed to be a win for the young militants. Up at Dharamsala, however, the Dalai Lama's government did not unanimously applaud Lodi's political coup. Some members feared that it might redound against their efforts to maintain their valued status and support from the Indian government, which was essential to their survival. But Lodi had made his mark, and five years later, as chairman of the Assembly of Tibetan People's Deputies, he had flown to Beijing in April 1982 as one of a three-man delegation to negotiate with the Chinese on the future status of Tibet. Lodi was able to represent his fellow Khampas in attempting to ensure that any settlement recognize their interests, and his claim to a berth on the negotiating team had been established. He was to become the dogged and skilled chief of the team engaged in the marathon talks three decades later.

Lodi's International Campaign for Tibet was ready to take on the challenge of enlisting the support of the new team that took over the White House and the State Department when Bill Clinton was elected in November 1992 to replace Tibet's newly found sympathizer George Bush. At the Senate Foreign Relations Committee hearings on January 13, 1993, on his confirmation as secretary of state, Warren Christopher was given full notice by the Senate stalwarts on Tibet that this issue would be one that they expected him to take on. Christopher ruled out unilateral recognition of Tibet, but he agreed, "When we meet with the Chinese we ought to make it a strong point that they need to have a good deal more respect for the unusual dignity of the Tibetan people, and to make that a high priority in our meetings with them." He punted in his response to Senator Chuck Robb's probing whether he would favor using the Most Favored Nation (MFN) provision in negotiations with the Chinese on trade issues as a prod to forcing the Chinese to extend further rights to the Tibetans.

Christopher's initial reluctance to commit himself to tying MFN status for China to its observance of human rights foreshadowed the continuing contention that was to involve the White House, Congress, human rights advocates, and Tibet supporters over the next two years and continues, albeit in a diluted form, today. From the beginning the debate and consequent actions have involved powerful personalities, potent political and economic interests, and strong emotions—a formidable and enduring combination.

Tibet's original key champions in the debate were Congresswoman Nancy Pelosi, Senator George Mitchell, and Assistant Secretary of State Winston Lord. Pelosi had been elected to Congress for her third term. Her constituency in downtown San Francisco was liberal and had a natural interest in China for a variety of reasons. In November 1989 Congress, in response to the suppression of the student movement at Tiananmen, by a vote of 403 to 0 had passed legislation sponsored by Pelosi temporarily suspending the requirement that Chinese students return home for at least two years after completing their studies in the United States. Bush vetoed the bill, announcing that he would grant the students the same protection by issuing an executive order. This he did, but his action in sending General Scowcroft on his unproductive mission to Beijing immediately afterward was highly criticized and fortified congressional opposition to Bush's policy of attempting to return to a normal relationship with China. Two years later, when Bush vetoed legislation introduced by Senate Majority Leader George Mitchell to impose strict conditions on the annual renewal of China's MFN trade privileges, he made Mitchell and Pelosi natural allies. Both had seen their legislative intentions concerning China vitiated by executive orders and were willing to see this bureaucratic device now used to further rather than frustrate their objectives.

After consultations and reassurances from the new assistant secretary of state for East Asia, Winston Lord, Pelosi and Mitchell accepted Clinton's conciliatory offer to incorporate in an executive order their attempts to condition MFN status for China on its observance of specific human rights. The resultant order was signed by Clinton on May 28, 1993, with a great flourish and a gift of pens to representatives of the beneficiaries of its provisions, including Lodi Gyari. The drafters' original language calling for China to "make overall, significant progress in the next twelve months" on "seeking to resume dialogue with the Dalai Lama or his representative, and taking measures to protect Tibet's distinctive religious and cultural heritage" had been watered down to include only the latter, less provocative provision of "protecting Tibet's distinctive religious and cultural heritage." But the executive branch had gone on record on the situation in Tibet which Congress had been pressing them to acknowledge, so it seemed like a reasonably good trade.

The sponsors from Capitol Hill who were advocates of the use of human rights to promote a more democratic China had acquired unusual support from the State Department when Winston Lord, the former Kissinger protégé who had defected to the Clinton camp, was appointed assistant secretary for East Asian affairs. His support was significant given his role as policy

FIGURE 17 The Dalai Lama meets with Nancy Pelosi, one of his strongest congressional supporters.

drafter, note taker, and confidante in Kissinger's dramatic opening to China a decade earlier and later one of Reagan's ambassadors to Beijing. Ironically Lord now had the support of Tibet's most conservative congressional advocate, Jesse Helms, who had held Lord's ambassadorial appointment hostage for several months as part of his campaign to deny contributions to any program that carried out family-planning assistance to China.

Lord had moved on to become a more outspoken supporter of the human rights movements that were gathering momentum in China, especially within the universities and other academic circles during the last years of the Reagan administration. He had then blotted his copy book with the succeeding Bush administration by including the well-known Chinese astrophysicist and human rights activist Fang Lizhi among the unpublicized guests at the Texas barbeque that Bush was hosting for Chinese leaders on his first visit to Beijing as president, in February 1989. The embassy had worked out what they and Bush's assistant for national security affairs, Brent Scowcroft, accepted as a satisfactory immunizing formula with the Chinese government. Fang was to be seated at a table in the Great Wall Sheraton Hotel banquet hall sufficiently distant from the Chinese leaders that they could eat their Texas beef with the dissident out of their sight. The Chinese, however, pulled a last-minute switch by sending a contingent of secret police to prevent Fang and his wife from reaching the banquet. This received heavy press coverage and soured what Bush had hoped would be a good start to a new, more productive relationship with China. Lord identified the originator of a publicized "background briefing" of the event as Scowcroft, to whom he protested that this had damaged his reputation as an ambassador, but even more important, scuttled concern about human rights as a legitimate element in United States relations with China.

The debate over the role of human rights in the formulation and conduct of relations with China came into even more dramatic focus a few months after Lord's departure as ambassador, when Beijing's leaders conducted a violent crackdown on the students whom Lord had been cultivating. After his return to the United States Lord became an outspoken critic of Bush's failure to take a stronger public stand against "the butchers of Beijing." These sentiments, coming from a Republican protégé of Kissinger schooled in realpolitik, made him an appealing candidate as a standard-bearer for an administration seeking a satisfactory formula for dealing with this difficult country. Clinton consequently offered, and Lord accepted, the post of assistant secretary of state for East Asian and Pacific affairs, with the responsibility for formulating and carrying out United States policy toward this rising economic giant and power broker. This put Lord in the middle, between powerful American business interests who argued that participation in the growing Chinese economic boom would serve the interests of both the Chinese and the American people, and those who would exact greater observance by the Chinese government of human rights as the price for such participation.

Looking back some years later, Lord said that prior to Tiananmen he had opposed linking MFN status for China to its observance of human rights. He also believed that Clinton had used excessive rhetoric in denouncing China during the 1992 campaign, which had forced him to carry out this linkage being pushed in Congress by Nancy Pelosi and George Mitchell. However, when Clinton came up with his political maneuver of offering to issue an executive order encompassing this linkage and thereby ensuring White House rather than congressional control over this critical element of United States policy, Lord, in his new role as a member of the administration, supported it. Among the provisions requiring China to make "significant progress" with respect to human rights was one calling for "protecting Tibet's distinctive religious and cultural heritage" as a condition for extension of MFN status the following year. Senator Moynihan ebulliently issued a press release declaring, "Today President Clinton has made history. He has told Congress that the movement of Chinese to Tibet threatens Tibet's unique identity and culture. More importantly, he has told China that significant progress must be made in protecting Tibet's unique identity or he will effectively sever trade with China. He has not submerged this issue within others. It stands alone as a separate MFN condition, a start—declaration—for the first time since the invasion of Tibet—that the Chinese subjugation of Tibet is a central issue in our relations."[3]

In retrospect some years later, Lord felt it had been a mistake to be so specific in the demands contained in the order. He believes this placed the administration in the difficult position of defining Chinese compliance the following year. This problem, he said, was compounded by the open "sabotage" conducted by the "business" components of the cabinet at the Treasury and Commerce Departments and the special trade representatives. Their active and open campaigns for "delinkage" were readily apparent to the Chinese, who rightly decided that they could sit back and let the administration sweat out a position. This left Warren Christopher, who was a human rights supporter, with three alternatives—all bad. He could pretend the Chinese had made some progress, a case that was hard to make; he could cut off the MFN linkage and go for specific lesser sanctions; or he could try to pursue the human rights objective through other channels. Lord recalled computer runs being made to see where selective cases for these options could be made. None emerged.[4]

In the autumn of 1993 the Washington establishment was sending out mixed signals concerning its intentions to enforce the MFN–human rights linkage. Robert Rubin, the chairman of the President's National Economic Council, had persuaded Clinton to grant waivers on the administration's announced intention to impose sanctions on China for selling missile parts to Pakistan. At the same time Congress passed a resolution condemning China as unfit to host the Olympic Games in 2000 because of its human rights record. Implementation of the president's executive order was put on hold while another review of China policy was conducted. It was decided to "engage" the Chinese in implementing the order. As the chief human rights official of the Clinton administration, John Shattuck, the assistant secretary of state for democracy, human rights and labor, was given the Sisyphean task of working out an accommodation with the Chinese. Shattuck had come to his post after a career as a lawyer for the American Civil Liberties Union and had been a vice president of Harvard. There he had helped President Derek Bok persuade the board of trustees to divest the university of its stock in companies doing business in South Africa and expand its assistance to racially mixed schools and universities there. He had also helped Bok organize a group of college presidents to support American and international sanctions against the apartheid regime. He was no stranger to controversy and the conflict between American business interests and human rights as a factor in United States foreign policy.

In October 1993 Shattuck was sent to Beijing to measure how effective the six-month threat of MFN revocation was in moving the Chinese to improve their actions in the human rights situations cited in the executive order. He had a message to deliver. Clinton needed the Chinese to provide evidence of their willingness to cooperate in his efforts to work with Congress on his China policy. The Chinese accordingly treated Shattuck to a week's "dialogue" with appropriate officials. This included a two-day tour of Tibet, where Shattuck took the usual guided tour of the seventh-century Jo-khang and the Dalai Lama's empty Potala Palace. He noted the "tens of thousands of fortune-seeking workers pouring into the city from China, dramatizing the slow strangling of traditional Tibetan culture." In an incident similar to the one that Ambassador James Lilley had encountered on a visit to Drapchi Prison two years before, a Tibetan managed to slip a note into the hand of the American embassy officer escorting Shattuck. The one given to Lilley said, "We are being tortured." The one intended for Shattuck reported, "More than thirty monks from this monastery are in prison."[5] This was a sour note, but a high-ranking American official had been permitted to visit the forbidden land.

This period was to be the high point of Beijing's effort to meet some of the requirements of the White House. The following month Clinton had a standoff session with President Jiang Zemin on linking MFN status to human rights when they met for the first time in Seattle. Winston Lord continued to hold weekly meetings of the interagency China Steering Group, but Shattuck noted that it was becoming increasingly obvious that "there were many China policies, and that each [United States government] agency was essentially pursuing its own China agenda."[6] He cited a particularly revealing indicator in the leak in December by an unidentified "White House official" who was quoted as saying that American business interests in China were so important that "[the administration was] not going to let something like MFN stand in its way." The human rights "dialogue" between Washington and Beijing sputtered along for a few months.

This all came to an inglorious climax in March 1994, when Secretary Christopher traveled to Beijing in a final effort to work out some accommodation with the hardball-playing Chinese that would allow Clinton to jettison what was becoming an increasingly apparent losing cause. Prior to the secretary's scheduled visit to Beijing, an evidently resigned Shattuck had gone there to review the prospects for getting the Chinese to make some moves that would permit Clinton to extend China's MFN status without a messy fight with Congress. Some evidence of Chinese concessions was especially critical in light of the bleak assessment of their human rights performance in the State Department's annual human rights report. Shattuck and Ambassador J. Stapleton Roy, the old China hand who was no enthusiast for the MFN–human rights linkage but was a loyal exponent of policies determined by the president he represented, agreed on their strategy. They would make the point that as a Democrat Clinton could work with a Democratic Congress to move the by then annual MFN debate away from the center of United States–China relations. But they first needed to measure the demonstrable progress that China had made on human rights since the Tiananmen events which they could present as evidence to the Congress.[7]

Since Shattuck's trip to Beijing the previous autumn embassy officers had met several times with Wei Jingsheng, one of Beijing's more outspoken dissidents, without provoking protests from the Chinese government. Shattuck suggested that if he were to meet with Wei to get his views on the current political climate for dissidents he could offer this as evidence of progress to congressional skeptics. Roy agreed and proceeded to set up a meeting that same evening; it was held in the coffee garden of one of Beijing's popular tourist hotels. Unfortunately, without consulting Shattuck, Wei informed the press of the meeting, and the resultant international publicity made it impossible for the Chinese government to ignore the event. Wei was arrested, and the roundup of more dissidents began. The question then was whether Christopher should cancel or postpone his scheduled visit to protest this latest crackdown on human rights.

Shattuck's advice that Christopher should cancel the visit was overruled by both Lord and Roy, and the secretary arrived in Beijing on March 11. There he was subjected to a vicious diatribe from China's hard-line premier Li Peng, who told him, "The sky will not fall for China if MFN is revoked." For good measure, he went on to assert that Christopher's generally well-regarded role as chairman of the commission which investigated the brutal beating of Rodney King by Los Angeles police officers showed that he was not objective about his own country. He concluded his tirade with the observation, "Human rights are not universal and China will not accept the human rights concepts of the United States." The next day Christopher was subjected to an equally tense meeting with representatives of the American business community in China, who argued against Clinton's MFN policy. The beleaguered secretary returned to Washington, where his reception "was almost as frosty as the greeting he had received a week earlier from the Chinese when he arrived in Beijing. The U.S. foreign policy establishment, which had hailed the executive order as a brilliant political compromise when it was unveiled by Clinton in May 1993, now turned on those seeking to implement it."[8]

In the midst of this brouhaha the Dalai Lama visited Washington and was accorded another "drop-by" meeting with Clinton and Vice President Al Gore, at which they discussed violations of religious and cultural rights in Tibet. "These issues are of concern to the Administration, especially as it views the conditions required for renewal of most favored nation status for China," the White House said.[9] This "concern," however, was not evident in the interagency policy meetings which were held in the following weeks to determine what policy to follow in face of the publicly admitted failure of the Chinese to meet the conditions laid down in the executive order. On May 26 Clinton announced that he was renewing China's MFN status, revoking the controversial executive order, and abandoning the linkage between trade and human rights policies. He rationalized that the new policy of engagement would produce greater progress for human rights than the proscriptive course that was being abandoned.[10]

Postmortem

Their supporters are still debating the consequences for the Dalai Lama and the Tibetans of having been included in the linkage of China's MFN status to human rights. One of the strongest proponents of the linkage, Joel Mc-Cleary, recalls having had vigorous arguments at the time with Gyalo Thondup, who asserted that the imposition of the requirement demanding Chinese protection of Tibet's heritage was impeding the negotiations that the Beijing government had recently resumed with him.[11] Gyalo was apparently in tune with his brother, the Dalai Lama, who with prescience opposed tying the Tibetan cause to economic trading stock as both morally inappropriate and a tactical political error. By this time Gyalo had been negotiating with the Beijing leaders for five years, trying to find a political solution to their differences that both parties could live with. This was more his style than trusting in human rights appeals, the approach he had reluctantly accepted at the United Nations in 1959. When the Tibetan ruler visited Washington as this issue was being debated he too spoke of his preference for inducing the Chinese to observe human rights as a matter of enlightened self-interest, presumably in the form of a mutually acceptable bilateral agreement affecting governance and boundaries, rather than being forced to do so because of external pressure. This forced the International Campaign for Tibet, another one of the linkage strategy's more ardent supporters and grateful legatees of Clinton's inclusion of their cause in his executive order, to make a quiet and reluctant withdrawal. McCleary still believes the Chinese leaders were particularly vulnerable at that time, as they began their move toward a market economy, and the withdrawal of linkage was a lost opportunity—one that seems lost for good with the drastically changed equities involved between an economically distressed United States and a China that is now one of its principal creditors.

In contrast, Mary Beth Markey, then a leading member of the Tibet Mafia of congressional staff promoting the Tibetan cause and now director of the International Campaign, believes that the debate in 1993–94 and the incorporation of the human rights requirement in the executive order were a critical achievement in solidifying congressional support for Tibet. In her words they moved Tibet from being a "boutique" to a "bread and butter" issue, forcing congressmen to go on record on an issue that was politically sensitive for them. This was especially true for those from districts for which trade with China was important. They had to make—and many did—the tough decision to vote on an issue that affected the pocketbooks of their constituents and, even more important, those of their campaign contributors. The consequences for them could be substantial. Although hard-core supporters of linkage such as Pelosi and Rose were not happy about trading their legislation for the executive order, they were willing to settle for a mechanism that had the public support of the president. By then they had become weary of continuing to push for legislation that never made it. Besides, Markey believes, Pelosi thought at the time that this was their best hope for accomplishing her side's goals. Clinton could inspire people, and he had become publicly committed by the executive order to deliver the result the human rights proponents were seeking. Lodi Gyari and his International Campaign staff who were supporting this tactic had helped to draw up the reasonably pragmatic list of human rights requirements, including the uncontroversial one on Tibet, that would be "winnable" and would ensure that the White House remained committed. Markey ruefully said this turned out not to have been an accurate calculation. Clinton's assumption that he could satisfy both his human rights constituents and his business supporters was a miscalculation, and the whole maneuver diverted, at least temporarily, the strong active congressional support the Tibetans had built in Congress.

Helping the Tibetans to exit Shangri-La would happen only with full regard for American commercial relations with China.

A New High in White House Support

During the last years of the twentieth century American support for the Dalai Lama and his people, both official and private, reached a new high. The White House and the State Department became more deeply involved in their affairs than any of their predecessors had been since the Ford administration severed official contact with the Tibetans twenty years earlier. Congress meanwhile maintained and strengthened the proprietary role in Tibetan affairs that it had assumed in the late 1980s. These efforts were supplemented by extramural personal initiatives undertaken by two major Washington power brokers: former president Jimmy Carter and Senator Dianne Feinstein.

In the public sector America's fascination with Tibet and its leader continued, while the organizational structure to maintain it was being created. Tibet House, founded in New York in 1987 by Robert Thurman, Richard Gere, and Philip Glass, was the site of the preservation and presentation of Tibetan culture to a receptive American public. The Shangri-La appeal was reintroduced to a greater public in 1997 by Martin Scorsese's *Kundun* and in 1998 by Brad Pitt's portrayal of the Dalai Lama's former tutor Heinrich Harrer in *Seven Years in Tibet*. By this time the romantic legend had been given new substance and meaning by the extraordinary and unique character and appeal of the Dalai Lama. He had moved on from being a displaced ruler of a remote exotic land to leader of a worldwide Buddhist revival and a widely admired and respected moral force. The State Department had given up its efforts to close down the Office of Tibet in New York. It continued to operate as the official agency of the Dalai Lama and the Tibetan government-in-exile and was joined by similar offices in London, Paris, Brussels, Budapest, Geneva, Moscow, Tokyo, Taipei, Canberra, Pretoria, New Delhi, and Kathmandu. The international campaign envisaged by Joel McCleary and institutionalized in the Washington law office of Lloyd Cutler ten years earlier was flourishing.

In Beijing President Jiang Zemin and Premier Zhu Rongji seemed prepared to match Bill Clinton's interest in reestablishing the pre-Tiananmen relationship between their two countries. By reaching a settlement with the Dalai Lama, Beijing could make a major contribution toward achieving this mutually desired amity with Washington while muting the "turbulent priest" and his international supporters, who were detracting from the trading-partner image Jiang and Zhu were seeking to establish. There seemed reason to hope that the new leadership in Beijing, then setting out to implement the new economy and society put in place by Deng Xiaoping, would find it to their advantage to come to terms with this Tibetan so admired and championed by the Americans.

New Teams in Beijing and Washington

On January 23, 1997, Madeleine Albright was sworn in as secretary of state to replace Warren Christopher, whose dealings with post-Tiananmen China during Clinton's first term had been unproductive. Another key figure, Winston Lord, had retired in January from his post as assistant secretary of state for East Asian affairs, where he had been a leading, though not always predominant, voice of Washington's efforts to find a solution to the unsettled relationship with China that he had helped establish twenty years earlier. Four weeks later Deng Xiaoping died at the age of ninety-three, leaving behind a record that Secretary Albright said called for "mixed assessment" and a number of issues that remained unresolved. These included Washington's continuing objections to China's human rights policies, particularly in Tibet. The principal question was whether Deng's successors would be willing to proceed any further toward a settlement that he seemed to have opened up but then set the limits on some years before.

Albright, who was on a round-the-world tour, stopped in Beijing as the security forces were clearing Tiananmen Square for the official memorial service for Deng. A senior embassy officer described her discussion on human rights with Li Peng as "a bit sharp," but he added that the hard-line premier had not been "sarcastic, acerbic or dismissive," as he often was. Albright left Beijing "satisfied with the meetings but foresaw no breakthroughs."[1] Vice President Gore visited Beijing the following month, the highest-ranking United States official to visit the Chinese capital since the crackdown on the democracy movement in Tiananmen Square eight years earlier. His visit was generally reported not to have been a great success. Gore's relationship with Li Peng had gotten off to a bad start at a UN World Summit for Social Development in Copenhagen two years earlier. When Gore arrived late for a meeting Li angrily attacked him on America's human rights position.[2] Gore's foreign policy aide Leon Fuerth described their meeting in Beijing in 1997 as "very different," but still no great success. Li was prepared to disrupt any efforts President Jiang might be disposed to make to consolidate relations with Washington. He knew that he was still regarded by the international community as the man who had declared martial law in Beijing to quell the Tiananmen demonstrations. This seemed to have made him particularly defensive about and opposed to any concessions on human rights issues, especially on such spotlight situations as Tibet.

These tepid readings of the post-Deng waters seemed to confirm the decision that the White House had nothing to lose by proceeding with plans for Clinton to meet with the Dalai Lama in a "drop-by" visit when the Tibetan leader met with Gore at his White House office four weeks later, on April 24, 1997. The Chinese Foreign Ministry complained that Beijing was strongly dissatisfied with the United States for allowing the Dalai Lama to carry out "splittist" activities in the United States and with American leaders for meeting with him.[3] This was, however, a more muted protest than Beijing's reaction to a similar low-key meeting that Clinton had held with the Dalai Lama two years earlier, when it had summoned the American chargé to deliver a strong protest. The White House press secretary said Clinton had used the present meeting to "convey to His Holiness the President's willingness to suggest to the People's Republic of China that they enter into a dialogue with the Dalai Lama or his representative and [inform them] that he intended to raise the issue when he meets with President Jiang Zemin in a Washington summit in the fall." Speaking to reporters before his meeting with Clinton, the Dalai Lama reiterated his Middle Way position, stressing, "We have tried to make very clear to the Chinese government that we are seeking self-rule, not independence."[4]

This effort to push the new team in China into taking action that would remove the chronic irritant hindering a relationship acceptable to both the White House and Capitol Hill was loudly echoed in the hearings by the full

Senate Foreign Relations Committee the next month on "the situation of Tibet and its people."[5] The redoubtable chairman Jesse Helms led off by applauding the "very welcome statement" by the president urging China to enter into a dialogue with the Dalai Lama. He took the occasion to remind Clinton, "[Your] wish to play a constructive role in Tibet can best be fulfilled by the immediate appointment of a special envoy or coordinator for Tibet, followed by a serious undertaking to persuade the Government of China to allow that special envoy into Tibet and allow him access to prisons.... [This] would emphasize the administration's sincerity about human rights in China and Tibet." Helms's prod turned out to be fruitful when Secretary Albright appointed such a coordinator five months later.

The liberal senator from Wisconsin, Russell Feingold, called the Committee's attention to the bipartisan support within the Senate for exerting pressure on the Chinese to improve its observance of human rights, especially in Tibet. He cited the "rare occurrence in Congress to have a Helms-Feingold bill," referring to the joint effort of these two usually ideological opponents to tie China's MFN status to its human rights performance. He ended his questioning of the sympathetic State Department representative Jeffrey Bader with a request that he provide whatever details the Department had on what Gore had discussed concerning Tibet during his recent trip to Beijing. Senator John Kerry then noted that the United States had "got trounced in Geneva" at the recent international conference on human rights, where several of America's allies had "gone south on us." He suggested, "It is high time for the United States to begin, assuming we still have some economic clout left with which to do that, within the context of the World Trade Organization or otherwise, to really raise these issues." In response to Bader's defense of Albright's and his colleagues' "vigorous" lobbying efforts at Geneva, Helms noted that they had been a bit late in "putting the pedal to the metal."

Senator Dianne Feinstein expressed exasperation over the negative responses she and her husband had been receiving from the Chinese leadership for the past several years to their efforts to persuade them to enter into negotiations with the Dalai Lama: "As late as November [1996], every time I have done this, what has come back has been very clear, which is the Chinese belief that the Dalai Lama is a 'splittist.'" She asked that the State Department "become much more dominant in reinforcing the 'middle way approach' that the Dalai Lama had publicly adopted ten years ago asking the Chinese to enter into negotiations that do not include independence." Here Helms intervened to ask Bader to answer yes or no, whether the United States supported the autonomy promised by Beijing. Bader responded, "Let me try to go beyond a yes or no on this one. . . . What we stress is the unique culture and religious tradition of Tibet. The Chinese Government has promised autonomy. The Dalai Lama has talked about autonomy. We will support any resolution that the two can reach through dialogue." Eleven years later Bader was still wriggling with this deadlock as he accompanied his present boss to Beijing after the White House had iced a meeting with the Dalai Lama until after they had first met with Hu Jintao.

Feinstein was followed by another woman known for her blunt and candid views, Ambassador Jeane Kirkpatrick, who argued that using the threat of denying China MFN status would not be useful. She would encourage the Chinese to become worthy members of the world community rather than isolating them. She would encourage trade with China, but not in high-tech weapons of mass destruction or in products produced by slave labor, and press Beijing more vigorously on the issue of China's violation of Tibetan human and political rights. She asserted, "The U.S. Government needs to be willing to be boorish about it. We need to talk about it a lot—week in and week out. We need to broadcast it . . . to bore our friends and allies with it until finally they begin to talk about it more."

An Advocate at Court

This hearing, with its outspoken bipartisan support for the Tibetans, which was preceded by Clinton's demonstrable willingness to take on the Tibet issue by meeting with the Dalai Lama despite Beijing's objections, made it clear that the State Department had to make some move if it wished to retain a voice in United States policy on the issue as part of the greater China account. Albright had heard Helms's renewed pitch for a special envoy or coordinator on Tibet. She would have noted that with Lord's departure from the State Department the National Security Council was assuming more policy and operational direction of the China account, in which the Tibet issue played a disproportionate role. Jeffrey Bader was soon to move from his post as desk officer in charge of Chinese affairs at the State Department, where he had been during Lord's tenure, to become the China officer at the NSC. These signals reflected the interest that NSC Director Samuel "Sandy" Berger had assumed in affairs affecting China in consonance with Clinton, who wanted to renovate the United States–China relationship. It had been eight years since the events in Tiananmen Square had chilled the connection, and the mangled debate over the renewal of the MFN statute had done little to restore it. Berger believed that Tibet was an issue that Americans really cared about, and if the Chinese would hold a meaningful dialogue with the Tibetans it would greatly enhance the Chinese relationship with both the American people and Congress.

Bader said that it was Clinton who set the tone in promoting the Tibetan issue with the Chinese. When Clinton "dropped in" on the meetings with the Dalai Lama in Gore's office he took the initiative in discussing the issues involved in the Dalai Lama's efforts to enter into a dialogue with the Chinese leadership. He also insisted that Tibet be included in policy papers prepared for American officers who were negotiating with their Chinese counterparts.

Both the White House and Congress knew that they were going to take some heat for their apparent abandonment of principle when they dropped the linkage between human rights and the renewal of China's MFN status three years before, in 1994. At that time the administration had assured congressional staffers that it would exert pressure on China through "other available means." Key Senate staff members, led by Jonathan Stein of Senator Simon's office, had met with the State Department's undersecretary of political affairs to discuss how to make it clear to the Chinese that the human rights issues involved in the Tibet question were still an important element of United States foreign policy. They had been unable to come up with an agreement on a coordinated approach when Morton Halperin approached Stein asking for ideas on how to carry out his mission as the newly appointed National Security Council officer responsible for promoting democracy worldwide. Stein suggested that Halperin start by husbanding the appointment within the State Department of a special envoy responsible for promoting the restoration of democracy in Tibet.[6]

A civil liberties veteran, Halperin might have been expected to be sympathetic to such a proposal. He was, however, still bruised and understandably cautious about promoting any proposals vulnerable to being tagged as quixotic after his recent unsuccessful battle to obtain confirmation for a senior Pentagon post in charge of nation building. He cited the State Department's stock technical questions about Tibet's legal status and pointedly asked if Stein's principal, Senator Simon, was going to sponsor such a proposal. Although Stein's fellow members of the Tibetan coterie among the congressional staffs were eager, his boss was not sufficiently fired up at that time to sponsor such a proposal as a separate bill. Simon was willing, however, to see it incorporated in the annual State Department authorization bill, as were the other pro-Tibetan senatorial stalwarts, Pell, Moynihan, and Helms. After considerable maneuvering it was included in the authorization bill of 1995, but it failed to pass.

By 1997, however, Albright could see the advantage of accepting Helms's renewed suggestion that the Department appoint a special envoy or coordinator for Tibet. Her personal priorities and interests were more attuned to the problems of the former Communist countries in Eastern Europe, but she wanted to retain a voice in relations with the Chinese. Fulfilling the wishes of the chairman of Senate Foreign Relations Committee would serve this purpose. Albright did not want to see a special envoy provision enacted into law because of the implications this would have concerning the status of the Dalai Lama's government-in-exile, which would produce a predictably bitter and unproductive exchange with China. She therefore offered a compromise. She would appoint a special coordinator for Tibetan affairs within the State Department whose "central objective [would] be to promote substantive dialogue between the Government of the People's Republic of China and the Dalai Lama or his representatives." The coordinator would "maintain close contact with religious and cultural leaders of the Tibetan people, including travel to Tibet." She stipulated, "Since the United States regards Tibet as part of China, however, these contacts will not constitute any form of diplomatic recognition of a Tibetan government-in-exile or promote the independence or secession of Tibet from China."[7]

Ellen Bork, Helms's foreign policy advisor, negotiated further commitments. She specified, and Albright agreed, that the coordinator would be appointed by November 1 of that year, after consultations with Congress on who that person would be; that the person would have authorization to travel to Tibetan regions; and that he or she would be provided with "adequate resources, staff and bureaucratic support."[8] The deadline proved awkward for the State Department, as it turned out to be the last day of President Jiang's first visit to the United States. Albright was able to finesse this potential diplomatic incident by waiting until Jiang left Washington on October 30 to announce the appointment of her director of the Department's Policy Planning Staff, Gregory B. Craig, to this post.

Although Jiang may have appreciated this bit of diplomatic politesse, he well knew that Tibet was to be a continuing issue in the new relationship he was hoping to establish with Washington. Prior to going to the United States he had held a rare interview in Beijing in which he sketched his positions on various subjects that he expected to discuss in Washington. On Tibet he stated the stock position of reaffirming China's claim to sovereignty. While in Washington he went little further in his response when asked at the joint press conference with Clinton about the possibility of "allowing greater religious freedom in Tibet." It was Clinton who took the initiative in assuring the press that "every aspect of this issue [political prisoners and religious freedom in Tibet] had been discussed in great detail." Jiang equivocated: "As for the issue concerning religion in Tibet, in China people have the freedom to exercise their different religious beliefs. However, on this question, I believe religious freedom in Tibet and violation of criminal law are issues within a different framework. And therefore, I hope that mutual understanding between us will be promoted."[9]

Jiang might have hoped to avoid the Tibet issue when he left Washington to make the visit to Harvard that he had asked for and looked forward to, but one of the three questions his host committee had permitted be asked following his speech there was why he had so far refused to meet with the Dalai Lama. In response Jiang recited the stock formula: "[The Dalai Lama] must recognize publicly that Tibet is an inalienable part of the People's Republic of China; . . . he must state publicly [his readiness] to give up Tibet independence; and . . . he must stop all activities aimed at splitting the motherland. . . . But much to [my] regret up until this date the fourteenth Dalai Lama has not stopped his separatist activities."[10]

Jiang then departed by way of the back entrance to Sanders Hall, a route selected by his hosts to avoid the demonstrations protesting his presence at Harvard, which had been actively debated on campus the week before he arrived. This exit, however, forced his cavalcade to pass by the small adjacent piece of land not owned by the university, but by the Swedenborgian church, which had provided hospitality to the Tibetan protest movement for some years. The Tibetans were able to take advantage of this serendipitous location to stand on the lawn in colorful national dress and with banners and flags and voice their sentiments of support for the Dalai Lama and their fellow countrymen as Jiang went by. For a man who had successfully walked through the political minefields of post-Tiananmen Beijing and survived, these American concerns about the situation in Tibet probably did not have high priority. Jiang, however, must have returned to Beijing with the message to his colleagues that failure to come to a demonstrably mutually satisfactory settlement with the Dalai Lama and his country was going to be a continuing major irritant in United States–China relations.

The First Coordinator of Tibetan Affairs

Jiang, a bureaucracy survivor, would also have understood the significance of the creation of a permanent institution within the State Department to monitor and promote what was becoming a shared objective of Congress, the White House, and the State Department. Albright had not only met Helms's deadline to appoint a coordinator to monitor Tibetan affairs. She had also appointed someone close to her to confirm to Helms and his congressional colleagues that she took the post seriously. Gregory Craig was a seasoned Washington insider, a Phi Beta Kappa Harvard graduate with a diploma in history from Cambridge University and a degree from Yale Law School, where he had known Hillary Rodham and Bill Clinton. In Washington Craig had represented a variety of high-profile defendants, ranging from Spiro Agnew, Richard Helms, and John Hinckley to Alexander Solzhenitsyn, and he had recently served as Senator Edward Kennedy's senior advisor on defense, foreign policy, and national security issues. The Tibetans had acquired a skilled political infighter as a champion.

Craig said that Albright made the new post responsible directly to her because she did not want to plant it either in her unreceptive East Asian and Pacific Bureau or in the Democracy, Human Rights and Labor Bureau, where it would not have the necessary political clout.[11] He believed that Albright brought a new approach to the United States–China relationship, which had grown bankrupt and single-track under her predecessor. She did this by walking a fine line between sticking to her principles and finding a way to work with a country like China with which the United States might disagree. She regarded China as a Great Power, with which it was necessary to find a working relationship. She believed that the Chinese had shown some initiative on a new approach to North Korea, and she wanted to work with them on this problem. Similarly she was looking for new approaches on the India-Pakistan problem. She thought that China was changing, and she was prepared to encourage it to open a window to the West. Problems like Taiwan and Tibet made it more difficult to find this working relationship. She was particularly anxious to find a solution to the seemingly more tractable Tibet situation to remove it as an issue. She was therefore prepared to take the Tibet coordinator role seriously. Moreover, Craig concluded, she liked the Dalai Lama.

Craig believes that in general Albright got the United States–China-Tibet balance "right." He initially assumed when he took the coordinator post that he might be able to do something to break the stalemate between the Dalai Lama and the Chinese leadership. Albright was able to persuade the reluctant Chinese to permit Craig to accompany her to Beijing to plan for Clinton's trip to China the following year. Although they accepted him as chief of her policy-planning staff, and not as the coordinator for Tibetan affairs, this did not prevent him from raising the issues of the Chinese dissidents and the human rights situation in Tibet. Both were subjects that Clinton raised with Jiang a few weeks later. Craig thought then, and continues to think, that Jiang was interested in coming to terms with the Tibetans. Craig found his contacts in the Chinese Foreign Office prepared to discuss the Tibet situation and expecting Clinton to include it on his agenda when he met with Jiang and other Chinese leaders on his forthcoming visit. He noted that it was Jiang, not Clinton, who raised "the Tibet issue" and the Dalai Lama at their joint press conference at Tiananmen. Craig believes that Jiang exceeded the agenda that his colleagues had agreed on and later had to pull back.

Craig had little opportunity, however, to explore this speculation or to promote what he considered Clinton's "fascination" with the Dalai Lama and the issues involved in the Tibet problem. In September 1998 Clinton summoned him to the White House, where Clinton was assembling a legal team to defend himself against impeachment charges. The Tibetans temporarily lost their on-the-scene spokesman.[12]

Julia V. Taft

The Chinese, who have been watching mandarins come and go for centuries, could have been expected to note that the man promoting the cause of the Dalai Lama on behalf of the Americans had been tapped to defend his own sovereign. This should have given enhanced stature to the cause that he represented. The Tibetans, although they had lost their high-profile advocate, could take comfort in knowing that the beleaguered defense of their cause had been institutionalized—not buried—within the executive branch of the United States government. On January 20, 1999, Julia V. Taft was named Craig's successor. Her political and professional credentials for performing this function were impressive. The wife of the State Department's legal advisor William Howard Taft IV, she had a distinguished résumé of her own as an expert on the affairs of refugees and displaced persons dating back to 1975, when she directed President Ford's program to resettle over 130,000 Indochinese refugees in the United States. Immediately prior to her present appointment she had been dealing with the crisis of the ethnic Albanians being forced from their homes in Kosovo by Serbian president Slobodan Milosevic.

Taft did not have the personal tie to Albright enjoyed by her predecessor, but she did have the appropriate bureaucratic territorial mandate as assistant secretary of the Bureau for Population, Refugees and Migration. In practice, she felt restricted by what she found to be the East Asian Bureau's consistent avoidance of any action on behalf of the Tibetans. She said she found this natural, as those working on China didn't want to get tagged with the Tibet label, which could make them persona non grata for assignments to mainland China and limit their China careers to working on Taiwan.[13]

She was a person of considerable enthusiasm and enterprise, but her tour as the Tibet coordinator was a frustrating experience. The Chinese would not permit her or her staff assistant, Kate Friedrich, to visit China and refused to recognize the existence of the Tibet Coordinator Office. She was similarly thwarted in her other initiatives. One major one was to push the White House to indicate its support by enlisting a high-level official who the Chinese would recognize spoke with authority—and consequently would respect—to complement her efforts. She proposed that either Defense Secretary William Perry or Joint Chiefs Chairman General John Shalikashvili carry a message to President Jiang that the United States was interested in seeing a solution to the Tibet situation and would be happy to organize a "stealth meeting" between a senior Tibetan and a Chinese official who could deal authoritatively with the issues outstanding between their two countries. The meeting would be held in a third country, away from the scrutiny of the press and constituents of both parties. Nothing came of this. Perry was named to handle the North Korean negotiations, and Shalikashvili was similarly employed elsewhere. No top member of the brass carried Taft's message to Jiang.

Her efforts to enlist the American business community to work in Tibet and thereby establish an American presence and an alternative to Chinese economic monopoly there also generally failed. Both the Erickson Company and BP had expressed willingness to cooperate in her efforts to force human rights concessions in return for doing business in Tibet. They, however, found the internal Chinese administrative and political structure too cumbersome or inadequate to proceed with investment there. She said the American consulate in Chengdu lacked both the staff and the imagination to exert the kind of quid pro quo business diplomacy that she had in mind. Despite these frustrations and disappointments, Taft strongly believed the Coordinator Office was worth preserving as the "burr under the saddle" that ensured that the Tibet issue wouldn't get lost among the other issues of more immediate concern and interest within the State Department.

Paula J. Dobriansky

The institution survived the change of parties controlling the White House. When Secretary of State Colin Powell appointed his number three officer, Paula J. Dobriansky, as the new special coordinator for Tibetan issues, she was in a stronger bureaucratic position to act as this "burr under the saddle" than either of her predecessors. Powell made the appointment on May 17, 2001, the week before the Dalai Lama was scheduled to arrive in Washington to meet with the new president. By this time Dobriansky had already traveled with Powell to Beijing, where she had her first opportunity to discuss Tibetan affairs in depth with the Chinese leaders. There was no breakthrough, but the protocol-conscious Chinese would have understood that when they met with either the president or his secretary of state from then on, they could expect Dobriansky to be sitting with them.

Dobriansky's appointment augured well for the Tibetans' prospects. She attributed her interest in the Tibetan cause to three factors: her long-standing involvement with human rights concerns; her regard for the Dalai Lama, whom she had met (she was particularly impressed that he did not sloganeer for Tibetan independence in his public appearances); and her Ukrainian heritage, because of which she appreciates the value of preserving a unique language and culture. She had grown up explaining to people that Ukraine was not part of Russia and that its language was not Russian. She disagreed with those who criticized the Dalai Lama's internationalization campaign as counterproductive. Citing her experience as a human rights negotiator, she found it most productive to begin by discussing the issues privately with the persons or countries involved. Then, if she obtained no satisfaction, it was time to go public. In the Dalai Lama's case, she felt the international campaign in support of his position was critical, pointing out that he had tried unsuccessfully for some years to negotiate with Jiang and his predecessors.[14]

Dobriansky's assistant for Tibetan affairs, Kate Friedrich, noted the even more active support for the Tibetans that came from the Bush II White House.[15] She attributed it to President George W. Bush's intense support for religious freedom, something he brought up in every discussion involving Tibet with the Chinese, at the expense of his wish for their support on other international issues. Secretary Powell was similarly supportive. He "packed" the room with everyone in the NSC and State Department staffs with an interest in Tibet when he met with the Chinese and made a point of including Dobriansky in meetings with them on other issues. Although the Chinese ambassador had apparently taken note of these protocol subtleties and met with Dobriansky and invited her to social functions at the embassy, Beijing's glacial movement toward granting any meaningful concessions on Tibet prevailed. Despite—or perhaps because of—being forced to circle around, but never inside, the corral for five years, Dobriansky reaffirmed her belief that continuance of the campaign was a critical requirement in pursuit of a long-term United States–China relationship. She had not participated in face-to-face negotiations with her Chinese counterparts on specific issues involving Tibet, and the urgings of her principals to engage in a meaningful dialogue did not produce concrete results. But she believed the process had provided the Dalai Lama with the opportunity to demonstrate his genuine desire to find a solution and maintain the Tibetan cause on the international scene.[16]

Maria Otero

As Dobriansky's successor, Maria Otero was introduced to the complexities she would confront when she traveled to Dharamsala in September 2009 with the White House advisor Valerie Jarrett. Jarrett was sent to inform the Dalai Lama that President Barack Obama was postponing their first meeting until after he met with Hu Jintao in Beijing. Acting as the new administration's focal point on Tibetan affairs was not going to be easy for Otero. She had worked for ACCION, an international microfinancing organization, in Inner Mongolia, where she launched and directed an antipoverty program which is still active; she thus knows both the potential and the limits of such endeavors in sensitive areas. This could cause her to favor participation in programs concerning specific human rights and relief programs rather than championing the Tibetans' political status within a divided State Department.[17]

The difficulty of practicing such delineation was demonstrated when she made a welcome visit in mid-February 2011 to Tibetan refugee camps in southern India and then proceeded to Nepal without stopping in Dharamsala to meet with the Dalai Lama. Banquo's ghost was waiting for her in Kathmandu; during her visit the Nepalese government initiated a crackdown on the elections being held for the leadership of the Chushi Gangdruk organization, composed of the veterans of the Tibetan resistance force that battled the Chinese People's Liberation Army (with American assistance) from 1958 to 1974. In addition to these fiduciaries from the past Otero felt obliged to speak on behalf of the refugees who continue to flee Tibet to a grudging reception in Nepal.

CHAPTER TWENTY-TWO

People-to-People Diplomacy

By the last decade of the twentieth century the Dalai Lama and his people had gained the enthusiastic support of a sizable number of influential members of the United States Congress and the pledged support of the White House and the State Department to help them find a peaceful resolution to their dispossessed status. These exertions were supplemented in private channels by Washington power figures.

Feinstein and Blum's Link with Jiang Zemin

One of more persistent and initially promising power-broker teams advocating for the Tibetans among the Chinese leadership is that of Senator Dianne Feinstein and her husband, Richard Blum, a banker in San Francisco. These two influential Americans, with a deep sympathy for the Dalai Lama and the Tibetans and a very strong interest in the Chinese economic and political scene, came together in time, location, means, and purpose as Jiang Zemin was making his way to becoming China's top political leader.

For Blum, this interest began when he went to Nepal on business in 1968 and met some of the displaced Tibetan guerrillas from Mustang, from whom the CIA and the Indian CIB had withdrawn their support. He determined to seek a remedy to the dismal prospects for these casualties of the Cold War. This led him to active involvement in the cause of the spiritual leader they revered. Blum recalled that when the Dalai Lama, the distinguished abbot of the Sherpa monastery Tengboche, and he celebrated their sixtieth birthdays together in 1995 Blum had joked that "they were all three obviously reincarnations: His Holiness that of the Thirteenth Dalai Lama, the abbot that of his predecessor at Tengboche, and he, for his sins, that of an investment banker."[1]

By 1978 Blum was in a position to bring all of his interests together. A better working relationship between the United States and China would permit him and his fellow businessmen in California to take part in the rapidly expanding economy on the mainland. One obstacle to the development of closer ties was Beijing's refusal to negotiate with Blum's friend, the Dalai Lama, who was about to make his first trip to the United States. The White House was skittish about encouraging such a visit at a time when it was maneuvering with Deng Xiaoping to complete and consolidate the normalization of relations that President Carter was working to achieve. Washington was using the excuse that because the Dalai Lama was not recognized as a head of state it couldn't provide the requisite security for his safety. Blum, who was both a personal friend of Mayor George Moscone of San Francisco and one of his most influential constituents, was able to persuade him to disregard such imagined sensitivities and pledge to provide full security and honors to the Dalai Lama if he visited San Francisco. By the following year Dianne Feinstein (whom Blum was to marry in 1980) had become mayor after the murder of Moscone, and the Dalai Lama was given a reception at City Hall and a podium at the politically influential Commonwealth Club.

During the Reagan years Blum continued his pursuit of the mountains, taking an expedition in 1981 to climb Mt. Everest, where he intended to plant a Tibetan flag given to him by the Dalai Lama. He and his party got as far as one of the base camps before bad weather forced them back. He also continued both his investments in China and his support of the Tibetans. These diverse interests, coupled with his vigor in pursuing them, have made for a complex but sustained effort that has kept him and his wife very much involved in the American efforts, official and private, to prod Beijing's leaders to come to a settlement with the Dalai Lama and his people. This constellation of power brokers first came together in 1985, when Jiang, who had been the local Chinese Communist Party boss, became mayor of Shanghai. Soon after, Feinstein, who was still mayor of San Francisco and supported a healthy trade with China, arrived in this major Chinese industrial and political city with her husband as part of the Sister City program. By then Blum had become a major figure in Asian financial affairs. Jiang thus sought and enjoyed the advice of these two powerful Americans with unique insights

FIGURE 18 Senator Dianne Feinstein, her husband, Richard Blum, their daughter Katherine, and granddaughter Eileen are welcomed to Beijing by their friend Jiang Zemin.

and connections in setting up the Shanghai Stock Exchange. The exchange was part of the new economic order in China which justified the incorporation of the new capitalist class into the Chinese Communist Party. On this visit the two Californians "brought up" the subject of Tibet with their new friend, but there was little substantive discussion of this issue.

When this influential trio next met, in 1991, the budding United States–China relationship had cooled in the public outrage that developed in the United States over the suppression of the student rebellion in Tiananmen Square. By then Jiang had become a member of the top leadership circle in Beijing as secretary general of the Communist Party, and he had begun sending subtle messages to Blum and the senator that they "must come" to Beijing to resume their relationship. When they met Jiang gave the standard Beijing response to Blum's presentation of the Tibetan grievances. Blum got increasingly angry during the exchange and began heatedly to cite the reports of injustice that he had heard from Tibetan refugees whom he had recently met in Nepal. Blum hauled out a bracelet which a nun had given him when he met her shortly after her flight from Tibet. It was one of two that she had made in the jail where she was imprisoned by the Chinese after her refusal to give up her vows. Blum had kept one to give to his daughter.

The other he wore, and it was this one that he flashed at Jiang. The Chinese leader's face turned white, and Feinstein thought that this was to be the end of both the interview and the relationship. Jiang regained his cool, however, and replied with platitudes about not believing everything you hear.

Two weeks later Richard Holbrooke, a Democratic Party foreign affairs insider, called Blum to tell him of the conversations he had just had with Jiang, in which he had raised the subject of Tibet. Jiang had told him, "Don't lecture to me on Tibet. Richard Blum is my expert on Tibet. But my revenge is to sing old Sigmund Romberg love songs to him." Blum confirmed that Jiang had serenaded Senator Feinstein with "O Sole Mio" at a dinner during their visit.

Blum later related this heated exchange followed by crooning to Jiang's son, who was studying at Drexel University, saying he was surprised that his father still considered him a friend. The well-trained young man replied with a Chinese proverb: "Until you have had a good argument, you can't be good friends."

When Clinton became president, Blum wrote a briefing paper for him to use in raising the subject of Tibet with Jiang when they met for the first time at a G-7 meeting in Vancouver in 1993. Afterward Clinton told Blum that he had raised all the issues with Jiang and had received the same polite brush-off. But Jiang had added that he assumed it was Blum who had put Clinton up to making the presentation.

Throughout the Clinton years Feinstein and Blum continued their efforts to persuade the Chinese to come to terms with the Tibetans. They acted as special couriers, delivering six messages from the Dalai Lama seeking to rejuvenate the stalled negotiations with Beijing. These messages, drafted by the Tibetans, were shown to the White House and on at least three occasions were discussed personally with Jiang, who had become president while retaining his top posts as secretary general of the Communist Party and chairman of the Central Military Commission. Feinstein and Blum personally like Jiang. They believe he was willing to accept a compromise solution on Tibet as inevitable—or at least not worth the continuing international opprobrium—but was constrained by his hard-line colleagues who feared it would lead to further dismemberment of the border area. Blum said that Jiang told Gore when they met in Kuala Lumpur in 1997 that he was prepared to meet with the Dalai Lama but was stymied by the opposition of his colleagues. He said that Jiang had told both President Jacques Chirac of France and Prime Minister Tony Blair of Great Britain the same thing, specifying to Chirac that it was Li Peng who was the strongest opponent of any accommodation with the Tibetan leader.[2] Feinstein said that the furthest she could ever get with Jiang was his agreement that after the problems of Hong Kong and Taiwan were solved, China would turn to Tibet.[3]

In 1999 a discouraged Feinstein informed Jiang of her intention to introduce the Tibet Policy Act unless his country changed its policies there. The Chinese ambassador in Washington subsequently called to dissuade her from sponsoring such legislation. At a later meeting with Jiang he refused to budge from his intransigent position, continuing to denounce the Dalai Lama as an untrustworthy "splittist," despite the Tibetan leader's disavowal of any demand for independence in one of the letters she had carried from him to Jiang.

In a final gracious but substantively empty gesture of goodwill, Jiang accepted Feinstein's persistence in promoting a cause that he could not approve of, characterizing the impasse as one of those things friends experience without its affecting their friendship. This exchange took place in 2002 as Jiang was beginning his long withdrawal from office, culminating in March 2005, when he gave up his last official post, chairman of the Central Military Commission, to Hu Jintao. He still plays a role in Chinese politics as the leader of the "Shanghai Gang," and Feinstein and Blum have maintained their friendship with him. When they met in China at an anniversary celebration of the Sister City relationship in 2005, they had a friendly conversation but did not mention Tibet. Jiang's son later told Blum that his father appreciated their courtesy in not revisiting this sore subject.[4] Presumably the channel to Jiang remains open in his present role as leader of a shadow group of senior backroom politicians—but unfortunately ones with declining influence in Beijing. Hu Jintao has shown no interest in taking up the personal relationship with Feinstein and Blum that his predecessor appeared to find pleasurable and profitable. By 2011 Blum did not believe the prospects of a renewed channel for negotiations on Tibet with Jiang were promising, and Jiang has shown little inclination to reinvolve himself either in the domestic politics of Beijing or in Tibet.[5]

The intended Tibetan beneficiaries of these efforts can take some comfort that the Tibet Policy Act which Senator Feinstein sponsored was signed into law by President Bush on September 30, 2002. This act solidified the various legislative actions and statements of policy by which Congress had carved out a position in America's course of action toward Tibet since 1987. Specifically it established in law the position of the special coordinator for Tibetan issues at the State Department and policy goals for international economic assistance to and in Tibet; called for the secretary of state to make "best efforts" to establish an office in Lhasa; provided support for consideration of

Tibet at the United Nations; ensured that Tibetan-language training is available for foreign service officers; and called on China to cease attacks on religious freedom in Tibet and to release political and religious prisoners while providing for the continuation of humanitarian assistance and scholarships for Tibetans in India and Nepal.

Each of the Tibet negotiations reports since the first was submitted to Congress in 2003 contained (with minor variations) the following sentence: Lack of resolution of these problems in Tibet leads to greater tensions inside China and will be a stumbling block to fuller political and economic engagement with the United States and other nations. In 2010 the report specified that failure to address these problems would lead to greater tensions inside China and would be "an impediment to China's social and economic development." The sentence describing the Tibetan people's view of the Dalai Lama was also changed from "He represents the views of the vast majority of Tibetans" to "His views are widely reflected within Tibetan society, and he commands the respect of a vast majority of Tibetans."

It remains to be seen whether the United States government will continue to repeat these worthy statements of support and act to give them substance.

The Tiananmen Press Conference

One of the more spectacular episodes in the history of Washington's efforts to find a modus vivendi with Jiang and his successors occurred on June 27, 1998, against the dramatic background of Tiananmen Square. President Jiang Zemin and President Bill Clinton held a press conference following their discussions during the visit Clinton was making to Beijing after Jiang's visit to Washington the previous autumn.[6] There had been some unfriendly press and congressional criticism of Clinton's visit, which fulfilled the sequential arrangement Warren Christopher had negotiated in 1996. His partisan critics suggested that Clinton found it useful to get out of town to escape the mounting adverse publicity concerning his relationship with Monica Lewinsky. In Congress 152 members had passed a resolution condemning any negotiations with the Chinese because of their human rights record. Even Dianne Feinstein had questioned the utility of a meeting with her uncooperative friend Jiang. The Democratic Party pols opposed the trip, as they considered Clinton's China initiative to be a loser. Clinton's NSC advisor, Jeffrey Bader, believed Clinton demonstrated real courage by proceeding with his initiative to improve relations with China, which he knew was not going to be a political win.[7]

Both Jiang and Clinton were mindful of the ghosts still present at the site of the events that had abruptly chilled the evolving relationship that their predecessors had failed to establish a decade earlier. Each took advantage of the forum to address both his and the other's constituents.

Jiang led off with a homily on the improvement in relations between the two countries, demonstrated by their agreement not to target their strategic nuclear weapons at each other and the mutually beneficial growth of economic cooperation and trade. He made a passing reference to the Taiwan question, "the most sensitive issue at the core of China-U.S. relations," expressing "the hope that the U.S. side will adhere to the principles set forth in the three China-U.S. joint communiqués and statement, as well as relevant commitments it has made in the interest of a smooth growth of China-U.S. relations." Jiang, who was well aware that some of his colleagues—and some of his guest's—did not share his professed benign interest in closer ties with the United States, said, "The improvement and the growth of China-U.S. relations have not come by easily. The world is a colorful one, and China and the United States have different social systems, ideologies, values and cultural traditions . . . [but] they should not become obstacles in the way of the growth of China-U.S. relations."

Clinton, equally mindful of his critics at home who had reservations about reviving the relationship with China, responded:

> Clearly, a stable, prosperous China, shouldering its responsibilities for a safer world, is good for America. Nothing makes that point better than today's agreement not to target our nuclear missiles at each other and do more to shore up stability in Asia, on the Korean Peninsula, and the Indian subcontinent. . . . [We have] reaffirmed our longstanding one-China policy to President Jiang and urged the pursuit of [the] cross-strait discussions recently resumed as the best path to a peaceful resolution. In a similar vein, I urged President Jiang to assume a dialogue with the Dalai Lama in return for the recognition that Tibet is a part of China and in recognition of the unique cultural and religious heritage of that region.[8]

Clinton then discoursed on the need for the observance of human rights as the basis for a civil society: "For all our agreements [with China], we still disagree about the meaning of what happened then [at Tiananmen in 1989]. I believe, and the American people believe, that the use of force and the tragic loss of life was wrong. I believe, and the American people believe, that freedom of speech, association and religions are recognized by the U.N. Charter, the right of people everywhere and should be protected by their governments." He went on to acknowledge the painful moments in America's own history "when fundamental human rights were denied," and concluded, "Whatever our disagreements over past action, China and the United States must go forward on the right side of history for the future sake of the world."

The session continued with a glancing dismissal of recent press reports of Chinese involvement in contributions to Democratic Party campaigns and a further exchange in response to a question concerning China's policy on human rights and the events at Tiananmen nine years earlier. Jiang repeated his stock defense, "Had the Chinese government not taken resolute measures, then we could not have enjoyed the stability we are enjoying today." Clinton once more urged that China take the gamble of allowing greater personal freedom as "stability in the 21st century will require high levels of freedom."

This gentlemanly draw might well have ended in a polite stalemate. But for seemingly inexplicable reasons Jiang brought Banquo's ghost back to the banquet by asking for five additional minutes "to say a few words on the Dalai Lama, a question [in which] President Clinton is also interested." He began with a short recital of the "earthshaking changes" in Tibet, where "the system of bureaucracy has forever become bygones . . . and more than one million serfs under the rule of the Dalai Lama were liberated." After further citations of the financial resources and reforms which the Chinese brought to Tibet, he referred to Clinton's call for the Chinese government to enter into a dialogue with the Dalai Lama. "Actually," Jiang said, "as long as the Dalai Lama can publicly make the statement and a commitment that Tibet is an inalienable part of China and he must also recognize Taiwan as a province of China, then the door to dialogue and negotiation is open. Actually [a word Jiang used repeatedly], we are having several channels of communication with the Dalai Lama. So I hope the Dalai Lama will make a positive response in this regard."

Having dutifully declaimed the official litany that would satisfy his hardline colleagues like Li Peng, Jiang declared that although he, as a Communist, was an atheist, this "by no means affects [his] respect for religious freedom in Tibet." He added, "Although education in science and technology [in the United States] have developed to a very high level, and people are now enjoying modern civilization, still quite a number of them have a belief in Lamaism. So this is a question that I'm studying and still looking into. I want to find out the reason why."

Jiang's coda permitted Clinton to have the last word. Clinton pointed out that most of the supporters of the Dalai Lama in the United States that Jiang spoke about had not given up their own religious beliefs, but rather believe in the unity of God and that the Dalai Lama is a holy man. "But for us, the question is not fundamentally religious, it is political. That is, we believe that other people should have the right to fully practice their religious belief, and that if he, in good faith, presents himself on those terms, it is a legitimate thing for China to engage him in dialogue." Clinton's conclusion was characteristic of the man from Hope speaking to another pol, the former mayor of Shanghai: "And let me say something that will perhaps be unpopular with everyone. I have spent time with the Dalai Lama. I believe him to be an honest man, and I believe if he had a conversation with President Jiang, they would like each other very much." There was laughter and applause.[9]

The Academicians' Mission

Whatever momentum there might have been in the summer of 1998 to take up Clinton's challenge was soon lost. Both Clinton and Jiang were to become preoccupied with their own political futures. The promoter returned to Washington to face impending impeachment charges, and his host was entering into what turned out to be a losing battle for primacy within the Beijing hierarchy. Tibet was not to be a priority item in either of their agendas.

It was in the wake of this cooling of the atmosphere favoring the Tibetan cause that a four-man team of U.S. academicians went to China and Tibet in November 1998 with the stated mission of looking into the issues that were causing "considerable misunderstanding about Tibet in the United States, in China, and also in the Tibetan exile community." This statement reflected the intended appearance of objectivity concerning the purpose of the mission and the professional background of the members conducting it. Their "Reflections" report was prepared to help inform the Carter Center's work to monitor, prevent, and resolve conflicts worldwide.

Two of the members, Harry Barnes and Michael Oksenberg, had been studying the political situation in Tibet and China and that of the Dalai Lama and American policy toward Tibet for some time. Barnes had insights into the Sino-Tibetan situation derived from his tour as ambassador to India from 1981 to 1985. Oksenberg had been the NSC officer on China who had worked twenty years before to complete negotiations for the resumption of diplomatic relations with Beijing. He thus maintained a strong desire to remove the obstacles to achieving their objectives. He well knew the limits and the possibilities of what the United States government could and would be inclined to promote with the Chinese. Barnes and Oksenberg were accompanied by two of America's most distinguished scholars on Tibet, the anthropologist Melvyn Goldstein of Case Western University and the Tibetan Buddhism specialist Matthew Kapstein of the University of Chicago.

The four men spent eighteen days traveling and interviewing leading officials in Beijing, the Tibet Autonomous Region, and the Tibetan regions in Sichuan and Gansu. Their report, which was completed in December 1998, was a somber estimate of the prospects for a settlement of the differences between the Dalai Lama and the Chinese leaders. They noted that security regarding Tibet was of crucial concern to the Chinese military, quoting a very high-ranking military official who opened their first meeting by declaring, "The issue of Tibet involves our territorial integrity and national sovereignty. We will not compromise on those issues. Those come first." They found the outlook for the Tibetan leader equally bleak: "Although no one voiced this view specifically, we have concluded that the Chinese do not feel impelled to reach an accommodation with the Dalai Lama. Vexing though his international acclaim may be to them, the Chinese appear to believe that time is in their favor and that they can wait him out."[10] Fourteen years later this conclusion seems to have been discouragingly prophetic.

The drafters noted that the Chinese policy, "as elsewhere in China, [was] to develop Tibet as rapidly as possible and to raise the standard of living of the people.... [However,] even under the best of circumstances and with massive subsidies, the 2015 average per capita income is targeted to reach only the average per capita income for all of China in 2000 [and] even this optimistic projection means that the Tibetan Autonomous Region will have one of the lowest per capita incomes of any of China's provinces"[11] (and this goal is not totally realistic if China's growth rate should falter and the subsidies have to be curtailed). Further, the drafters also noted the following:

> There are many indications that the Chinese development strategy does not adequately take into account the desires, needs and capabilities of the indigenous people.... [Tibet's ecology] is quite fragile, and it seems likely that the land is vulnerable to excessive timbering, overgrazing and soil erosion. Moreover, Tibet's high altitude and mountainous terrain make its vegetation particularly sensitive to variation in temperature. Global warming could have major consequences for its glaciers, which in turn would affect its water flow. It is worth remembering that most of Asia's major rivers arise in Tibetan inhabited regions. From this perspective, the hundreds of millions of people who inhabit the Asian littoral have an interest in the development strategy pursued in Tibet.

The observers noted that the Chinese had adhered until 1955–56 to the agreement signed by the Chinese government and the Dalai Lama in 1950 to grant greater political autonomy to the Tibetans. But Beijing had "not exempted the Tibetan regions from the collectivization of agriculture, thereby disrupting traditional land holding and tenure patterns and laying the basis for a Tibetan rebellion." In any event, "the Chinese government no longer consider[ed] the agreement valid due to the 1957–59 rebellion, the fleeing of the Dalai Lama to India, and the establishment of the government-in-exile in Dharamsala. Nonetheless, that earlier agreement had been endorsed by Mao, and it provides a benchmark against which to judge subsequent policies. It may also contain elements to which China's leaders may be willing to return, if they can be assured that the result will not yield another era of rebellion."

As for the indigenous Tibetan culture, the team asserted:

Despite the officially stated desire (to preserve Tibetan culture), we conclude that the unstated current policy is to cultivate and assimilate a Tibetan Chinese political elite into the dominant culture. Another related objective is to weaken the grip of Tibetan Buddhism upon the popular culture. . . . The government's objective is to weave Tibetans firmly into the national social fabric. So far, four massive transformations are taking place in Tibet simultaneously: from relative isolation to extensive contact with the rest of the world; from a largely self-sufficient and planned economy to a state guided market economy; from a traditional to a modern society; and from a fusion of religion and the state to state control of religion.

They continued, "Rapid economic growth is taking place in Tibet, as in the rest of China. Urban areas are in the midst of a building boom, and the gap between urban and rural income levels is widening, with the Han Chinese residing in the TAR [Tibet Autonomous Region] benefiting disproportionally. . . . The vast majority of ethnic Tibetans are simply ill-equipped educationally to take advantage of the opportunities that Beijing is trying to create by pouring investment funds into the TAR, especially into its two major cities."

The team's observations on education in Tibet were mixed. They found that although to the government's credit a major push is now underway to make education mandatory and universal through the ninth grade throughout China, including the Tibetan inhabited regions, there were serious problems in finding qualified teachers and keeping primary-age children in class. "Moreover, the effort to expand education is not being pursued with an unambiguous emphasis upon education in the Tibetan language.... The government's objective seems to be for educated Tibetans to be able to function effectively in Mandarin and for Mandarin to dominate as the official and public language, especially in the urban areas."

Despite the officially stated desire to preserve Tibetan culture, [we] conclude that the unstated current policy is to cultivate and assimilate a Tibetan Chinese political and economic elite into the dominant culture. Another related objective is to weaken the grip of Tibetan Buddhism upon the popular culture.... [However,] it is obvious, even to the most superficial of visitors, that popular Buddhism survives despite government constraints and persecution. [But High Tibetan Buddhism, the religious and philosophic traditions in their full richness and sophistication,] is hanging by a thread.... It is worth stating explicitly what humanity and China would lose, should High Tibetan Buddhism see further erosion of its vitality.

The observers concluded that the Dalai Lama did not seek independence, but a high degree of political autonomy for a democratic Tibet within the People's Republic of China. "Indeed, he recognizes that an independent Tibet would not be economically viable without considerable outside assistance." He wants "a democratic Tibet and insists that any agreement reached with Beijing would have international guarantees and be approved by ethnic Tibetans in a plebiscite." He would permit the stationing of Chinese forces in a nuclear-free Tibet where the Chinese Communist Party would retain a presence. The PRC would represent Tibet in international organizations, though he "favors the ability of Tibet to have representatives abroad."

On the gut issue of territory they wrote, "His Holiness does not limit his interest to the TAR but envisions all the regions inhabited by Tibetans being reunited into the autonomous entity he seeks.... The territory that his supporters claim, as shown on the maps distributed by the exile community, is one-sixth of the total area of China and includes many areas inhabited by non-Tibetans."

As for the Dalai Lama himself, they wrote:

[He] integrates four roles: being the spiritual leader of Tibetan Buddhism; articulates and pursues a vision for Tibet's political future; gives hope to and unifies the ethnic Tibetan diaspora that now resides outside Tibet, many of whom might not return to Tibet even if the situation there greatly improved from their perspective; and finally, he is an ecumenical figure, seeking to invigorate Buddhism worldwide after its tragic twentieth century, and to bring together all the world's religions, and to champion the causes of democracy and justice for all oppressed ethnic minorities. . . . His personality and his intellect enable him to combine these four roles into an extraordinary whole [and] he appears to look upon them as reinforcing rather than establishing a sense of priority among them.

They questioned, however, "whether there are tensions among these roles, not in his mind, but among the constituencies they serve and the consequences they produce." Specifically they noted that his ministry to the diaspora probably constrained the political solutions that he can pursue for Tibet, citing the fact that two-thirds of the diaspora and a somewhat higher portion of the legislature of the government-in-exile came from outside the Tibet Autonomous Region. "This appears to make His Holiness more insistent upon bringing all the Tibet inhabited regions in China under one political entity." (The Dalai Lama had issued a statement in Strasbourg on June 15, 1988, introducing his Middle Way approach, by which Tibet would give up its claim to independence and accept "voluntary association , i.e. autonomy, in a unified Tibet which would include the four provinces outside the Tibet Autonomous Region where over half the Tibetan population lives." It had been extensively debated at a four-day special conference at Dharamsala prior to its release, and thus had been part of the Dalai Lama's negotiating team's brief for a decade by the time the mission arrived in Dharamsala.)

The observers noted, "[The Dalai Lama's] ecumenical activities generate Chinese mistrust of him. . . . More pointedly, his patronage of the government-in-exile makes accommodation with Beijing very difficult [and] generates Chinese mistrust of him." This led them to "wonder whether the international campaign ha[d] reached its apogee in actually promoting the welfare of the people of Tibet."

The report examined the motivation and justification for the interest in Tibet of the American people and the government. The authors sternly rejected as unworthy those who saw it as an opportunity to "weaken China and perhaps split it apart and thwart China's rise in world affairs by generating resistance to it from among its own people." Conversely, they appreciated the motivation of those concerned for the preservation of Tibetan Buddhism who found Chinese oppression of it and other religions to be intolerable, those who were concerned about the abuses of human rights in Tibet, and "still others who have simply fallen under the magnetic influence of the Dalai Lama."

They then cited three additional reasons for American interest in the Tibet issue:

First, as we earlier noted, Tibetan Buddhism is a cultural legacy that belongs not just to China but to all humanity. Second, the United States has an interest in a unified, stable, and justly governed China. Should ethnic tensions arise in China, the stability of the country would be adversely affected as in the Soviet Union. While some policies toward Tibet seem to be yielding stability, some of the most knowledgeable American observers are warning that the situation could turn violent.[12] Finally, Tibet is an indicator of the Chinese future. China is poised to achieve greatness in the twenty first century: to become as President Jiang Zemin stated at the Fifteenth Party Congress, a prosperous, socialist, democratic and culturally advanced country by 2050. To achieve that lofty goal will require drawing upon the diverse talents and traditions of all its people. Such a China will be a natural partner of the United States. But China also could become a militaristic and oppressive state. Such a China would likely be an adversary. Tibet then provides a significant litmus test; its future will reveal much about the direction in which China is headed. . . . It is therefore quite appropriate for the United States and the American people to be concerned about Tibet, to observe its evolution, to assist in the efforts to develop Tibet and improve its educational system, and to encourage a reconciliation between the government of China and the followers of the Dalai Lama.

An appendix took note of the Chinese policies which have had an adverse effect on the practice of Tibetan Buddhism. They cited the strict control of the number of monks in monasteries and the legal requirement that those entering monasteries be eighteen years old, "perhaps too late an age to attain mastery of the requisite religious rituals and laws and to have acquired an education which would enable [and encourage] them to earn a living in other pursuits." They pointed out, "[There are] precious few living Buddhas and master Buddhist teachers now, and they are aged." These obstacles were compounded by the fact that "several of the major monasteries in the TAR [were] under special political control as a result of the 1987 riots, and by the constraint on contacts between monasteries in the TAR—the mother churches—so to speak and with monasteries in other Tibetan inhabited regions." (The riots and demonstrations in the widely scattered areas of Inner and Outer Tibet decades later would indicate that these controls have been ineffective in quashing the zeal of the Tibetans for their religion and its leader.)[13]

CHAPTER TWENTY-THREE

An Uncertain Future

Tibet dropped off the White House agenda as a priority item during the last years of the Clinton administration, but the Dalai Lama and his cause retained the backing of their congressional supporters and their growing constituency among the American public. They acquired new support from the Bush II White House, where the Tibetans found the occupant even more prepared to take up their cause than his father had been. Michael Green, Bush's national security advisor on Asian affairs, said that in addition to his personal religious convictions, the president frequently cited his political belief that more religious freedom and the rule of law were indispensable for achieving the economic and social development for which China was striving.[1] Whatever the reasons, he was one of the strongest supporters that the Dalai Lama and the Tibetans have had in the White House. On his last meeting as head of state with his Chinese counterpart, Hu Jintao, Bush expressed his "longstanding commitment to religious freedom and encouraged [Jintao] to continue China's dialogue with the Dalai Lama."[2]

Bush's advocacy of the Dalai Lama and his cause was amplified by continuing bipartisan support from the other end of Pennsylvania Avenue. Under the leadership of the faithful Nancy Pelosi, Congress nominated him to receive the Congressional Gold Medal at a ceremony at the Capitol Rotunda on October 17, 2007. This honor was first awarded to George Washington and has included

FIGURE 19 The Dalai Lama pulls President George W. Bush and Speaker of the House Nancy Pelosi (D-CA) together during the ceremony where His Holiness received the Congressional Gold Medal in the Capitol Rotunda, October 17, 2007. President Bush participated in the ceremony despite Beijing's strong disapproval of the recognition for the seventy-two-year-old exiled leader from Tibet.

distinguished foreigners such as Winston Churchill, Mother Teresa, Pope John Paul II, and Aung San Suu Kyi.

Beijing's protests indicated that they had taken full note of the event and the fact that this was the first time a United States president both attended the ceremony and made the award. Bush had chosen to meet with the Dalai Lama the day before in the private quarters of the White House rather than in the Oval Office. His spokesperson explained, "We in no way want to stir the pot and make [the] Chinese feel that we are poking a stick in their eye." Following that meeting, however, Bush volunteered a reprise of Clinton's folksy urging of President Jiang at Tiananmen almost a decade earlier, that "if he had a conversation with the Dalai Lama they would like each other very much." Bush "had consistently told the Chinese that religious freedom [was] in their nation's interest ... [and] if they were to sit down with the Dalai Lama they would find him to be a man of peace and reconciliation."[3]

At the ceremony in the Rotunda Speaker Pelosi referred to America's long relationship with the Dalai Lama, noting that it had begun sixty-five years earlier, when President Franklin Roosevelt sent an emissary to Lhasa bearing a gold watch as a gift, along with his letter asking him to open his country to the transport of wartime aid to China.[4] Tenzin Gyatso, the Fourteenth Dalai Lama, smilingly held up his wrist to demonstrate that he still wears and values the watch presented to him by Ilya Tolstoy. The top-drawer audience, which included the president's wife, his secretary of state, and all of the surviving senators and congressmen who had been the Dalai Lama's stout supporters for the past two decades, rose to applaud.

In Tibet security forces quickly repressed demonstrations in Lhasa by both monks and the lay public to celebrate the honor bestowed on their absent leader. All media coverage was blacked out, but foreign observers reported that the Lhasa faithful had full knowledge of it and had quietly taken their banned celebratory incense up in the mountains and burned it there. These demonstrations of continuing loyalty to their absent leader foreshadowed those that erupted in Lhasa and throughout Tibet five months later.

2008: A Year of Critical Events

June 19, 2008, was the hundredth anniversary of America's first meeting with a Dalai Lama, the predecessor of the current one. The Thirteenth Dalai Lama had sought—and been denied—Washington's support for the right to govern his own country, free from the strictures of his Chinese overlords. Ambassador William Rockhill had made it very clear that such support was simply not in the cards then. The United States had just fulfilled its own Manifest Destiny, and the concept of acting as the champion of the human rights of the people of other nations was decades away.

A century later his successor is still striving for the same goals, but the dynamics among those involved have changed dramatically. He and his people have acquired international support, albeit of varying constancy. The China that the Great Powers felt it in their interest to protect one hundred years ago is now a Power itself—one to be challenged and bargained with rather than succored. And it is the Tibetans that the United States is now more ready, but not guaranteed, to defend. But their plight appears uncertain.

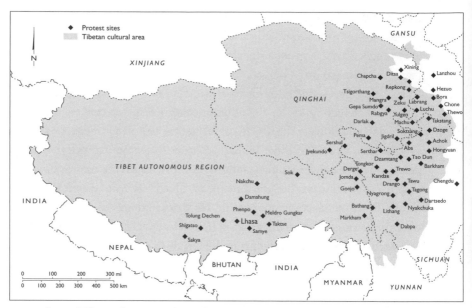

MAP 1 Sites of Tibetan demonstrations and protests, compiled from various sources where protests are reported to have taken place since March 10, 2008.

The centennial year of that first meeting and polite rebuff by America was marked by demonstrations that began in Lhasa on March 10, 2008, the forty-ninth anniversary of the failed revolt that resulted in the flight of the Dalai Lama into exile, where the end of the way of life he embodied for his countrymen had seemed imminent. The protests were initially peaceful, sparked by a march of three hundred monks from the local monasteries, demanding the release of monks who had been detained by the Chinese authorities during similar protests the previous autumn. But within four days they developed into widespread violence directed against non-Tibetans living in the Tibetan capital, in a scene which the *Economist* described as "fire on the roof of the world."[5] Similar demonstrations broke out in the ethnic Tibetan areas outside of the Tibet Autonomous Region in Gansu, Qinghai, Yunnan, and Sichuan, about which Beijing had grown increasingly sensitive.

Beijing reacted by deploying the People's Armed Police. On March 20 the BBC reported mobilization of four hundred troop carriers dispatched to the riot scenes. This publicity was followed shortly after by what the *London Times* called "a public [relations] disaster for Beijing" as the Olympic Torch was lit in Greece on March 24 and arrived in Beijing on March 31, from where it began a 130-day tour that Beijing ironically hailed as a "journey of harmony." Protestors attempted to extinguish the flame when the torch arrived in London; they were briefly successful in Paris. Similar protests occurred throughout the six-continent tour before the torch bearers scaled the Tibetan side of Mt. Everest by way of a specially constructed 108-kilometer blacktop road on the return to Beijing.

Resumption of Negotiations

It was against this backdrop of supportive protests and threatened boycotts abroad and continuing unrest in Tibet that the dialogue between Dharamsala and Beijing was resumed and again sputtered into a stalemate. On May 4, 2008, Lodi Gyari and Kelsang Gyaltsen met with two representatives of the United Front Department, the agency to which the Chinese government had consigned negotiations concerning Tibet since 1979, when Deng Xiaoping first met with the Dalai Lama's brother Gyalo Thondup. After two dozen negotiating trips and sessions in Beijing in the intervening two decades, Gyalo had been sidelined in favor of Gyari and Gyaltsen.[6] At the meeting, their sixth since 2002, when they assumed the role of Dharamsala's designated negotiators, and the first since the March riots, both parties agreed to a further round of talks.

Gyari reported that when the talks did take place in Beijing, from June 30 to July 3, he was disappointed to find the Chinese negotiators preoccupied with past history and with concerns that Tibetans, particularly the Tibetan Youth Congress, might take actions to sabotage the forthcoming Olympics. Their United Front counterparts seemed seriously upset by the March riots in Tibet and strenuously demanded to know what Dharamsala would do to prevent such violent protests and disruptions in the future.[7]

Beijing had apparently taken note of the unfavorable international publicity which the March riots and consequent Chinese crackdown had generated.[8] Members of the United States Congress had responded with legislation demanding that American officials boycott the opening ceremony of the Olympics, asking Beijing to hold talks with the Dalai Lama, and forming a new Tibet Caucus.[9] The Tibetans' longtime champion and White House monitor Speaker Pelosi had taken the message directly to Dharamsala, where she met with the Dalai Lama and called for an international investigation to "clear the Dalai Lama's name" of Beijing's allegations of his involvement in the riots: "If freedom-loving people throughout the world do not speak out against China's oppression in China and Tibet, we have lost all moral authority to speak on behalf of human rights anywhere in the world. It is our karma, we know, to help the people of Tibet."[10] The senior Republican member of her delegation, Congressman James Sensenbrenner, supported her comments.

The Tibetan envoys Lodi Gyari and Kelsang Gyaltsen and their senior aides returned to Beijing on October 30. In response to the Chinese demand to hear what the Dalai Lama would do to prevent future riots, they reiterated the Middle Way, which the Dalai Lama had been calling for since 1979: "The Tibetan people are striving for the right of a distinct people to be able to preserve that very distinctiveness through a single administrative entity."[11] This would encompass all the Tibetan people, both those living in the present Tibet Autonomous Region and the more than half who live "across the river" in Qinghai, Gansu, Sichuan, and Yunnan provinces, where Tibetans do not constitute majorities.

By this time over one hundred world leaders, including George Bush and Vladimir Putin, had arrived at the Beijing Olympics, China's international coming-out party, and the protests during the torch relay and threatened boycott of the games by world leaders were yesterday's news. International attention was absorbed by a colossal financial crisis which made events in Tibet seem very remote, and the impasse remained stalled.

After a week of inconclusive discussions the Tibetan envoys returned to Dharamsala on November 6, 2008. There preparations were in process to hold the conference at which the Tibetan exile community would confront both their present situation and their future. Vice Minister Zhu Weigun held a press conference in Beijing to denounce the Tibetan proposal as covert independence, which is not tolerated in the Chinese Constitution. He declared that the Chinese government "would never make a concession" and urged the Dalai Lama "to do something beneficial" before he died.

A Himalayan Runnymede

Against this stalemate Gyari released to the press the Memorandum on Genuine Autonomy for the Tibetan People, calling for all of the currently designated Tibetan autonomous areas to become one single administrative entity with its own regional self-government and autonomy within the People's Republic of China.

The governing mode would be the "romantic moonshine" derided by the British Foreign Office critic a half-century earlier, when the Dalai Lama set out to transfer official decision making from his sole authority to one shared with his constituents. At that time this referred to those in exile with him, but it was the pattern that he envisaged for all the Tibetan people in a reunited Tibet. He himself was an Amdo, born in Qinghai province, then governed by a Muslim warlord under the authority of Chiang Kai-shek, from whom the Lhasa government had to ransom his release in order that he might be enthroned. He fully appreciated that the majority of the Tibetan resistance forces that had initiated and manned the revolt in the 1950s were

Khampas and other Tibetan tribespeople living in Chinese provinces outside the Tibet Autonomous Region. They constituted a significant number among the Tibetans who had fled into exile with him in 1959.

Self-governance was the legacy for which the Dalai Lama had been preparing his people over the past fifty years. At a special convocation in Dharamsala on November 17–22, 2008, he asked them to accept his Middle Way. It had been formulated "as a result of much deliberation and discussion with leaders who represented the Tibetan people." Once again, as he had "specifically stated in the Strasbourg Proposal [in 1988,] the Tibetan people [would] make the final decision."

The Middle Way is a humbling revelation to those of us who supported and aided the Dalai Lama's efforts to prepare his people to govern themselves. We originally encouraged these aspirations for their immediate pragmatic value in establishing his claim to represent a democratic state worthy of the backing of like-minded nations in the international community. Such a program gave substance to the Tibetans' claim of self-determination which Secretary Herter recognized on behalf of the United States in early 1960 and which won votes for a similar resolution at the United Nations the following year. The United States considered these to be diplomatic victories. The Dalai Lama and his political counselors, while appreciative of this affirmation of their status, considered it an acknowledgment of the "genuine autonomy" that they would continue to fight for.

And they and their constituents have fought. This contest was recorded in the resignation, effective June 1, 2012, of Lodi Gyari and Kelsang Gyaltsen, the interlocutors in the nine rounds of negotiations that the Dalai Lama's government has been engaged in with Beijing since 2002 seeking an agreement on "genuine autonomy" for Tibet. They cited their frustration over the stonewall response they have received, but declared that "given the deterioration inside Tibet since 2008 leading to increasing cases of self-immolation by the Tibetans [at least thirty-eight] we are compelled to submit our resignations." The resignations were accepted by Kalon Tripa Lobsang Sangay, who was appointed to his post as administrative head of the Tibetan government-in-exile in 2011. His government said that a new task force on talks will meet again in December 2012 after China announces its new leadership in the fall.

But when the 581 delegates from the Dalai Lama's worldwide constituency had met in Dharamsala in November 2008 the stalemate with the Chinese negotiators that was brewing was not that generally apparent. The Dalai Lama's older brother, Gyalo Thondup, expressed his "shock" that the current United Front official who was negotiating with his successor denied that Deng had said on March 12, 1979, "Except independence all other issues can be settled through discussions." Thondup, then eighty years old, advised his younger brother, "It's essential for the Tibetan people not to lose hope in pleading for our rights to the Chinese government."[12]

The Dalai Lama has critics. Jamyang Norbu, despite being the son-in-law of the late Lhamo Tsering, Gyalo's longtime friend, ally, and associate in challenging the Chinese occupation of Tibet, spoke vigorously for *rangzen* (independence) now. He asserted that the Dalai Lama's Middle Way "depends on China democratizing, but that premise has so far not materialized in any way and has even gotten worse." An independence movement, he argued, would unite the exile community, keep Tibet in the headlines, and increase pressure on the Chinese government. Similarly Tenzin Dorjee, an officer of the Students for a Free Tibet, headquartered in New York City, and his cohorts expressed their position that ratifying the Dalai Lama's Middle Way policy of settling for "real and meaningful autonomy" instead of outright independence for Tibet would be a mistake. They did not prevail, but Dorjee gave notice: "It's significant that we'll continue the Middle Way for a defined amount of time, maybe two or three years."[13] He left unstated what course of action they might resort to if the Dalai Lama or his successors aren't able to deliver the "real" autonomy they seek.

The week-long conference concluded with a majority vote "to stand firm on the Middle Way Approach to resolve the issue of Tibet." The following day the Tibetan leader gave a press conference, explaining that he had absented himself from the convocation so that the participants would feel free to express themselves, and he was convinced and reassured that they had done so. He reaffirmed his commitment to lead the people of Tibet "till death," but said that he had devolved most of his administrative responsibilities to Samdhong Rinpoche, the democratically elected head of the Tibetans in exile. He concluded with a reaffirmation of his position that it is up to the Tibetan people to decide whether they need and want the institution of Dalai Lama to continue: "I may be the last Dalai Lama."

Six months later he amplified his position concerning his role, saying, "The Dalai Lamas have held temporal and spiritual leadership over the past 400 to 500 years.[14] It may have been quite useful. But that period is over. Today, it is clear to the whole world that democracy is the best system despite its minor negativities. That is why it is important that Tibetans also move with the larger world community." He confirmed his strong position that the Dalai Lama should not bear the sole responsibility for the leadership of the Tibetan people. "When we put the whole responsibility in the person of the Dalai Lama it is dangerous. It is appropriate that a democratically elected leader lead a people's movement. In reality, a change is happening in the responsibility of the Dalai Lama as the temporal and spiritual leader. This I think is very good. A religious leader having to assume political leadership, that period is over."[15]

The Dalai Lama was then seventy-three years old. He was giving notice to his people that he would not be with them forever and they must soon carry on the work that he had been preparing them to assume for the past half-century. Two years later he took the first formal step to begin the withdrawal process when he announced that he would ask the Tibetan Parliament to consider his retirement from his ceremonial responsibilities as head of the Tibetan government-in-exile. In response to the concerns of his exile constituents he reassured them, "This did not mean that I will forget the Tibetan struggle. I am a Tibetan and every Tibetan has the moral obligation to carry out our own struggle."[16]

It took some centuries for the consequences of the meeting at Runny-mede to become fixed principles and practices in the country of its origin and democratic societies throughout the world. The Himalayan rerun in 2008 of a compact between a sovereign and his people dedicated to a common goal of a peaceful society is facing tough odds in being transformed into practice in Tibet. The will and the way have been forcefully expressed by both the Tibetan people and their leader, imposing a challenge to their American supporters to continue to support these common goals in our own country's self-interest. As one of Tibet's most dedicated American advocates, Nancy Pelosi, declared at Dharamsala following the protests that year in Tibet, "If we do not support human rights in China and in Tibet, we lose all moral authority to speak about human rights any place in the world."[17] Whether America's support continues or fades, as Pelosi and the Dalai Lama feared it could fifteen years ago, becoming a casualty of the drastically changed international status of both Beijing and Tibet's international sponsors, will be a critical test in determining the ultimate destiny of both the Tibetans and the Americans.

On the centennial of American involvement in the affairs of Tibet, the strategic positions of the country that Tibet hoped could be its principal international champion and the country to be challenged have been reversed. Then the United States had just completed its intervention in Cuba and the Philippines; had reduced its native Indian inhabitants to about one-third of 1 percent of its population; and a reserved interest in defending those that a decadent and bankrupt Manchu government claimed as its suzerain subjects. Today the United States is asking the holder of approximately one-sixth of its public debt to observe in Tibet a universal code of human rights that has been evolving over the past half-century on behalf of a people and a way of life the United States has come to admire—and the present rulers of Beijing would like to consign to history.

The limits of this prudent support were demonstrated in 2009, however, when White House Advisor Valerie Jarrett informed the Dalai Lama that President Obama preferred to postpone their first meeting until after he had gone to Beijing to meet with President Hu Jintao in November. The Tibetan leader quietly swallowed this decision. He went to Washington to accept the Lantos Human Rights Award and to present the International Campaign for Tibet's Light of Truth Award posthumously to his stalwart champion Julia Taft. In an interview with Wolf Blitzer on October 8, 2009, he maintained that he wasn't disappointed that he was not seeing the president on this visit, nor did he acknowledge that Obama was kowtowing to Beijing.

The pontiff maintained his judicious display of acceptance and good manners when Obama finally received his politically sensitive guest in the White House. On February 18, 2010, they met not in the Oval Office, which would stamp the visit as official, but in the Map Room, which adjoins the family quarters. Clinton had used a similar subterfuge by "dropping in" for unofficial chats while the Dalai Lama was visiting either Vice President Gore or Hillary Clinton in other parts of the White House. The Bushes, father and son, had chosen to offer him tea and cookies in the family quarters upstairs.

The two men met for an hour's conversation, following which the Dalai Lama playfully tossed a bit of snow at the reporters waiting outside and expressed himself "very happy" with the visit. The White House press secretary released a statement describing the meeting: "The President stated his strong support for the preservation of Tibet's unique religious, cultural and linguistic identity and the protection of human rights for the Tibetans in the People's Republic of China. The President commended the Dalai Lama's 'Middle Way' approach, his commitment to nonviolence and his pursuit of dialogue with the Chinese Government ... something he has consistently encouraged ... [and] was pleased to hear about the recent resumption of talks." The statement concluded piously, "The President and the Dalai Lama agreed on the importance of a positive and cooperative relationship between the United States and China."

From Capitol Hill Speaker Pelosi commended the president for "meeting with His Holiness, a champion of peace and non-violence, and a voice for

FIGURE 20 President Barack Obama meets with His Holiness the Fourteenth Dalai Lama in the Map Room of the White House, July 16, 2011.

dignity, justice, and respect for all humanity . . . a powerful spokesman for the moral duty and inherent worth of every person, and a force for human rights across the globe." She concluded, "[Their meeting] marks another chapter in the long friendship and close ties between the United States and the people of Tibet. As Americans, we must continue to stand with His Holiness to promote, preserve, and protect the rights of all people to live in freedom worldwide."[18]

Seventeen months later the Dalai Lama renewed his ties with both the White House and Congress when he visited Washington to conduct a Buddhist teaching conference. On the Hill he met with Pelosi and her Republican replacement, John Boehner. The president then met with him in a forty-five-minute closed-door conference—again in the Map Room. According to press accounts, the Dalai Lama restated his stand for self-rule rather than independence in Tibet, and Obama expressed "strong support" for direct talks and a resolution that protects both the Tibetans' rights and China's claim to the territory.

Envoi

When Washington first took official note of the Tibetan situation one hundred years ago, the White House was reluctant to sap the authority of the imperial mandarins then in charge of a declining and bankrupt Chinese nation. Today Beijing's new mandarins have succeeded in creating a dramatically less vulnerable regime. It calls rather than responds to the shots on the international scene.

As this process unfolded the Dalai Lama felt forced to leave his country when it fell under the total occupation of the new China. He knew as he left Lhasa in 1959 that he was leaving an imperfect country, not a Shangri-La where harmony and unity prevailed. He had also learned the limits of support that he could expect from the free world, beginning with his brief exodus from Lhasa in the winter of 1950 and resigned return seven months later to begin a decade of failed accommodation with Mao. His response has been to spend the past five decades building a Tibetan form of self-governance to unite his people and challenge their occupiers.

The Tibetan cause appeared on America's horizon a half-century ago as an appealing and substantive vehicle to use in challenging a mutual enemy, but it has moved far beyond that image to become a mode of life that we can believe in and support for itself. The Tibetans brought with them a battered and imperfect model of what compassion and determination can achieve. They have shown "a decent respect to the opinions of mankind," observing Jefferson's maxim of "declaring [and challenging] the causes which impelled them to a separation," and moved on to create an effective challenge to Beijing's efforts to destroy one of the world's most unique cultures, exploit its natural resources, and turn Lhasa into a Disneyland and Tibet into a military and industrial base, rather than a refuge and an active model for an increasingly materially and spiritually exhausted but interconnected world.

In a Panglossian best of all possible worlds Beijing would have shrugged and chosen some time ago to end the conflict that has been going on for the past two thousand years over the right to self-government by their neighbors of a distinct origin and identity. The likelihood of this happening seems increasingly lost as China grows richer, more secure, and seemingly more oblivious "to the decent respect of the opinions of mankind." But these Himalayan proponents and practitioners of self-determination are owed support, lest they and their civilization silently disappear as an admired Lost Cause consigned to history and Beijing is granted another bye in the continuing struggle to maintain a free world.

The Dalai Lama, whose title Kundun means "the Presence," has kept the present and future existence of Tibet and the Tibetans very much alive in a complex world. Bhuchung Tsering, a member of the Tibetan team that has been negotiating the future of Tibet, pointedly reminded his fellow countrymen of this fact when the Dalai Lama recently announced his decision to

FIGURE 21 The Dalai Lama passes the mantle of political direction of the Tibetan government-in-exile to Lobsang Sangay (left), August 8, 2011.

retire. On December 15, 2010, Tsering wrote, "The Dalai Lama has been making efforts to shake off the Tibetan people's overdependence on him and this is one more step toward that objective. Then there have been some individuals who have said that the absence of the Dalai Lama from the government system would not altogether be a bad thing for the Tibetan struggle. The Dalai Lama's statement [of his intention to retire from the political direction of his government] will now be a challenge to these individuals to rise to the occasion and play a responsible role in preparing Tibetan society for such a development. This will be the time for these people to walk the talk."[19]

This awesome challenge became more immediate on August 8, 2011, when the Dalai Lama formally turned over political leadership of the Tibetan government–in-exile to Lobsang Sangay, a forty-three-year-old Harvard Law School graduate and the son of a former resistance leader. The test will be whether Sangay and his countrymen who aspire to follow in his footsteps will rule with the same combination of humility, grace, and keen insight into the political aspirations, actions, and limitations of his fellow man that has made the Dalai Lama one of the world's most respected leaders. He has led his people out of the mountains into an increasingly complex and interconnected world and spent the past half-century developing and maintaining a living culture and mode of governance far beyond the quaint and exotic image to which they had been relegated. It has imperfections, but it represents

FIGURE 22 Tenzin Gyatso, the Fourteenth Dalai Lama, "Kundun, the Presence," prepares his people to govern themselves when he is no longer with them.

a fulfilled act of self-determination that gives the Tibetans a valid claim to self-government. The free world has come to find it in its self-interest to ally with him, his people, and the government they have created in exile across the mountains from their homeland.

By continuing to fulfill the commitments they have made to Tibet over the past half century, the United States and other freedom-seeking nations serve their common interest in an increasingly interdependent world. There would be two prizes to gain. The immediate one would be to convince the coming administrations in Beijing that China would benefit by ridding itself of a persistent domestic problem and international opprobrium. The other prize, a derivative one, would be for the citizens of the free world to discover that the way of life they have supported and promoted as a means of confronting Chinese expansionism continues and merits both sustained support and practice in their own increasingly uncertain, interconnected world beyond Shangri-La.

Abbreviations

CIA CREST	Central Intelligence Agency project file
DCI	Director of Central Intelligence, Central Intelligence Agency
DDE	Dwight D. Eisenhower Library, Abilene, Kans.
FO	Foreign and Commonwealth Office, London
FRUS	Foreign Relations of the United States, University of Wisconsin Digital Collections Center, Madison, Wis.
JFD	Papers of John Foster Dulles, Mudd Library, Princeton University
JFK	John F. Kennedy Library, Boston
NARA	National Archives, College Park, Md.
NSC	Records of the National Security Council, National Archives, College Park, Md.
OSS	Office of Strategic Services Records, National Archives, College Park, Md.
RL	Franklin D. Roosevelt Presidential Library and Museum, Hyde Park, N.Y.
Rockhill	Papers of William W. Rockhill, Houghton Library, Harvard University
TR papers	Theodore Roosevelt Papers, Library of Congress, Washington, D.C.
USGPO	United States Government Printing Office, Washington, D.C.
USUN	United States delegation to the UN, New York

1. Washington Discovers the Hidden Land

1. Letter from W. W. Rockhill, National Archives, American Legation, Peking, June 30, 1908.
2. TR papers, series 1, reel 83.
3. Ibid.
4. Memo, April 29, 1904, Rockhill papers, 46M-386.
5. TR papers, series 2, reel 350, vol. 83, p. 213.
6. His skepticism about the Dalai Lama's appreciation for things outside his ken might have been encouraged by the report in the London *Times* of June 30, 1908, that the Dalai Lama and his entourage were preserving as a devotional work an illustrated book on German arsenals that the Kaiser had sent him as a gift.
7. TR papers, series 1, reel 84.

8. Ibid.

9. Rockhill dispatch to Roosevelt, November 8, 1908, TR papers, series 1, reel 85.

10. *New York Times*, October 7, 1908.

11. A compromise was worked out whereby the Dalai Lama was required to make only genuflections.

12. Rockhill, dispatch to Roosevelt, November 8, 1908.

13. Rockhill letter to Secretary Root, November 10, 1908.

14. Rockhill, dispatch to Roosevelt, November 8, 1908.

15. Rockhill would seem to have been expounding a more hopeful view to the entrapped Tibetan leader concerning the administrative reforms that the Manchu government was promoting than he was reporting to his own government. In a dispatch to the State Department a month earlier he concluded, "The present program clearly indicates the tendency of the statesmen in charge of the reform movement, the limitations they hope to impose on it, the object they seek to attain, which would seem to be no other than a perpetuation of the existing system under a thin veil of constitutional guarantees." American Legation, Peking, No. 1005, September 12, 1908.

16. Rockhill's account of his discussion with Dorzhiev about the Dalai Lama's political concerns is contained in a dispatch re-sent from the American Legation, Peking, November 10, 1908.

17. Ibid.

18. Enclosure 1 to Rockhill, dispatch to Roosevelt, November 8, 1908.

19. Rockhill account, re-sent from the American Legation, Peking, November 10, 1908.

20. Charles Bell, in *Portrait of a Dalai Lama*, notes that Rockhill was the victim of a sham prophecy invented by monks of the Tibetan monastery of Tengyeling whom the Dalai Lama had punished for having plotted against his life. In current speculation about the future of this institution, the Dalai Lama over the past decade has raised the possibility that future events could obviate the need for the creation of a successor following his death.

21. FRUS, 1908, p. 118.

2. The Long Journey Home

1. *North China Daily News*, March 2, 1909.

2. Rockhill papers, Houghton Library, folder 87, 49M-284.

3. Ibid.

4. These are the areas included in the present Dalai Lama's Middle Way.

5. Bell, *Portrait of a Dalai Lama*, p. 94.

6. Quoted in *New York Times*, February 26, 1910.

7. London *Times*, February 22, 1910.

8. "Hillside" became the site of the Tibetan Refugee and Rehabilitation Center in 1959, when his successor fled to India.

9. Younghusband, the leader of the 1904 expedition to Lhasa, participated in the debate and later published a book pointing out the irony of the new policy. He asked, "Was there ever a more tragic reversal of an old position. When the Tibetans did not want us we fought our way to Lhasa to insist upon their having us; when they did want us, and had come all the way from Lhasa to get us, we turned them the most frigid of shoulders." Francis Younghusband, *India and Tibet* (London: Murray, 1910), p. 380.

10. William Woodville Rockhill, *The Dalai Lamas of Lhasa 1644–1908* (Leiden: E. J. Brill, 1910).

11. Letter to the Dalai Lama, September 30, 1910, Rockhill papers, Houghton Library, 49M-284.

12. Ibid.

13. Bell, *Tibet Past and Present*, p. 120.

14. In contrast to the Tibetans' acts of mercy, the commander of the ill-fated Chinese garrison was executed by his own government upon his return to China. Ibid., p. 143.

15. Dispatch No. 57, American consulate, Chungking, April 10, 1913, NARA, 741/93/2.

16. *New York Times*, September 2, 1912.

17. Bell, *Tibet Past and Present*, p. 156.

18. Richardson, *A Short History of Tibet*, p. 111.

19. Ibid., p. 105.

20. Ibid.

21. Bell, *Portrait of a Dalai Lama*, p. 235, noted that there weren't enough rifles in Tibet to equip such a force, and the few that were there were needed for Tibet's own defense.

22. Richardson, p. 119.

23. One went on to study electrical engineering at an English university and had a distinguished career in Tibet as a district magistrate and engineer; one was killed during the First World War while serving with an Indian battalion; and the other two became middle-level monastic and civil officials, respectively.

24. Logbook, December 23, 1913, Rockhill papers, Houghton Library.

25. American consulate, Chungking, dispatch, November 2, 1914, NARA, 741.93/8.

26. American consulate, Chungking, dispatch, January 19, 1915, NARA, 741.93/10.

3. Beyond the Horizon

1. Letter from Polk to acting secretary of state, September 12, 1919, NARA, 741.93/12. There is no record that Polk or the State Department made any effort to obtain confirmation from their British colleagues that such a proposal had been made.

2. Christian Herter, February 20, 1960, FRUS 1956–60, vol. 19, p. 809.

3. This statement did not include the guarantee to go to China's aid if she were threatened by an unprovoked attack, which Koo said was the reciprocal part of a bargain offered by Britain before the war, whereby China would accept autonomous status for Tibet.

4. Goldstein, *A History of Modern Tibet*, cites a letter from R. Peel, India Office, London, to the Foreign Office, London, dated May 7, 1943.

5. Richardson, *High Peaks, Pure Earth*, p. 124.

6. He had also been made one of the four Shapes, who were the top government administrators below the prime minister.

7. Bell, *Tibet Past and Present*, p. 184.

8. William M. McGovern, *To Lhasa in Disguise* (New York: Century, 1924).

9. File number 893.00/3912, May 7, 1921, microfilm roll M329, National Archives.

10. F. B. Shelton, *Shelton of Tibet*, p. 262.

11. Shelton records in his autobiography that the local Tibetan governor had forwarded a letter from him to the Dalai Lama seeking his permission to establish a hospital in Lhasa to train Tibetans to provide health care to their people. He received in reply

what, "as far as he knew, [was] the only letter ever written by the Dalai Lama to a missionary": "I [the Dalai Lama] know of your work and that you have come a long way to do good, and, so far as I am concerned, I will put no straw in your way, providing there are no foreign treaties to prevent your coming." A. E. Shelton, *Pioneering in Tibet*, p. 135.

12. NARA, RG Entry 165 MID correspondence, 1917–41, box 769, 2055-1-2066.

13. Magruder, Records of the OSS, National Archives, p. 13.

14. Magruder's powers of observation and candor in reporting got him into trouble in 1942. As head of the Lend-Lease mission in China, he recommended that in view of the poor contribution that Chiang Kai-shek's government was making to the war effort, the United States government provide only sufficient supplies to keep the Chinese government from falling. When a White House Secretary showed a copy of Magruder's cable making this recommendation to T. V. Soong, Chiang's brother-in-law, Magruder was put in jail. This incident apparently did Magruder's distinguished career no lasting damage, as he returned to Washington as deputy director of the Office of Strategic Services, where he served until the end of the war. NARA RG 225, box 742, entry 190, official history of the OSS, pp. 82–83.

4. The United States Sits Out

1. Cutting, *The Fire Ox and Other Years*, p. 176.

2. NARA, State Department file 983.00-Tibet/16, microfilm file 187, reel 45.

3. Memo to Phillips, January 25, 1934, NARA, State Department file 983.00-Tibet/16, microfilm file 187.

4. Letter to Mr. Roosevelt, February 2, 1934, RL, PPF 4596.

5. Dispatch, Yunnanfu consulate, January 24, 1935, NARA, microfilm 187, reel 45.

6. Dispatch, Nanking consul, January 21, 1935, NARA, microfilm 187, reel 45.

7. Snow, *Red Star over China*, p. 214.

8. Ibid.

9. American consulate, Yunnanfu, September 1936, NARA 893.00, LM182, reel 45.

10. Phuntsok Wanggyal is alive today in Beijing after an extraordinary career during which he became a close friend and supporter of the Dalai Lama, spent eighteen years in prison, and since his release in 1978 has acted as an advocate for the Dalai Lama and sometimes tolerated gadfly of the government of the People's Republic of China.

11. Richardson, *A Short History of Tibet*, p. 148.

12. Richardson became an ardent supporter of the Tibetans and harshly critical of his government's postwar policy toward Tibet. He wrote, "The British government, the only government among Western countries to have had treaty relations with Tibet, sold the Tibetans down the river and since then have constantly cold-shouldered the Tibetans so that in 1959 they could not even support a resolution in the UN condemning the violation of human rights in Tibet by the Chinese." *The Scotsman*, December 7, 2000.

13. McKay, *Tibet and the British Raj*, pp. 156–57.

14. Ibid.

15. Teichman, *Affairs of China*, p. 226.

16. Dispatch, American legation, Peking, January 16, 1934, NARA 893.00 Tibet/18, microfilm 182, reel 45.

17. Dispatch, American consulate general, Calcutta, March 29, 1939, NARA 893.00 Tibet/38.
18. Dispatch 3408, Nanking, March 5, 1935, NARA 893.00/13063.
19. Meyer and Brysac, *Tournament of Shadows*, p. 536. Schafer's trip to Lhasa in 1938 was approved by Whitehall, which was then attempting to find some accommodation with Hitler. Schafer regarded the Tibetans as much degraded Aryans. McKay, *Tibet and the British Raj*, pp. 176–77.
20. Dispatch, American consulate general, Calcutta, October 7, 1937, NARA 893.00 Tibet/34.
21. Cutting, an army major in charge of the United States Observer Group in New Delhi, was able to use his contacts five years later to support the wartime OSS mission being undertaken by his old friend Dolan and Major Ilya Tolstoy. They were seeking Tibetan approval for an overland route by which to transport supplies to the beleaguered forces of Chiang Kai-shek. The mission had the full support of the only other American to have made an official journey into Tibet, John Magruder, who was then a brigadier general and the deputy director of OSS.
22. *New York Times*, July 26, 1936.

5. Washington Discovers Tibet

1. Charles Bell, letter dated May 4, 1942, to Lord Halifax, FO 371/31637.
2. Foreign Office minute, May 21, 1942, FO 371/31637.
3. Foreign Office minute, June 19, 1942, FO 371/31638.
4. Foreign Office minute, May 27, 1942, FO 329/3026.
5. India Office minute, June 2, 1942, FO 371/31638.
6. Tolstoy was thirty-nine, with an impressive biography which his friend Archibald MacLeish forwarded to his friend Bill Donovan, suggesting he hire him for the OSS. In his CV Tolstoy described working as a livestock breeder on a Soviet farm and later as a volunteer with the American Friends Relief Committee in Turkestan and Siberia. He had then studied at a Quaker college in Oskaloosa, Iowa, and at Iowa State College. The Depression foreclosed employment in the farm belt, but the American Museum of Natural History asked him to organize and lead expeditions to the Arctic Circle, Central America, and the British West Indies. When he was accepted by the OSS he was vice president of Marineland in Florida. His professional and social credentials made him a natural to lead an expedition to a sensitive unknown area which relied on the support of the British Raj. MacLeish to Donovan, January 27, 1942, NARA RG 226.
7. OSS background report, NARA RG 226, E092, folder 39. The details of their mission and its results are described in Knaus, *Orphans of the Cold War*, pp. 5–18.
8. OSS background study, NARA RG 226, E190, box 583, folder 435. Relations with Chiang's ambassador were further strained when the Tibetans again asserted their claim to independence by reopening the Foreign Affairs Bureau, which had been briefly utilized during the Thirteenth Dalai Lama's tenure. The British, Nepalese, and Chinese representatives were all notified that all matters "big and small" between their governments and the Tibetan government should be discussed with this office.
9. Report by Tolstoy, NARA RG 165, entry 79, box 1995.
10. Goldstein, *A History of Modern Tibet*, p. 392.

11. FRUS, 1942, China:

> Your Holiness,
>
>> Two of my fellow countrymen Ilia Tolstoy and Brooke Dolan, hope to visit your Pontificate and the historic and and widely famed city of Lhasa. There are in the United States of America many persons, among them myself, who, long and greatly interested in your land and people, would highly value such an opportunity.
>>
>> As you know, the people of the United States, in association with those of twenty-seven other countries, are now engaged in a war which has been thrust upon the world by nations bent on conquest who are intent on destroying freedom of thought, of religion, and of action everywhere. The United Nations are fighting today in defense of and for preservation of freedom, confident that we shall be victorious because our cause is just, our capacity is adequate and our determination is unshakable.
>
> With cordial greetings [etc.] Franklin D. Roosevelt

12. Memorandum, January 3, 1943, FO 70371/35754.

13. Meyer and Brysac, *Tournament of Shadows*, pp. 545–46, notes that it was at one of these parties that Dolan met the sister of a Tibetan noble with whom he fathered a child. Meyer states that although Dolan returned to the Tibetan borderlands shortly before his suicide in April 1945, he did not make it to Lhasa to see his wife and daughter, who were drowned near Gyantse a few years later.

14. Memorandum from Ludlow to political officer, April 11, 1943, FO 371/35756.

15. A State Department study reported that "the United States was most careful to respect Chinese suzerainty over Tibet and that Roosevelt in his letter addressed him [the Dalai Lama] in his capacity of religious leader rather than in his capacity of secular leader in order to avoid any possible offense to the Chinese Government." It also cited a telegram from Secretary Cordell Hull to the American ambassador at Chungking: "As you are aware, the Chinese Government has long claimed suzerainty over Tibet, the Chinese constitution lists Tibet among areas constituting the territory of the Republic of China, and this Government has at no time raised question regarding either of these claims." NARA, Historical Project No. 403, November 1957.

16. Ibid.

17. Cable, Tolstoy to Donovan, January 31, 1943, NARA RG 226, microfilm M1642, roll 41.

18. Letter, FDR to Dalai Lama, July 1, 1943, NARA RG 226, entry 92, box 354.

19. NARA, microfilm M1642, roll 116.

20. British mission, Lhasa, to Tolstoy, November 22, 1944, B644, FO 918 NARA, E190.

21. The only record that can be located is a cable Tolstoy sent from Lhasa on February 11, 1943, asking OSS headquarters in Washington, "For information only, please give the approximate date, if possible, of the Pacific [*sic*] Conference." He "strongly suggested that in the interest of peace Tibet be independently represented at the conference." NARA RG 226, microfilm 1642.

22. Letter from F. Ludlow Esq., British mission, Lhasa, to Sir Basil Gould, political officer in Sikkim, Gangtok, February 24, 1943, FO 371/35755.

23. Demiofficial letter, British Mission, Lhasa, to political officer in Sikkim, March 14, 1943, FO 371/35755.

24. Viceroy to secretary of state for India, May 3, 1943, FO 371/35755.

25. White House memorandum, May 20, 1943, RL, Map Room files, box 168.

26. There is some evidence that Soong may not have felt fully confident about his claim to China's sovereignty over Tibet. In a memorandum prepared on June 1, 1943, presumably prompted by Soong's exchange with Churchill two weeks earlier, a Chinese Foreign Ministry officer, Liu Chieh, reassured Soong, "The Chinese government regards Tibet as an integral part of China, and any attempt by a foreign power to interfere with the administration and control of Tibet would be looked upon as an infringement of China's sovereignty and her administrative and territorial integrity." This opinion by Liu, who was destined to be the man who led the Chinese Nationalist delegation out of the United Nations General Assembly when it voted to admit Communist China and expel his government on October 26, 1971, was challenged three days later by the Ministry's international law expert, Shuhsi Hsu, in an opinion requested by Soong. Hsu wrote:

> The problem of Tibet is ticklish because it involves a non-Chinese race in the face of a strong sentiment in the world for liberalizing government over subject peoples. If diplomacy is to succeed at all, some definite policy toward Tibet and Outer Mongolia, and perhaps the minorities in the provinces, will probably have to be adopted by the Government first. Mere assertion of sovereignty, proper though it may be, will not carry us very far, even if it is effectively supported by political arguments. It may be added that the problem of Tibet is not among the most urgent, for as long as Britain cannot handle India, she can do little in Tibet. If rapprochement with the Tibetans is desired, direct approach is preferable. The National Government has got on quite well with them so far. It can do more if it employs the right kind of man and tries again. (T. V. Soong Archives, Hoover Institution, Stanford University)

27. War Cabinet memorandum, June 1943, FO 371/35756.

28. Minute, September 9, 1944, FO 371/41588. This concern came into play again fifteen years later, when the British abstained on October 21, 1959, on a UN resolution deploring the denial by the Mao government of "the fundamental human rights and freedoms of the people of Tibet." Sir Pierson Dixon, in defending his vote, cited Britain's doubts about "the status of Tibet, which [was] in itself, a matter of differing opinion." This was consonant with the concern expressed earlier by Foreign Minister Selwyn Lloyd to Secretary Christian Herter that even debate on Tibet "would open the way to discussion in the UN of subjects like Oman, Nyassaland, Ulster and even segregation in the United States." FO 371/141600.

29. Ibid.

30. American embassy, Chungking, dispatch 1482, August 17, 1943, FRUS, 1943, China, p. 629.

31. British embassy, Washington, to Foreign Office, October 23, 1944, FO 371/41588.

32. Telegram from Lhasa to the Foreign Office, New Delhi, January 3, 1944, FO 371/41585.

33. OSS Records, NARA RG 226, entry 169A, folder 1178.

34. NARA RG 226, entry 196, box 226, folder 358.

35. Memo from Tolstoy to his OSS commander, January 20, 1944, NARA, E190, B644, folder 918.

36. FRUS, 1944, China, p. 960.

37. FRUS, 1944, China, p. 961. Washington was forced to take notice of Tibet's equivocal international status some months after Tolstoy left Lhasa, when a United States Air

Force plane flying off course ran out of fuel, forcing the five members of the crew to parachute into Tibet near Tsetang on November 30, 1943. They were taken to Lhasa, where they were met with some hostility by the local citizens who were reportedly angered that the plane had overflown the Potala, thus committing an act of sacrilege against the Dalai Lama. They were housed at the British mission, given unwanted hospitality by the overly proprietary Chinese representative, and hastened on their way to India by a friendly but nervous Tibetan government.

38. James Dunn, Office of European Affairs, to General Donovan, May 17, 1944, NARA, E190, B644.

6. A Small Part of the Bigger Picture

1. It is ironic that the Tibetans, many of whom had not favored the Allied cause, should have chosen such a vehicle. In a dispatch describing the three-day V-E Day celebration he hosted at the mission headquarters in Lhasa on May 15–17, Hugh Richardson wrote, "It was a pleasant incident when on arrival, members of what may be called the Tsarong-Tering [pro-British] set offered scarves of congratulations on the allied victory; the Kashag [the cabinet, containing more Japanese sympathizers], however, was dumb on the subject." The usually sympathetic but objective Richardson also made an unflattering observation concerning the reaction of the Tibetan guests to the display of photographs of German concentration camps: "In a country where public floggings are a normal event and the victims if not killed at once, are left to die a lingering death, it is doubtful whether the horror expressed over the German atrocities was anything more [than] life [lip?] service to the cause of humanity." Memorandum, May 20, 1945, FO 371/46122.

2. Goldstein describes the origin, contents, and purpose of this bold declaration of Tibetan independence in a detailed chapter of his book, *A History of Modern Tibet*, pp. 522–559.

3. A. J. Hopkinson, the political officer in Sikkim who had escorted them on a month's tour of India prior to their travel to China, reported, "[The] poor opinion I had already formed of the leading members of the Mission, evidently shared by many in Lhasa, more than justified itself during the tour." He went on to lament, "It is to be regretted, and evidently a mark of their present supineness, that the Tibetan Government took no trouble over the important matter of personnel. I fear they have done Tibet a disservice; possibly they thought it best to send fools to lie abroad for the good of their country as least likely to do any positive harm." In addition to these perceived character defects Hopkinson objected that the mission members, rather than wearing Tibetan dress and following Tibetan custom, "frequent[ed] public places such as the dining room of the Great Eastern Hotel looking like a pack of Chinese coolies, in shirt sleeves with their braces outside." May 2, 1946, FO 371/53614.

4. Goldstein, *A History of Modern Tibet*, p. 561.

5. Quotation from a report on Indo-Tibetan relations, November 7, 1947, FO 371/63943.

6. Goldstein, in his book *A History of Modern Tibet*, records Lhasa's concerted efforts to establish Tibet's independent identity. See chapter 16.

7. American embassy, New Delhi, January 13, 1947, FRUS 1947, pp. 588–93.

8. State Department cable to Merrell, April 14, 1947, FRUS 1947, vol. 7; p. 594.

9. American embassy, New Delhi, No. 100, August 1, 1947, FRUS 1947, vol. 7.

10. American embassy, New Delhi, Dispatch 142, August 21, 1947, FRUS 1947, vol. 7.

11. Ibid.

12. State Department, Dispatch 46, October 28, 1947, FRUS 1947, vol. 7.

13. The British embassy in Nanking had apparently not received the instruction not to issue visas on the Tibetan passports. When it learned of the minister's cavalier act the Foreign Office in London was only mildly dismayed, dismissing the anticipated Chinese displeasure with the comment "Our shoulders are broad enough to withstand any reproaches from the Chinese, though [we] had sooner this had not happened." Minute, May 31, 1948, FO 371/70042/.

14. On April 3, 2004, the Dalai Lama's government announced that Shakabpa's original passport with the visa stamps intact had been retrieved from an antique dealer in Nepal. It is to be part of a traveling exhibition of old photographs and documents intended to validate Tibet's claim to independence.

15. Secretary of state to ambassador in China, 1086, Washington, July 28, 1949, FRUS 1948, vol. 7.

16. On February 29, 1960, Secretary of State Christian Herter formally announced, "It is the belief of the United States Government that this principle [of self determination] should apply to the people of Tibet."

17. Memorandum of conversation, Washington, August 6, 1948, FRUS 1948, vol. 7, p. 775.

18. Prince Peter acquired a certain notoriety from these anthropological studies, conducted primarily in Kalimpong among the Tibetans and the hill tribes. He became a friend and tennis partner of Gyalo Thondup, which made him a natural candidate to be listed among the "nest of spies" that Peking charged had directed the Tibet revolt in 1959. Thondup laughingly related some years later that the Prince's only interest in the seven thousand Tibetans he met was to measure their skulls as part of his authoritative study on Himalayan polyandry. Nehru expelled him from Kalimpong in April 1959 after he spoke out on India's passive policy concerning the occupation of Tibet by China. After the Prince returned to Denmark he became an active supporter of programs on behalf of Tibetan refugee children.

19. Secretary of state to the secretary of the treasury, August 27, 1948, FRUS 1948, vol. 7, p. 780.

20. Goldstein, *A History of Modern Tibet*, p. 607.

21. Memorandum from Harry S. Evans, public relations manager for *Business Week*, who escorted the delegation, Hoover Institution Archives.

7. The United States Enters the Scene

1. Isaacson and Thomas, *The Wise Men*, p. 475.

2. Memorandum, April 12, 1949, FRUS 1949, vol. 9, pp. 1065–71.

3. Ibid., p. 1065.

4. American embassy, New Delhi, dispatch 302, April 12, 1949, FRUS 1949, vol. 9, pp. 1073–75.

5. American embassy, Moscow, airgram A-577, June 4, 1949, FRUS 1949, vol. 9, p. 1075.

6. American embassy, Nanjing, cable 1459, July 8, 1949, FRUS 1949, vol. 9.

7. See Knaus, *Orphans of the Cold War*, pp. 41–42.

8. Indian mission, Lhasa, memorandum, September 15, 1949, FO 371/76315.

9. Lowell Thomas Jr., *Out of This World* (New York: Greystone Press, 1950).

10. Dean Acheson and Lowell Thomas, memorandum of conversation, February 17, 1950, Dean Acheson papers, Truman Library.

11. Conversation, February 17, 1950, Dean Acheson papers, Truman Library.

12. Speech by Mao, July 1, 1949, twenty-eighth anniversary of the CCP.

13. American embassy, New Delhi, telegram, November 21, 1949, FRUS 1949, vol. 9, p. 1080.

14. American embassy, New Delhi, telegram, December 2, 1949, FRUS 1949, vol. 9, p. 1087.

15. American embassy, New Delhi, Embassy telegram 91, January 20, 1950, NARA decimal file, 793B/1-2050.

16. Indian mission report, January 15, 1950, FO 371/84453. This was the first of other temporary landing fields built in Lhasa and was never used for the arrival of foreign assistance and personnel.

17. American embassy, New Delhi, cable, January 10, 1950, FRUS 1950, vol. 6.

18. Memorandum of conversation, Office of Chinese Affairs, December 21, 1949, FRUS 1949, vol. 9.

19. Memorandum of conversation, Ambassador Henderson and U.K. high commissioner, New Delhi, December 8, 1949, Embassy telegram 1523, FRUS 1949, vol. 9.

20. American embassy, New Delhi, telegram 1558, December 15, 1949, FRUS 1949, vol. 9, pp. 1092–93.

21. American embassy, New Delhi, airpouch, January 9, 1950, NARA 793B/1-950.

22. In reporting the arrival of Shakabpa as head of a mission to contact the Chinese the consulate in Calcutta were told that he had been chosen by "divine prognostication" to lead the group. A member of the group observed, "The people of Tibet are so simple and superstitious that many of their most important decisions are made in such a way." The writer noted that although Shakabpa had let it be known that he preferred not to go to the American consulate, it would be impossible "for the members of the mission to remain inconspicuous in any city of the Far East outside of southwest China, since they dress in the typical Tibetan robes of wool with pastel-colored silk linings; wear their hair in braids wound around their head; are decorated with bright and gangling turquoise earrings; are of unusual height, several of them being somewhat over six feet; wear snappy Western-style hats made in Lhasa and have a singular resemblance to the American Indian." American embassy, New Delhi, dispatch 683, March 27, 1950, NARA decimal file 793B.

23. Department of State telegram 380, April 19, 1950, FRUS 1950, vol. 6, p. 330.

24. American embassy, New Delhi, telegram 839, June 9, 1950, FRUS 1950, vol. 6, p. 361.

25. Footnote to Department of State telegram 2945, June 16, 1950, FRUS 1950, vol. 6.

26. American embassy, New Delhi, Embassy telegram 302, August 7, 1950, FRUS 1950, vol. 6.

27. American embassy, New Delhi, Embassy telegram 390, August 14, 1950, FRUS 1950, vol. 6.

28. American embassy, New Delhi, telegram 799, June 3, 1950, FRUS 1950, volume 6.

29. Thomas Laird describes the whole Mackiernan-Bessac saga in his book *Into Tibet*. The magazine article appeared in the November 13, 1950, edition. Mackiernan's star was the first one placed on the memorial wall at CIA Headquarters.

30. American embassy, New Delhi, Embassy telegram, October 28, 1950, NARA 793B.00/10-2850.

31. American embassy, New Delhi, Embassy telegram 1030, October 31, 1950, FRUS 1950, vol. 6.

32. American embassy, New Delhi, Embassy telegram 1072, November 3, 1950, NARA decimal file 793B.0011-350.

33. UN document, A11549-11, November 1950.

34. Ibid.

35. American embassy, New Delhi, airpouch, November 13, 1950, NARA decimal file.

36. American embassy, New Delhi, Embassy telegram, November 3, 1950, FRUS 1950, vol. 6, pp. 550–51.

37. Office of China Affairs, memorandum, November 13, 1950, NARA DC/R Central Files.

38. Department of State telegram 4567, November 14, 1950, NARA decimal file 793B.00/11-1450.

39. General Assembly No. 117, November 16, 1950, FRUS 1950, vol. 6, p. 577.

40. Interview with the author, November 28, 1994.

41. American embassy, New Delhi, Embassy telegram 1350, November 30, 1950, FRUS 1950, vol. 6.

42. American embassy, New Delhi, Embassy telegram 1509, December 18, 1950, FRUS 1950, vol. 6.

43. Memorandum of conversation, November 21, 1950, NARA DC/R Central Files 693.93B/11-2150.

44. State legal advisor, memorandum to Clubb, December 5, 1950, digested in aide-mémoire given to the British embassy, December 30, 1950, FRUS 1950, vol. 6, p. 612.

8. Washington and Lhasa Regroup

1. American embassy, New Delhi, Embassy telegram, January 25, 1951, FRUS 1951, vol. 7, p. 1529.

2. Footnote to Office of Chinese Affairs, Department of State, FRUS 1951, vol. 7, p. 1528.

3. Department of State telegram 1047, January 6, 1951, FRUS 1950, vol. 6, p. 618.

4. Ibid.

5. American embassy, New Delhi, Embassy telegram 1691, January 12, 1951, FRUS 1951, vol. 7, pp. 1506–8.

6. It was to be another ten years before Secretary Herter, in defining Tibet's international statutes, specified that autonomy means self-determination. Statement of Policy, February 20, 1960. FRUS 1958–1960, vol. 19, p. 809.

7. NIE-10, January 17, 1951, FRUS 1951, vol. 7, pp. 1510–14.

8. MacArthur had also proposed consideration of atomic bombing in North Korea and "hot pursuit" of enemy aircraft into Manchuria. Acheson, *Present at the Creation*, p. 514.

9. Ibid., p. 513.

10. American embassy, London, 5089, March 27, 1951, FRUS 1951, vol. 7, p. 1610.

11. Aufschnaiter had also remained in Lhasa when he and Harrer fled the invading Chinese army. He helped Lhasa plan a hydroelectric power plant and a system of canals and worked as a cartographer. After leaving Tibet he worked as an engineer in Nepal and India. He died in his native Austria in 1973. Harrer returned to Austria in 1952. There he maintained his relationship with the Dalai Lama and his family; wrote *Seven Years in Tibet*, which was made into a movie in 1997; and continued vigorously to deny having participated in any political activities of the ss, which he had agreed to join as an athletic instructor in 1938. He died on January 14, 2006.

12. Henderson described the meeting with Harrer and his self-initiated advice and plan for the Dalai Lama to seek asylum abroad in a cable to the Department's director of the Office of South Asian Affairs, FRUS 1951, vol. 7, pp. 1610–12. Henderson's background and active role in counseling the Tibetans is described in Knaus, *Orphans of the Cold War*, pp. 79–103.

13. Henderson's description of his letter is in his report to the Office of China Affairs, March 29, 1951. FRUS 1951, vol. 7, p. 1610.

14. Footnote to New Delhi Embassy telegram 1673, April 4, 1951, FRUS 1951, vol. 7, p. 1619.

15. American embassy, Colombo, Top Secret letter, April 13, 1951, NARA 793B.11/4-1351.

16. Top Secret letter, April 24, 1951, NARA 793B.11/4-1351.

17. State Department, OIR 6000.7, June 4, 1951, NARA RG 59, box 292.

18. American embassy, New Delhi, Embassy telegram 2891, May 24, 1951, FRUS 1951, vol. 7, pp. 1682–84.

19. American embassy, New Delhi, Embassy telegram 3398, May 29, 1951, FRUS 1951, vol. 7, pp. 1687–91.

20. Ibid.

21. Ibid.

22. American embassy, New Delhi, Embassy telegram 3433, May 29, 1951, FRUS 1951, vol. 7, pp. 1691, 1693.

23. Department of State, cable 2051, June 2, 1951, FRUS 1951, vol. 7, p. 1693.

24. The State Department may have overestimated the Dalai Lama's personal financial resources based on an earlier report from the New Delhi embassy (Embassy telegram 1658, January 9, 1951, NARA 693.93/1-951), sent while he was en route to his refuge. It stated, "The Dalai Lama with enormous treasures is now day's march from the Indian frontier."

25. Ibid.

26. Quoted in Brands, *Inside the Cold War*, p. 208.

27. Rusk, *As I Saw It*, p. 172.

28. Telephone interview with the author, May 27, 1994.

29. American embassy, New Delhi, airpouch 70, July 11, 1951, FRUS 1951, vol. 7, pp. 1743–44.

30. Department of State telegram 91, July 12, 1951, FRUS 1951, vol. 7, pp. 1748–49.

31. Historical Division of the Department of State, Research Project, November 1957, NARA RG 59, 793B.00/11-57, box 3949.

32. Ibid., p. 15.

33. Outlined in American consulate general, Calcutta, No. 52, July 17, 1951, FRUS 1951, vol. 7, p. 1754.

34. In a series of interviews with the author at his home in New Jersey in January through March 1995, Patterson described his role in the rescue plan and in translating the documents given by the consulate to the Tibetans.

35. Historical Division of the Department of State, Research Project, November 1957, NARA RG 59, 793B.00/11-57, box 3949, p. 16. The "lots" he is referring to, which consisted of swinging mud balls in a basket, is described in Knaus, *Orphans of the Cold War*, p. 100.

36. See Knaus, *Orphans of the Cold War*, p. 101.

37. American embassy, New Delhi, Embassy telegram 1749, November 15, 1951, FRUS 1951, vol. 7, pp. 1848–49.

9. On the Sidelines

1. Memorandum of conversation, FRUS 1952–54, vol. 14, pp. 8–10.
2. Ibid.
3. Interview with the author, Bloomington, Ind., May 16, 1995.
4. Memorandum of conversation, February 13, 1952, FRUS 1952–54, vol. 14, p. 8.
5. American consulate, Calcutta, dispatch 5, July 2, 1952; Historical Division of the Department of State, Research Project, November 1957, NARA RG 59, 793B.00/11-57, box 3949. Princess Coocoola was the granddaughter of a Tibetan general who continued her interest in Himalayan politics until her death fifty-six years later.
6. Ambrose, *Eisenhower*, p. 55.
7. Ibid., pp. 29–31.
8. Ibid., p. 35.
9. Ibid., p. 197.
10. Michael Warner, "The CIA under Harry Truman," History Staff, Center for the Study of Intelligence, CIA, 1994, p. xxv.
11. Tenzin Gyatso, *Freedom in Exile*, p. 122.
12. Although I came to regard him as a personal friend, this did not foreclose strong arguments between us, as he argued for support for the cause of the Dalai Lama and his people and I defended what I knew was reasonable and appropriate to expect from the United States government.
13. Tsering, *Dalai Lama, My Son*, p. 146.
14. Interview with the author, January 16, 2003.
15. Her son Khedroob said that the family was finally reconciled in 1956. His mother was one of the founders of the Tibetan Self Help Center in Darjeeling and one of its principal officials until her death forty years later. Interview with the author, Darjeeling, November 1995.
16. Tenpa Thondup said Chu Shih-kuei took this action when Zhu De was captured by the Kuomintang Army during the Red Army's retreat to Yenan. Interview with the author, Annisquam, Mass., September 27, 2006.
17. There is no record in the United States Archives that these messages were ever shown or discussed by Gyalo with the United States government.
18. Craig, *Kundun*, p. 120.
19. Interview with the author, Kalimpong, November 1995.
20. According to Craig, *Kundun*, p. 120, Gyalo's older sister, Tsering Dolma, asked Lhamo Tsering to keep a watchful eye over her brother, who was ready to enjoy the full worldly pleasures of life in the Chinese capital. Apparently they cut a wide swath together, making full use of Gyalo's allowance and the Jeep that the Gimo had given him. This image of Lhamo Tsering as a swashbuckling collegian is hard to reconcile with the man that those of us who worked with him in supporting the Tibetan resistance fifteen years later knew. It was he who arrived at all operational planning sessions with the meticulously prepared notebooks concerning the biographies and missions of the Tibetans the CIA was training and dispatching into Tibet. He kept careful account of how well the Agency was delivering the arms and other commitments it had promised. He did this not as a bookkeeper but as a man who was fully aware of the responsibility he had assumed for protecting the Tibetans for whom he was acting as spokesman.

21. Lhamo Tsering, *Resisting Oppression and Protecting the Country*, vol. 1, pp. 107–8.

22. Interview with the author, Kalimpong, November 1995.

23. Ibid.

24. Dispatch 560, February 4, 1955, NARA RG 59, 793B.00/2-455, box 3949.

25. Their relationship survived crushing experiences, which both of them were later subjected to by Mao and his successors, and still endures today.

26. Tenzin Gyatso, *Freedom in Exile*, p. 89.

27. Ibid.

28. Ibid., p. 99.

29. The leader of this group was a ne'er-do-well businessman named Alo Chondze, who returned to Lhasa after 1959, after squandering money lent him by Gyalo and the Dalai Lama Trust. When he returned to Lhasa the Chinese gave him a job which he later lost, and he was forced to emigrate to Australia. His son, however, remained in India and worked with the Tibetan government-in-exile.

30. Gyalo made full use of this privilege, including offering "abundant quantities of food and drink, including Scotch whisky for the more sophisticated," at the annual party given for the Tibetan community in Kalimpong on the Dalai Lama's birthday in 1955. Calcutta Consulate General, July 21, 1955, NARA RG 59. This fortuitous privilege had a more significant benefit, as Gyalo used it to import significant quantities of White Horse whisky, which he used in a profitable cross-border trade to supply the Chinese occupation troops. The muleteers who transported his whisky (whose price was highly inflated) also carried with them pamphlets urging resistance which they distributed to sympathizers and from whom they gathered intelligence, which they brought back to Gyalo. The loss of this valuable enterprise due to the muleteers' diversion of the whisky to their private use is described in Knaus, *Orphans of the Cold War*, pp. 123–24.

31. American embassy, New Delhi, dispatch 506, August 20, 1952, FRUS 1952–54, vol. 14, p. 96n.

10. The Stalemate Breaks

1. Tenzin Gyatso, *Freedom in Exile*, p. 100.

2. American consulate, Calcutta, 828, June 27, 1956, NARA RG 59 793B/6-2757,

3. Ibid.

4. Tenzin Gyatso, *Freedom in Exile*, p. 104.

5. Ibid.

6. State Department, telegram 23, July 24, 1956, NARA RG 59, box 3951, italics added.

7. State Department, Historical Division, Project 403, November 1957, NARA RG 59, box 3951.

8. Ibid.

9. Tenzin Gyatso, *Freedom in Exile*, p. 113.

10. Ibid., p. 117.

11. Interview with the author, Kalimpong, November 10–21, 1995.

12. The Five Principles, first stated in the preamble to the Sino-Indian Agreement on Tibet on April 29, 1954, were mutual respect for each other's territorial integrity and sovereignty, mutual noninterference in each other's internal affairs, equality, mutual benefit, and peaceful coexistence.

13. U.K. High Commission in India, telegram 61, May 20, 1954, FO 371/10647.

14. Tenzin Gyatso, *Freedom in Exile*, p. 118.

15. Ibid.

16. Ibid., p. 119.

17. Ibid., p. 120.

18. Interviews with the author in New Delhi and Kalimpong, 1995 and 1996.

19. Interview with the author, March 8, 1995.

20. All of the Tibetans regarded as agents or assets were given American first names.

21. George Patterson described the political structure in eastern Tibet as like that of the rival Scottish clans portrayed in the movie *Braveheart*. Interview with the author, Roseland, N.J., January 1995.

22. Lhamo Tsering, *Resisting Oppression*, vol. 2, p. 42.

23. A half-century later he confronted the same dilemma, when his loyal subjects rebelled against the continuing occupation of their country, and he gave the same response, threatening to step down if they resorted to violence. A year later the stubbornly resolute leader reaffirmed his conviction that despite the Chinese having created a "hell on earth" in his homeland, he "had no doubt that the justice of the Tibetan cause [would] prevail if [they] continue[d] to tread a path of truth and nonviolence." Associated Press, Dharamsala, March 19, 2009.

24. The task force chief, "Slim," who trained these men, reminded Walt when he debriefed him in Darjeeling in 1959 that he had refused to take radio training and had also persuaded another member of the team to decline it. Therefore when the team's only radio operator was killed they lost the only means of providing the information necessary to make the requested arms drop. Walt countered that if the drops had been made as soon as he had reported his presence with a force ready to use the arms, without waiting for the detailed location of an appropriate site, he and his forces would have found and used them to repel the Chinese. Slim said he recognized that this argument was going nowhere, so he and Walt, "a helluva man but stubborn to the core," hugged and parted. Email to the author, May 5, 2004.

25. The throne still sits in the assembly hall of the Dalai Lama's summer palace, the Norbulingka, ironically surrounded by a mural containing the only image in a public building in Lhasa of the Dalai Lama. To add to the irony the mural depicts the Dalai Lama as a young man surrounded by his family, including his two older brothers, who were the first to defy the Chinese occupation. They all look from the back wall toward the throne that was an organizing centerpiece for the resistance.

26. Gompo Tashi Andrustang, *Four Rivers, Six Ranges: Reminiscences of the Resistance Movement in Tibet* (Dharamsala, 1973).

27. Ibid., p. 73. Gompo writes, "The relatively lower losses were perhaps because of the holy charm boxes which our freedom fighters wore around their waists."

28. Interview with the author, Dharamsala, October 26, 1996.

29. Conboy, *The CIA's Secret War in Tibet*, p. 79.

11. Promises Kept

1. Tenzin Gyatso, *Freedom in Exile*, p. 131.

2. Ibid., p. 136.

3. Ngabo Ngawang Jigme, who signed the Seventeen-Point Agreement and whose relationship with the Chinese was to remain ambiguous, stayed behind. He later made his way to Peking, where he spent the remaining fifty years of his life in apparent physical comfort but equivocal moral status. One of his sons, who left China in the mid-1980s, now heads Radio Free Asia's Tibetan-language section. He commented that "history would judge his father's career and actions" (from a conversation that the author had on January 7, 2010).

4. This was a specific point that he volunteered in an interview with the author at Dharamsala on November 18, 1995, in which we discussed the pros and cons of the United States government's aid to the Tibetan resistance forces.

5. Briefing, March 23, 1959, JFD.

6. FRUS 1958–60, vol. 19, p. 751.

7. Ibid.

8. Department of State, press release 222, March 26, 1959, National Archives Library, American Foreign Policy Documents, 1959, p. 1162.

9. Ibid.

10. On December 24, 1958, the State Department sent a guidance to all its posts regarding how to respond to a manifesto issued by Gyalo Thondup's group in India to bring the growing rebellion in Tibet to the attention of the international community: "Your reply should be phrased in a low key designed to convey a sympathetic U.S. attitude toward the group as being a bona-fide anti-Communist organization, but at the same time not to encourage speculation that the United States Government is connected with its activities. The line should be that detailed knowledge is lacking concerning the organization's structure and operations, but that on the basis of information available via various sources, including domestic and international news media, it appears to be a genuine resistance group representing the aspirations of the Tibetan people." CA 5482, December 24, 1958, NARA RG 793B00/12-2458.

11. Republic of China, Government Information Office, press release, March 26, 1959.

12. Memorandum, Frederic Bartlett, March 27, 1959, NARA RG 59.

13. *St. Petersburg Times*, March 3, 1959.

14. American embassy, New Delhi, telegram, March 30, 1959, NARA RG 59.

15. *New York Times*, April 3, 1959. Nehru did not cite some of the more exotic residents, such as Adrian Conan Doyle, who had spent considerable time there attempting a spiritualist reunion with his late father; the mystic Roerich, known as Vice President Henry Wallace's "Dear Guru"; or any of Gyalo Thondup's resident kitchen cabinet. However, three weeks later, when the anthropologist Prince Peter of Greece, who had been there for some time collecting data for his study on Himalayan polyandry, spoke out against India's passive policy, the annoyed prime minister did expel him. Thondup dismissed Nehru's charges against his former tennis partner as nonsense, saying all the Prince did was measure the skull of any Tibetan he could find there. After his banishment the Prince and his White Russian wife took an active role in the support of refugee Tibetan children.

16. Department of State telegram 654, April 2, 1959, FRUS 1958–60, vol. 19, p. 754E.

17. Message, White House staff, "Intelligence Matters," DDE.

18. Gompo Tashi, *Four Rivers, Six Ranges*, p. 103.

19. Ibid.

20. Memorandum from DCI to President Eisenhower, Washington, April 1, 1959, FRUS 1958–60, vol. 19, p. 753.

21. Email message from "Slim" to the author, July 5, 2004.

22. Ibid.

23. Mark Udall, speech, Camp Hale, Colo., September 10, 2010, at which the author was present.

24. Memorandum of the proceedings of the March 27 meeting of the 5412 Group, FRUS 1958–60, vol. 19, p. 555.

25. Chairman's daily log, April 20, 1959, phone call from Allen Dulles, Twining Papers, Library of Congress.

26. FRUS 1958–60, vol. 19, p. 755.

27. Memorandum, May 7, 1959, DCI to President Eisenhower, FRUS 1958–60, vol. 19, p. 768.

28. CIA CREST document: RDP79T01049A001900130001-6.

29. See Roderick MacFarquhar, *The Politics of China* (Cambridge: Cambridge University Press, 1993), p. 100.

30. A more detailed description of these teams, their missions, and their fate is provided in Conboy, *The CIA's Secret War in Tibet*; Knaus, *Orphans of the Cold War*, pp. 222–35.

31. From frequent conversations between the author and his colleagues, 1963–67.

32. Meetings with the author in Dharamsala and Darjeeling, 1995 and 1996; meetings with McCarthy in Kathmandu and Dharamsala, 1998.

12. Tibet on the International Scene

1. State Department, intelligence brief, April 14, 1959, British FO file 371/141595.

2. Quoted in *New York Times*, April 5, 1958.

3. *Sarasota Herald Tribune*, April 17, 1959.

4. *New York Times*, April 4, 1959.

5. Memorandum of conversation, April 2, 1959, Chatterjee and Hart, NARA RG 59, box 3950.

6. Memorandum of conversation, April 1, 1959, de la Mare and Lutkins, NARA RG 59, box 3950.

7. United States Embassy telegram, London, April 7, 1959, NARA RG 59, box 3950.

8. NSC 5412/2 memorandum, March 27, 1959, FRUS 1958–60, vol. 19, p. 556.

9. Department of State telegram 654 to Taipei, April 2, 1959, NARA RG 59, box 3950.

10. Memorandum of conversation, Liebman and Fisk, March 30, 1959, NARA RG 59, 793B.00/3-3059.

11. Letter, Case to Herter, April 7, 1959, NARA RG 59, box 3950.

12. Letter, Walter Robertson to Senator Humphrey, April 29, 1959, NARA RG 59.

13. TDCS-3/396,258, April 23, 1959, DDE, Whitman file.

14. New Delhi Embassy telegram 2532, April 22, 1959, NARA RG 59 box 3950; Nehru press conference, April 7, 1959, New Delhi Embassy telegram 2362, April 8, 1959, NARA RG 59, box 3950.

15. Dalai Lama press statement, April 18, 1951.

16. Knaus, *Orphans of the Cold War*, p. 173.

17. White House Staff Security Files, Intelligence Briefing folder, box 14, Eisenhower Library.

18. Mullik, *The Chinese Betrayal*, pp. 180–81.

19. United States Consulate General, Hong Kong, No. 1597, April 21, 1959, NARA RG 59, box 3950.

20. *New York Times*, April 28, 1959.

21. Memorandum of conversation, Robertson and Herve Alphand, April 10, 1959, NARA RG 59.

22. Circular 1218, April 29, 1959, NARA RG 59, box 3950.

23. Knaus, *Orphans of the Cold War*, p. 189; DDE, Whitman file, box 44, Eisenhower Library.

24. Memorandum, May 5, 1959, Robertson to Herter, FRUS 1958–60, vol. 19, pp. 765–67.

25. Editorial note, FRUS 1958–60, vol. 19, p. 770.

26. Memorandum of conversation, George Yeh and Walter Robertson, April 29, 1959, FRUS 1958–59, vol. 19, pp. 760–61.

27. United States Embassy telegram, Taipei, April 28, 1959, NARA RG 59.

28. Gyalo described this meeting in an interview with the author in Kalimpong in November 1996.

29. U.K. High Commission, New Delhi, telegram 1523, October 3, 1959, FO 371/141602.

13. The United States Remains Involved

1. *New York Times*, June 21, 1959.

2. State Department, memorandum for the president, April 30, 1959, DDE, Ann Whitman file, box 44.

3. Memorandum for the president, June 16, 1959, DDE, International file, box 13.

4. Message from Acting Secretary Douglas Dillon, FRUS 1958–60, vol. 19, p. 773.

5. Ibid.

6. Letter addressed to "His Holiness," dated July 6, 1959, DDE, MR Case No. 94-168.

7. American embassy, El Salvador, dispatch 517, April 17, 1959; American embassy, Dublin, dispatch 323, April 15, 1959; State Department, telegram, April 9, 1959.

8. Memorandum of discussion in New York, September 18, 1958, FO 37/141/6000.

9. USUN telegram 82, FRUS 1958–60.

10. Memorandum, Parsons to the secretary, September 16, 1959, NARA RG 59, box 3951.

11. USUN telegram 137, October 8, 1959, FRUS, vol. 19, pp. 791–792.

12. All quotations from the UN debate are from the official records of the Plenary Meetings of the Fourteenth Session of the United Nations General Assembly, Autumn 1959.

13. The United States did not sever relations with Castro until January 1961.

14. Article 2 states, "Nothing contained in the present Charter shall authorize the United Nations to intervene in matters which are essentially within the domestic jurisdiction of any state."

15. American embassy, New Delhi, Embassy telegram 812, September 5, 1959, FRUS 1958–60, vol. 19, p. 781.

16. USUN 251, October 23, 1959, FRUS 1958–60, vol. 19.

17. State Department, telegram to USUN and New Delhi embassy, October 26, 1959, NARA RG 59 793B.00/102659, box 3951.

18. Memorandum, October 14, 1959, FRUS 1958–60, vol. 19, pp. 792–95.

19. Memorandum, October 29, 1959, FRUS 1958–60, vol. 19, pp. 797–800.

20. Memorandum, Parsons to Yeh, November 3, 1959, FRUS 1958–60, vol. 19, pp. 800–802.

21. Personal letter from Murphy to Thondup, November 4, 1959, NARA.

22. American embassy, New Delhi, Embassy telegram 1858, November 23, 1959, FRUS 1958–60, vol. 19, pp. 804–5.

23. The author's personal knowledge of and role in this effort is described in Knaus, *Orphans of the Cold War*, pp. 211–12.

24. White House Office of the Staff Secretary, DDE, Intelligence file, box 13, Tibet (2).

25. Department of State to Embassy, New Delhi, November 25, 1959, FRUS 14, pp. 806–7.

14. New Commitments

1. The Tibetan task force chief described his meeting with Gompo and the decisions that grew out of it in correspondence with the author on May 6 and 7 and July 20, 2004.

2. Lhamo Tsering, in correspondence with the author on November 18, 1995, provided his understanding of the plan that was finally agreed to.

3. Calcutta *Statesman*, August 1, 1960.

4. Memorandum of conversation, October 27, 1960, FRUS 1958–60, vol. 19.

5. FRUS, 1951, vol. 7, p. 1815.

15. A New Ballgame

1. Theodore C. Sorenson, *Kennedy* (New York: Harper and Row, 1965), p. 334.

2. The CIA released a set of these journals to the Library of Congress on August 4, 1963.

3. Galbraith to Ball, November 30, 1961, FRUS 1961–63, vol. 22.

4. Telegram to Bundy for the president, November 27, 1961, JFK, Country Series, Tibet.

5. Personal letter from Galbraith to JFK, December 6, 1961, JFK, Country Series, Tibet.

6. Interviews with the author, Cambridge, Mass., March 14, 1994, December 8, 2004.

7. . When Nehru offered Dharamsala as a relocation site for the displaced Tibetan leader in 1960, it was a ghost town. An earthquake in 1905 had caused the British to opt for Simla rather than Dharamsala as the summer capital of the British Raj. Its relative isolation at the end of the railway line to Kashmir served the interests of the Dalai Lama while he reorganized his political and religious establishment and relationship with his Indian hosts. In the forty years since the Dalai Lama and his small retinue of family and officials settled in these bungalows, Dharamsala has served well as the seat of a functioning though officially unrecognized government-in-exile.

8. *Times of India*, August 8, 2006.

9. Menon, however, was the only non-family member at Nehru's birthday breakfast on November 14. He moved to a house near Nehru's and spent the rest of his days practicing law at the Supreme Court, never again holding high office.

10. Galbraith, *A Life in Our Times*, p. 450.

11. Ibid., p. 428.

12. Or with which he felt constrained to share power. Ibid., p. 429.

13. Ibid., p. 437.

14. See Knaus, *Orphans of the Cold War*, p. 257.

15. Galbraith, *A Life in Our Times*, p. 441.

16. Memorandum from Kaysen to President Kennedy, November 3, 1962, FRUS 1961–63, vol. 19, pp. 363–68.

17. Editorial note, FRUS 1961–63, vol. 22, p. 321.

18. Interview with Dean Rusk, March 30, 1970, JFK, Oral History Program.
19. "Memorandum on United States Policy in the Sino-Indian Conflict," November 3, 1962, JFK, Roger Hilsman Papers, folder 18, box 1.
20. American embassy, New Delhi, telegram 1891, and Indian embassy, Washington, letter from Nehru, both dated November 19, 1962, JFK.
21. Presidential meeting, November 19, 1962, FRUS 1961–63, vol. 19, pp. 394–96. Symington was a member of the special Executive Committee advising JFK during the Cuban missile crisis.
22. Memorandum for the record, November 22, 1962, JFK, Hilsman Papers, folder 18.
23. Ibid.
24. Author interviews with Galbraith, Cambridge, Mass., March 1994 and December 2004, and with Critchfield, Washington, July 1998.
25. FRUS 1961–63, vol. 19, pp. 414–16.

16. The United States and India as Allies

1. Memorandum, Kaysen to JFK, December 9, 1962, JFK, NSF, Galbraith special file.
2. Letter, JFK to Nehru, December 11, 1962, JFK, NSF file, India.
3. Memorandum of conversation, JFK and Macmillan, Nassau, December 20, 1962, FRUS 1961–63, vol. 19, p. 452.
4. Department of State telegram 3098, February 6, 1963, FRUS 1961–63, vol. 19, p. 491.
5. Department of State, survey, JFK, Hilsman Papers, folder 18.
6. Mullik, The Chinese Betrayal, pp. 437–38.
7. In a letter to the author dated September 7, 1999, Galbraith wrote, "I am not writing to offer a serious defense of action in those distant times or to recall my difficulties with Desmond FitzGerald. There was indeed a strong difference of purpose between his adventuresome Cold War activities and my responsibilities as ambassador." In reference to my account of the CIA's support of the Tibetan guerrillas at Mustang, he wrote, "You will not be surprised that I have a somewhat different view of events out of Mustang in those years, but I readily concede you a point on my description of those there engaged. My reference to an unhygienic force was inappropriate and certainly not intended as a public characterization." He never completely mellowed, however. My last memory of him shortly before he died in 2006 was his cackling shout from his bed as I was going down the stairs that it was time for me to move on from "those deeply unhygienic tribesmen."
8. American embassy, New Delhi, Embassy telegram 4334, May 8, 1963, JFK, NSF, India.
9. JFK to Galbraith, March 22, 1963, FRUS 1963, vol. 19, pp. 523–24.
10. Official informal letter, March 17, 1962, NARA RG 59, box 2161.
11. President Ayub eventually addressed his concerns about the aid the United States was providing India, hinting in a letter to President Johnson the following year that it was causing him to reevaluate the desirability of Pakistan's alliance with the United States. He asked to come to Washington to present his case in person, a potentially ticklish occasion that LBJ had no interest in hosting, especially in an election year. Johnson, as one frontier poker player to another, called the bluff, telling his staff, "Ayub says he'll take a look at his hole card. Let's wait till he does and then we will look at ours. Isn't that good poker?" FRUS 1964–68, vol. 25, p. 138.
12. Remarks, National Security Council, January 22, 1963, FRUS 1961–63, vol. 19, p. 480.

13. The "Young Turk" training program carried out at Cornell University from 1964 to 1967 is described in Knaus, *Orphans of the Cold War,* pp. 284–85. Most of the two dozen young Tibetan men and women who were trained there in government, world history, and English composition served in the Dalai Lama's exile government either in India or abroad. Generally this CIA project, which William Colby enthusiastically supported, proved highly rewarding.

14. In a meeting in Darjeeling in November 1996, one of the participants, Gyesang Chamatsang (known as Ngadruk), and I recalled our respective regretful memories of these meetings and what became their unfulfilled conclusions.

15. Letter to the author, April 11, 1996.

16. From the first time I met Lhamo Tsering in the late 1950s until his death forty years later, he was constantly suffering from a nervous stomach. This disability, however, never caused him to let up on his relentless pursuit of his duties and obligations. The constant tension under which this gentle but conscience-driven person lived might well have contributed to his death from stomach cancer in 1999.

17. Interview with the author, New York, February 1997.

18. Memorandum for the 303 Committee, January 26, 1968, FRUS 1964–68, vol. 30, p. 739.

19. Sonam Palden, interview with the author, Cambridge, Mass., September 6, 1997.

20. S. S. Uban, *The Phantoms of Chittagong* (New Delhi: Allied Press, 1985).

21. Interview with the author, Kalimpong, November 1996.

22. Dean Rusk, telephone interview with the author, May 24, 1994.

17. The United States Disengages

1. Interview with the author, November 6, 1997.

2. "Polo" was the White House code name for the visits to China that Nixon had inaugurated.

3. Telefax from Lord to the author, February 14, 1997.

4. Interview with the author, November 6, 1997.

5. The gossip at Mustang was that Birendra was particularly sensitive about what he considered the Mustang commander Wangdu's superior manner toward him, which he felt he demonstrated by dominating him with his greater height in photographs taken during their meetings.

6. A fuller account of the dismantling of the Mustang operations and its consequences is included in Knaus, *Orphans of the Cold War,* pp. 296–314.

7. Lhamo Tsering's jail mate, the hero of the October 1961 ambush which netted the document trove, was unable to accept refugee life in India and was rearrested when he attempted to steal back into Nepal, in violation of the terms of his release. He died in prison there. Conboy, *The CIA's Secret War in Tibet,* p. 259.

8. Memorandum, Kissinger for the president, "My Talks with Chou En-lai," July 14, 1971, NARA, NSC Files, Lord, box 847.

9. Department of State, memorandum for Mr. Kissinger, February 19, 1970, NARA RG 59, 1970–73, box 2628.

10. Memorandum from the White House, April 1, 1970, NARA RG 59, 1970–73, box 2628.

11. Assurances given by American embassy officer Nicholas G. Thatcher to Tsepon Shakabpa, June 1951, American consulate, dispatch 615, June 25, 1951, NARA RG 59, NND 822910, box 4227.

12. American Embassy, New Delhi, telegram 9883, April 24, 1970, NARA RG 59, 1970–73, box 2628.

13. American Embassy, New Delhi, Embassy telegram, May 21, 1970, NARA RG 59, 1970–73, box 2628.

14. Letter, Ernest A. Gross to Undersecretary Alexis Johnson, December 10, 1970, NARA RG 59, 1970–73, box 2628.

15. Approval, Secretary Rogers, December 26, 1970, NSC approval, March 1, 1971, NARA RG 59, 1970–73, box 2628.

16. Oval Office conversation, July 22, 1971, Nixon, Rogers, and Kissinger, White House tape cassette 543-1.

17. Alexis Johnson, letter to John Ball, January 19, 1972, NARA RG 59, box 2628.

18. Action memorandum, Green to Johnson, August 27, 1971, NARA RG 59, box 2628.

19. Interview with the author, Washington, July 7, 1996. "Li Mi" referred to the problem created by the Chinese Nationalist soldiers who had set up an enclave in northern Burma, which they refused to leave. They fled there after Chiang and the remnants of his army escaped to Taiwan in 1949.

20. American consulate, Hong Kong, telegram, September 24, 1971, NARA RG 59, box 2628.

21. Lodi Gyari became the executive chairman of the International Campaign for Tibet, and is now the special envoy in the negotiations which the Dalai Lama's government-in-exile has been conducting with Beijing since Gyalo began them in 1982.

22. Memorandum of conversation, Lodi Gyari and William A. Brown, American embassy, New Delhi, December 19, 1969, NARA RG 59, Central Policy Files, 1967–69.

23. In their initial discussions Nixon and Kissinger considered various candidates to be the envoy on the "secret" trip to set up Nixon's visit. They both dismissed George Bush "as too soft and not sophisticated enough" and Elliot Richardson, the attorney general who refused to comply with Nixon's order to sack the Watergate special prosecutor, as "too close to them" and unacceptable to Secretary Rogers. When Nixon came up with Nelson Rockefeller, John D. Rockefeller's Wall Street lawyer and grandson, Kissinger at first dismissed his old sponsor and boss as "not disciplined enough." But Nixon later returned to Rockefeller, musing, "The Chinese would consider him important and he would be—could do a lot for us in terms of the domestic situation." However, he again rejected him: "No, Nelson is a wild hair [hare] running around." Kissinger then reassured Nixon that "for one operation" he could keep him under control, adding, "To them a Rockefeller is a tremendous thing." After discussing and dismissing other candidates, Kissinger again proposed his old boss, saying the Chinese "would jump at a Rockefeller, a high visibility one." This prospect intrigued Nixon, who agreed that "the visibility would be enormous": "Can't you just see what that would do to the Libs in this country, oh, God. Rockefeller over there, Jesus Christ!" Teleconference, Nixon and Kissinger, April 27, 1971, NARA NSC files, box 1031. Despite Nixon's mischievous glee at this prospect, Kissinger eventually was able to claim the post for himself.

24. NARA, Polo I Briefing Book, NSC, File for the President, box 1032.

25. Kissinger memorandum to Nixon, July 17, 1971, NARA, NSC Files for the President, China, box 1036.

26. Memorandum of conversation, Zhou and Kissinger, July 9, 1971, NARA, NSC file, box 846.

27. Memorandum of conversation, Zhou and Kissinger, October 21, 1971, NARA, NSC files, box 846.

28. The whole venture appealed to both Kissinger and Yahya Khan, and both would have regretted being forced to call it off. In a private briefing given to the White House staff on July 15, 1971, Kissinger said, "The cloak and dagger exercise in Pakistan [from where a PIA Boeing aircraft flew him to and from Beijing] arranging the trip was fascinating. Yahya hadn't had such fun since the last Hindu massacre." NARA, NSC Files for the President, box 1036.

29. Kissinger, *White House Years*, p. 854.

30. Memorandum of conversation, Zhou and Kissinger, July 10, 1971, NARA, NSC, box 1032.

31. Oval Office conversation, August 11, 1971, NARA, White House cassette tape 561D.

32. Memorandum of conversation, Huang Hua and Kissinger, November 23, 1971, New York, NARA, National Security files, box 849.

33. Memorandum of conversation, Kissinger and Huang Hua, October 3, 1972, NARA RG 59, Policy Planning Staff Director's Files (Winston Lord), box 332.

34. Nixon and Kissinger, January 1, 1972, White House tape cassette 17F.

35. NARA, NSC Office files, box 9.

36. Memorandum of conversation, Nixon and Zhou, February 21, 1972, NARA, NSC files, box 92. Nixon's conversation with Mao on February 23 is filed in NSC files, box 9.

37. Tyler, *A Great Wall*, p. 440. A year later Beijing agreed to accept a CIA officer as a member of the American Liaison Office in Beijing in order to preserve a separate channel of communication apart from the regular diplomatic channel.

38. United States House of Representatives, document 92-337, *Impressions of the New China*.

39. Cable, Scowcroft to Kissinger, February 9, 1973, NARA, National Security Files, Kissinger Office files, box 29.

40. Memorandum of conversation, Nixon and Huang Zen, July 6, 1973, NARA, NSC files, box 328.

41. Memorandum of conversation, Tsien Ta-yung and Armstrong, July 30, 1974, NARA RG 59, NMD 979520, box 376.

42. Interview with the author, New York, April 30, 1997.

43. Teleconference, Mr. Habib and the Secretary, October 13, 1975, NARA, Kissinger telecoms.

44. Ibid.

45. *New York Times*, October 15, 1975.

46. Bilateral Issue Book, Kissinger visit to Peking, PPS Director Lord Files, box 373.

47. United States Liaison Office, Peking, telegram 1897, November 3, 1974, NARA RG 59, box 375.

48. Memorandum of conversation, Deng and Kissinger, November 27, 1974, NARA RG 59.

49. The ambassador, Leonard Unger, had presented his credentials to the Republic of China on May 25, 1974.

50. Memorandum, Kissinger to Ford, "Possible Approaches to Your China Trip," RG 59, Winston Lord files, box 379. Kissinger later said that forebodings about the Chinese sensitivity over the choice of Vladivostok as a meeting site were well founded. He had to pass off Deng's opening inquiry about "how he had found Vladivostok" by saying he had never been so cold in his life and could well understand why the Chinese

had never settled there. Deng immediately took him to task for implying that this territory, which the Russians had wrested from China in the previous century, had always been Russian. He noted that in the past the inhabitants were mainly Chinese. Although the Russians gave it its present name, which means "Rule of the East," the Chinese still used their name for it, which translates as "sea slug." Kissinger, *Years of Renewal*, p. 870.

51. "Bei-jing" translates as "north capital." It was named in 1421 AD when the Yongle emperor moved the capital there. Beijing was later named Beiping in 1928 when Jiang Kai-shek moved his government to Nanjing. Once again, the city's name became Beijing when the Chinese Communist Party decided to relocate the capital once more.

52. Memorandum of conversation, Mao and Kissinger, October 21, 1975, NARA RG 59, Director PPS files, box 372, folder 1.

53. New China News Agency, December 2, 75.

54. Memorandum of conversation, Deng and Ford, December 4, 1975, NARA RG 59, PPS Lord, box 372.

18. Rescue from Limbo

1. Tyler, *A Great Wall*, pp. 235–37.

2. Interview with the author, Cambridge, Mass., January 10, 2002.

3. *New York Times*, September 9, 1976.

4. Thirty-two years later a similar snub in the form of President Obama's delaying his first meeting with the Dalai Lama until he had met with his Chinese counterpart received wide coverage of the new equities and consequent protocol involved.

5. *New York Times*, September 4, 1979.

6. Geshe, meaning "spiritual friend," is a title given to a spiritual teacher.

7. *New York Times Magazine*, May 5, 1996, pp. 46–49.

8. McCleary interview with the author, Roland Farms, Va., May 26, 2000.

9. Geshe La's involvement in the affairs of the Fourteenth Dalai Lama and with the CIA is a rich historical irony. As a young Kalmyk monk he was a protégé of the Buryat Mongol Dorzhiev, whose relationship with the Thirteenth Dalai Lama was one of the prime factors precipitating the Younghusband expedition that caused the Tibetan pontiff to flee Lhasa a half-century earlier. Although Dorzhiev first appeared on the American diplomatic screen when, as the Dalai Lama's emissary, he met with Ambassador Rockhill in 1908, that was a piece of diplomatic history long forgotten. When the Thirteenth Dalai Lama returned to Lhasa and immediately fled to India in 1910, Dorzhiev went back to Russia. It was there that he became the root lama of Geshe La and encouraged him to go to Lhasa in 1920 to study at Drepung monastery. Geshe La left Lhasa when the Dalai Lama fled to Yatung in 1950. When the Dalai Lama decided to return to Lhasa for another go at trying to rule under Mao, Geshe La went to the United States, where he established his monastery in New Jersey. Geshe maintained his regard for Dorzhiev and consecrated his memory by hanging a portrait of him at his monastery. The complexity and sensitivity of this relationship was demonstrated when Geshe carefully took down this portrait when His Holiness visited. Joshua Cutler, the director of the monastic center, recalls that the Dalai Lama ex-

pressed some surprise—but made no comment—when he visited there after Geshe's death and Cutler had neglected to remove the portrait of this controversial figure of central Asian Buddhist history. Interview with the author, November 12, 2005.

Geshe La was highly regarded and valued by all of us CIA officers who worked with him as he devised the telecodes and translated the messages sent by the members of the Tibetan resistance movement that the Agency was supporting. None of us, however, was aware of the richness of our colleague's background in central Asian politics.

10. Email note to the author, July 1, 2005.
11. Interview with the author, University of Virginia, Charlottesville, October 25, 2001.
12. *New York Times,* October 21, 1979.
13. Email to the author, June 27, 2005.
14. Interview with the author, Alexandria, Va., September 2001.
15. Interview with the author, Chevy Chase, Md., August 3, 2005.
16. Meeting with the author, January 20, 2009.
17. Shakya, *Dragon in the Land of Snows,* p. 384.
18. Conversation with the author, Kalimpong, November 1995.
19. Interview with the author, August 3, 2005.
20. Gyalo's description of Dharamsala's role in their negotiations with Beijing—and of his role in them—was obtained during discussions with him in Kalimpong and New Delhi on November 10–21, 1995.
21. These terms are basically those embodied in the Dalai Lama's "Middle Way" proposal and have been the basis for the Tibetan negotiating position pursued by Dharamsala and rejected by the Chinese government ever since.

19. America Rediscovers Tibet

1. McCleary, in a meeting at his home in the Plains, Va., August 28, 2001, lent a copy of this document to the author for his education.
2. See previous note; this information is from the introduction within McCleary's study.
3. Ibid.
4. Lantos's death on February 11, 2008, deprived the Dalai Lama and the Tibetans of one of their most dedicated and effective champions in the United States Congress, where he had promoted their cause for two decades. The memorial service held by the Tibetan community in Washington, with its humming of Buddhist prayers for a departed Jew, was an eloquent and moving testimonial to this bridging of two worlds.
5. All quotations are from the text of the five-point peace plan published by the Office of H. H. the Dalai Lama.
6. *New York Times,* October 7, 1987.
7. Lantos's aide Kay King, who was orchestrating this event, said that the *Washington Post* declined to send a reporter to cover the event, but it did print a photograph of the Dalai Lama speaking to the hearing in its local news section. She later discovered that this modest note of his presence in Washington was due to an intern in Lantos's office who was interested in Tibet and who fortuitously happened to be working on that section of the newspaper. Interview with King, June 16, 2000.

8. Quotations provided by general news coverage supplied by the China Tibet Information Center.

9. The lawyer was John Ackerly, who became president of the International Campaign for Tibet when it was formed the following year, and the physician was his Dartmouth classmate Blake Kerr. Both were mountain climbers who were on vacation in Tibet. They were released four days later.

10. *New York Times*, October 7, 1987.

11. Ibid.

12. Hearing, October 14, 1987, Subcommittees on Human Rights and International Organizations and on Asian and Pacific Affairs, USGPO, 1988, pp. 24–36. The diplomat William W. Rockhill and his travels to Tibet and dealings with the Thirteenth Dalai Lama are described in the first chapter of this book. Roy did not note that the ambassador under whom Rockhill served looked with considerable disfavor on what he considered Rockhill's personal boondoggling in trying to reach Lhasa. Neither did he cite Rockhill's advice to the Dalai Lama to make the best deal he could with those then ruling in Peking and remain "a portion of the Manchu Empire" for Tibet's own good because "the Great Powers of the world deem[ed] it necessary for the prosperity of their own peoples" (see chap. 2).

13. *New York Times*, October 15, 1987.

14. Interview with the author, Washington.

15. Pell had ensconced the controversial Uri Geller in a secluded nook in the Capitol to continue his controversial studies in psychokinesis.

16. This background data concerning Berkowitz, his relationships with his fellow congressional aides and the advice he provided them and the Tibetans, and the substance and documentation of the legislative action they generated come from seven packing cases of congressional legislation and documents covering these activities that Berkowitz made available to the author.

17. Maura Moynihan, in an interview with the author in Washington in June 2000, described being regularly taken into custody by the District of Columbia police, who asked her and her colleagues to do their picketing in the mornings so that they could be arrested, charged, and discharged before lunch and they would not have to incarcerate the daughter of one of the Capitol's more prominent and articulate senators.

18. Interview with the author, Washington, June 2000.

19. Galbraith had been egged on by his assistant, Mary Beth Markey. She was to continue promoting and authoring various projects which Galbraith willingly took on in support of the Tibetans for many years, until she joined the staff of the International Campaign for Tibet as their legislative counsel to conduct the Campaign's highly successful lobbying activities. She is now director of the Campaign.

20. Interview with the author, Newton, Mass., July 31, 2000.

21. As the situation calmed down, Ambassador James Lilley persuaded Washington to limit the evacuation to dependents.

22. Quoted in Tyler, *A Great Wall*, p. 366.

23. Ibid.

24. Winston Lord, "Misguided Mission," *Washington Post*, December 19, 1989.

25. Interview with the author, Washington, June 12, 2002.

26. These quotations are from House Document 102-150, USGPO, 1992.

27. Paal, meeting with the author, August 10, 2001.

28. *Washington Post*, April 17, 1991; House Document 102-150.

20. Collateral Diplomacy

1. Proceedings, USGPO document ISBN 16-039892-4.

2. Moynihan continued to promote the Tibetan cause for the duration of his term. In recognition of his efforts on behalf of his people, the Dalai Lama visited the future site of the Moynihan train station in New York City on September 25, 2005, where Mayor Michael Bloomberg presented the Tibetan leader with keys to the city.

3. Press release, Moynihan office, May 28, 1993.

4. Lord made these retrospective comments in an interview with the author on April 19, 2001.

5. These incidents are recorded in Lilley, *China Hands*, p. 203; Shattuck, *Freedom on Fire*, p. 240.

6. Shattuck, *Freedom on Fire*, p. 242.

7. Twenty years later there was a repeat performance of this contest, but the equities of the participants had changed, and accordingly so did the script. It was the American president who postponed his first meeting with the Dalai Lama until after he had made his trip to Beijing for his first meeting with the Chinese president, whose country holds a significant amount of the current United States debt. Roy again defended this show of deference, noting that the sensitivities of one billion Chinese toward the two million Tibetans cannot be ignored. Symposium, Brookings Institute, November 6, 2009.

8. Shattuck, *Freedom on Fire*, pp. 272–73.

9. *New York Times*, April 30, 1994.

10. This description of the genesis and abandonment of the MFN–human rights linkage for China policy is based on Shattuck's book *Freedom on Fire* and conversations with him on July 19, 2001, and November 16, 2005.

11. Discussions with McCleary, Washington, November 2005.

21. A New High in White House Support

1. Reuters, Beijing, February 25, 1997.

2. *Michigan Daily Online*, quoting *Los Angeles Times*, March 26, 1997.

3. CNN, Washington, April 24, 1997.

4. Reuters, Washington, April 24, 1997.

5. United States Senate, Hearing 105-124, May 13, 1997, USGPO.

6. Stein described the origin of this proposal in an interview with the author, Washington, July 11, 2000.

7. Secretary of State to the chairman of the Foreign Relations Committee, July 29, 1997.

8. Joint House-Senate Conference Committee, July 30, 1997, described in the *New York Times*, November 1, 1997.

9. Transcript of press conference, Executive Office, October 29, 1997.

10. Speech at Sanders Hall, Harvard University, November 1, 1997.

11. Interview with the author, Washington, August 21, 2001.

12. The Tibetans were to lose it again eleven years later, when Craig resigned, this time from his even more key post as Obama's White House counsel.

13. Interview with the author, Washington, September 5, 2001.

14. Interview with the author, Washington, November 20, 2001.
15. Interview with the author, Washington, October 9, 2003.
16. Interview with the author, May 6, 2009.
17. Interview with the author, October 14, 2010.

22. People-to-People Diplomacy

1. Interview with the author, Washington, June 17, 2002.
2. Ibid.
3. Interview with the author, Senate Office Building, January 23, 2004.
4. In a conversation with the author on March 6, 2006, Blum said that Feinstein had received little or no criticism from her constituents for her outspoken support of Tibet. He believes even those who are pro-Taiwan, including those who want to do business with the Mainland, want to see the Tibet issue peaceably solved.
5. Blum conversation with the author, March 1, 2011.
6. The conference was fully recorded in the *Washington Post* on June 28, 1998.
7. Interview with the author, Washington, March 16, 2006.
8. Official press conference transcript, Associated Press News Archive, June 27, 1998.
9. *Washington Post*, June 27, 1998.
10. Final report, December 1998. Copy provided to the author by Mr. Barnes.
11. According to official China Tibet Information Center figures, the average per capita income of rural people in the Tibet Autonomous Region in 2008 was 3,170 yuan (U.S.$1 equals 6.84 yuan). The per capita disposable income of urban residents in Tibet in 2007, according to the *People's Daily*, was 11,131 yuan.
12. This observation was to prove prophetic a decade later.
13. Generally the conclusions and proposed solutions follow the analysis that Goldstein outlined in his book, *The Snow Lion and the Dragon*. He recommended that the Dalai Lama return to Tibet and accept Chinese sovereignty and the current political system in the Tibet Autonomous Region, while the Chinese in stages appointed Tibetans to head all party and government offices there, phase in Tibetan as the operating language of government, and reduce substantially the number of Chinese living and working there. Goldstein wrote, "One of the greatest stumbling blocks to such a solution is the exile's demand for a Greater Tibet. Amdo and Kham, to be sure, are ecologically, culturally and religiously similar to political Tibet, but historical differences and current political realities make the creation of a Greater Tibet extremely improbable, at least initially" (128).

23. An Uncertain Future

1. Interview with the author, Washington, June 28, 2006.
2. The Dalai Lama reciprocated this regard, but with reservations. In a lecture in New Delhi on January 17, 2009, he "evoked a stunned silence" from his audience when he described how he and Bush "struck a chord immediately in their first meeting," but then added that he had told Bush, "I love you, but some of your policies I oppose." (New Delhi PTI, January 17, 2009.) He reaffirmed this measured view in response to a question posed after a lecture at MIT on May Day about whom he regarded as a model leader: "I love him [Bush] as a model leader but as far as his policies are concerned I have reservations." *The Tech*, MIT, May 1, 2009.

3. Reuters, Washington, October 17, 2007.

4. Cf. chapter 5.

5. *Economist*, March 14, 2008.

6. Lodi Gyari, who became the official negotiator for Dharamsala in 2002, suggests that Thondup's predominant role before he was sidelined may have reflected a snobbish Chinese preference to deal with an "insider" member of the Dalai Lama's family while avoiding official recognition of someone who represented what Beijing considers a rebel government. At Dharamsala some members of the Dalai Lama's government who were nervous about Gyalo's freewheeling style of negotiating may have felt relief. At the present time Gyalo is reportedly writing his long-promised memoirs, which may provide some insights—or at least another perspective on these intracourt politics.

7. Lodi Gyari, speech, Kennedy School of Government, Harvard University, October 10, 2008.

8. On May 14, five hundred monks attended a Buddhist service at Drepung monastery to pray for and collect funds for the victims of the earthquakes in Sichuan. (They collected 38,000 yuan; U.S.$5,440.) The Chinese official news agency made no comment on the donors, whom Beijing blamed as instigators of the subsequent riots. The Dalai Lama praised the Chinese authorities for their swift relief and reconstruction response and offered his prayers and condolences for the victims of the earthquakes.

9. HR 5668, 1075, 1077, USGPO.

10. *London Telegraph*, March 21, 2010; *New York Times*, March 12, 2010.

11. Speech, Kennedy School at Harvard University, October 8, 2008.

12. Press conference, Dharamsala, India, described in the *New York Times* (Asia Pacific edition), November 22, 2008.

13. Letter to the author, March 6, 2007.

14. He was obviously aware that his predecessors made a late entry into Tibet's history; Tibetans as a distinct people have been sparring with the Chinese for some two thousand years.

15. Press statement, Dharamsala, India, June 20, 2009, recorded by Reuters, June 21, 2009.

16. Report filed by *Sheja* editor Kelsang Khuduo from Kalimpong, December 15, 2010.

17. *New York Times*, March 21, 2008.

18. Statement to the press, February 19, 2010.

19. *Tibet Report*, November 30, 2010.

Publications

Acheson, Dean. *Present at the Creation.* New York: W. W. Norton, 1969.

Ambrose, Stephen E. *Eisenhower: The President.* New York: Simon and Schuster, 1984.

Anand, Dibyesh. *Geopolitical Exotica.* Minneapolis: University of Minnesota Press, 2007.

Andreyev, Alexandre. *Soviet Russia and Tibet.* Leiden: Brill, 2003.

Avedon, John F. *In Exile from Land of Snows.* New York: Alfred A. Knopf, 1984.

———. *An Interview with the Dalai Lama.* New York: Littlebird, 1978.

Barnett, Robert. *Lhasa: Streets with Memories.* New York: Columbia University Press, 2006.

Beckwith, Christopher I. *The Tibetan Empire in Central Asia.* Princeton: Princeton University Press, 1987.

Bell, Sir Charles. *Portrait of a Dalai Lama.* Somerville, Mass.: Wisdom Publications, 1987.

———. *The Religion of Tibet.* Oxford: Oxford University Press, 1931.

———. *Tibet Past and Present.* Delhi: Oxford University Press, 1962.

Bishop, Peter. *The Myth of Shangri-La: Tibet, Travel Writing and Western Creation of Sacred Landscape.* Berkeley: University of California Press, 1989.

Brands, H. W. *Cold Warriors.* New York: Columbia University Press.

———. *Inside the Cold War: Loy Henderson and the Rise of the American Empire, 1918–1961.* New York: Oxford University Press, 1991.

Brauen, Martin. *Peter Aufschnaiter's Eight Years in Tibet.* Bangkok: Orchid Press, 2002.

Brecher, Michael. *Nehru: A Political Biography.* New York: Oxford University Press, 1959.

Burr, William. *The Kissinger Transcripts.* New York: New Press, 1998.

Cater, Harold Dean. *Henry Adams and His Friends.* Boston: Houghton Mifflin, 1947.

Chace, James. *Acheson.* New York: Simon and Schuster, 1998.

Chang, Jung. *Mao: The Unknown Story.* New York: Alfred A. Knopf, 2005.

Chapman, Spencer. *Lhasa: The Holy City.* London: Chatto and Windus, 1940.

Conboy, Kenneth. *The CIA's Secret War in Tibet.* Lawrence: University Press of Kansas, 2002.

———. *Elite Forces of India and Pakistan.* Oxford: Osprey, 1992.

Conboy, Kenneth, with M. S. Kohli. *Spies in the Himalayas: Secret Missions and Perilous Climbs.* Lawrence: University Press of Kansas, 2002.

Craig, Mary. *Kundun: The Biography of the Family of the Dalai Lama*. Berkeley: Counterpoint, 1997.

Crossley, Pamela Kyle. *Orphan Warriors: Three Manchu Generations and the End of the Qing World*. Princeton: Princeton University Press, 1990.

Cutler, Joshua, and Diana Cutler. Introduction to *The Door of Liberation*. Marblehead, Mass.: Wisdom Publications, 1973.

Cutler, Joshua, and Diana Cutler. Introduction to *The Jeweled Staircase*, by Geshe Wangyal. Ithaca, N.Y.: Snow Lion Publications, 1986.

Cutting, Suydam. *The Fire Ox and Other Years*. New York: Charles Scribner's, 1940.

Douglas, William O. *Beyond the High Himalayas*. New York: Doubleday, 1951.

Dunham, Mikel. *Buddha's Warriors*. New York: Tarcher/Penguin, 2004.

Fergusson, W. N. *Adventure Sport and Travel on the Tibetan Steppes*. London: Constable and Company, 1911.

Fleming, Peter. *Bayonets to Lhasa*. New York: Harper and Brothers, 1961.

French, Patrick. *Tibet, Tibet*. New York: Alfred A. Knopf, 2003.

Galbraith, John Kenneth. *A Life in Our Times: Memoirs*. Boston: Houghton Mifflin, 1981.

Gilmour, David. *Curzon: Imperial Statesman*. New York: Farrar, Straus and Giroux, 1994.

Goldstein, Melvyn C. *A History of Modern Tibet*. Berkeley: University of California Press, 1989.

———. *A Tibetan Revolutionary*. Berkeley: University of California Press, 2004.

Goldstein, Melvyn C., Ben Jiao, and Tanzen Lhundrup. *On the Cultural Revolution in Tibet: The Nyemo Incident of 1969*. Berkeley: University of California Press, 2009.

Gordon, Antoinette K. *The Iconography of Tibetan Lamaism*. North Clarendon, Vt.: Charles E. Tuttle, 1959.

Gould, B. J. *The Jewel in the Lotus*. London: Chatto and Windus, 1957.

Harrer, Heinrich. *Seven Years in Tibet*. New York: E. P. Dutton, 1954.

Hopkirk, Peter. *Trespassers on the Roof of the World*. New York: Kodansha International, 1995.

Isaacson, Walter, and Evan Thomas. *The Wise Men*. New York: Simon and Schuster, 1986.

Iyer, Pico. *The Open Road*. New York: Vintage Books, 2009.

Kamenetz, Rodger. *The Jew in the Lotus*. New York: Harper, 1995.

Kimura, Hisao. *Japanese Agent in Tibet*. London: Serindia, 1990.

Kirkpatrick, W. *An Account of the Kingdom of Nepal*. 1811. New Delhi: Manjusri, 1969.

Kissinger, Henry A. *White House Years*. Boston: Little, Brown, 1979.

———. *Years of Renewal*. New York: Simon and Schuster, 1999.

Knaus, John Kenneth. *Orphans of the Cold War: America and the Tibetan Struggle for Survival*. New York: PublicAffairs, 1999.

Laird, Thomas. *Into Tibet*. New York: Grove Press, 2002.

———. *The Story of Tibet: Conversations with the Dalai Lama*. New York: Grove Press, 2006.

Lamb, Alastair. *Britain and Chinese Central Asia*. London: Routledge and Kegan Paul, 1960.

Landon, Perceval. *The Opening of Tibet*. New York: Doubleday, Page, 1905.

Lang-Sims, Lois. *The Presence of Tibet*. London: Cresset Press, 1963.

Latourette, Kenneth Scott. *The Chinese: Their History and Culture*. New York: Macmillan, 1964.

Lauf, Detlef Ingo. *Tibetan Sacred Art*. Berkeley: Shambala, 1996.

Lilley, James. *China Hands*. New York: Public Affairs, 2004.

MacMillan, Margaret. *Nixon in China*. Toronto: Viking, 2006.

McGranahan, Carole. *Arrested Histories*. Durham, N.C.: Duke University Press, 2010.

McKay, David. *Tibet and the British Raj*. London: Curzon Press, 1997.

Meyer, Karl E., and Shareen Brysac. *Tournament of Shadows*. Berkeley: Counterpoint, 1999.

Moberly, Alan. *God Spoke Tibetan*. Nampa, Id.: Pacific Press Publishing Association, 1971.

Mullik, B. N. *The Chinese Betrayal: My Years with Nehru*. Bombay: Allied, 1971.

Mullin, Glenn H. *The Fourteen Dalai Lamas*. Santa Fe, N.M.: Clear Light Publishers, 2001.

Phuntsok Wanggyal. *Liquid Water Does Exist on the Moon*. Beijing: Foreign Languages Press, 2002.

Pomfret, John. *Chinese Lessons*. New York: Henry Holt, 2006.

Reinsch, Paul S. *An American Diplomat in China*. New York: Doubleday, Page, 1922.

Richardson, Hugh E. *High Peaks, Pure Earth: Collected Writings on Tibetan History and Culture*. London: Serindia, 1998.

———. *A Short History of Tibet*. New York: E. P. Dutton, 1962.

Rockhill, William Woodville. *Diary of a Journey through Mongolia and Tibet*. Washington: Smithsonian Institution, 1894.

Rusk, Dean. *As I Saw It*. New York: W. W. Norton, 1990.

Schaeffer, Howard B. *Ellsworth Bunker: Global Troubleshooter and Vietnam Hawk*. Chapel Hill: University of North Carolina Press, 2003.

Schell, Orville. *Virtual Tibet*. New York: Henry Holt, 2000.

Shakya, Tsering. *The Dragon in the Land of Snows: A History of Tibet since 1947*. New York: Columbia University Press, 1999.

Shattuck, John. *Freedom on Fire*. Cambridge: Harvard University Press, 2003.

Shelton, Albert E. *Pioneering in Tibet*. Grand Rapids, Mich.: Revell, 1921.

Shelton, Flora B. *Shelton of Tibet*. New York: Doran, 1923.

Shen, Tsung-lien. *Tibet and the Tibetans*. Stanford: Stanford University Press, 1953.

Smith, Warren W., Jr. *Tibetan Nation*. Boulder, Colo.: Westview Press, 1996.

Snelling, John. *Buddhism in Russia*. Perth, Wash.: Element, 1993.

Snow, Edgar. *Red Star over China*. New York: Modern Library, 1938.

Spence, Jonathan D. *The Search for Modern China*. New York: W. W. Norton, 1990.

Strober, Deborah Hart, and Gerald S. Strober. *His Holiness the Dalai Lama*. New York: John Wiley and Sons, 2005.

Teichman, Eric. *Affairs of China*. London: Methuen, 1938.

Tenzin Gyatso, XIV Dalai Lama. *The Dalai Lama at Harvard*. Translated by Jeffrey Hopkins. Ithaca, N.Y.: Snow Lion, 1988.

———. *Freedom in Exile: The Autobiography of the Dalai Lama*. New York: HarperCollins, 1990.

Thurman, Robert. *Inner Revolution: Life, Liberty and the Pursuit of Real Happiness*. New York: Riverhead Books, 1998.

———. *Why the Dalai Lama Matters: His Act of Truth as the Solution for China, Tibet, and the World*. New York: Simon and Schuster, 2008.

Tsarong, Dasang Damdul. *In the Service of His Country*. Ithaca, N.Y.: Snow Lion, 2000.

Tsering, Diki. *Dalai Lama, My Son*. New York: Viking/Arkana, 1997.

Tsering, Lhamo. *Resisting Oppression and Protecting the Country*. 2 vols. Dharamsala: AMI, 1998.

Tuttle, Gray. *Tibetan Buddhists in the Making of Modern China*. New York: Columbia University Press, 2005.

Tyler, Patrick. *A Great Wall*. New York: Public Affairs, 1999.

Van Walt van Praag, Michael C. *The Status of Tibet*. Boulder, Colo.: Westview Press, 1987.

Varg, Paul A. *Open Door Diplomat*. Champaign: University of Illinois Press, 1952.

Wilson, Dick. *The Long March*. London: Hamilton, 1971.

Wolpert, Stanley. *Nehru: A Tryst with Destiny*. New York: Oxford University Press, 1996.

Document Collections

Papers of Dean Acheson, Beinecke Library, Yale University.

Papers of Dean Acheson, Harry S. Truman Library, Independence, Mo.

Papers of American Emergency Committee for Tibetan Refugees, Hoover Institution, Stanford University.

Paul Berkowitz, congressional correspondence concerning Tibet, 1987–1991, private collection.

Papers of Chester Bowles, Beinecke Library, Yale University.

Documents relating to the British government's relationship with Tibet, Public Record Office, Kew, Richmond, Surrey.

Papers of McGeorge Bundy, John F. Kennedy Library, Boston.

Ellsworth Bunker correspondence, Columbia University.

Papers of Edmund Clubb, Hoover Institution, Stanford University.

Oral history of Edmund Clubb, Harry S. Truman Library, Independence, Mo.

Papers of Allen W. Dulles, Seeley G. Mudd Library, Princeton University.

Papers of John Foster Dulles, Dwight D. Eisenhower Library, Abilene, Kan.

Papers of President Eisenhower, Dwight D. Eisenhower Library, Abilene, Kan.

Papers of President Ford, Gerald R. Ford Library, Ann Arbor.

Papers of Averell Harriman, Library of Congress.

Papers of Christian A. Herter, Dwight D. Eisenhower Library, Abilene, Kan.

Papers of Roger Hilsman, John F. Kennedy Library, Boston.

Papers of Stanley Hornbeck, Hoover Institution, Stanford University.

Papers of President Johnson, Lyndon B. Johnson Library, Austin, Tx.

Papers of President Kennedy, John F. Kennedy Library, Boston.

Papers of Robert A. Lovett, New York Historical Society.

Joel McCleary, papers relative to the Tibetan international campaign, 1986–1990, private collection.

Papers and Recorded Conversations of Richard M. Nixon, Department of State Records, Office of Strategic Services Records, National Archives, College Park, Md.

Papers relating to Observation Mission, 1998, Jimmy Carter Library, Atlanta.

Papers of William W. Rockhill, Houghton Library, Harvard University.

Papers of William W. Rockhill, Litchfield, Conn., Historical Society.

Papers of Theodore Roosevelt, Library of Congress.

Oral history of John S. Service, Harry S. Truman Library, Independence, Mo.

Papers of T. V. Soong, Hoover Institution, Stanford University.

Papers of Adlai E. Stevenson, Seeley G. Mudd Library, Princeton University.
Papers of James C. Thomson, John F. Kennedy Library, Boston.
Papers of President Truman, Harry S. Truman Library, Independence, Mo.
Papers of General Nathan Twining, Library of Congress.
U.S. support for Tibetan resistance, 1958–68, records of the late Lhamo Tsering, Records Center, Dharamsala, India.

FIGURE CREDITS

FIGURE 1. National Anthropological Archives, Smithsonian Institution, MNH 5720.

FIGURE 2. National Anthropological Archives, Smithsonian Institution, MNH 5332.

FIGURE 3. Reproduced from the collections of the Library of Congress.

FIGURE 4. Personal photograph provided by Gyalo Thondup for use in book.

FIGURES 5, 6, 7, AND 8. Personal photographs from the author's collection.

FIGURES 9 AND 10. Personal photographs provided by protégées of Geshe Wangyal for use in this book.

FIGURES 11, 12, AND 16. Photographs provided by Joel McCleary for use in this book.

FIGURES 13 AND 15. Photograph provided by Mary Beth Markey for use in this book.

FIGURE 14. Photograph provided by Mary Beth Markey on behalf of the widow of Tom Lantos and his congressional staff for use in this book.

FIGURE 17. Photograph provided by the Office of the Speaker of the House for use in this book.

FIGURE 18. Photograph given to the author by Senator Dianne Feinstein for use in this book.

FIGURE 19. Photo by Chip Somodevilla/Getty Images News.

MAP 1. International Campaign for Tibet, 2008.

FIGURE 20. Official White House Photo by Pete Souza.

FIGURE 21. By permission of the Department of Information and International Relations, Central Tibetan Administration, Dharamsala, India.

FIGURE 22. Photo by Don Farber/buddhistphotos.com.

INDEX

Britain: India aided by, 179–80; Tibet and, 25–26, 55, 94, 146; at UN hearing of Tibet, 155

British Foreign Office: on Chiang's road, 40; on Tibet, 47–48, 78, 138; on Tibetan trade mission documents, 309 n. 13; on UN hearing of Tibet, 151

British government: China resented by, 46; First World War distracting, 16; Lhasa, Tibet, presence, 34–36; nation building of, 22–25; negotiations of, 15–17; Panchen Lama influencing, 25; proposal on Tibet made by, 22, 303 n. 1; on Tibet, 137–38, 307 n. 28; Tibet aided by, 22–25, 76, 303 n. 3; Tibetan officials paid by, 35; Tibetan policy of, 12, 15, 24, 47, 48, 68, 137–38, 302 n. 9 (chap. 2), 304 n. 12 (chap. 4); Tibetans supplied by, 20; on Tibetan trade mission documents, 58–59; US government deferring to, 22, 26; Younghusband influencing, 5

Bryce, James, 5

Brysac, Shareen Blair, 306 n. 13

Brzezinski, Zbigniew, 215, 219

Buddha, celebrations for, 111

Buddhism in Tibet, 283. See also Tibetan Buddhism

Bunker, Ellsworth, 159; Dalai Lama responded to by, 144; Dalai Lama role of, 146–47; letter delivered by, 160; on Tibetan uprising, 125

Burke, James, 81

Bush, George H. W., 239, 240, 245–46, 247, 253

Bush, George W., 270, 287, 288–95, 328 n. 2 (chap. 23)

Byelorussia, 155–56

Byrd, Robert, 233

Cabell, Charles, 129–30

Camp Hale, 123, 128–29, 130, 131

Carter, Jimmy, 214–15, 259

Carter Center, 280

Carver, George, 205

Case, Clifford, 138

Central Intelligence Agency, US (CIA): CIB as partner of, 183; covert action within, 98; Gyalo's relationship with, 181; Indian government blind to activities of, 161; Kissinger on, 201, 202; SFF supported by,

184; on supply routes, 132; Tibetan resistance supported by, 126–28, 129–32, 161–62, 177–78, 183, 190; Tibetans named by, 315 n. 20; Tibetans trained by, 115–16, 123, 127–29; TIM supported by, 201; Young Turk training program of, 321 n. 13; Zhou on, 201–2. See also Trainees

Central Intelligence Bureau (CIB), 104–5, 181, 183, 184

Chamberlain (lord), 61–62

Chamorro, Violeta, 243

Chang Ching-wu, 103

Chang Kuo-hua, 103

Chang Kuo-tao, 34

Chao Erh-fang, 11

Chen, Ivan, 15–16

Chiang, Madame, 33, 49

Chiang Kai-shek, 304 n. 14 (chap. 3); Acheson on, 63; Gyalo as protégé of, 99; Gyalo turning to, 115; India supplies obtained by, 39; Mao fighting with, 31, 33; Marshall persuading, 55; pronunciamento of, 124; resignation of, 63; road of, 39, 40–41; on Tibet, 47; Tibetan government congratulating, 49; Tibetan mission's letter to, 52–53

Ch'ien Lung, 13

China: Albright in, 260–61; Albright's thoughts on, 267; ambassadors to, 18; Berger interested in, 263; British government resenting, 46; Christopher in, 256–57; Clinton in, 277–80; Dalai Lama capture plan of, 11; Dalai Lama's authority encroached on by, 7–9; Dalai Lama's dialogue with, 261–62, 262–63, 266, 279, 280, 288–95; Ford visiting, 192, 205, 208–12; Gore in, 261; Gyalo in, 99, 195, 223; human rights influencing, 251–52; India attacked by, 170–71; India's relationship with, 72; Japanese military occupying, 39; Johnson, L., seeking reconciliation with, 193; Kissinger in, 191, 192, 193, 200–201, 208–9, 321 n. 2; Kissinger seeking accommodation with, 191, 195–96, 200–201; Nixon in, 193, 200–201, 321 n. 2, 322 n. 23; Nixon seeking accommodation with, 191, 200–201; Scowcroft in, 251; Shattuck in, 255–56; Soviet Union attacking, 206; Soviet Union's relationship with, 136–37, 172; Tibetan mission sent to,

51–53, 308 n. 3; Tibetans' dialogue with, 263–64; Tibet invaded by, 45, 69–71, 72–75, 78–79, 80; Tibet's relationship with, 15, 35–36, 52–53, 73, 94, 95, 100, 227, 307 n. 26; US government's interest in, 31; US government's policy regarding, 174–75, 241, 255; US's relationship with, 94, 191, 193, 196, 205–6, 208, 214–15, 222, 246, 251, 253, 254, 256, 258, 260, 261–62, 263, 266, 267, 278, 295–96, 297–98; US's sanctions placed on, 240–41. *See also* Most Favored Nation status

"China's Illegal Control of Tibet," 237–38

Chinese Communists, 33–34, 88, 139

Chinese Foreign Ministry, 261

Chinese Foreign Office, Dalai Lama secluded by, 6

Chinese government: on British proposal, 22, 303 n. 1; Dalai Lama influenced by, 122; Dalai Lama on, 14; Dalai Lama replaced by, 125; Dalai Lama's congressional appearance influencing, 232–33; on Dalai Lama traveling, 112; diplomatic channel of, 323 n. 37; Germany making peace with, 21–22; Great Leap Forward influencing, 133; Gyalo negotiating with, 101, 247, 291, 313 n. 17, 329 n. 6; Gyari negotiating with, 291–98; Indian government recognizing, 69; invitation declined by, 111; on Kalimpong, India, 125; Middle Way rejected by, 16, 325 n. 21; military campaign of, 19–20; national intelligence estimate on, 80; negotiations of, 15–17, 81, 86, 101, 171, 173, 178, 226–27, 228, 260, 262–63, 269, 291–98, 313 n. 17, 325 n. 21; Nehru's ire roused by, 125; on Office of Tibet, 207; Panikkar warning, 70–71; Rockhill on, 13–14; Tibetan mission exploited by, 53; Tibetan policy of, 110, 111, 222–23, 224–25, 227, 249; Tibetans challenging, 298; on Tibetan trade mission, 58–60; Tibetan uprisings subdued by, 18–19; Tibet challenging, 27; Tibet population transfers of, 230; Tibet-US relationship raised by, 206; UN influencing, 74–75; US government accommodating, 241; US government challenging, 80

Chinese military, 14–15, 19–20, 46, 303 n. 14. *See also* People's Liberation Army

Chinese Nationalist government, 124, 138, 145–46

Chinese occupation: economic development emphasized by, 227; film on, 198; Khampas and, 111; Tibetan nobility paid off by, 105; Tibet freed from, 174

Chinese People's Liberation Army. *See* People's Liberation Army

Chinese Revolution of 1911, 73

Christopher, Warren, 250, 254, 256–57

Churchill, Winston, 46, 62

Chushi Gangdruk (Four Rivers, Six Ranges), 117–18, 119, 271, 315 n. 27

Chu Shih-kuei, 100–101, 313 n. 16

CIA. *See* Central Intelligence Agency, US

CIB. *See* Central Intelligence Bureau

Clinton, Bill: Bader on, 264; campaign of, 253; in China, 277–80; China-Dalai Lama dialogue encouraged by, 261, 262, 264; on Dalai Lama, 279–80; Dalai Lama meeting with, 257, 261; executive order signed by, 251, 253, 254, 257, 258; Helms, J., on, 262; on human rights, 278–79; Jiang and, 277–80; Jiang meeting with, 275; Jiang's standoff session with, 255; Lord supporting, 253; MFN status extended by, 255–56, 257; MFN status renewed by, 257; Moynihan, D., on, 253–54; special envoy to Tibet and, 262; on Tibet, 266; US-China relationship reestablished by, 260

Clubb, Oliver, 76

Colby, William, 321 n. 13

Colman, Ronald, 38

Committee of the One Million, 138

Communism, Dalai Lama and, 105–6

Conboy, Kenneth, 120

Congress, US: Anderson, Desaix, appearing before, 247–49; Bush, G. H. W., pressured by, 247; Clinton's executive order influencing, 258; Dalai Lama appearing before, 231–33, 325 n. 7; Dalai Lama honored by, 243–45; Dalai Lama lunching with, 222; Dalai Lama's appeal to, 220–21; Dalai Lama supported by, 233, 272; Reagan influenced by, 233; riots in Tibet influencing, 291; State Department pressured by, 247; Tibetan policy executed by, 235; Tibetans supported by, 272; Tibet hearings of, 261–62; Zhao's letter from, 231–32

106, 112–13, 114, 141; Nobel Peace Prize awarded to, 241; *North China Daily News* on, 10–11; Obama giving letter to, 42; Obama meeting with, 271, 296–97, 324 n. 4, 327 n. 7 (chap. 20); peace proposal of, 231–32; in Peking, China, 5–6, 9; Pelosi meeting with, 252, 288; Phala's request of, 117; pilgrimage of, 114; in political limbo, 21; political role of, 23; prime ministers dismissed by, 105; as religious leader, 164, 165; retirement of, 295, 298–99; Rockhill's advice to, 7–9, 10, 12–13, 17, 302 n. 15; Rockhill's letter from, 11, 14; Rockhill's letter to, 13–14; Rockhill's meeting with, 1, 3–5; roles of, 283–84; Roosevelt, F., addressing, 306 n. 15; Roosevelt, F., gifts from, 44; Roosevelt, F., letter to, 42, 306 n. 11; Roosevelt, F., messages to, 32–33, 44; Roosevelt, T., gifts to, 4–5, 301 n. 6; with Rose, 221; Rose supporting, 243; Rose welcoming, 244–45; Roy on, 234–35; Russian tsar communicating with, 12; Shelton's letter from, 303 n. 11 (chap. 3); Simonov and, 199–200; State Department on, 32, 111, 149–50, 196, 216, 312 n. 24; State Department supporting, 272; statement of, 139–40; on successor, 302 n. 20; Taktser influencing, 89; Taktser's letter from, 95; Taktser's letter to, 93, 94; theatrical performance invitation for, 122; on Tibetan autonomy, 139; Tibetan Buddhism promoted by, 122; Tibetan cabinet investing authority in, 73; on Tibetan government, 14; on Tibetan government-in-exile, 148; Tibetan government-in-exile created by, 141; Tibetan government modernized by, 169–70; Tibetan resistance united by, 225–26; Tibet left by, 85, 86, 88–90, 91, 92, 93–94, 95–96, 111, 113, 114–15, 122–23, 137, 298; with Tibet Mafia, 238; Tibet returned to by, 225–26; Tolstoy giving gift to, 42, 289; UN appealed to by, 145, 151; on UN hearing of Tibet, 151; US Congress appealed to by, 220–21; US Congress appeared before by, 231–33, 325 n. 7; US Congress honoring, 243–45; US Congress lunching with, 222; US Congress supporting, 233, 272; US government's commitments to, 136, 149–50,

300; US government supporting, 93–94, 136, 289; US's recognition requested by, 144; US visited by, 196–99, 216, 217, 219–20; violence and, 117, 315 n. 23; Wangyal, P., as friend of, 105; Wangyal, P., request pertaining to, 110; Wangyal (spiritual teacher) visited by, 218; White House supporting, 272; Zhang meeting with, 92; Zhou influenced by, 113; Zhou meeting with, 113–14

Darjeeling, India, 100, 106–7
Davitt, Michael, 154
Dayal, Harishwal, 69
Democracy, Dalai Lama promoting, 169–70, 292–99, 294–95, 299–300
Demonstrations, 233, 266, 289, 290–97
Deng Xiaoping: Albright on, 260; on Dalai Lama, 211; Dalai Lama's letter to, 225; death of, 260; on détente, 208; Ford's conversations with, 210–12; Gyalo meeting with, 223; Mao and, 209, 213; on Office of Tibet, 210–11; sidelining of, 213; on Taiwan, 210; Tibet and, 207–8, 211, 226; Tibetans influenced by, 223; on US's sanctions on China, 241; on Vladivostok, Russia, 323 n. 50
Department of Defense (DOD), 145
Détente, 208
Dewey, Thomas Edmund, 61
Dharamsala, India, 195, 293–94, 319 n. 7
Dixon, Pierson, 151, 155, 307 n. 28
Dobriansky, Paula J., 269–71
DOD. *See* Department of Defense
Dolan, Brooke, 30, 36–37, 305 n. 21; child of, 306 n. 13; Gould meeting with, 42; as Lhasa social scene part, 42–43; as Roosevelt, F., envoy, 43–44; on Tibet, 49; Tibetan government inviting, 41–42, 43; Tibet receiving, 41
Dole, Robert, 244
Donovan, Bill, 43, 49–50, 305 n. 6
Dorjee, Tenzin, 294
Dorzhiev, Agvan, 6–7, 324 n. 9
Douglas-Home, Alec, 170
Drumright, Everett, 126, 138, 145–46
Dulles, Allen, 124, 127, 130–31, 168, 185
Dulles, John Foster, 149
Dumra, 128–29, 130, 131
Dutt, Subimal, 159

East Asian Bureau, 268–69

East Pakistan, 185, 190–91, 202–3

Eden, Anthony, 146

Eisenhower, Dwight D.: covert action capability used by, 97; Dalai Lama meeting with, 159; Dalai Lama replied to by, 149–50; Dulles, A., informing, 127, 131; Eisenhower, M., influencing, 97; in India, 159; on Korean War, 96–97; on nuclear weapons use, 96–97; Smith influencing, 97; Tibetan resistance assisted by, 130, 133; Tibetan resistance plan stood down by, 163

Eisenhower, Milton, 97

El Salvador, 74–75, 150

Empress Dowager, 5–6, 8, 9

Erickson Company, 269

Establishment 22, 190–91

Fairbank, John King, 203–4

Fang Lizhi, 252–53

Fecteau, Richard, 205

Feingold, Russell, 262

Feinstein, Dianne: on China-Dalai Lama negotiations, 262; Jiang and, 273–75, 276; Tibetans supported by, 259, 272, 275, 276–77, 328 n. 4

First World War, 16, 17, 303 n. 21, 303 n. 23

FitzGerald, Desmond, 115–16; covert action and, 177; death of, 189; description of, 129; Galbraith, J., on, 177, 320 n. 7; Tibetan resistance and, 127, 177

Fitzwater, Marlin, 246

Five Principles of Peaceful Coexistence, 113, 142, 314 n. 12

Foley, Tom, 243–44

Ford, Gerald, 192, 205, 208–12

Foreign Affairs Bureau (Tibet), 305 n. 8

Foreign Relations Authorization Act, 235

Four Rivers, Six Ranges: Reminiscences of the Resistance Movement in Tibet (Gompo), 315 n. 27

Frank, Barney, 239

Free Tibetan government. *See* Tibetan government-in-exile

Friedrich, Kate, 269, 270

Fuerth, Leon, 261

Gaden Chokor, 119

Galbraith, John Kenneth: covert action and, 181–82; on FitzGerald, 177, 320 n. 7; to India, 172–73; Indian-Chinese negotiations and, 171, 173; Kaysen and, 173; on Menon, K., 169; on Rusk, 173; on Tibetan cause, 182; on Tibetan resistance, 320 n. 7; on Tibetan resistance assistance, 168–69; Tibetan resistance assistance opposed by, 166–67; on war, 173

Galbraith, Peter, 237

Gandhi, Mahatma, 54

Gang of Four, 209

Geller, Uri, 326 n. 15

George VI (king), 62

Gephardt, Richard, 244

Germany, 21–22

Geshe (doctor of Buddhist theology), 121–22

Ghegen (teachers), 134–35

Gilman, Ben, 236

Golden throne, 118, 315 n. 25

Goldstein, Melvyn C., 53, 280, 328 n. 14

Goldwater, Barry, 208

Gompo Tashi Andrutsang, 315 n. 27; covert action proposed by, 132; Gaden Chokor as objective of, 119; golden throne project of, 118; guerrilla groups and, 133, 134; letter of, 159; Lithang A., contacting, 116–17; Lithang A., meeting with, 126; Lithang L., contacting, 116–17; Lithang L., meeting with, 126; as NVDA leader, 118; PLA engaged by, 121; Tibetan government replied to by, 119; on Tibetan resistance, 119; Tibetan resistance effort led by, 161–62; Tibetan resistance's role for, 118

Gore, Al, 257, 261

Gould, Basil, 36, 42, 45

Gray, Gordon, 145

Great Britain. *See* Britain

Great Game, US engaging in replay of, 175–76

Great Leap Forward, 133, 167

Green, Marshall, 198, 199

Green, Michael, 287

Grey, Edward, 5

Gross, Ernest, 74–75; Dalai Lama invited by, 164; on Dalai Lama's US visit, 197–98; Gyalo meeting with, 206–7; Johnson, A., knowing, 198; Office of Tibet guided by,

206; UN hearing of Tibet analyzed by, 152–53

Guatemala, 97

Gyalo Thondup, 293–94, 309 n. 18, 313 n. 12; Chang C., pressuring, 103; Chang Kuo-hua pressuring, 103; Chiang as mentor of, 99; Chiang turned to by, 115; in China, 99, 195, 223; Chinese government negotiating with, 101, 247, 291, 313 n. 17, 329 n. 6; CIA's relationship with, 181; CIA training Tibetans for, 115–16; CIB's relationship with, 181; contacts of, 107–8; on Dalai Lama, 112–13; Dalai Lama influenced by, 89; Dalai Lama on, 98, 100; Dalai Lama's US visit and, 196–97; in Darjeeling, India, 100, 106–7; Deng meeting with, 223; description of, 98; Gross meeting with, 206–7; Gyen Yeshe influencing, 188; Herter meeting with, 163–64; history of, 98–105, 106–7; Hu sidelining, 100; in India, 104–5; as intermediary, 226, 247; Jyin, Khen, Tsi Sum and, 106–7; Lhasa, Tibet, returned to by, 102; Lodge meeting with, 153; on MFN–human rights linkage including Tibetans, 257; Mullik approached by, 115; Mullik's association with, 104–5; Murphy speaking with, 158; Mustang force plans of, 190, 192, 193–95; negotiations of, 101, 247, 291, 313 n. 17, 329 n. 6; Nehru's association with, 104–5; Nehru's communications with, 104; Nehru supporting, 142; on Office of Tibet, 206–7; Pant giving guarantee to, 113; Phuntso Thonden on, 206; on self-determination of Tibet, 158–59; smuggling, 107, 314 n. 30; State Department meeting with, 92–93; Taiwan card played by, 100; Tibetan government reform plan of, 102–3; with Tsering, L., 102, 104, 106, 313 n. 20; Tsering on, 102; at UN hearing of Tibet, 157; UN hearing of Tibet and, 152; in US, 101, 102; White, R., advising, 146; Zhu D., approaching, 100–101

Gyaltsen, Kelsang, 291–98, 293

Gyari, Lodi, 322 n. 21, 329 n. 7; Chinese government negotiating with, 291–98; on Dalai Lama, 100, 224; description of, 249–50; human rights requirements

written by, 258; on Middle Way, 291–98; proposals carried by, 228; resignation of, 293; Simonov and, 199

Gyen Yeshe, 163, 186, 188–89, 194

Habib, Philip, 207

Haig, Alexander, 196

Halperin, Morton, 264

Hammarskjold, Dag, 152

Harrer, Heinrich, 68, 81–82, 89, 91, 92, 311 n. 11

Harriman, Averell, 138–39, 176–78

Helms, Jesse, 220, 231–32, 233; Bader questioned by, 262–63; on Clinton, 262; Lord supported by, 252

Helms, Richard, 177

Helsinki Accords, 212

Henderson, Loy, 63–64; Bajpai communicating with, 70–71; Bowles succeeding, 93; on Chinese invasion, 73, 80; Dalai Lama and, 81–84, 88–90, 164; description of, 79–80; Indian external affairs minister briefed by, 78; Indian government challenged by, 87–88; letters of, 82–84, 89–90, 92; officers of, 87, 88, 92; orders of, 87; Shakabpa meeting with, 72; State Department communicating with, 83; Tibetan government's offer accepted by, 71–72; on US mission to Lhasa, Tibet, 68–69

Herter, Christian, 307 n. 28, 309 n. 16, 311 n. 6; Dalai Lama's correspondence with, 160; Gyalo meeting with, 163–64; on Tibetan uprising, 124

Hillside, 12, 302 n. 8 (chap. 2)

Hilsman, Roger, 176

Hilton, James, 38

Holbrooke, Richard, 214–15, 275

Holdridge, John, 193

Holocaust, 231

Hopkins, Jeffrey, 217, 242

Hopkinson, A. J., 56, 308 n. 3

Huang Hua, 204

Huang Zen, 205–6

Hu Jintao, 16, 300; Gyalo sidelined by, 100; Obama meeting with, 271, 296

Hull, Cordell, 306 n.15

Human rights: Carter and, 215; China influenced by, 251–52; Christopher's options regarding, 254; Clinton on,

Mao Tse-tung: Chiang fighting with, 31, 33; Dalai Lama meeting with, 105–6; Dalai Lama on, 109–10; death of, 213; Deng and, 209, 213; Ford meeting with, 209–10; on Ford's China visit, 209; Khrushchev influencing, 136–37; on Kissinger, 209–10; Stalin meeting with, 67; on turnips, 34; Zhou's policy endorsed by, 67

Ma Pu-fang, 38

Markey, Mary Beth, 235, 258, 326 n. 19

Marshall, George, 55, 60–61

Marxism. *See* Communism, Dalai Lama and

Matthews, Elbert, 83

McCarthy, Joseph, 96

McCleary, Joel, 216; Dalai Lama and, 221, 242; Dalai Lama's US visit enabled by, 217, 219; description of, 242; international campaign advocated by, 241–42, 260; on MFN–human rights linkage, 258; Rose's conversation with, 219–20; study of Tibetan situation of, 229–31; with Tibetans, 243

McCone, John, 174, 182–83

McKay, David, 35

McMahon, Henry, 16

McMahon Line, 170–71

McNamara, Robert, 175

Memorandum on Genuine Autonomy for the Tibetan People, 292

Menon, Krishna, 155, 168–69, 171, 319 n. 9

Menon, P. N., 139

Merrell, George, 55

Meyer, Karl Ernest, 306 n. 13

MFN status. *See* Most Favored Nation status

Michel, Robert, 244

Middle Way, 27, 302 n. 4; Chinese government rejecting, 16, 325 n. 21; criticism of, 294; Dalai Lama on, 261, 293; Gyaltsen on, 291–98; Gyari on, 291–98

Mimang (the People), 107, 314 n. 29

Missionaries, 26–27, 303 n. 11 (chap. 3)

Mitchell, George, 244, 251

Monastic establishment, 23–25, 28, 81

Mongols, Dalai Lama and, 242

Monlam prayer festival, 121–22

Moscone, George, 273

Mossadegh, Mohammed, 97

Most Favored Nation (MFN) status, 250; Clinton extending, 255–56; Clinton

renewing, 257; human rights linked to, 251, 253–54, 255–56, 257–58, 262, 264

Moynihan, Daniel Patrick, 237, 248–49, 253–54, 327 n. 2 (chap. 20)

Moynihan, Maura, 237, 326 n. 17

Mullik, B. N., 104–5, 115, 141–42, 181

Murphy, Robert, 152, 158–59, 160

Mustang (Nepal area), 162, 163, 184–90, 192–94

Mutiny in Chinese military, 14–15, 303 n. 14

Nancy (Gyalo's wife), 100, 313 n. 15

National Constitutional Assembly, Tibetan mission at, 52, 53

National Security Council, Dulles, A. briefing, 124

National Volunteer Defense Army (NVDA), 118, 123

Nation building, 22–25

Negotiations: of British government, 15–17; of Chinese government, 15–17, 81, 86, 101, 171, 173, 178, 226–27, 228, 260, 262–63, 269, 291–98, 313 n. 17, 325 n. 21; of Dalai Lama, 260, 262–63; of Gyalo, 101, 247, 291, 313 n. 17, 329 n. 6; of Indian government, 171, 173, 178; Korean War, 96; monastic establishment on, 81; reports on Tibet, 277; on Sino-Indian War, 173; of Tibetan government, 15–17, 81, 86; of Tibetan government-in-exile, 226–27, 228, 269, 291–98, 325 n. 21; of Tsering, L., 188

Nehru, Jawaharlal: Chinese attack influencing, 171; Chinese government rousing ire of, 125; Chinese invasion and, 72–73; Dalai Lama meeting, 106, 112–13, 114, 141; Gyalo's association with, 104–5; Gyalo's communications with, 104; Gyalo supported by, 142; Harriman meeting with, 178; on Kalimpong, India, 125, 316 n. 15; Kennedy appealed to by, 172, 175; Kennedy influencing, 180; McMahon Line established as frontier by, 170–71; Menon, K., sacked by, 171, 319 n. 9; Mullik sent to Gyalo by, 141–42; Peter (prince) expelled by, 309 n. 18; policy rubric of, 140; Sino-Indian war influencing, 180–81; State Department on, 125; Tibetan autonomy suggested by, 139; Tibetan government-in-exile influenced by, 141;

Tibetan government invited by, 53; on Tibetan resistance, 146–47; on Tibetan uprising, 125, 142–43; US mission to India meeting with, 176; Zhou offending, 142; Zhou's agreement with, 113

Nepal, 154, 162, 163, 184–90, 192–95

Nepalese government, 271

Nepalese Gurkhas invading Tibet, 13

Ngabo Ngawang Jigme, 316 n. 3

Ngadruk. *See* Gyesang Chamatsang

Nixon, Richard: on Brezhnev, 205–6; in China, 193, 200–201, 321 n. 2, 322 n. 23; China accommodation sought by, 191, 200–201; on Rockefeller, N., 322 n. 23; on Tiananmen Square crackdown, 240–41; Zhou's dinner with, 204–5

Nobel Peace Prize, 241

North China Daily News, 10–11

North China Herald, 19

North East Frontier Agency, 171

Nuclear weapons, 96–97

NVDA. *See* National Volunteer Defense Army

Obama, Barack, 42, 271, 296–97, 324 n. 4, 327 n. 7 (chap. 20)

Observer Group, US, 41, 305 n. 21

Office of Strategic Services (OSS), 30, 41, 304 n. 14 (chap. 3), 305 n. 6, 305 n. 21

Office of Tibet, 206–7, 210–11, 260

Oksenberg, Mike, 214–15, 280

Olympic Torch, 290–97

Operation Ajax, 97

Osborn, David, 199

OSS. *See* Office of Strategic Services

Otero, Maria, 271

Outer Tibet, 16

Paal, Douglas, 245–46

Pacific War Council, 45, 46, 47, 306 n. 21

Pahlavi, Reza, 97

Pakistan, 178, 182, 191. *See also* East Pakistan

Palden, Sonam, 190–91

Pallis, Marco, 146

Panchen Lama, 13, 25

Pandya, Amit, 235, 237–39

Pangdatshang, L. Y., 56, 58–59, 309 n. 13

Panikkar, K. M., 70–71

Pant, Apa, 113

Parsons, J. Graham, 152

Pascal, Blaise, 235

Patterson, George, 89, 91–92, 187–88, 315 n. 21

Peking, China, Dalai Lama in, 5–6, 9

Pell, Claiborne, 231–32, 233; Anderson, Desaix, talking to, 248; Geller ensconced by, 326 n. 15; Tibetans supported by, 235; as Tibet Mafia member, 237

Pelosi, Nancy, 289; Dalai Lama meeting with, 252, 288; on human rights, 295; on Obama meeting with Dalai Lama, 296–97; on riots in Tibet, 291; Tibet supported by, 251

Peng Dehuai, 133

Peng Meng-min, 201

People's Liberation Army (PLA): Chushi Gangdruk's engagements with, 119, 315 n. 27; Gompo engaging, 121; Indian military engaging, 170, 171, 172; intelligence captured from, 167–68, 185–86; theatrical performance at compound of, 122; Tibetan resistance crushed by, 126; Tibetan resistance engaging, 167, 185–87

People's Militia (China), 167

Perry, William, 269

Peter (prince), 61, 309 n. 18, 316 n. 15

Phala Dronyerchemmo, 107, 117, 123

The Phantoms of Chittagong (Uban), 191

Phillips, William, 32–33

Phuntso Tashi, 88–89, 91

Phuntso Thonden, 206

Pitts, Keith, 221

Pius XII (Pope), 75

PLA. *See* People's Liberation Army

Polk, Franklin, 22, 303 n. 1

Porter, John, 231

Portrait of a Dalai Lama (Bell), 302 n. 20, 303 n. 22

Powell, Colin, 269–71, 270

Present at the Creation (Acheson), 311 n. 8

Protests. *See* Demonstrations

Public lashing, 72

Public Law 102–138, 237–39

Pu Yi, 14, 36

Ragashar Shape, 91

Raj, government of, 39

Rau, Benegal, 74, 75

State Department, US: on aid to Tibet,
86–87; on Chinese-Indian border, 174–75;
on Chinese invasion, 73, 78–79; on Dalai
Lama, 32, 111, 149–50, 196, 216, 312 n. 24;
Dalai Lama supported by, 272; Donovan's
proposal to, 49–50; Gyalo meeting with,
92–93; Henderson communicating with,
83; human rights supported by, 251–52; on
Jyin, Khen, Tsi Sum, 316 n. 10; on Nehru,
125; on Seventeen-Point Agreement, 84,
86; Taktser communicating with, 90–91,
101; Tibet and, 18, 55–56, 57, 64–65, 70,
76–77, 84, 199, 247–49, 309 n. 16; on
Tibetan government, 32; on Tibetan
government-in-exile recognition, 144,
149; Tibetan government's appeals to, 67;
Tibetans supported by, 272; Tibetan trade
mission and, 56–58, 59–60, 61; on Tibetan
uprising, 138; on Tibet as independent
state, 144–46, 158; on Tibet's legal status,
124, 125; US Congress pressuring, 247
Stein, Jonathan, 264
Stevenson, Adlai, 170
Stilwell, Joseph, 44
Stuart, John Leighton, 65
Sun Yat-sen, 14
Surkhang Shape, 89
Symington, Stuart, 175, 320 n. 21

Taft, Julia V., 268–69, 296
Taiwan: Deng on, 210; Gyalo playing card of,
100
Taiwan Independence Movement (TIM),
201
Taktser Rinpoche, 85; Allison's communica-
tions with, 95–96; Bowles's suggestion to,
93; Dalai Lama influenced by, 89; Dalai
Lama's letter from, 93, 94; Dalai Lama's
letter to, 95; State Department's com-
munications with, 90–91, 101
Teichman, Eric, 20, 26, 35–36
Tenpa Thondup, 313 n. 16
Tenzin Gyatso. See Dalai Lama
Tenzin Tethong, 216
Thagla Ridge, 170, 171
Third World War, 74, 80
Thomas, Lowell, Jr., 66
Thomas, Lowell, Sr., 65, 66–67
Thubten Norbu. See Taktser Rinpoche

Thurman, Robert, 216, 242, 243
Tiananmen Square, 240–41
Tibet: aid to, 66–67, 69–70, 72, 80, 85, 86–87,
96, 111–12, 117; academicians' mission to,
280–285; as autonomous state, 22, 47, 48,
76–77, 91–92, 124, 139, 164, 262–63, 283,
294, 311 n. 6; Bowles supporting cause of,
182; Britain and, 25–26, 55, 94, 146; British
Foreign Office on, 47–48, 78, 138; British
government aiding, 22–25, 76, 303 n. 3;
British government making proposal
on, 22, 303 n. 1; British government on,
137–38, 307 n. 28; British government's
policy regarding, 12, 15, 24, 47, 48, 68, 137–38,
302 n. 9 (chap. 2), 304 n. 12 (chap. 4);
Buddhism in, 283; Chiang on, 47; China
mission from, 51–53, 308 n. 3; China's
invasion of, 45, 69–71, 72–75, 78–79, 80;
China's relationship with, 15, 35–36, 52–53,
73, 94, 95, 100, 227, 307 n. 26; Chinese
government challenged by, 27; Chinese
government's policy regarding, 110, 111,
222–23, 224–25, 227, 249; Chinese
government's population transfers to,
230; Chinese military on border of, 46;
Chinese occupation and freedom for, 174;
Clinton on, 266; Clinton's executive order
influencing, 258; coordinator, 262, 264–65,
266–71; Dalai Lama leaving, 85, 86, 88–90,
91, 92, 93–94, 95–96, 111, 113, 114–15, 122–23,
137, 298; Dalai Lama returning to, 225–26;
declaring independence, 17; definition of,
226–27; delegations in, 224; demonstrations in, 290; Deng and, 226; Deng on,
207–8, 211; DOD on, 145; Dolan on, 49;
Dolan sent to, 41; expeditions to, 25–26;
Galbraith, J., on cause of, 182; Goldstein on,
328 n. 14; Gray on, 145; Hull on, 306 n. 15;
human rights in, 234, 235; as independent
state, 144–46, 149, 152, 158, 294; India
helping, 72; India mission sent from, 54;
India's relationship with, 68; intelligence
report on, 27–30; Jiang on, 265–66, 268,
279, 280; Jordan on, 6; Korostovetz on, 6;
legal status of, 78, 124, 125, 151, 152–53, 155,
207, 228; Liu C., on, 307 n. 26; Lord on,
207; Lord supporting, 251; McCleary's
study on situation of, 229–31; Mitchell
supporting, 251; modernization of, 25;

negotiations reports, 277; Nepalese Gurkhas invading, 13; Office of, 206–7, 210–11, 260; OSS mission in, 41; Pacific War Council representation of, 45, 46, 47, 306 n. 21; pack animal supply route through, 49–50; Pelosi supporting, 251; radio equipment sent to, 44–45; religious freedom in, 265–66; riots in, 290, 291–98, 329 n. 8; Rockhill on, 27–28; Roy on, 234; self-determination of, 158–59, 160, 170, 248–49; Shuhsi on, 307 n. 26; Soong and, 307 n. 26; special envoy to, 262, 264–65, 266–71; sponsors of, 150–54; State Department and, 18, 55–56, 57, 64–65, 70, 76–77, 84, 199, 247–49, 309 n. 16; Tibetan resistance relocating to, 186; Tolstoy on, 49; Tolstoy sent to, 41; UN hearing of, 80, 147, 150–57; as united identity, 226–27; UN resolution on, 156–57; uprisings in, 18–19, 110, 123–26, 137, 138, 142–44; US Congress's hearings on, 261–62; US government's analysis of, 227; US government's assistance to, 85; US government's interest in, 33, 48–50, 285, 297–98; US government's policy regarding, 63–65, 69–70, 76–77, 83, 86–87, 92, 93, 112, 120, 123–24, 145, 157, 160, 199, 201, 222, 235; US government's statements on, 96; US government's views of, 36–38, 307 n. 37; US's perspective of, 38; US's relationship with, 94, 95, 110, 120, 123–24, 206; viceroy (India) on, 46; violence in, 285, 290, 328 n. 12; wool of, 49–50. *See also* Inner Tibet; Lhasa, Tibet; Outer Tibet

Tibetan army. *See* Tibetan military

Tibetan Buddhism, 122, 283, 285

Tibetan cabinet, 43, 55, 73–74, 75, 76, 91

Tibetan Foreign Bureau, Jessup invited by, 67–68

Tibetan Foreign Office, 45, 306 n. 21

Tibetan government: Chiang congratulated by, 49; on Chiang's road, 40; Chinese invasion influencing, 72; Dalai Lama modernizing, 169–70; Dalai Lama on, 14; Dolan invited by, 41–42, 43; Foreign Affairs Bureau opened by, 305 n. 8; Gompo's reply to, 119; Gyalo's reform plan for, 102–3; Henderson's offer from, 71–72; Indian government policy of, 54–55;

Indian government suggesting pressuring, 40; Madame Chiang's medals from, 49; negotiations of, 15–17, 81, 86; Nehru inviting, 53; officials paid by British, 35; OSS on, 41; Richardson, H., counseling, 54; Rockhill on, 13; on Shakabpa's documents, 309 n. 14; State Department on, 32; State Department's appeals from, 67; Tolstoy invited by, 41–42, 43; trade mission of, 56–62, 309 n. 13, 309 n. 14; Truman's mission from, 55; US government supporting, 96

Tibetan government-in-exile: Dalai Lama creating, 141; Dalai Lama on, 148; Hopkins envied by, 242; Indian government's relationship with, 161; Indian Ministry of External Affairs on, 148; Mongols and, 242; negotiations of, 226–27, 228, 269, 291–98, 325 n. 21; Nehru influencing, 141; recognition of, 138–39, 144, 148, 149, 164; task force of, 293; Thurman envied by, 242; US government's relationship with, 161

Tibetan military, 17, 23–24, 29, 303 n. 22

Tibetan nobility, Chinese occupation paying off, 105

Tibetan politics, 89, 315 n. 21

Tibetan resistance: aid to, 124–25, 126–27; arms distributed to, 167; arms drops and, 120, 126, 127, 162–63, 167, 168, 186, 188; Blum meeting, 272–73; Chinese Nationalist government's pledge to, 124; CIA supporting, 126–28, 129–32, 161–62, 177–78, 183, 190; company commanders, 185; covert action influenced by, 97–98; Dalai Lama uniting, 225–26; dispute within, 188; Dulles, A., on, 130–31; in East Pakistan, 190–91; Eisenhower, D., approving assistance to, 130, 133; FitzGerald supporting, 177; Galbraith, J., on, 320 n. 7; Gompo leading effort of, 161–62; Gompo on, 119; Gompo's role in, 118; as guerrilla groups, 133, 134; Indian government using, 190–91; intelligence collected by, 189; Kennedy approving assistance to, 133; Khampas in, 292–99; in Mustang, 162, 163, 184–90, 192–94; Nehru on, 146–47; in Nepal, 194–95; Nepal left by, 186; PLA crushing, 126; PLA engaged by, 167, 185–86, 186–87; plan of, 161–63; Tibet relocated to by, 186; Tsering, L., supporting, 313 n. 20; US government supporting, 123–24, 166–67, 168–69, 192; veterans of, 109, 162–63, 185, 193–95. *See also* Chushi Gangdruk; National Volunteer Defense Army; Trainees

Tibetans, 212–13; Blum supporting, 272, 273, 274–75; Bowles supporting, 170; British government supplying, 20; Bush, G. W., supporting, 270, 287; Carter supporting, 259; China's dialogue with, 263–64; Chinese government challenged by, 298; CIA naming, 315 n. 20; CIA training, 115–16, 123, 127–29; covert action capability available to, 97–98; Craig, G., lost by, 268, 327 n. 12; Deng influencing, 223; description of, 310 n. 22; East Asian Bureau and, 268–69; Feinstein supporting, 259, 272, 275, 276–77, 328 n. 4; Ford repudiating, 211–12; Inner Tibet and, 20; Kao's relationship with, 184; Magruder on, 28–29; McCleary with, 243; MFN–human rights linkage including, 257–58; Pell supporting, 235; Powell supporting, 270; Red Army encountered by, 33–34; in SFF, 191; State Department supporting, 272; Thurman with, 243; UN and, 157; Upper Yangtze and, 19, 20; US arrived in by, 239; US Congress supporting, 272; US government's support for, 215–16, 220, 239–40; van Walt supporting, 241–42; V-E Day reactions of, 308 n. 1; White House supporting, 272

Tibetan Support Project, 128

Tibetan Welfare Association, 107

Tibetan Youth Congress (TYC), 249–50, 291

Tibet Autonomous Region, 224, 281, 328 n. 11

Tibet Communist Party, 110

Tibet Coordinator Office, 266–71

Tibet House, 259

Tibet Mafia, 236–39

Tibet Policy Act, 276–77

TIM. *See* Taiwan Independence Movement

Tolstoy, Ilya, 30, 37, 305 n. 21; CV of, 305 n. 6; Dalai Lama receiving gift from, 42, 289; diplomacy reacted to, 48–49; Donovan's message from, 43; Gould meeting with, 42; as Lhasa social scene part, 42–43;

Ludlow consulted by, 42; as Roosevelt, F., envoy, 43–44; on Tibet, 49; Tibet and, 41; Tibetan Foreign Office communicating with, 45, 306 n. 21; Tibetan government inviting, 41–42, 43; Tibetan trade mission and, 61

Tom. *See* Lithang Athar

Topgay Pandatsang, 89

Tournament of Shadows (Meyer and Brysac), 306 n. 13

Trainees, 115–18, 119–20, 315 n. 24; arms drops and, 126; Camp Hale and, 127–29; on covert action, 134–35; Dumra and, 127–29; on *ghegen*, 134–35; Mustang as destination for, 185; second group of, 123

Triplett, William, 235, 236–37

Truman, Harry S., 55, 59–60, 61, 88

Truman Doctrine, US government influenced by, 79

Tsarong, D. D., 24, 303 n. 6

Tsarong Shape, 23, 37

Tsering, Bhuchung, 298–99

Tsering, Lhamo: on arms drops, 120; arrest of, 194–95; on covert action, 134; in Darjeeling, India, 106; death of, 321 n. 16; Dharamsala, India returned to by, 195; on Gyalo, 102; with Gyalo, 102, 104, 106, 313 n. 20; jail mate of, 321 n. 7; in Mustang, 188; negotiations of, 188; Tibetan resistance supported by, 313 n. 20

Tsering Dolma, 313 n. 20

Twining, Nathan, 130

TYC. *See* Tibetan Youth Congress

Tyler, Patrick, 214

Uban, Sujan Singh, 190–91

Udall, Mark, 128–29

UK. *See* Britain

Ulanfu (United Front Department director), 223

UN. *See* United Nations

Unconventional warfare. *See* Covert action

Unger, Leonard, 208, 323 n. 49

United Kingdom (UK). *See* Britain

United Nations (UN): Chinese government influenced by, 74–75; Dalai Lama appealing to, 145, 151; front, 80; General Assembly, 170; Nepal at, 154; Tibetan cabinet's appeal to, 73–74, 75, 76; Tibetans

JOHN KENNETH KNAUS is an associate in research with the
Fairbank Center for East Asian Research at Harvard University.
He is the author of *Orphans of the Cold War: America and the
Tibetan Struggle for Survival.*

Library of Congress Cataloging-in-Publication Data
Knaus, John Kenneth, 1923–
Beyond Shangri-La : America and Tibet's move into the
twenty-first century / John Kenneth Knaus.
p. cm. — (American encounters/global interactions)
Includes bibliographical references and index.
ISBN 978-0-8223-5219-8 (cloth : alk. paper)
ISBN 978-0-8223-5234-1 (pbk. : alk. paper)
1. Tibet Autonomous Region (China)—History—1951–
2. China—Politics and government—1949–
3. United States—Relations—China—Tibet Autonomous
Region.   4. Tibet Autonomous Region (China)—Relations—
United States.   I. Title.   II. Series: American encounters/
global interactions.
DS786.K63 2012
303.48'2515073—dc23   2012011591